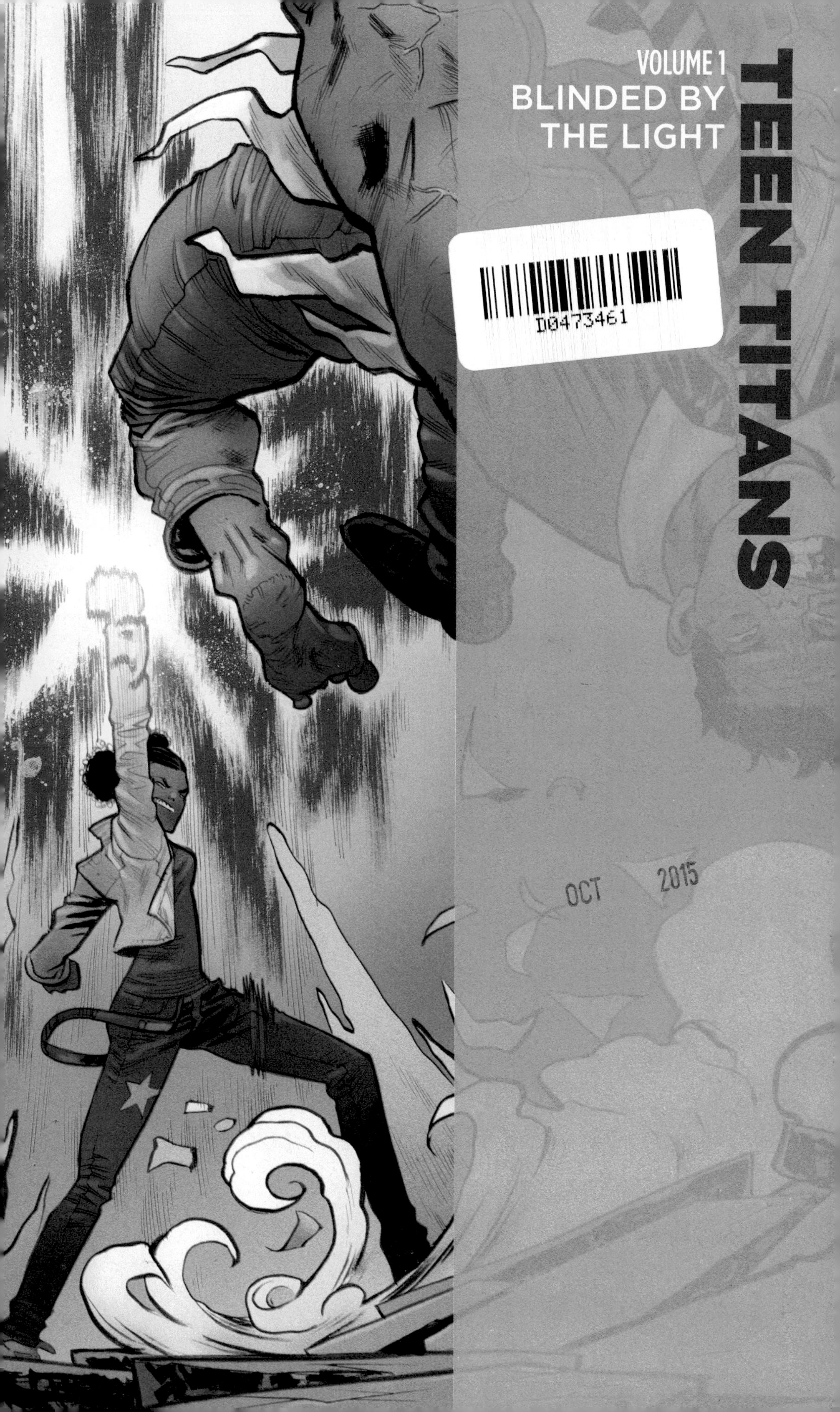

TEEN TITANS

VOLUME 1
BLINDED BY THE LIGHT

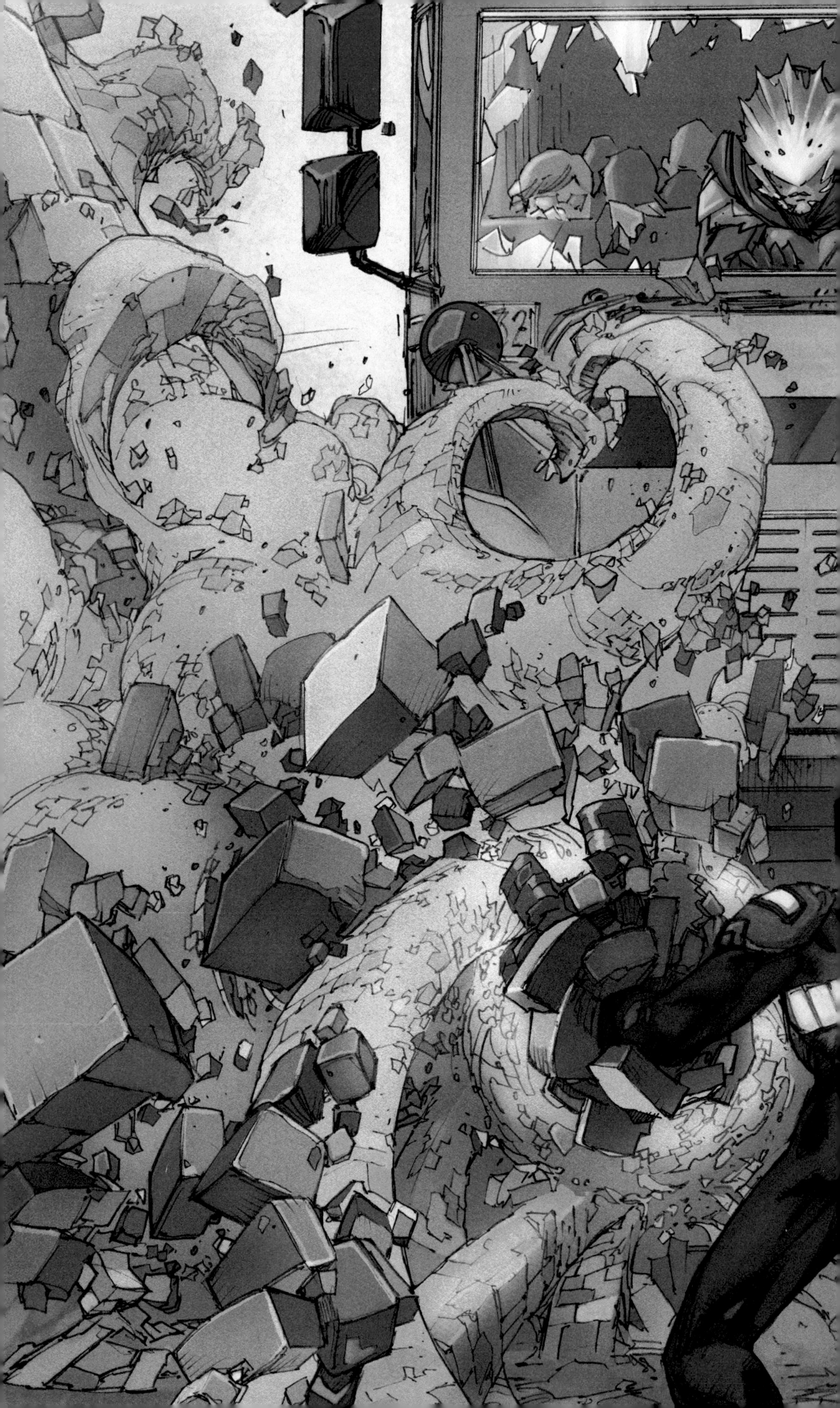

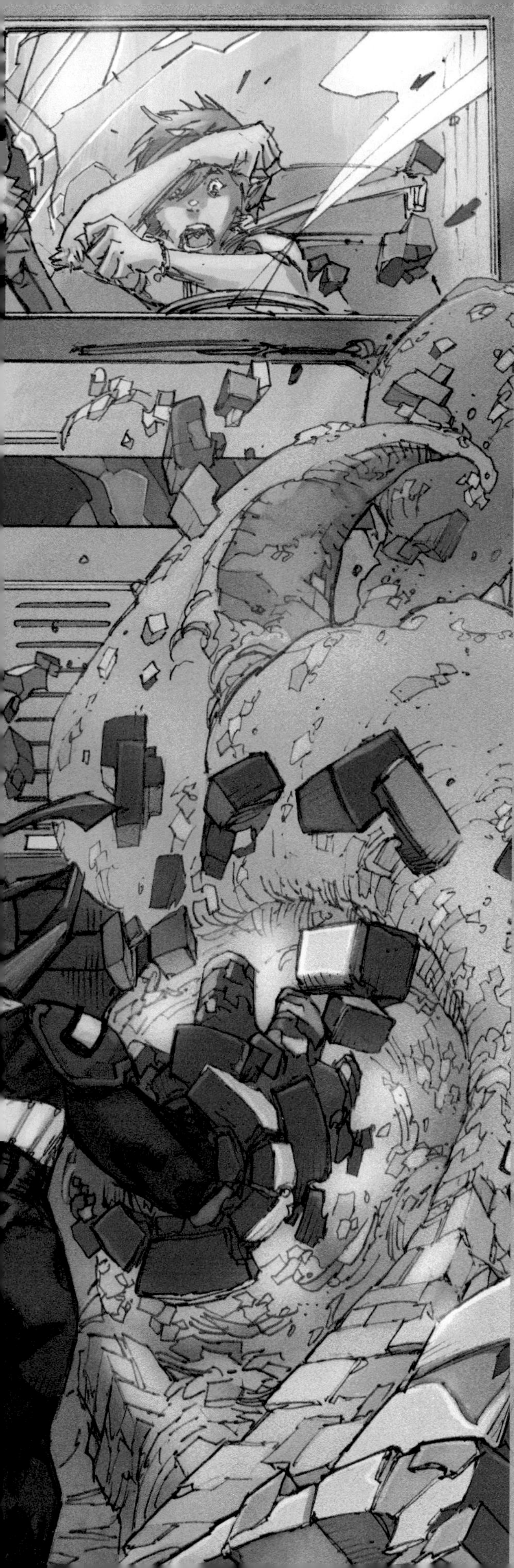

TEEN TITANS

VOLUME 1
BLINDED BY THE LIGHT

WRITTEN BY
WILL PFEIFER

ART BY
KENNETH ROCAFORT
SCOTT HEPBURN

COLOR BY
DAN BROWN
BLOND
HI-FI

LETTERS BY
JOHN J. HILL

COLLECTION COVER ART BY
KENNETH ROCAFORT

SUPERMAN CREATED BY
JERRY SIEGEL &
JOE SHUSTER
BY SPECIAL ARRANGEMENT
WITH THE JERRY SIEGEL FAMILY

MIKE COTTON Editor - Original Series
RICKEY PURDIN Associate Editor - Original Series
LIZ ERICKSON Editor
ROBBIN BROSTERMAN Design Director - Books
DAMIAN RYLAND Publication Design

BOB HARRAS Senior VP - Editor-in-Chief, DC Comics

DIANE NELSON President
DAN DIDIO and JIM LEE Co-Publishers
GEOFF JOHNS Chief Creative Officer
AMIT DESAI Senior VP - Marketing & Franchise Management
AMY GENKINS Senior VP - Business & Legal Affairs
NAIRI GARDINER Senior VP - Finance
JEFF BOISON VP - Publishing Planning
MARK CHIARELLO VP - Art Direction & Design
JOHN CUNNINGHAM VP - Marketing
TERRI CUNNINGHAM VP - Editorial Administration
LARRY GANEM VP - Talent Relations & Services
ALISON GILL Senior VP - Manufacturing & Operations
HANK KANALZ Senior VP - Vertigo & Integrated Publishing
JAY KOGAN VP - Business & Legal Affairs, Publishing
JACK MAHAN VP - Business Affairs, Talent
NICK NAPOLITANO VP - Manufacturing Administration
SUE POHJA VP - Book Sales
FRED RUIZ VP - Manufacturing Operations
COURTNEY SIMMONS Senior VP - Publicity
BOB WAYNE Senior VP - Sales

TEEN TITANS VOLUME 1: BLINDED BY THE LIGHT

DC Comics, 4000 Warner Blvd., Burbank, CA 91522
A Warner Bros. Entertainment Company.
Printed by RR Donnelley, Owensville, MO, USA. 7/3/15 First Printing.
ISBN: 978-1-4012-5237-3

Library of Congress Cataloging-in-Publication Data

Pfeifer, Will, author.
Teen Titans. Volume 1 / Will Pfeifer ; Kenneth Rocafort.
pages cm. — (The New 52!)
ISBN 978-1-4012-5237-3
1. Graphic novels. I. Rocafort, Kenneth, illustrator. II. Title.
PN6728.T34P44 2015
741.5'973—dc23
2015008052

SUSTAINABLE FORESTRY INITIATIVE
Certified Chain of Custody
20% Certified Forest Content,
80% Certified Sourcing
www.sfiprogram.org
SFI-01042
APPLIES TO TEXT STOCK ONLY

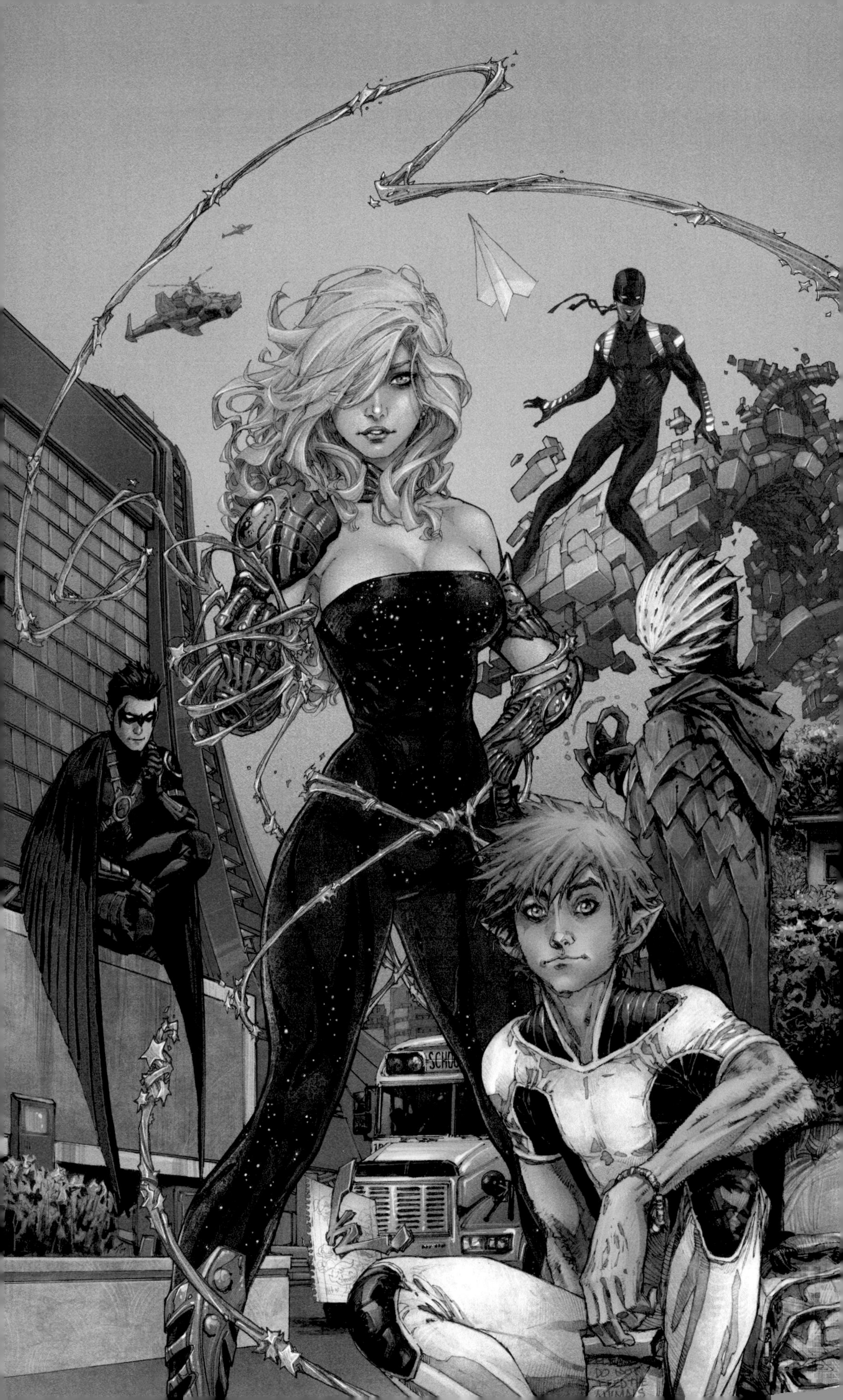

BLINDED BY THE LIGHT: PART 1

WILL PFEIFER writer KENNETH ROCAFORT artist DAN BROWN colorist JOHN J. HILL letterer cover art by KENNETH ROCAFORT

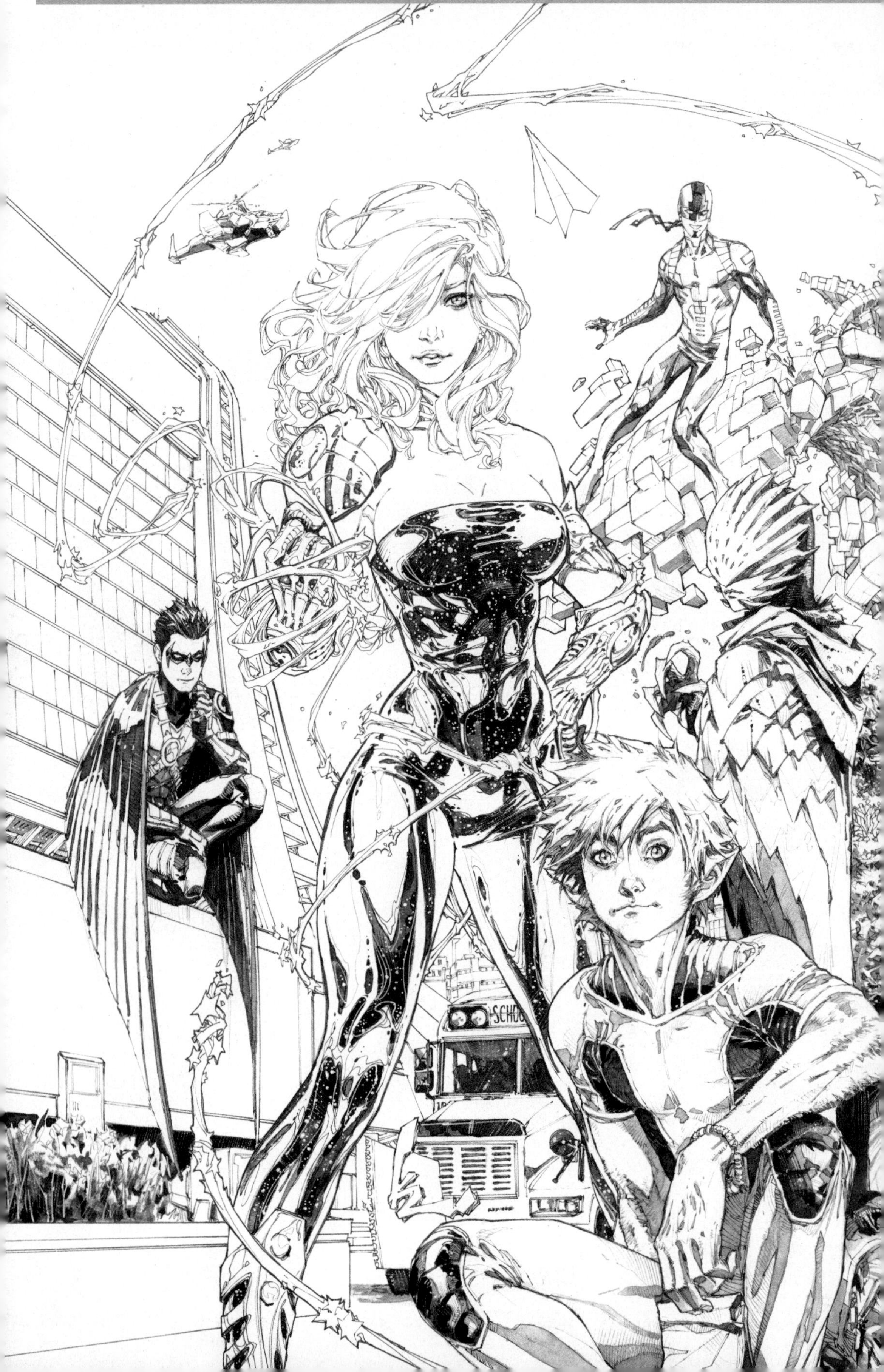

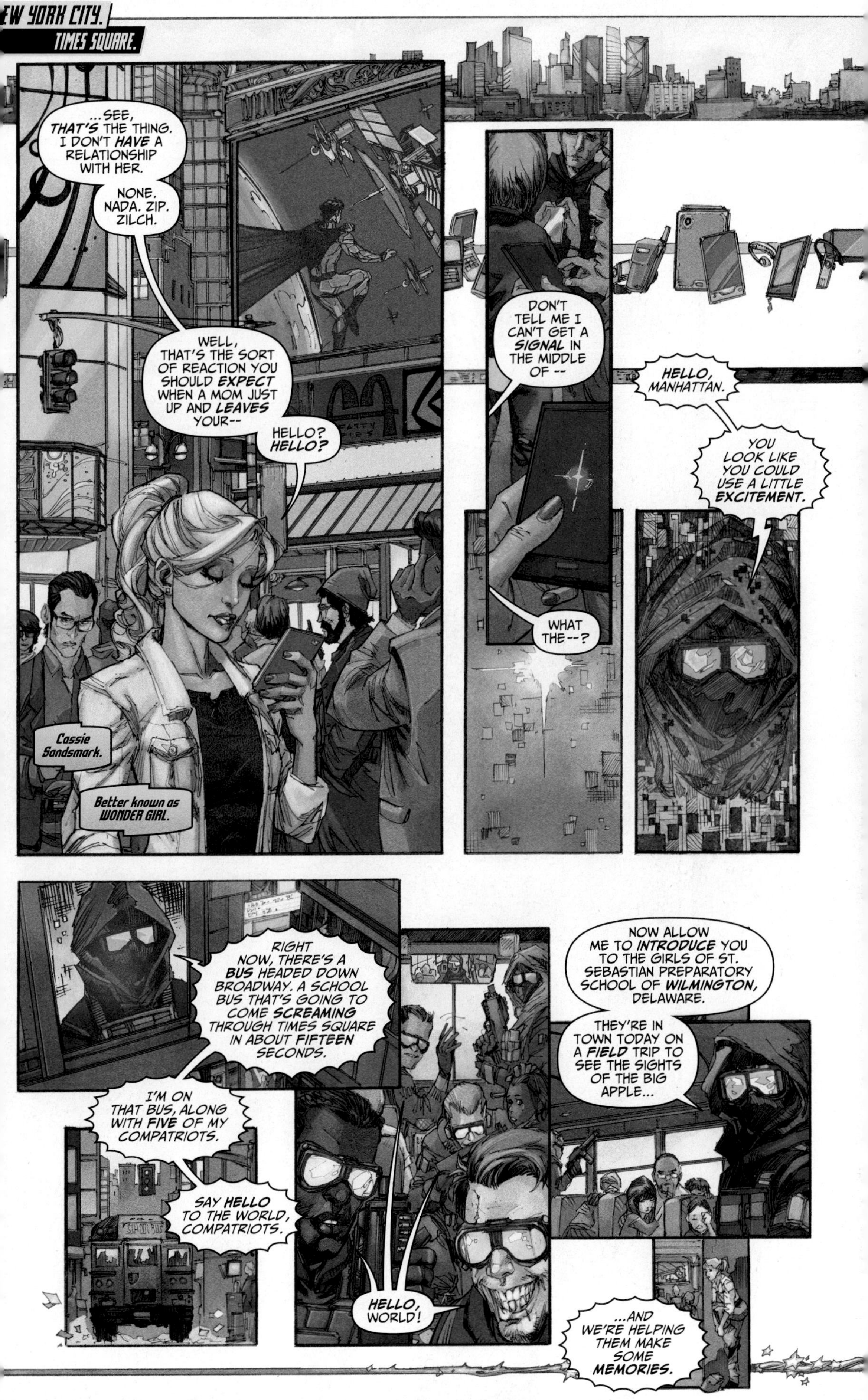

EW YORK CITY.
TIMES SQUARE.
...SEE, THAT'S THE THING. I DON'T HAVE A RELATIONSHIP WITH HER.
NONE. NADA. ZIP. ZILCH.
WELL, THAT'S THE SORT OF REACTION YOU SHOULD EXPECT WHEN A MOM JUST UP AND LEAVES YOUR--
HELLO? HELLO?
Cassie Sandsmark.
Better known as WONDER GIRL.
DON'T TELL ME I CAN'T GET A SIGNAL IN THE MIDDLE OF --
WHAT THE--?
HELLO, MANHATTAN.
YOU LOOK LIKE YOU COULD USE A LITTLE EXCITEMENT.
RIGHT NOW, THERE'S A BUS HEADED DOWN BROADWAY. A SCHOOL BUS THAT'S GOING TO COME SCREAMING THROUGH TIMES SQUARE IN ABOUT FIFTEEN SECONDS.
I'M ON THAT BUS, ALONG WITH FIVE OF MY COMPATRIOTS.
SAY HELLO TO THE WORLD, COMPATRIOTS.
SCHOOL BUS
HELLO, WORLD!
NOW ALLOW ME TO INTRODUCE YOU TO THE GIRLS OF ST. SEBASTIAN PREPARATORY SCHOOL OF WILMINGTON, DELAWARE.
THEY'RE IN TOWN TODAY ON A FIELD TRIP TO SEE THE SIGHTS OF THE BIG APPLE...
...AND WE'RE HELPING THEM MAKE SOME MEMORIES.

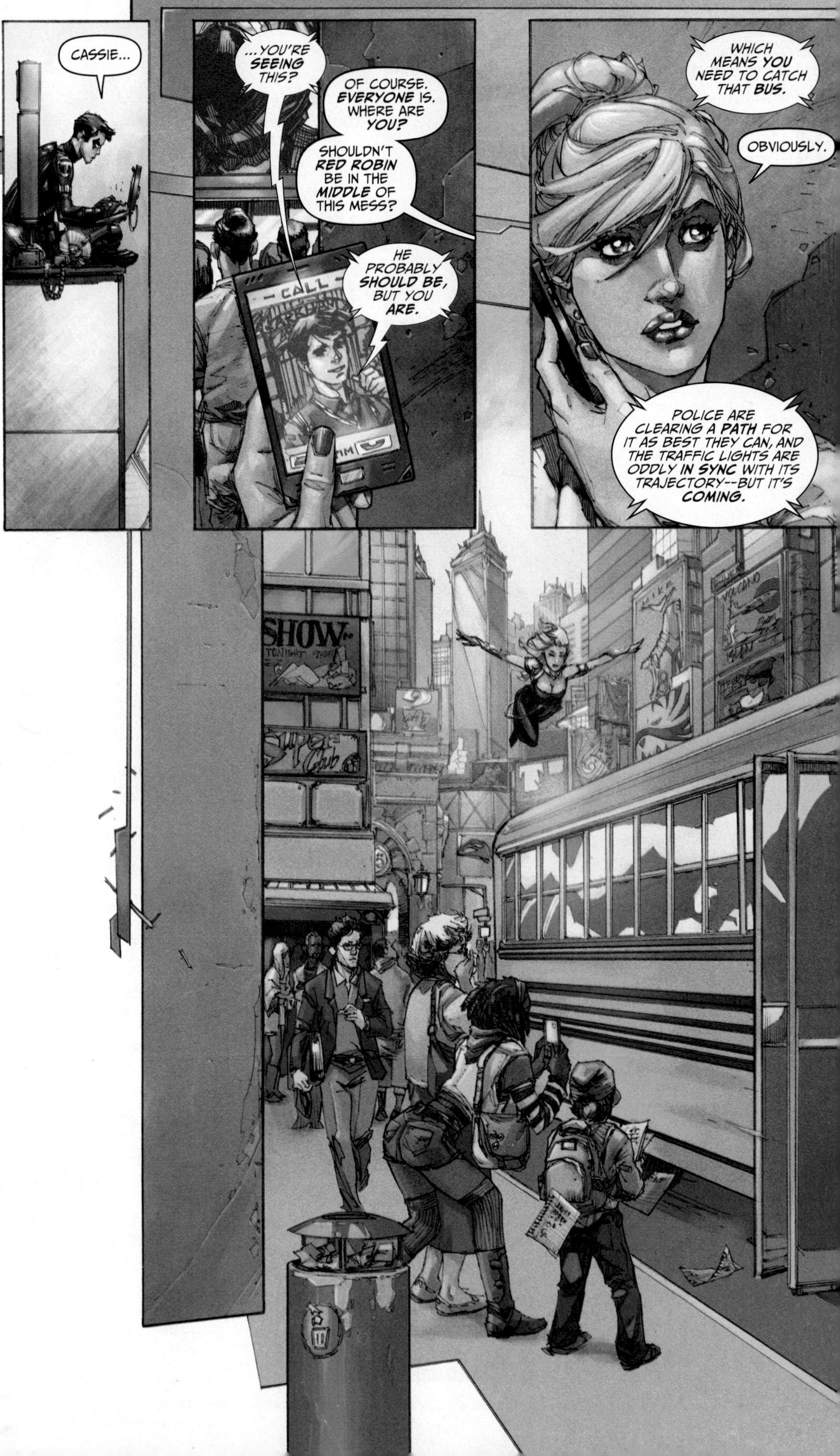

CASSIE...
...YOU'RE SEEING THIS?
OF COURSE. EVERYONE IS. WHERE ARE YOU?
SHOULDN'T RED ROBIN BE IN THE MIDDLE OF THIS MESS?
HE PROBABLY SHOULD BE, BUT YOU ARE.
CALL
WHICH MEANS YOU NEED TO CATCH THAT BUS.
OBVIOUSLY.
POLICE ARE CLEARING A PATH FOR IT AS BEST THEY CAN, AND THE TRAFFIC LIGHTS ARE ODDLY IN SYNC WITH ITS TRAJECTORY--BUT IT'S COMING.
SHOW

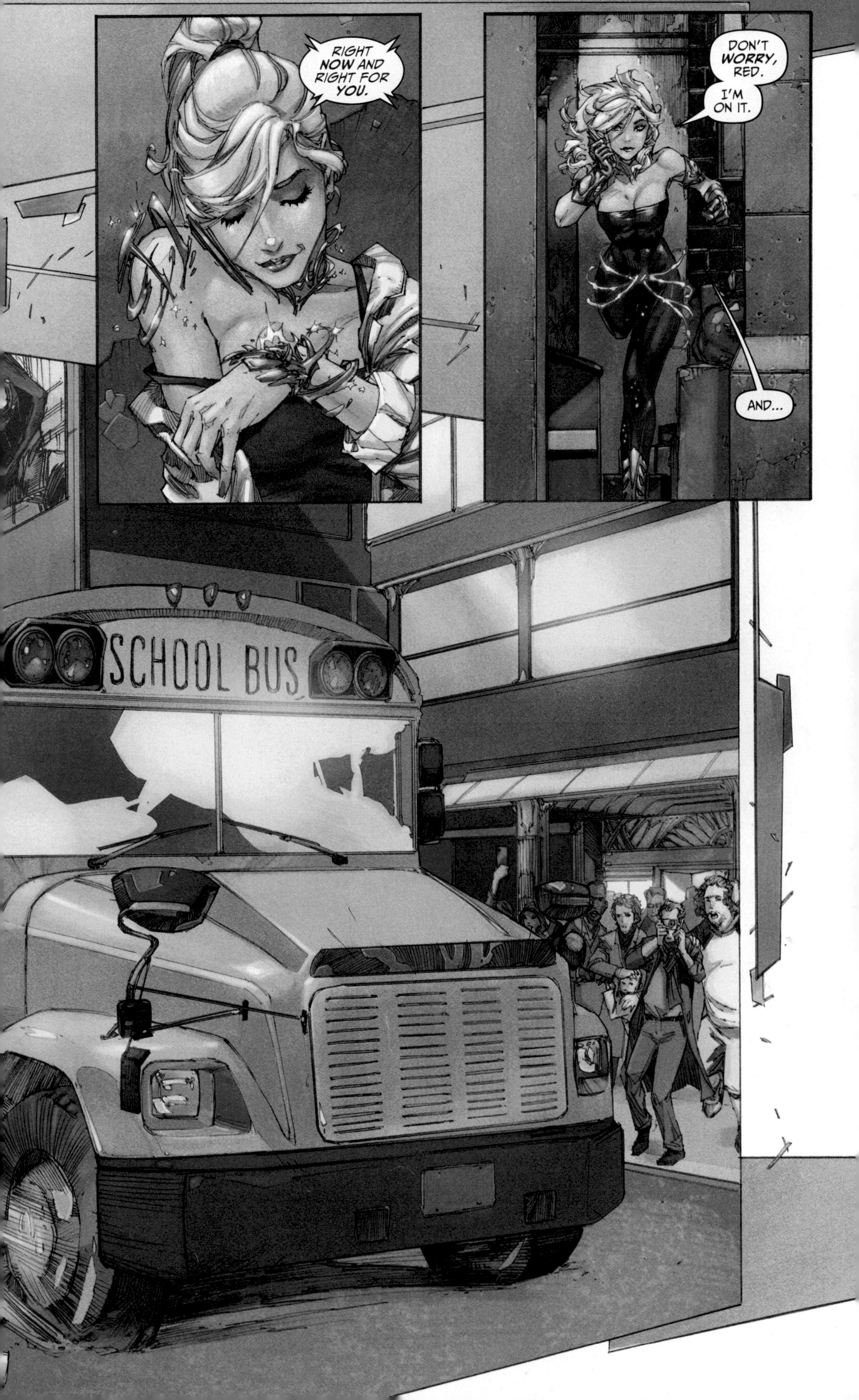
RIGHT NOW AND RIGHT FOR YOU.
DON'T WORRY, RED.
I'M ON IT.
AND...
SCHOOL BUS

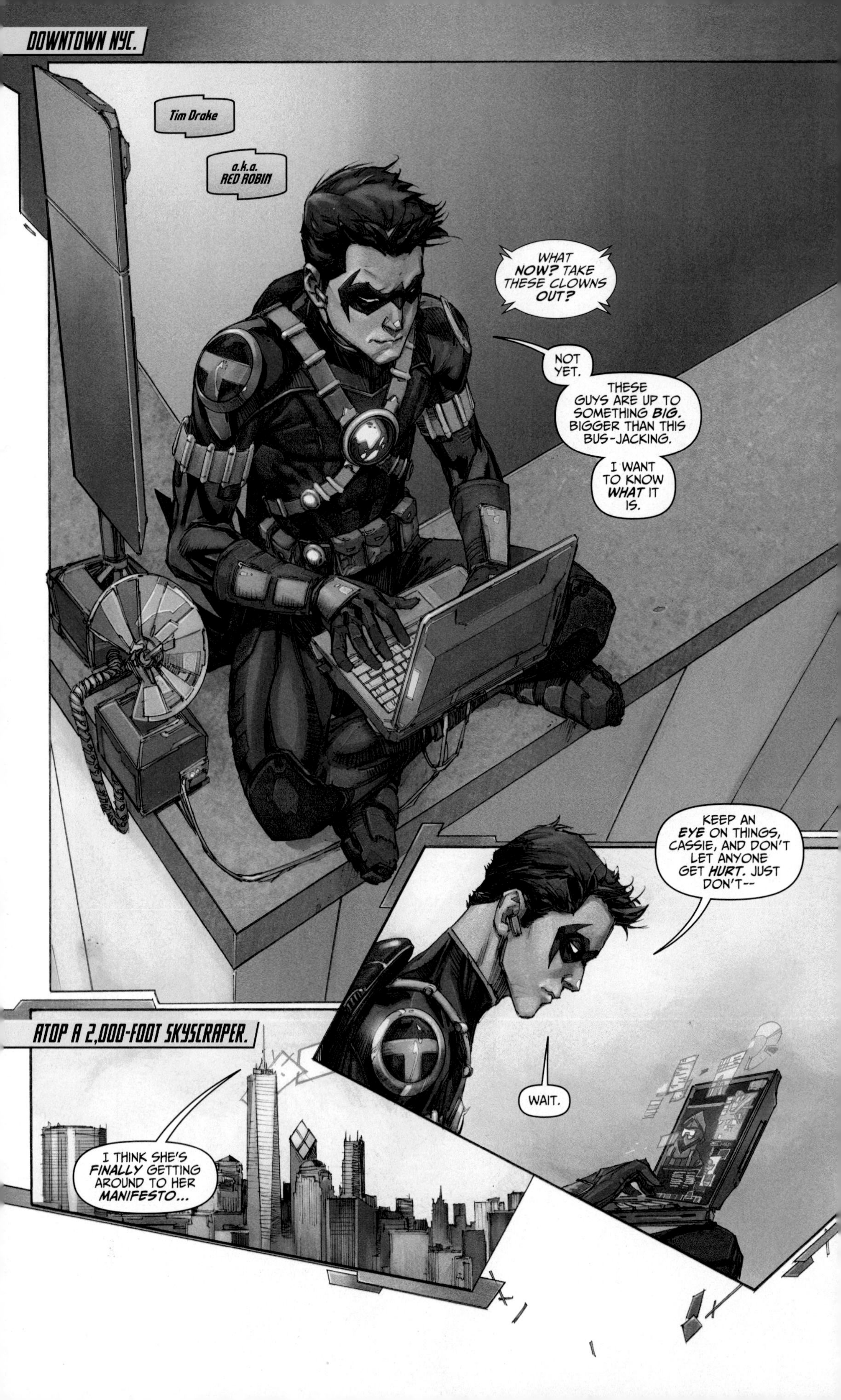
DOWNTOWN NYC.
Tim Drake
a.k.a. RED ROBIN
WHAT NOW? TAKE THESE CLOWNS OUT?
NOT YET.
THESE GUYS ARE UP TO SOMETHING BIG. BIGGER THAN THIS BUS-JACKING.
I WANT TO KNOW WHAT IT IS.
KEEP AN EYE ON THINGS, CASSIE, AND DON'T LET ANYONE GET HURT. JUST DON'T--
WAIT.
ATOP A 2,000-FOOT SKYSCRAPER.
I THINK SHE'S FINALLY GETTING AROUND TO HER MANIFESTO...

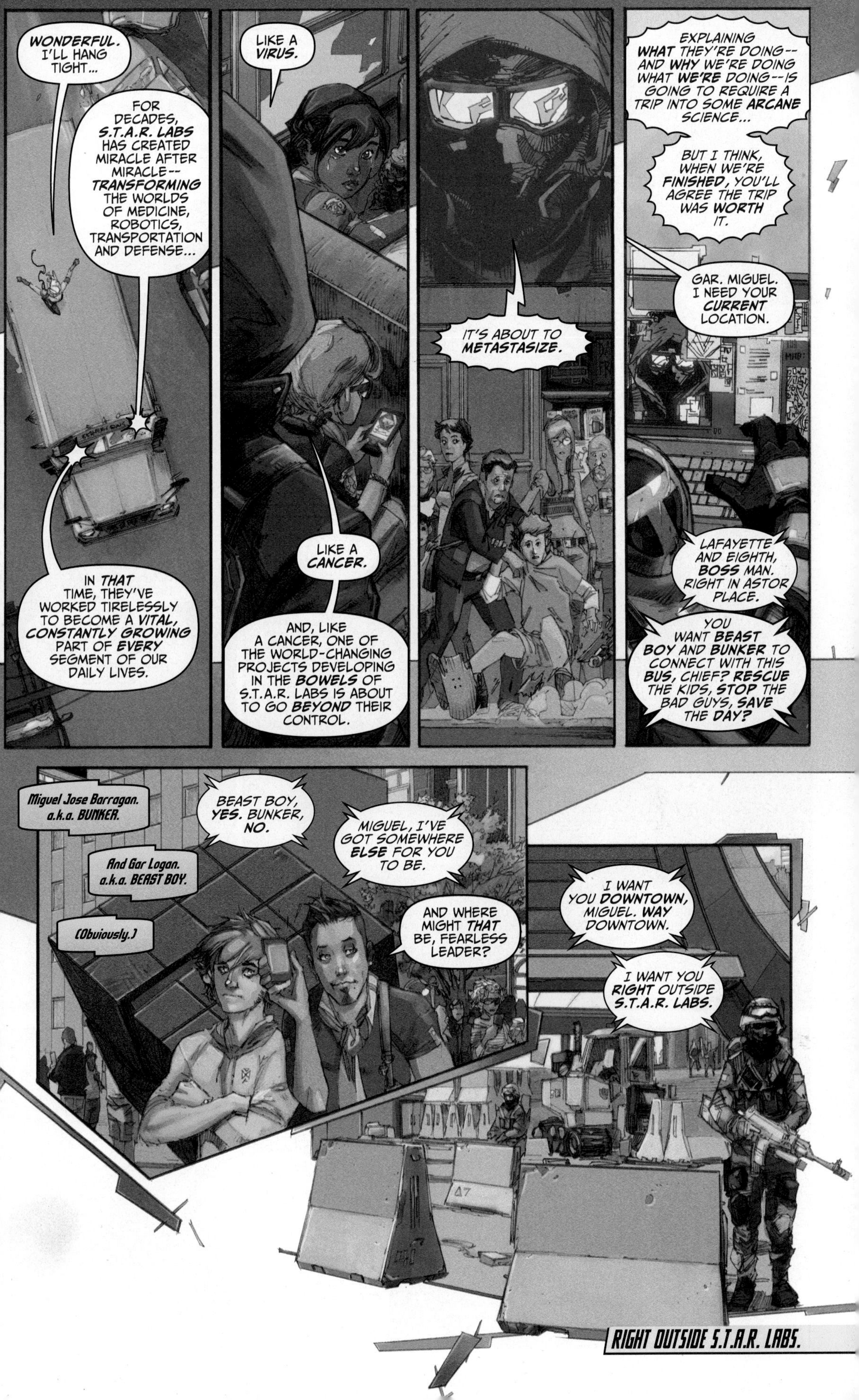
WONDERFUL. I'LL HANG TIGHT...
FOR DECADES, S.T.A.R. LABS HAS CREATED MIRACLE AFTER MIRACLE-- TRANSFORMING THE WORLDS OF MEDICINE, ROBOTICS, TRANSPORTATION AND DEFENSE...
IN THAT TIME, THEY'VE WORKED TIRELESSLY TO BECOME A VITAL, CONSTANTLY GROWING PART OF EVERY SEGMENT OF OUR DAILY LIVES.
LIKE A VIRUS.
LIKE A CANCER.
AND, LIKE A CANCER, ONE OF THE WORLD-CHANGING PROJECTS DEVELOPING IN THE BOWELS OF S.T.A.R. LABS IS ABOUT TO GO BEYOND THEIR CONTROL.
IT'S ABOUT TO METASTASIZE.
EXPLAINING WHAT THEY'RE DOING-- AND WHY WE'RE DOING WHAT WE'RE DOING--IS GOING TO REQUIRE A TRIP INTO SOME ARCANE SCIENCE...
BUT I THINK, WHEN WE'RE FINISHED, YOU'LL AGREE THE TRIP WAS WORTH IT.
GAR. MIGUEL. I NEED YOUR CURRENT LOCATION.
LAFAYETTE AND EIGHTH, BOSS MAN. RIGHT IN ASTOR PLACE.
YOU WANT BEAST BOY AND BUNKER TO CONNECT WITH THIS BUS, CHIEF? RESCUE THE KIDS, STOP THE BAD GUYS, SAVE THE DAY?
Miguel Jose Barragan. a.k.a. BUNKER.
And Gar Logan. a.k.a. BEAST BOY.
(Obviously.)
BEAST BOY, YES. BUNKER, NO.
MIGUEL, I'VE GOT SOMEWHERE ELSE FOR YOU TO BE.
AND WHERE MIGHT THAT BE, FEARLESS LEADER?
I WANT YOU DOWNTOWN, MIGUEL. WAY DOWNTOWN.
I WANT YOU RIGHT OUTSIDE S.T.A.R. LABS.
RIGHT OUTSIDE S.T.A.R. LABS.

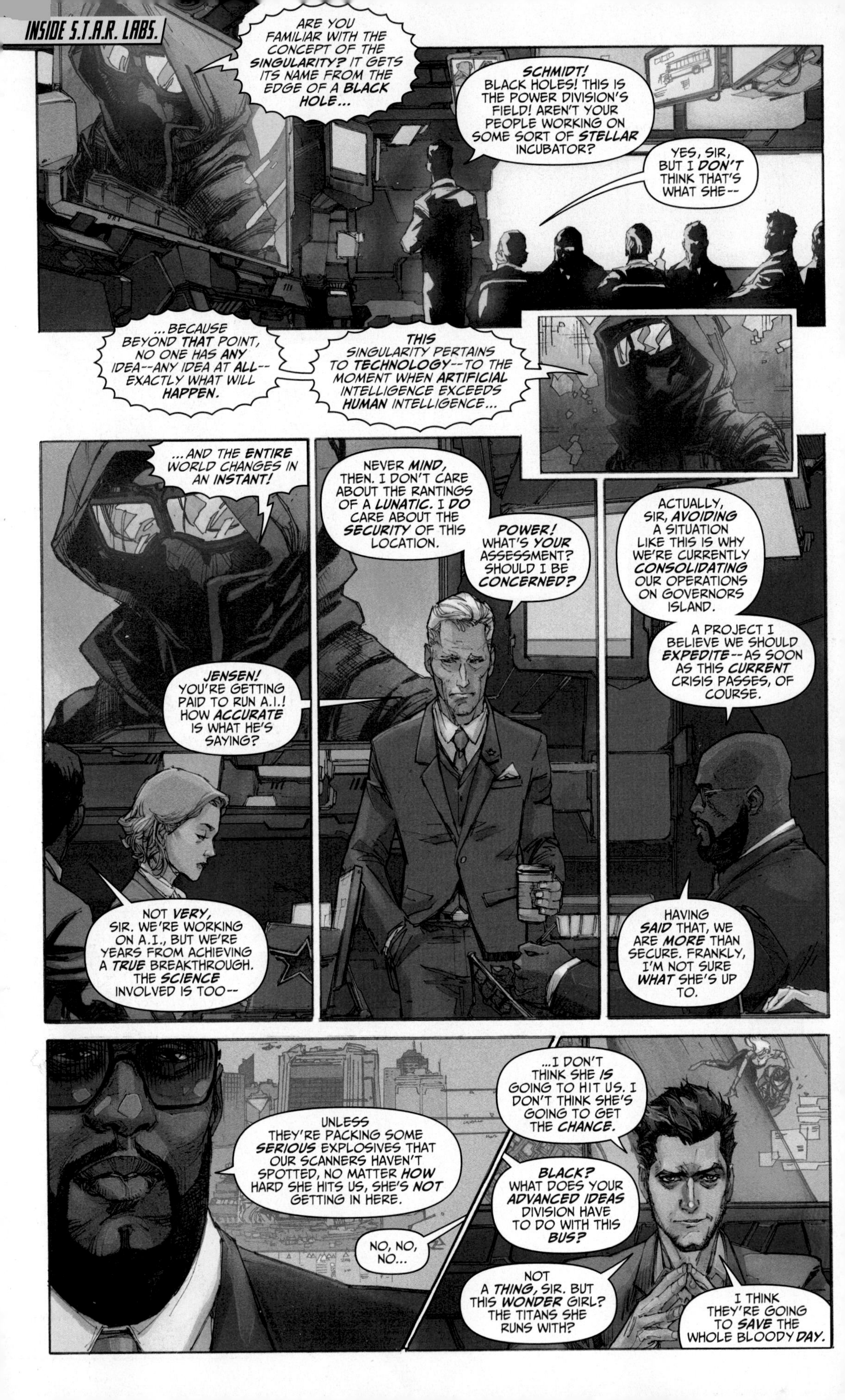
INSIDE S.T.A.R. LABS.
ARE YOU FAMILIAR WITH THE CONCEPT OF THE SINGULARITY? IT GETS ITS NAME FROM THE EDGE OF A BLACK HOLE...
SCHMIDT! BLACK HOLES! THIS IS THE POWER DIVISION'S FIELD! AREN'T YOUR PEOPLE WORKING ON SOME SORT OF STELLAR INCUBATOR?
YES, SIR, BUT I DON'T THINK THAT'S WHAT SHE--
...BECAUSE BEYOND THAT POINT, NO ONE HAS ANY IDEA--ANY IDEA AT ALL--EXACTLY WHAT WILL HAPPEN.
THIS SINGULARITY PERTAINS TO TECHNOLOGY--TO THE MOMENT WHEN ARTIFICIAL INTELLIGENCE EXCEEDS HUMAN INTELLIGENCE...
...AND THE ENTIRE WORLD CHANGES IN AN INSTANT!
JENSEN! YOU'RE GETTING PAID TO RUN A.I.! HOW ACCURATE IS WHAT HE'S SAYING?
NOT VERY, SIR. WE'RE WORKING ON A.I., BUT WE'RE YEARS FROM ACHIEVING A TRUE BREAKTHROUGH. THE SCIENCE INVOLVED IS TOO--
NEVER MIND, THEN. I DON'T CARE ABOUT THE RANTINGS OF A LUNATIC. I DO CARE ABOUT THE SECURITY OF THIS LOCATION.
POWER! WHAT'S YOUR ASSESSMENT? SHOULD I BE CONCERNED?
ACTUALLY, SIR, AVOIDING A SITUATION LIKE THIS IS WHY WE'RE CURRENTLY CONSOLIDATING OUR OPERATIONS ON GOVERNORS ISLAND.
A PROJECT I BELIEVE WE SHOULD EXPEDITE--AS SOON AS THIS CURRENT CRISIS PASSES, OF COURSE.
HAVING SAID THAT, WE ARE MORE THAN SECURE. FRANKLY, I'M NOT SURE WHAT SHE'S UP TO.
UNLESS THEY'RE PACKING SOME SERIOUS EXPLOSIVES THAT OUR SCANNERS HAVEN'T SPOTTED, NO MATTER HOW HARD SHE HITS US, SHE'S NOT GETTING IN HERE.
NO, NO, NO...
...I DON'T THINK SHE IS GOING TO HIT US. I DON'T THINK SHE'S GOING TO GET THE CHANCE.
BLACK? WHAT DOES YOUR ADVANCED IDEAS DIVISION HAVE TO DO WITH THIS BUS?
NOT A THING, SIR. BUT THIS WONDER GIRL? THE TITANS SHE RUNS WITH?
I THINK THEY'RE GOING TO SAVE THE WHOLE BLOODY DAY.

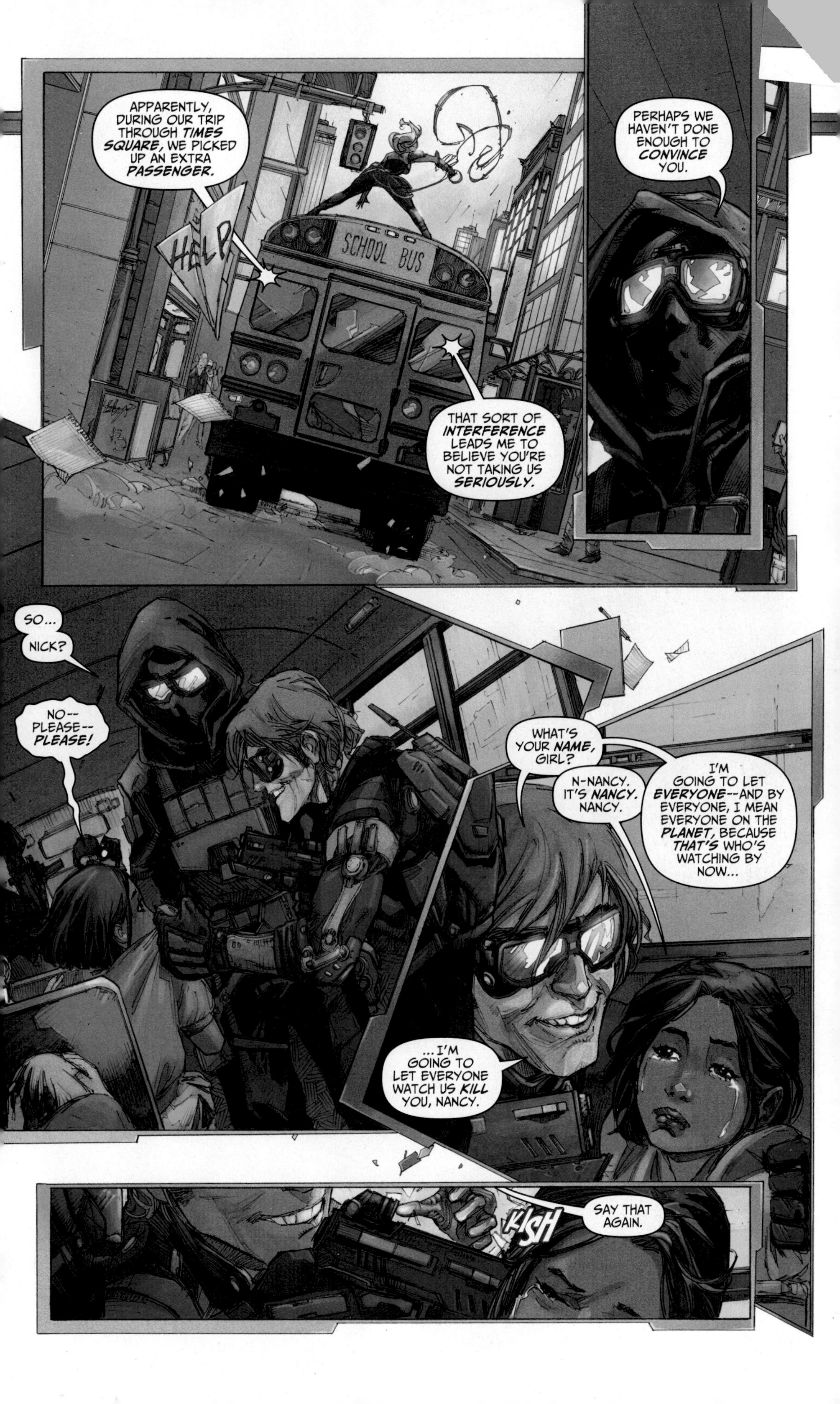

APPARENTLY, DURING OUR TRIP THROUGH TIMES SQUARE, WE PICKED UP AN EXTRA PASSENGER.
HELP
SCHOOL BUS
THAT SORT OF INTERFERENCE LEADS ME TO BELIEVE YOU'RE NOT TAKING US SERIOUSLY.
PERHAPS WE HAVEN'T DONE ENOUGH TO CONVINCE YOU.
SO...
NICK?
NO-- PLEASE-- PLEASE!
WHAT'S YOUR NAME, GIRL?
N-NANCY. IT'S NANCY. NANCY.
I'M GOING TO LET EVERYONE--AND BY EVERYONE, I MEAN EVERYONE ON THE PLANET, BECAUSE THAT'S WHO'S WATCHING BY NOW...
...I'M GOING TO LET EVERYONE WATCH US KILL YOU, NANCY.
KISH
SAY THAT AGAIN.

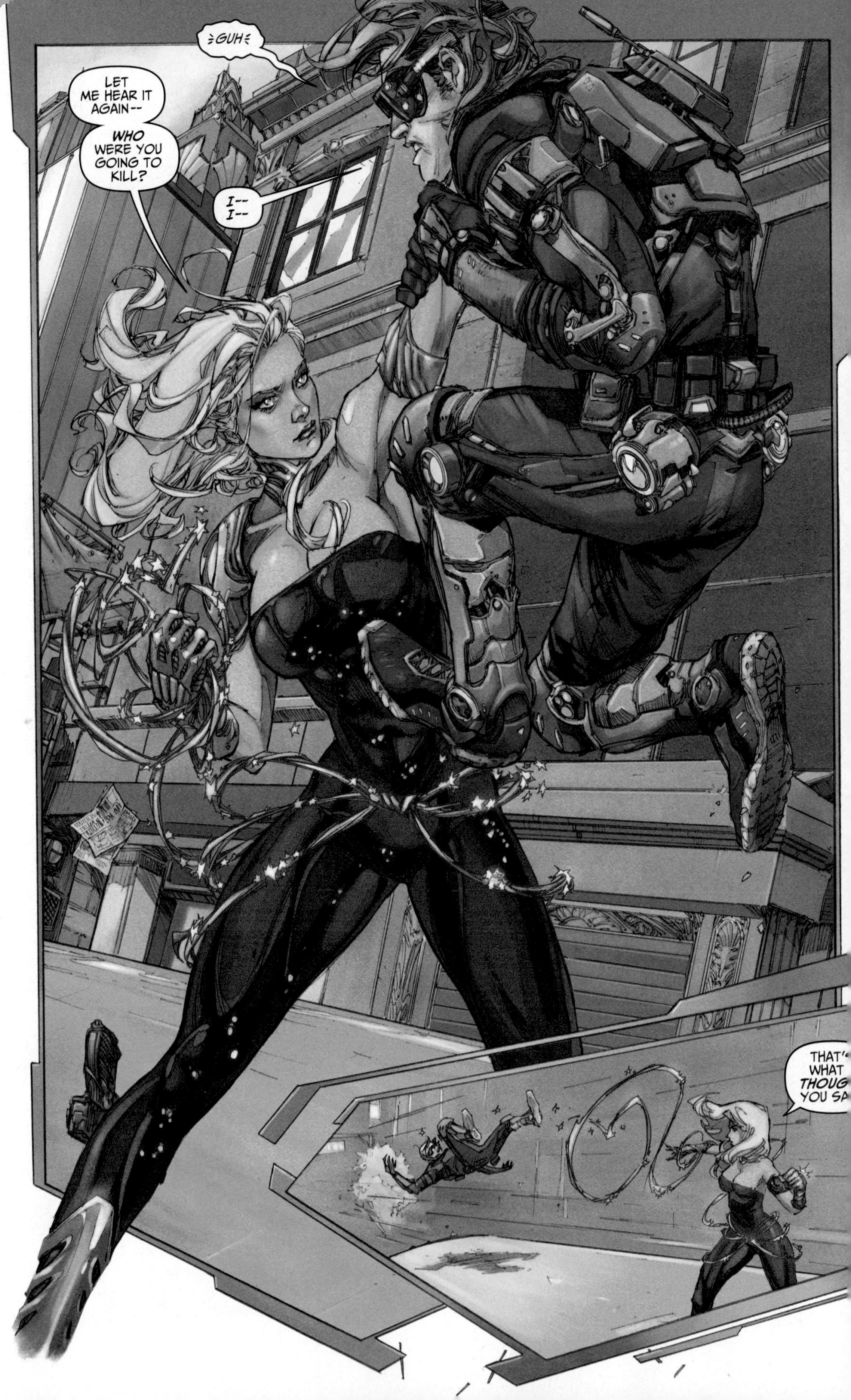
GUH
LET ME HEAR IT AGAIN--
WHO WERE YOU GOING TO KILL?
I-- I--
THAT' WHAT *THOUG* YOU SA

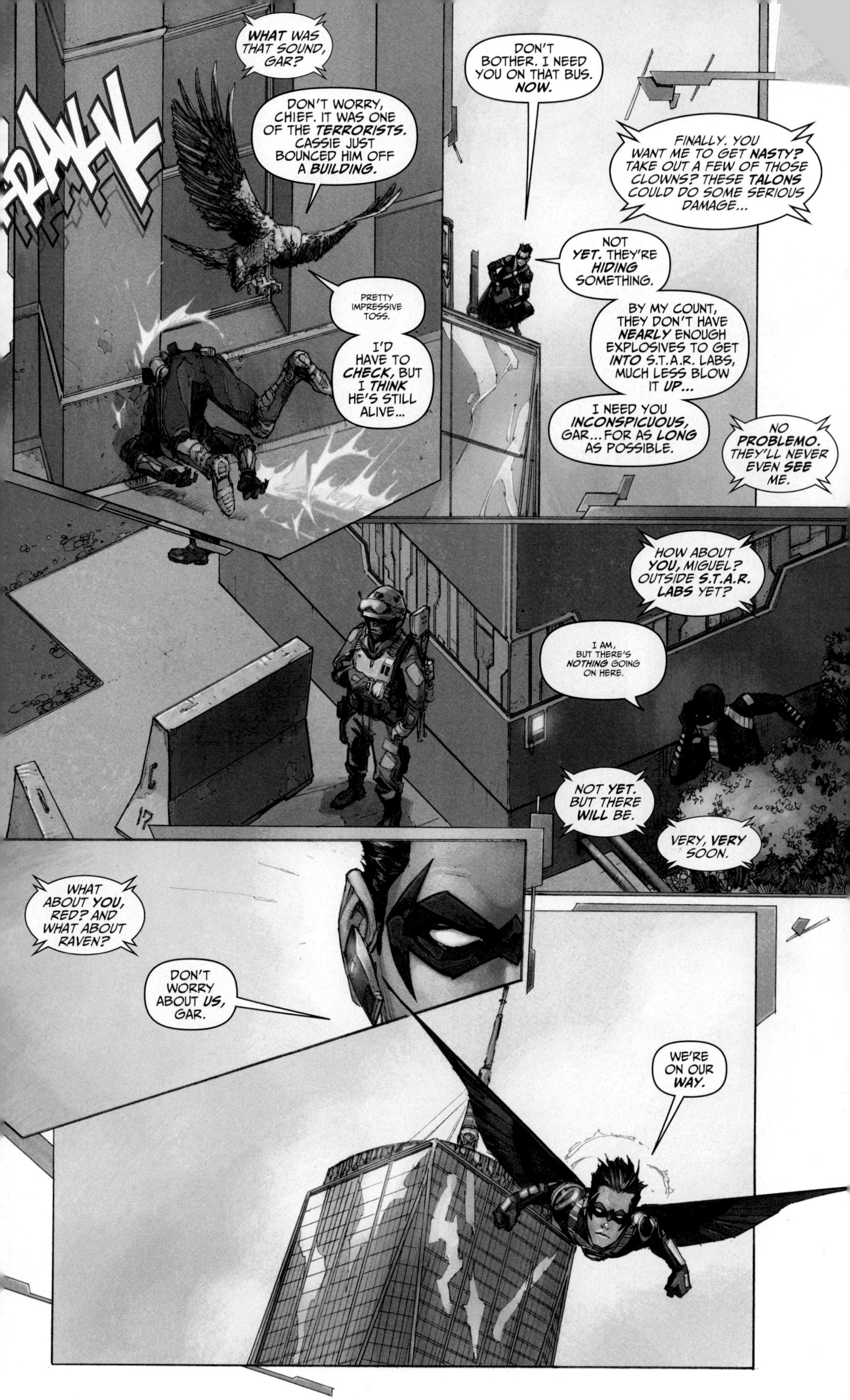
WHAT WAS THAT SOUND, GAR?
KRAKK
DON'T WORRY, CHIEF. IT WAS ONE OF THE TERRORISTS. CASSIE JUST BOUNCED HIM OFF A BUILDING.
PRETTY IMPRESSIVE TOSS.
I'D HAVE TO CHECK, BUT I THINK HE'S STILL ALIVE...
DON'T BOTHER. I NEED YOU ON THAT BUS. NOW.
FINALLY. YOU WANT ME TO GET NASTY? TAKE OUT A FEW OF THOSE CLOWNS? THESE TALONS COULD DO SOME SERIOUS DAMAGE...
NOT YET. THEY'RE HIDING SOMETHING.
BY MY COUNT, THEY DON'T HAVE NEARLY ENOUGH EXPLOSIVES TO GET INTO S.T.A.R. LABS, MUCH LESS BLOW IT UP...
I NEED YOU INCONSPICUOUS, GAR...FOR AS LONG AS POSSIBLE.
NO PROBLEMO. THEY'LL NEVER EVEN SEE ME.
HOW ABOUT YOU, MIGUEL? OUTSIDE S.T.A.R. LABS YET?
I AM, BUT THERE'S NOTHING GOING ON HERE.
NOT YET. BUT THERE WILL BE.
VERY, VERY SOON.
WHAT ABOUT YOU, RED? AND WHAT ABOUT RAVEN?
DON'T WORRY ABOUT US, GAR.
WE'RE ON OUR WAY.

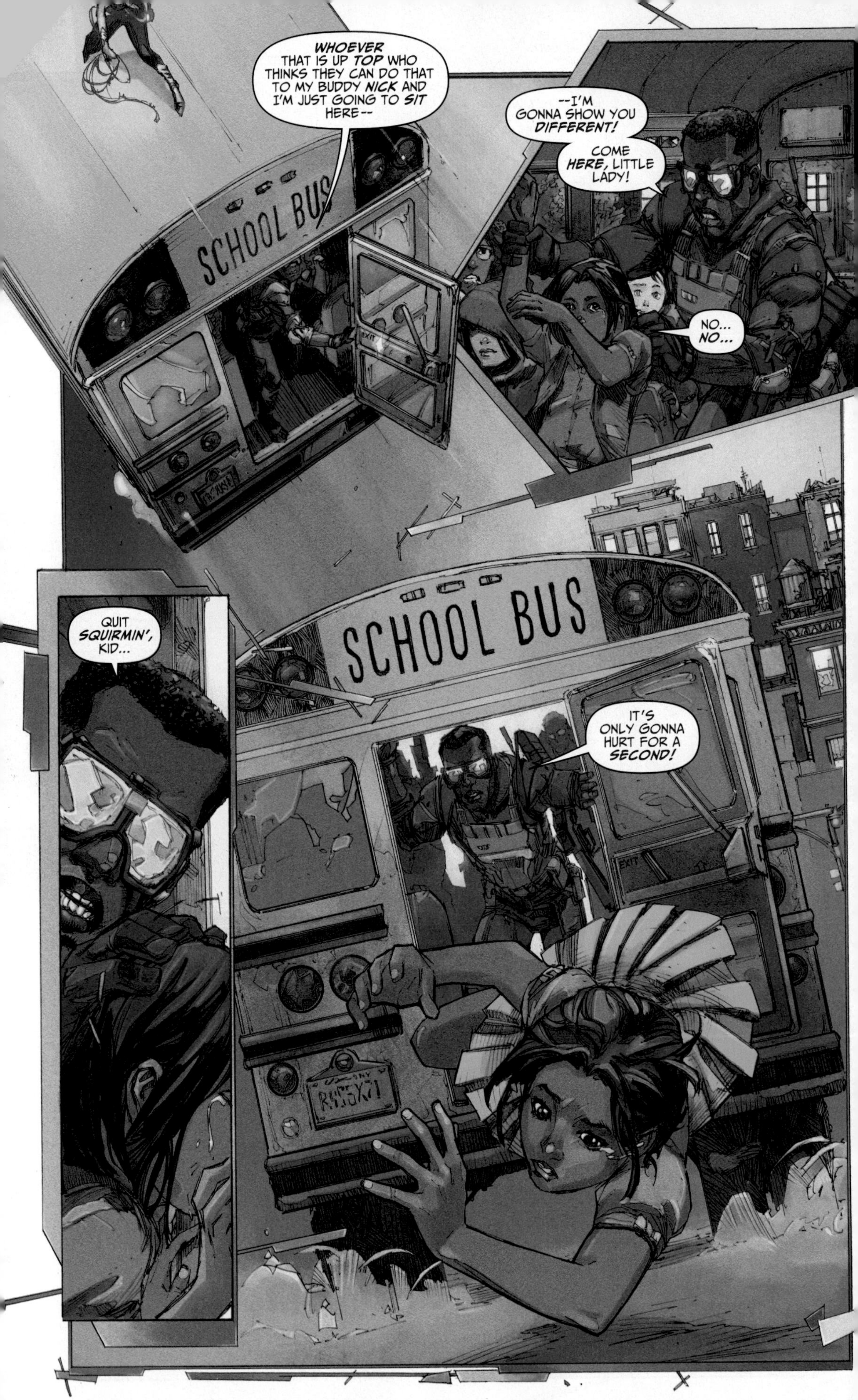

WHOEVER THAT IS UP TOP WHO THINKS THEY CAN DO THAT TO MY BUDDY NICK AND I'M JUST GOING TO SIT HERE--
SCHOOL BUS
--I'M GONNA SHOW YOU DIFFERENT!
COME HERE, LITTLE LADY!
NO... NO...
QUIT SQUIRMIN', KID...
SCHOOL BUS
IT'S ONLY GONNA HURT FOR A SECOND!

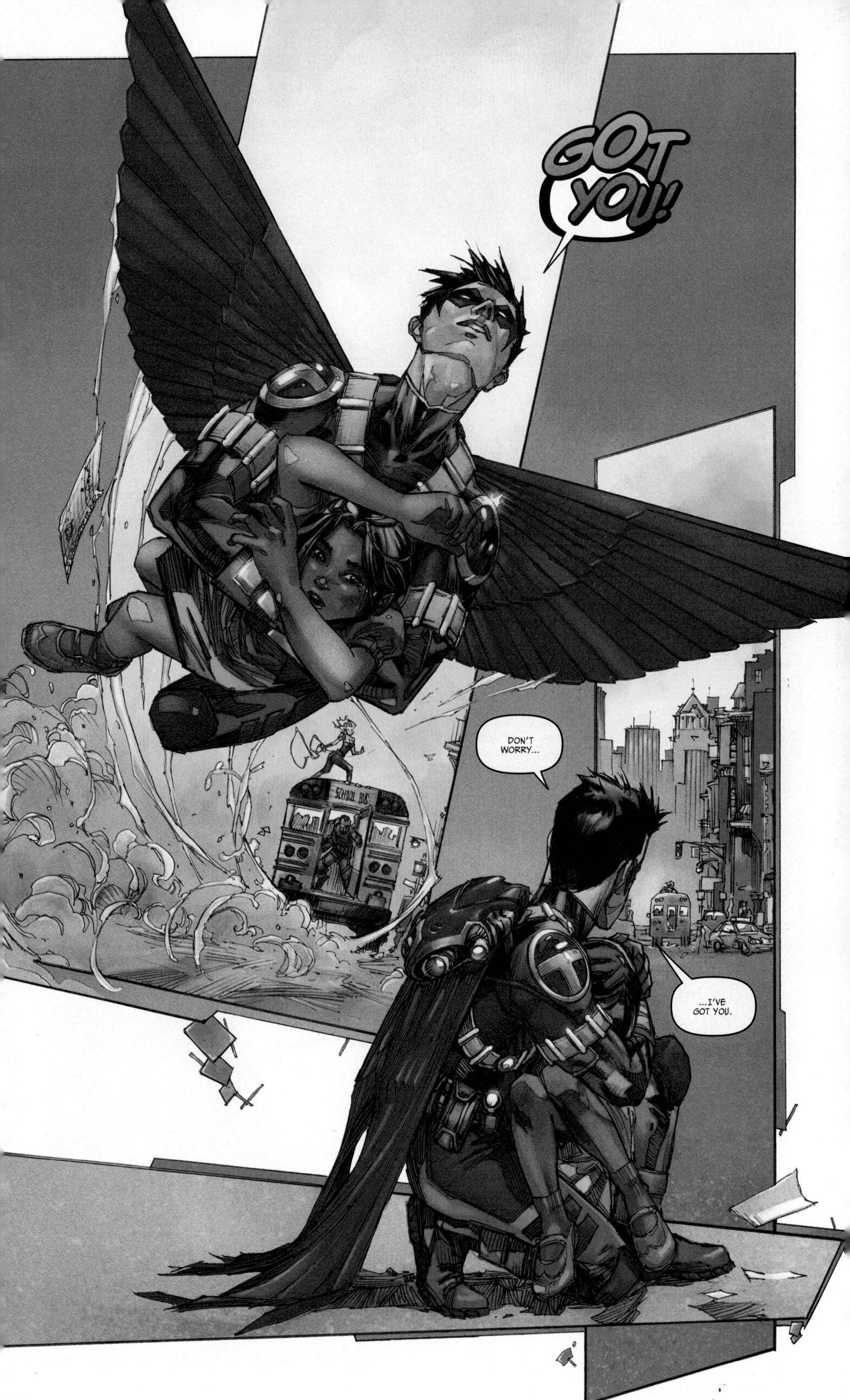
GOT YOU!
DON'T WORRY...
...I'VE GOT YOU.
SCHOOL BUS

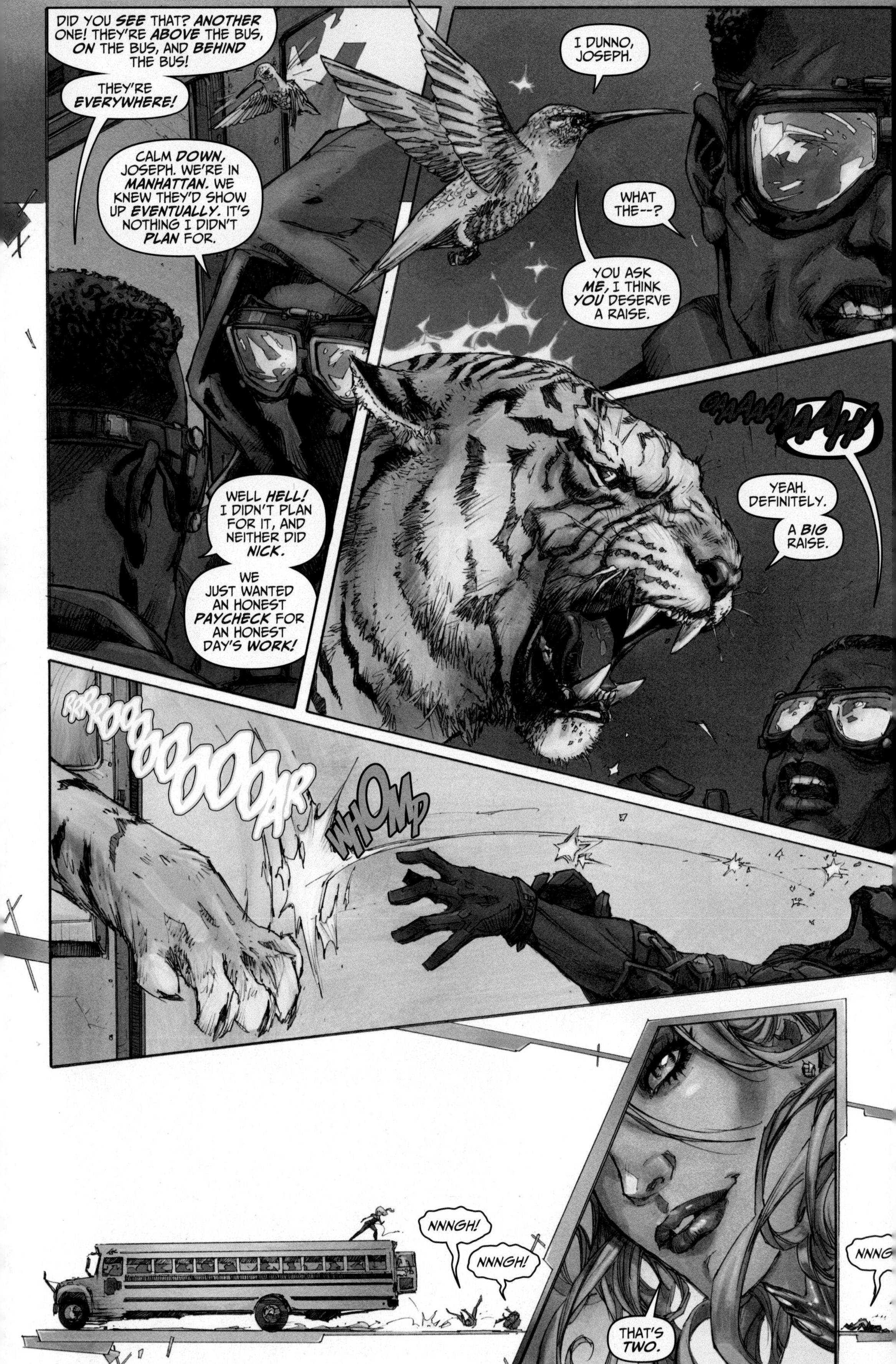

DID YOU SEE THAT? ANOTHER ONE! THEY'RE ABOVE THE BUS, ON THE BUS, AND BEHIND THE BUS!
THEY'RE EVERYWHERE!
CALM DOWN, JOSEPH. WE'RE IN MANHATTAN. WE KNEW THEY'D SHOW UP EVENTUALLY. IT'S NOTHING I DIDN'T PLAN FOR.
I DUNNO, JOSEPH.
WHAT THE--?
YOU ASK ME, I THINK YOU DESERVE A RAISE.
WELL HELL! I DIDN'T PLAN FOR IT, AND NEITHER DID NICK.
WE JUST WANTED AN HONEST PAYCHECK FOR AN HONEST DAY'S WORK!
YEAH. DEFINITELY.
A BIG RAISE.
RRRROOOOOOOOOAR
WHOMP
NNNGH!
NNNGH!
THAT'S TWO.

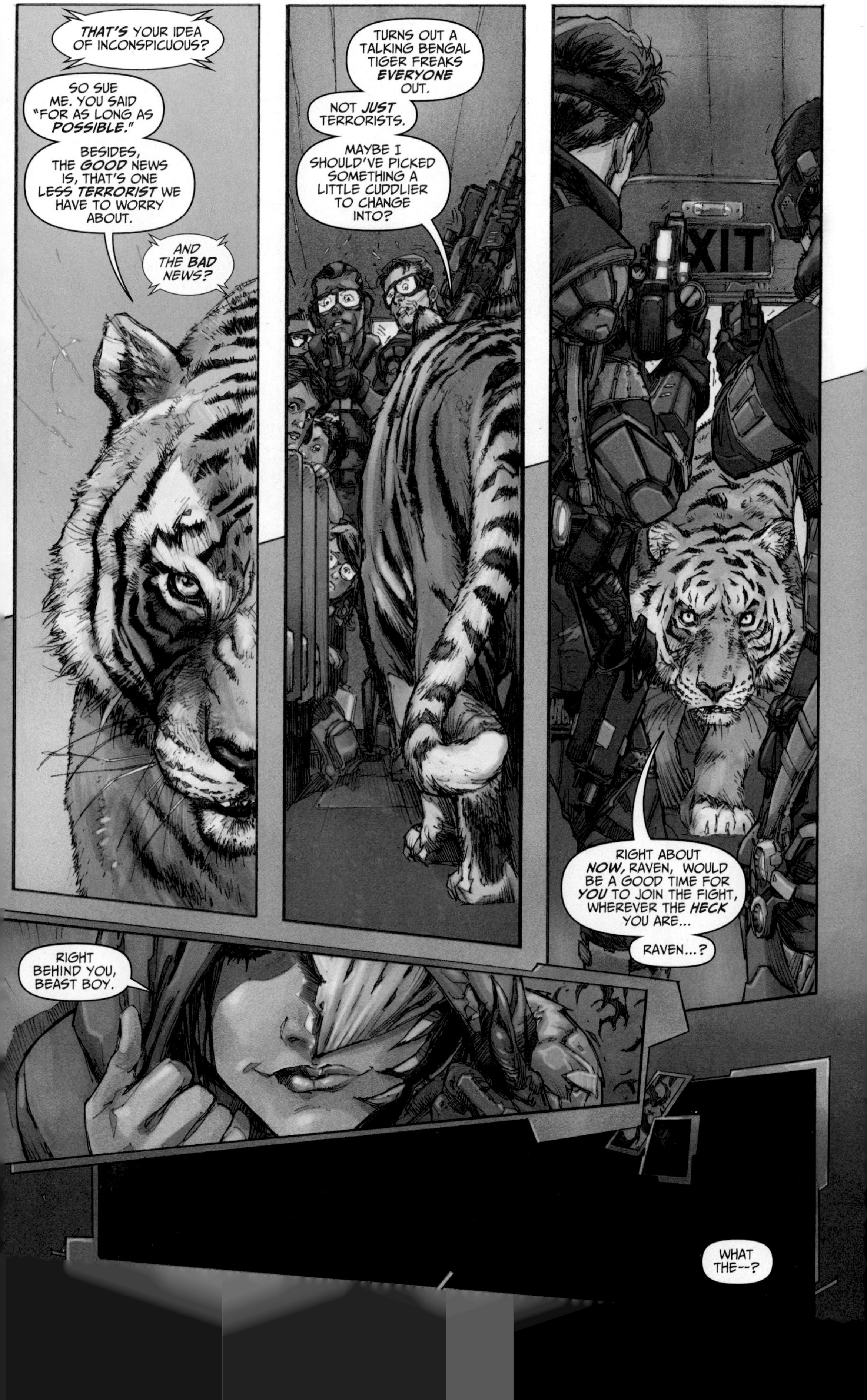
THAT'S YOUR IDEA OF INCONSPICUOUS?
SO SUE ME. YOU SAID "FOR AS LONG AS POSSIBLE."
BESIDES, THE GOOD NEWS IS, THAT'S ONE LESS TERRORIST WE HAVE TO WORRY ABOUT.
AND THE BAD NEWS?
TURNS OUT A TALKING BENGAL TIGER FREAKS EVERYONE OUT.
NOT JUST TERRORISTS.
MAYBE I SHOULD'VE PICKED SOMETHING A LITTLE CUDDLIER TO CHANGE INTO?
EXIT
RIGHT ABOUT NOW, RAVEN, WOULD BE A GOOD TIME FOR YOU TO JOIN THE FIGHT, WHEREVER THE HECK YOU ARE...
RAVEN...?
RIGHT BEHIND YOU, BEAST BOY.
WHAT THE--?

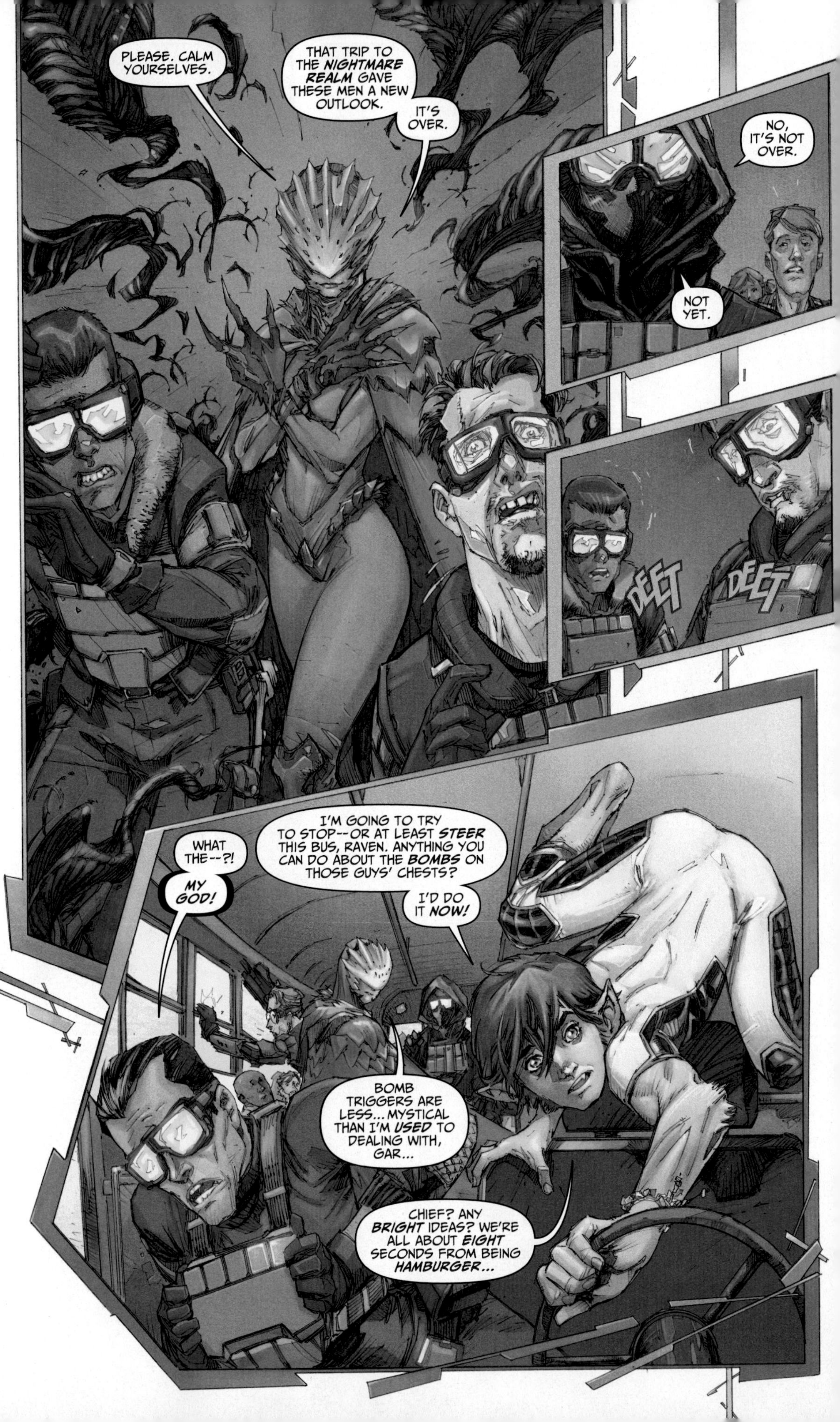
PLEASE. CALM YOURSELVES.
THAT TRIP TO THE *NIGHTMARE REALM* GAVE THESE MEN A NEW OUTLOOK.
IT'S OVER.
NO, IT'S NOT OVER.
NOT YET.
DEET
DEET
WHAT THE--?!
MY GOD!
I'M GOING TO TRY TO STOP--OR AT LEAST *STEER* THIS BUS, RAVEN. ANYTHING YOU CAN DO ABOUT THE *BOMBS* ON THOSE GUYS' CHESTS?
I'D DO IT *NOW!*
BOMB TRIGGERS ARE LESS...MYSTICAL THAN I'M *USED* TO DEALING WITH, GAR...
CHIEF? ANY *BRIGHT* IDEAS? WE'RE ALL ABOUT *EIGHT* SECONDS FROM BEING *HAMBURGER...*

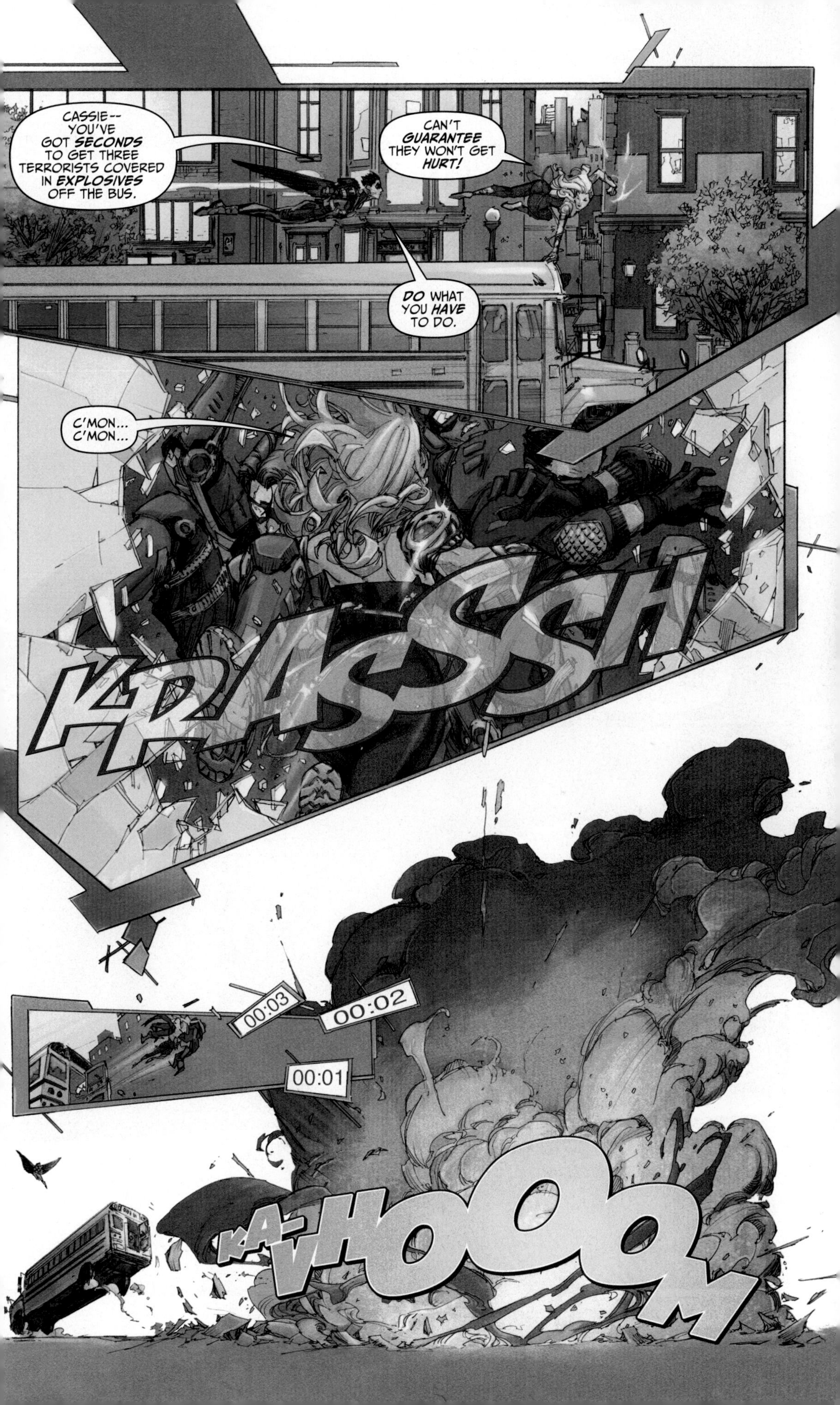
CASSIE-- YOU'VE GOT SECONDS TO GET THREE TERRORISTS COVERED IN EXPLOSIVES OFF THE BUS.
CAN'T GUARANTEE THEY WON'T GET HURT!
DO WHAT YOU HAVE TO DO.
C'MON... C'MON...
KRASSH
00:03
00:02
00:01
KA-VHOOOM

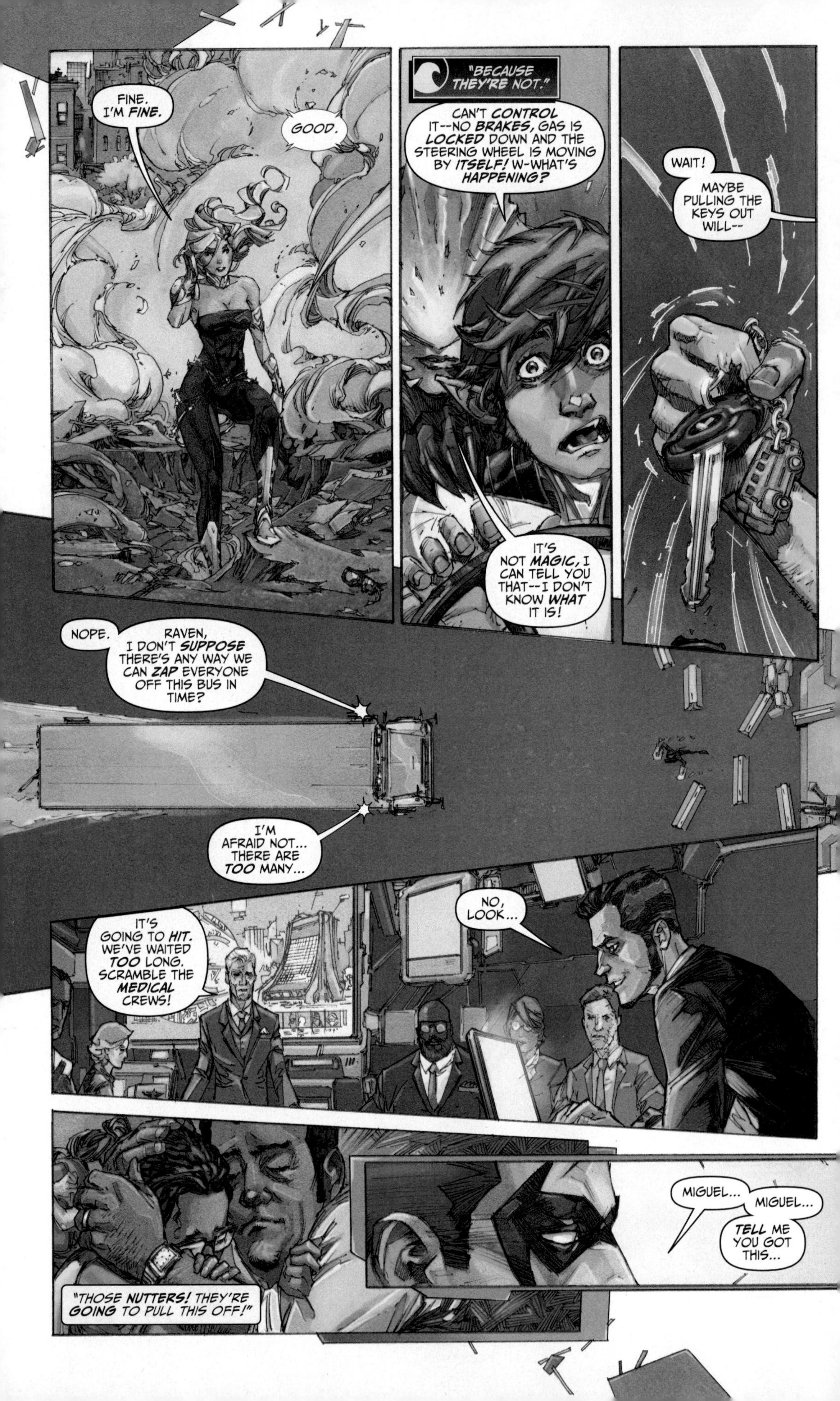
FINE. I'M FINE.
GOOD.
"BECAUSE THEY'RE NOT."
CAN'T CONTROL IT--NO BRAKES, GAS IS LOCKED DOWN AND THE STEERING WHEEL IS MOVING BY ITSELF! W-WHAT'S HAPPENING?
IT'S NOT MAGIC, I CAN TELL YOU THAT--I DON'T KNOW WHAT IT IS!
WAIT!
MAYBE PULLING THE KEYS OUT WILL--
NOPE.
RAVEN, I DON'T SUPPOSE THERE'S ANY WAY WE CAN ZAP EVERYONE OFF THIS BUS IN TIME?
I'M AFRAID NOT... THERE ARE TOO MANY...
IT'S GOING TO HIT. WE'VE WAITED TOO LONG. SCRAMBLE THE MEDICAL CREWS!
NO, LOOK...
"THOSE NUTTERS! THEY'RE GOING TO PULL THIS OFF!"
MIGUEL...
MIGUEL...
TELL ME YOU GOT THIS...

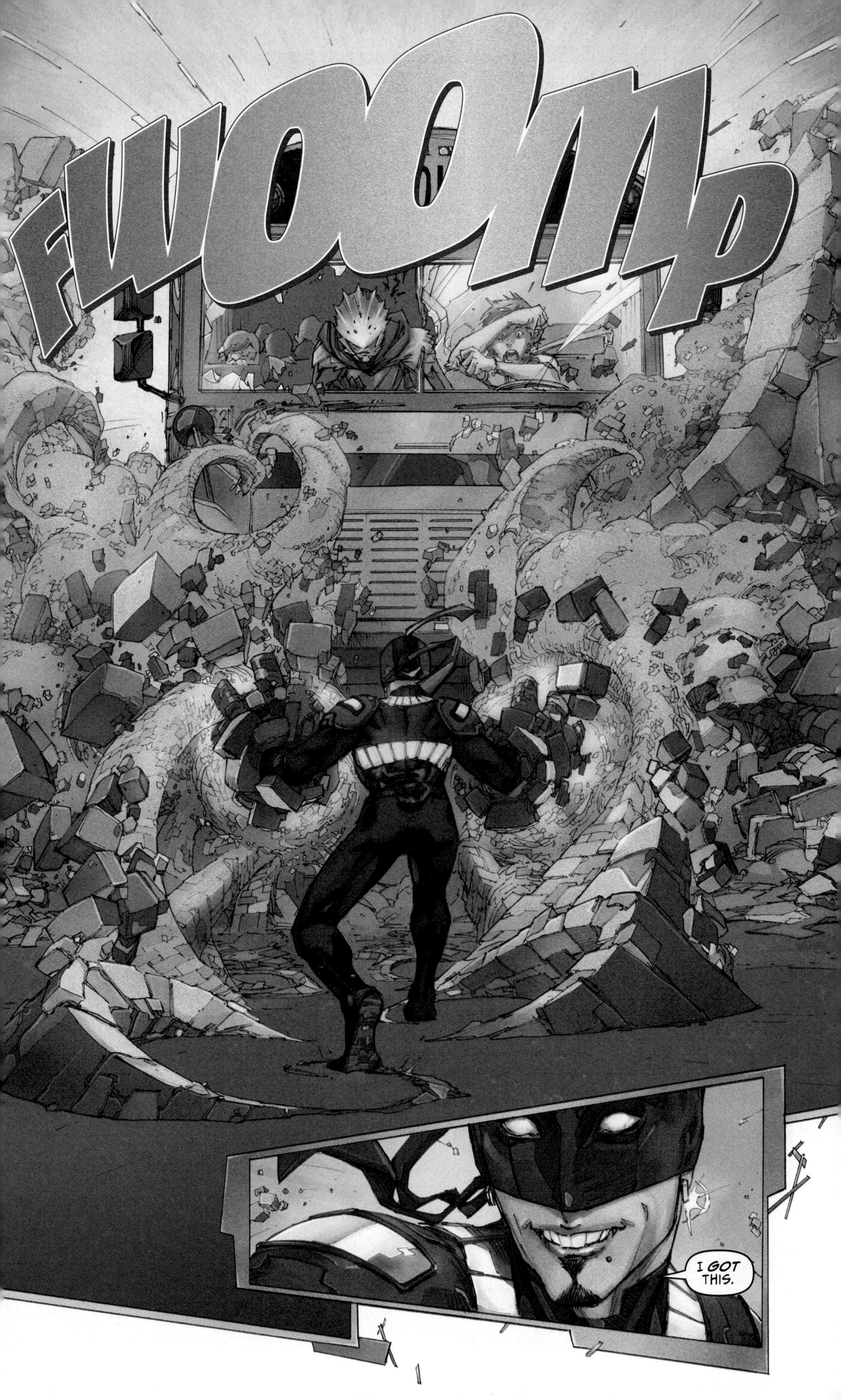
FWOOMP
I GOT THIS.

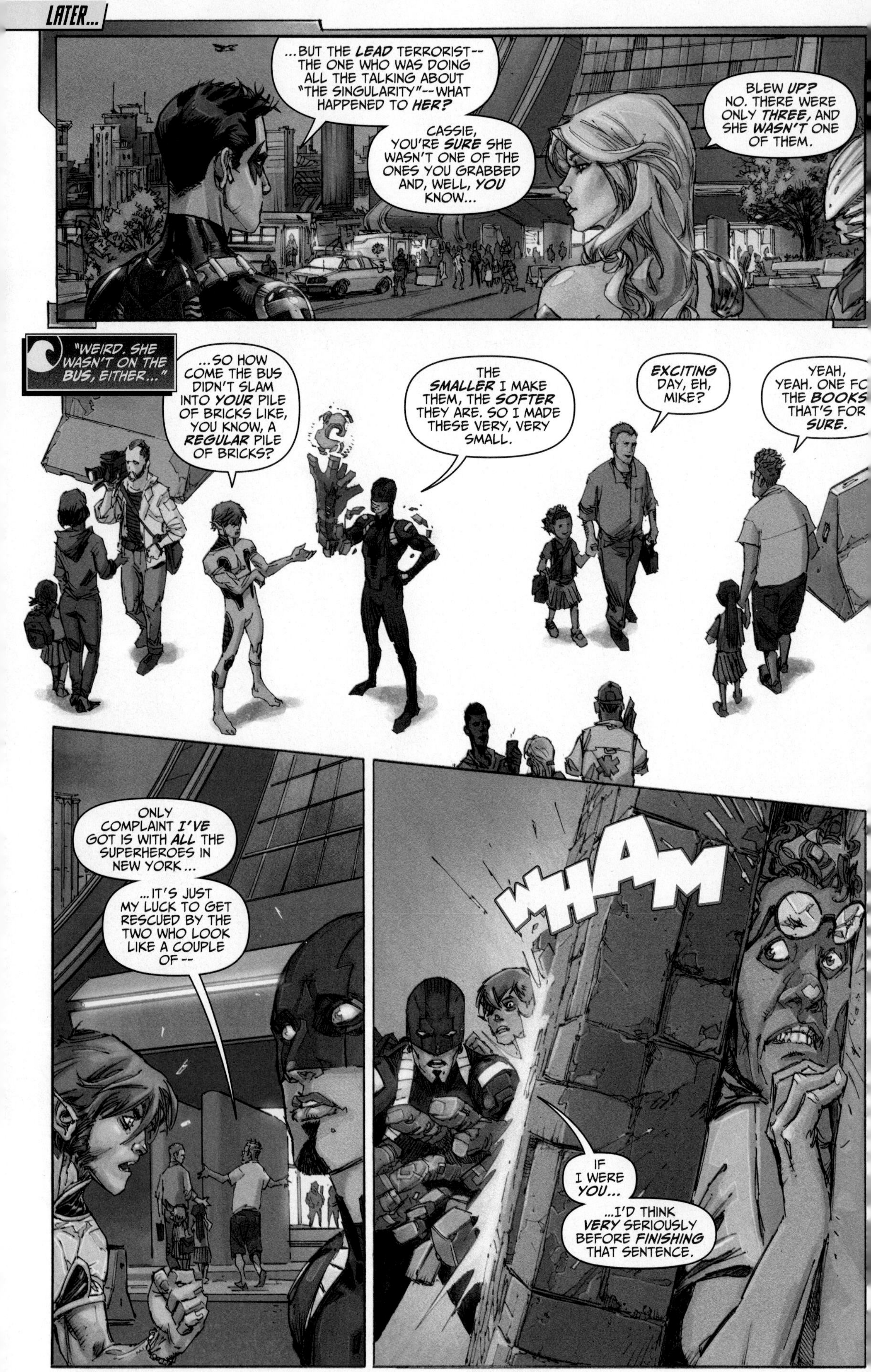
LATER...
...BUT THE LEAD TERRORIST-- THE ONE WHO WAS DOING ALL THE TALKING ABOUT "THE SINGULARITY"--WHAT HAPPENED TO HER?
CASSIE, YOU'RE SURE SHE WASN'T ONE OF THE ONES YOU GRABBED AND, WELL, YOU KNOW...
BLEW UP? NO. THERE WERE ONLY THREE, AND SHE WASN'T ONE OF THEM.
"WEIRD. SHE WASN'T ON THE BUS, EITHER..."
...SO HOW COME THE BUS DIDN'T SLAM INTO YOUR PILE OF BRICKS LIKE, YOU KNOW, A REGULAR PILE OF BRICKS?
THE SMALLER I MAKE THEM, THE SOFTER THEY ARE. SO I MADE THESE VERY, VERY SMALL.
EXCITING DAY, EH, MIKE?
YEAH, YEAH. ONE FO THE BOOKS THAT'S FOR SURE.
ONLY COMPLAINT I'VE GOT IS WITH ALL THE SUPERHEROES IN NEW YORK...
...IT'S JUST MY LUCK TO GET RESCUED BY THE TWO WHO LOOK LIKE A COUPLE OF --
WHAM
IF I WERE YOU...
...I'D THINK VERY SERIOUSLY BEFORE FINISHING THAT SENTENCE.

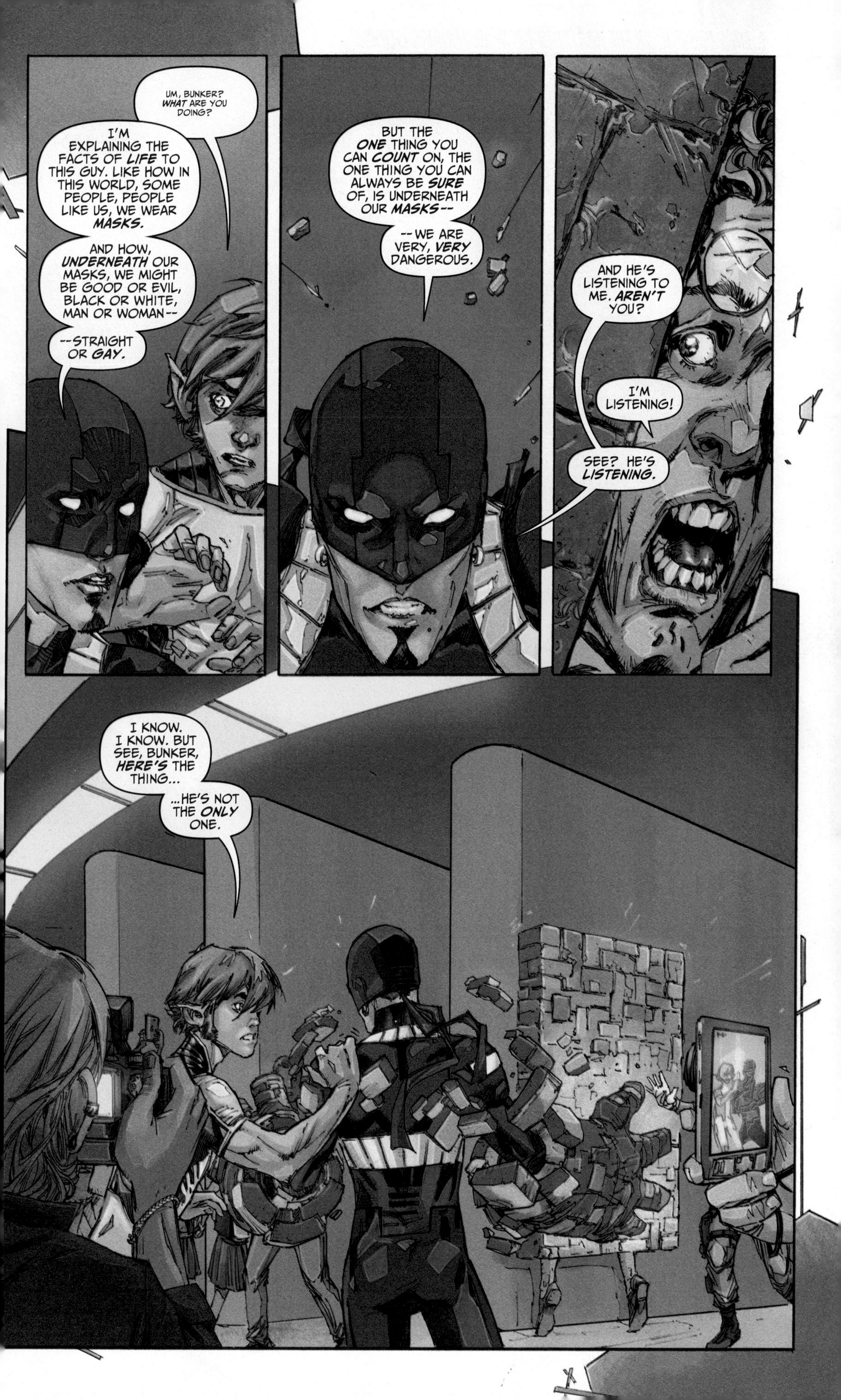

UM, BUNKER? WHAT ARE YOU DOING?
I'M EXPLAINING THE FACTS OF LIFE TO THIS GUY. LIKE HOW IN THIS WORLD, SOME PEOPLE, PEOPLE LIKE US, WE WEAR MASKS.
AND HOW, UNDERNEATH OUR MASKS, WE MIGHT BE GOOD OR EVIL, BLACK OR WHITE, MAN OR WOMAN--
--STRAIGHT OR GAY.
BUT THE ONE THING YOU CAN COUNT ON, THE ONE THING YOU CAN ALWAYS BE SURE OF, IS UNDERNEATH OUR MASKS--
--WE ARE VERY, VERY DANGEROUS.
AND HE'S LISTENING TO ME. AREN'T YOU?
I'M LISTENING!
SEE? HE'S LISTENING.
I KNOW. I KNOW. BUT SEE, BUNKER, HERE'S THE THING...
...HE'S NOT THE ONLY ONE.

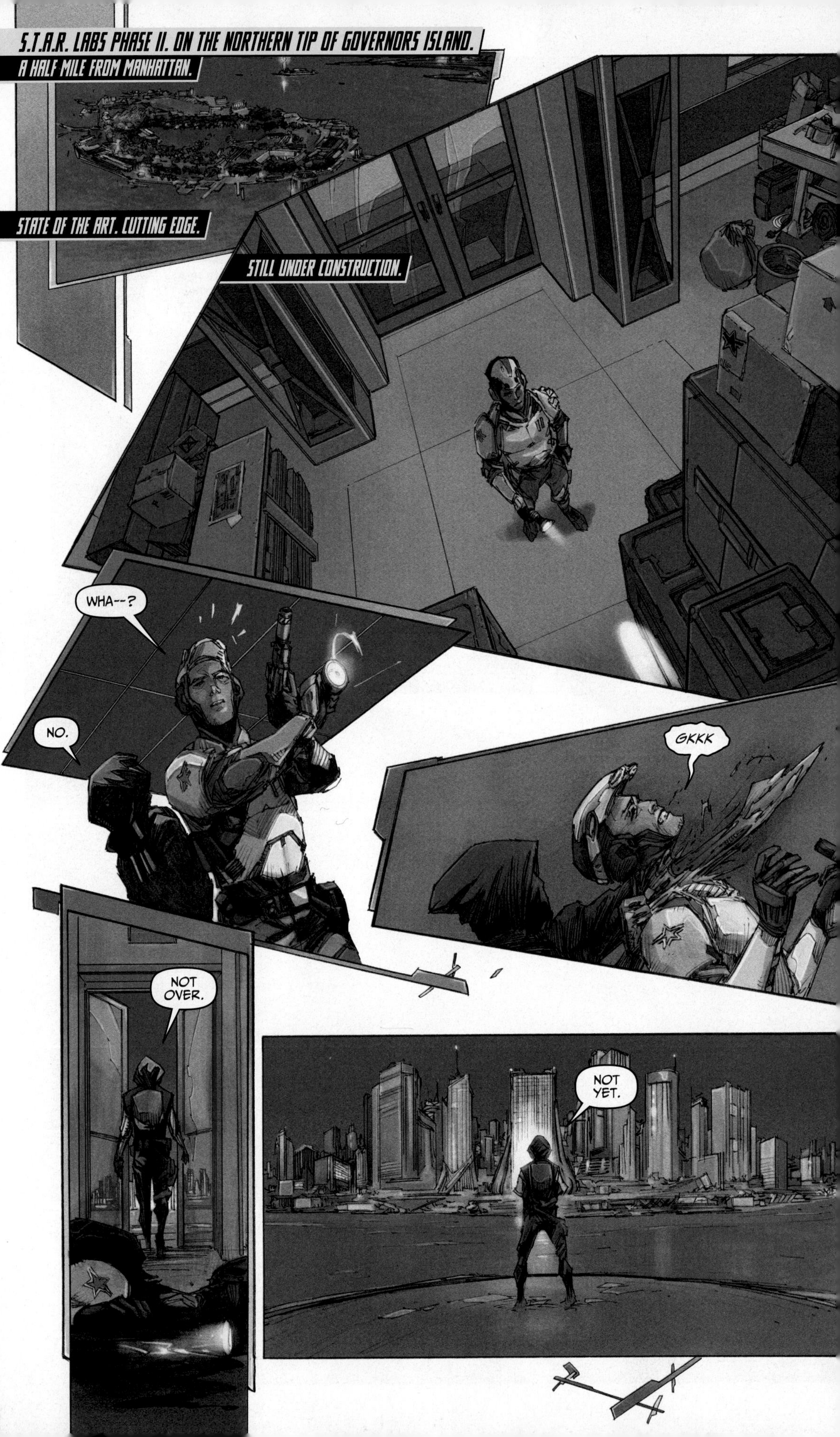

S.T.A.R. LABS PHASE II. ON THE NORTHERN TIP OF GOVERNORS ISLAND.
A HALF MILE FROM MANHATTAN.
STATE OF THE ART. CUTTING EDGE.
STILL UNDER CONSTRUCTION.
WHA--?
NO.
GKKK
NOT OVER.
NOT YET.

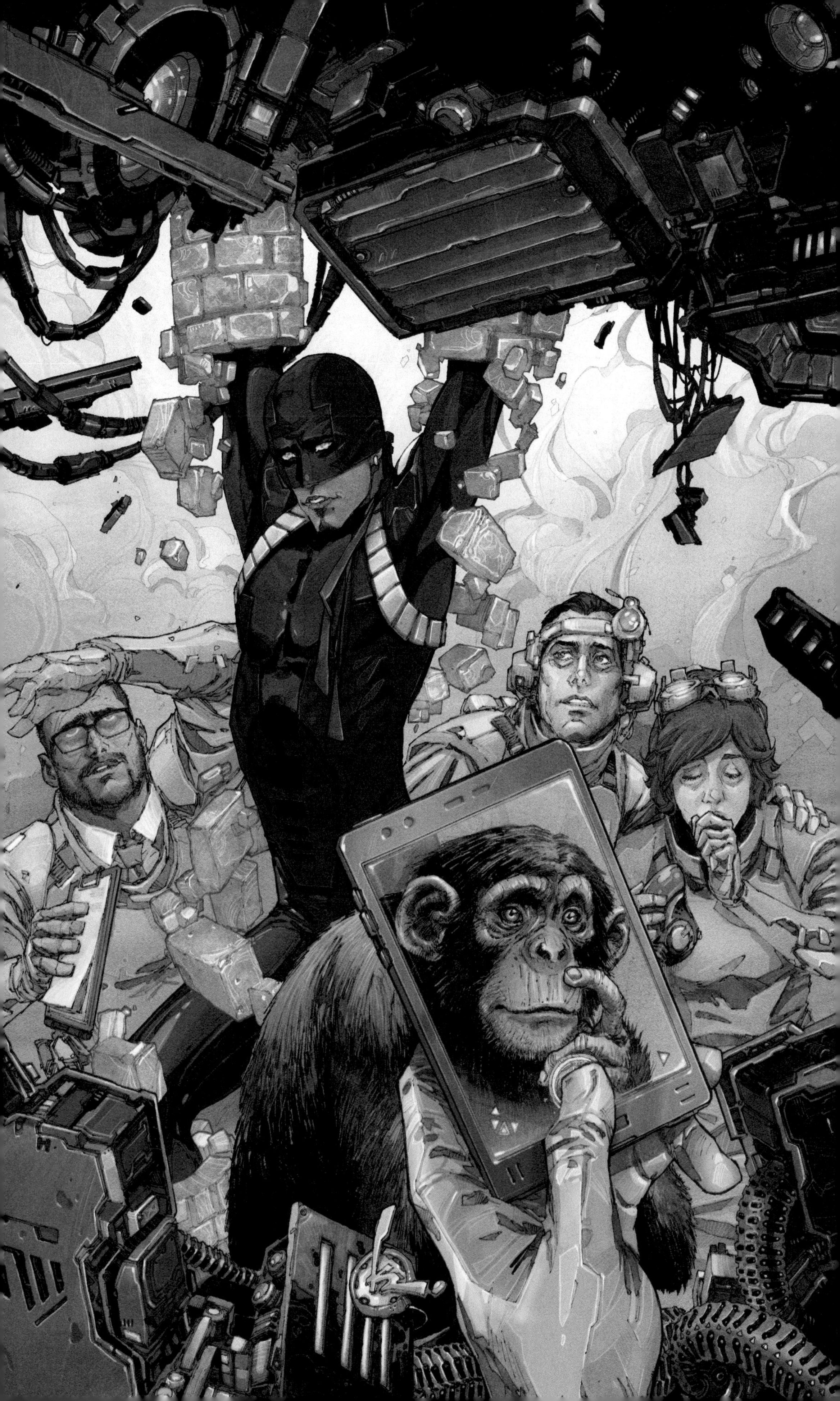

BLINDED BY THE LIGHT: PART 2

WILL PFEIFER writer KENNETH ROCAFORT artist DAN BROWN colorist JOHN J. HILL letterer cover art by KENNETH ROCAFORT

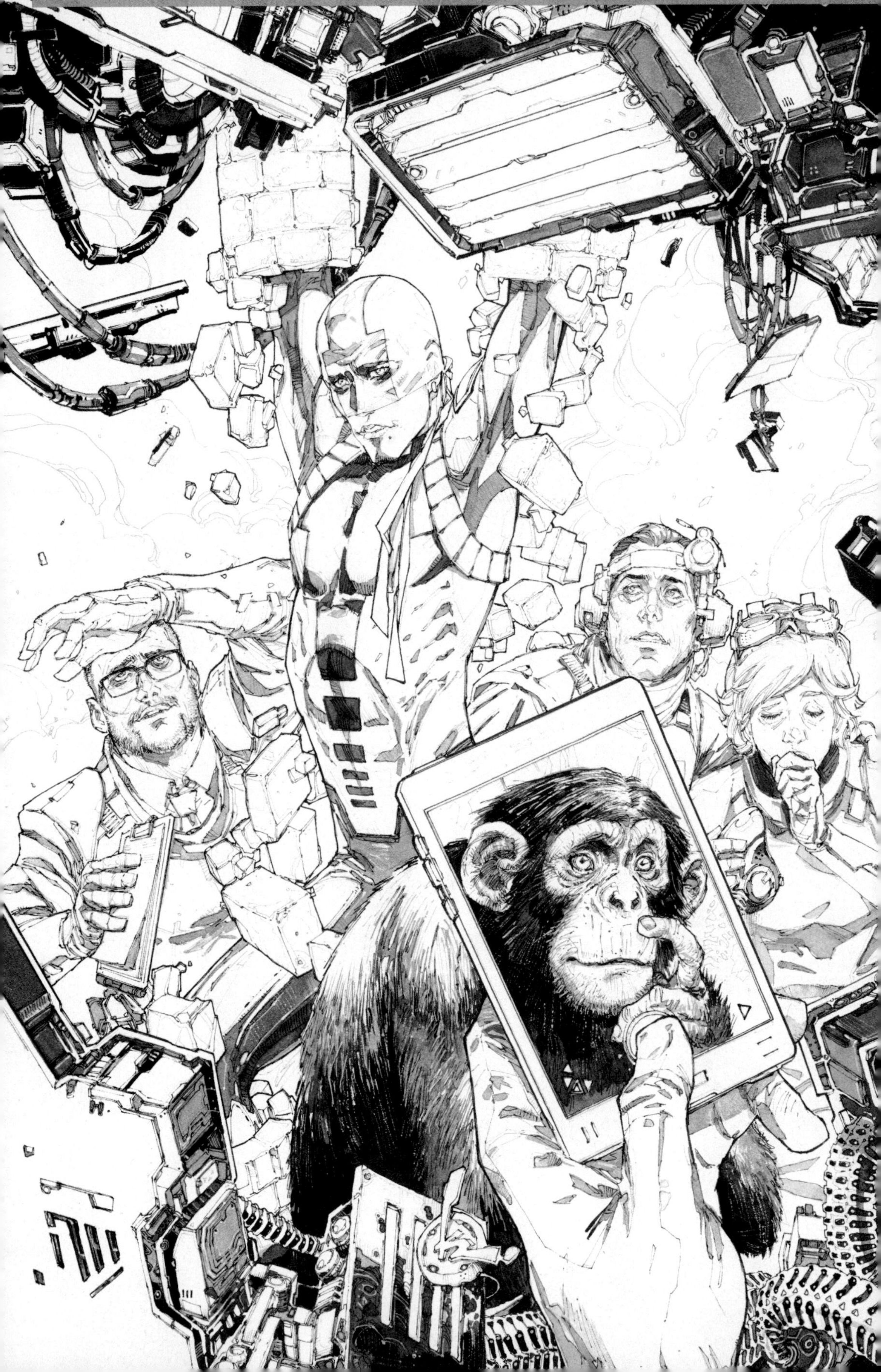

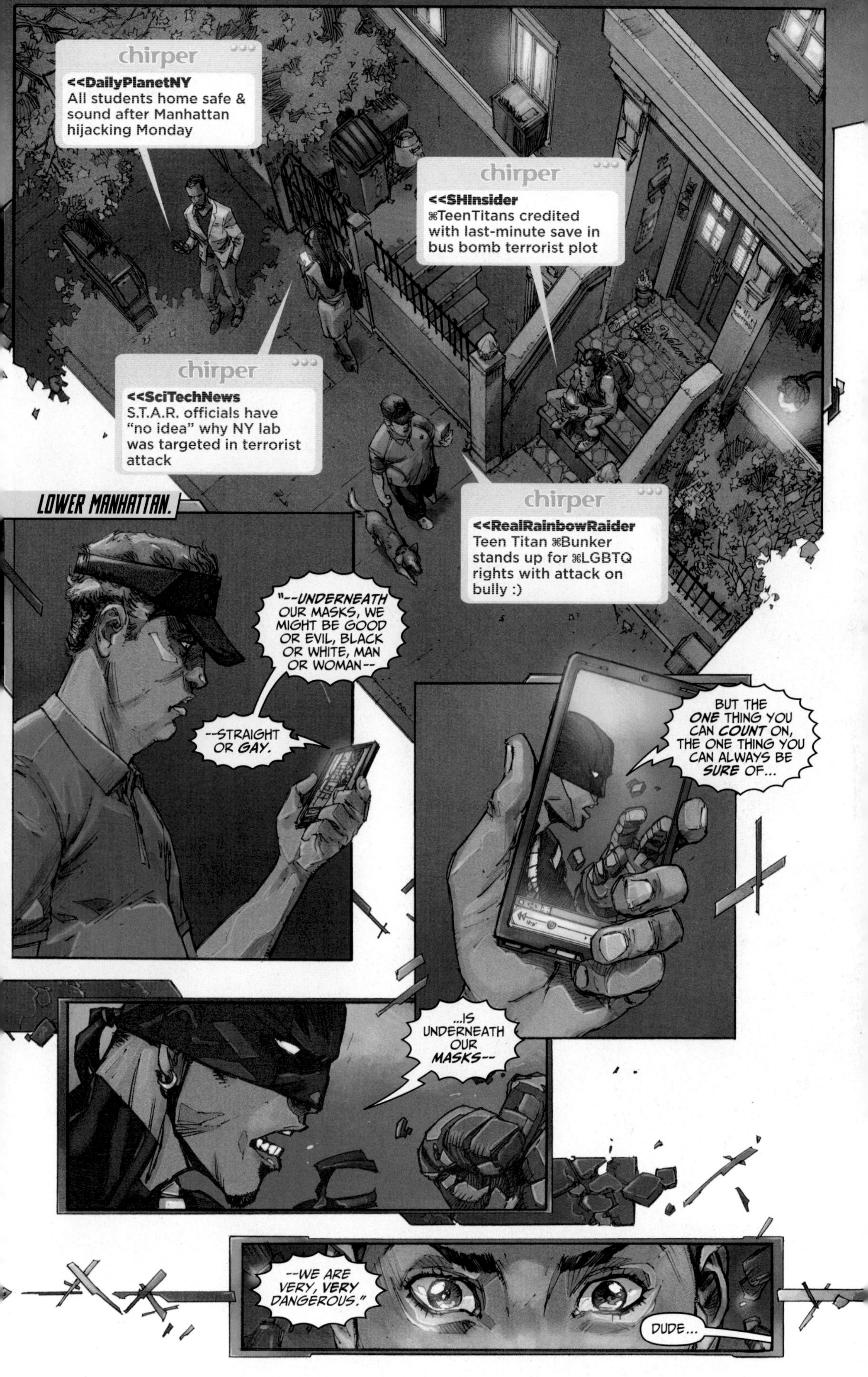
chirper
<<DailyPlanetNY
All students home safe & sound after Manhattan hijacking Monday
chirper
<<SHInsider
⌘TeenTitans credited with last-minute save in bus bomb terrorist plot
chirper
<<SciTechNews
S.T.A.R. officials have "no idea" why NY lab was targeted in terrorist attack
chirper
<<RealRainbowRaider
Teen Titan ⌘Bunker stands up for ⌘LGBTQ rights with attack on bully :)
LOWER MANHATTAN.
"--UNDERNEATH OUR MASKS, WE MIGHT BE GOOD OR EVIL, BLACK OR WHITE, MAN OR WOMAN--
--STRAIGHT OR GAY.
BUT THE ONE THING YOU CAN COUNT ON, THE ONE THING YOU CAN ALWAYS BE SURE OF...
...IS UNDERNEATH OUR MASKS--
--WE ARE VERY, VERY DANGEROUS."
DUDE...

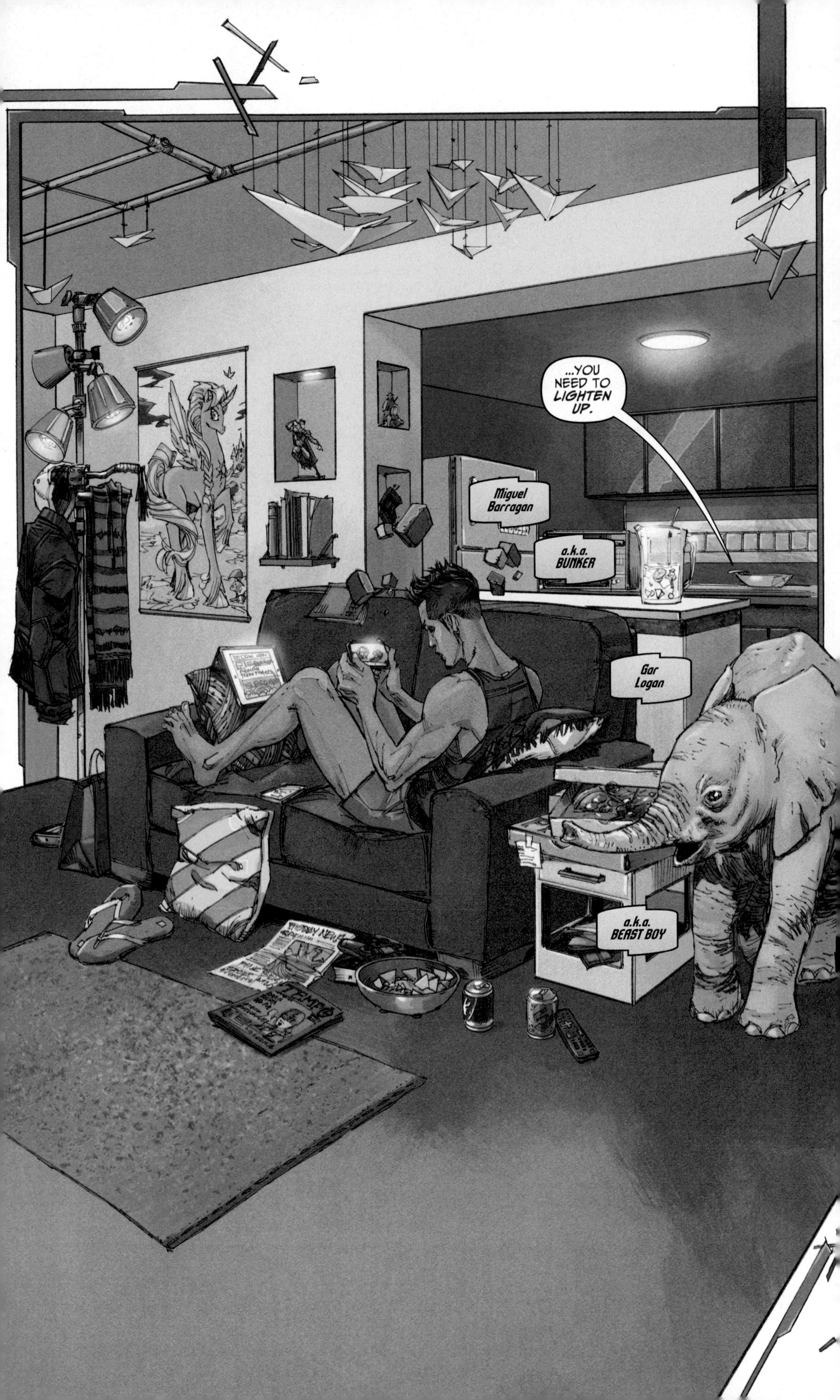
...YOU NEED TO LIGHTEN UP.
Miguel Barragan
a.k.a. BUNKER
Gar Logan
a.k.a. BEAST BOY

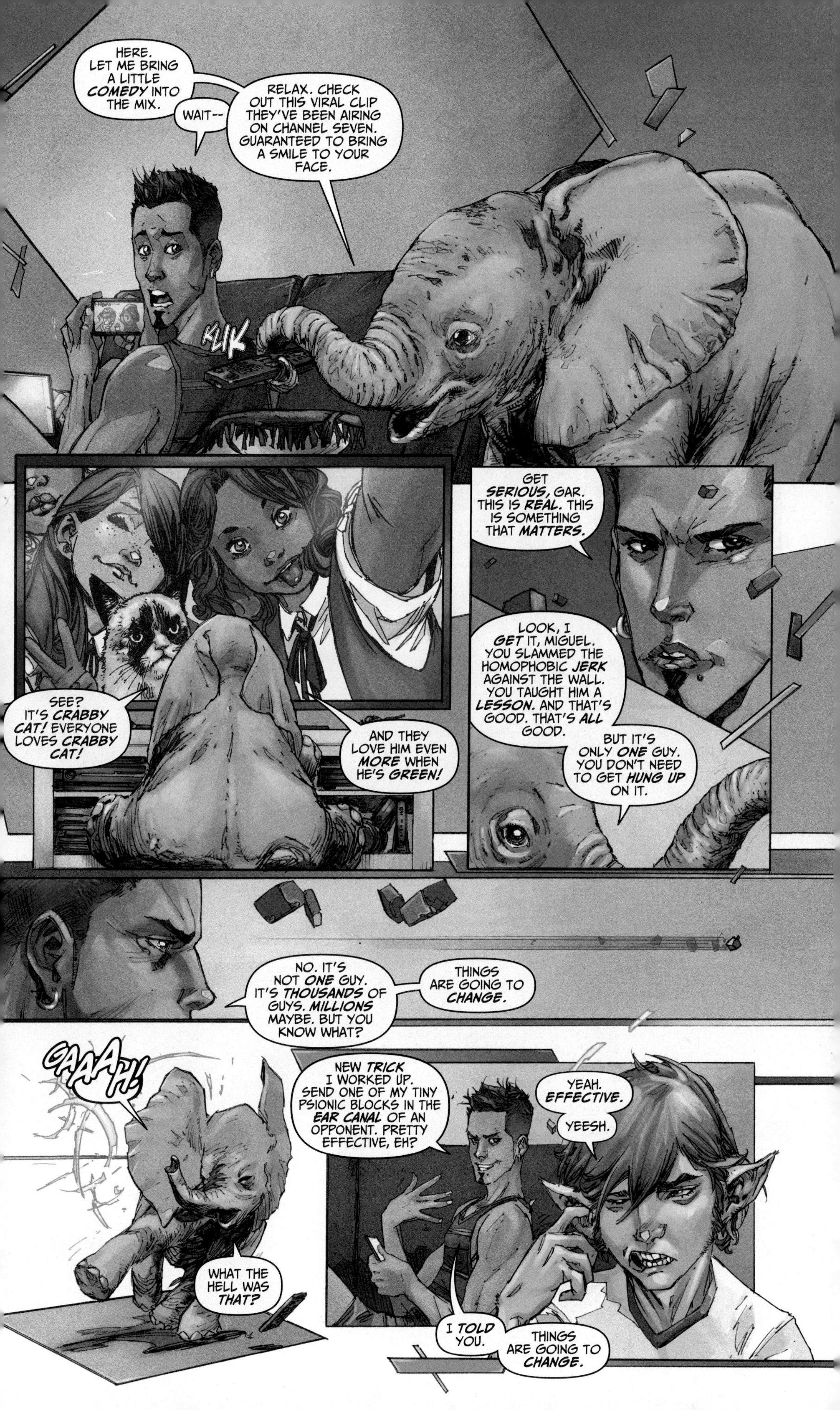

HERE. LET ME BRING A LITTLE COMEDY INTO THE MIX.
WAIT--
RELAX. CHECK OUT THIS VIRAL CLIP THEY'VE BEEN AIRING ON CHANNEL SEVEN. GUARANTEED TO BRING A SMILE TO YOUR FACE.
KLIK
SEE? IT'S CRABBY CAT! EVERYONE LOVES CRABBY CAT!
AND THEY LOVE HIM EVEN MORE WHEN HE'S GREEN!
GET SERIOUS, GAR. THIS IS REAL. THIS IS SOMETHING THAT MATTERS.
LOOK, I GET IT, MIGUEL. YOU SLAMMED THE HOMOPHOBIC JERK AGAINST THE WALL. YOU TAUGHT HIM A LESSON. AND THAT'S GOOD. THAT'S ALL GOOD.
BUT IT'S ONLY ONE GUY. YOU DON'T NEED TO GET HUNG UP ON IT.
NO. IT'S NOT ONE GUY. IT'S THOUSANDS OF GUYS. MILLIONS MAYBE. BUT YOU KNOW WHAT?
THINGS ARE GOING TO CHANGE.
GAAAH!
WHAT THE HELL WAS THAT?
NEW TRICK I WORKED UP. SEND ONE OF MY TINY PSIONIC BLOCKS IN THE EAR CANAL OF AN OPPONENT. PRETTY EFFECTIVE, EH?
YEAH. EFFECTIVE.
YEESH.
I TOLD YOU.
THINGS ARE GOING TO CHANGE.

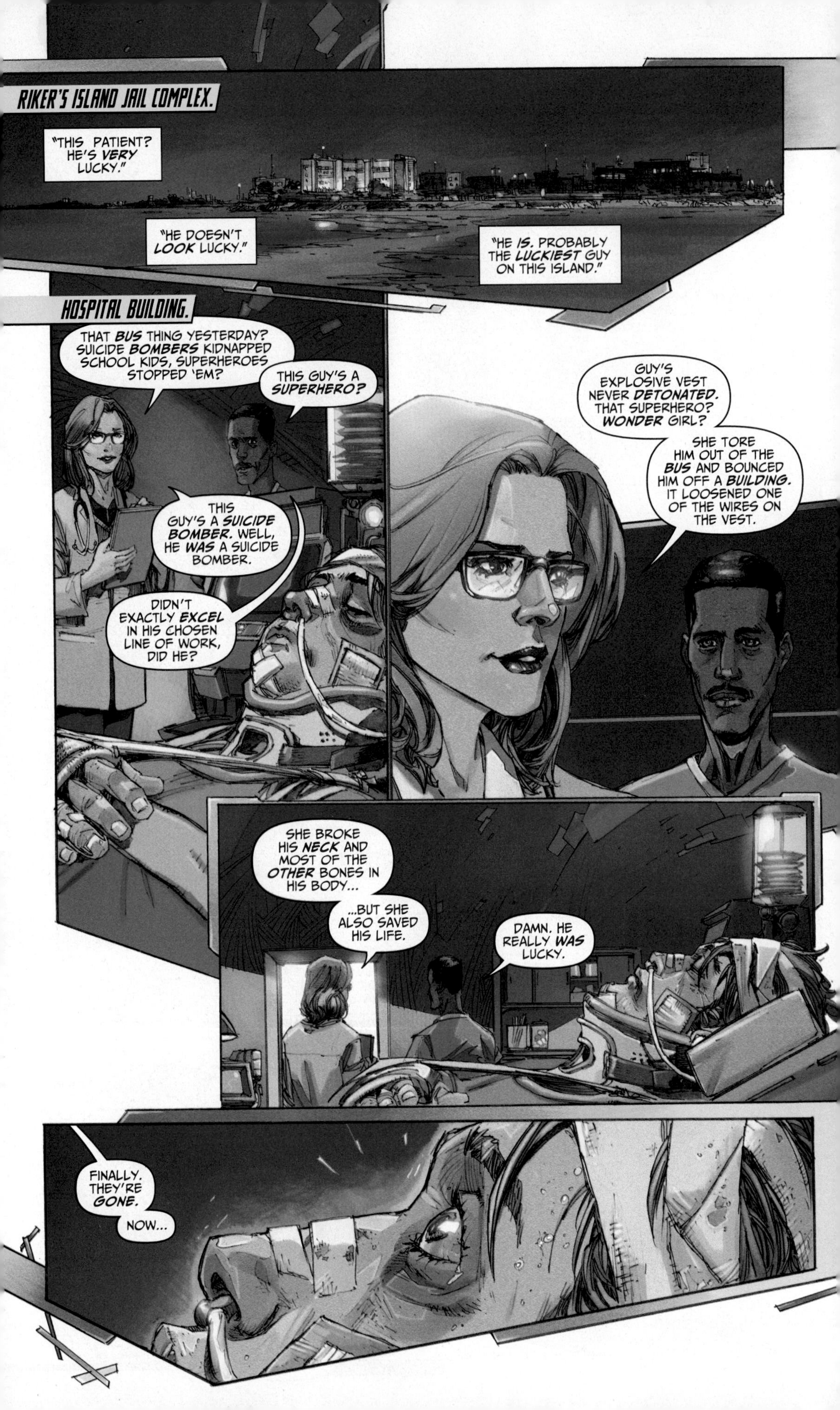
RIKER'S ISLAND JAIL COMPLEX.
"THIS PATIENT? HE'S VERY LUCKY."
"HE DOESN'T LOOK LUCKY."
"HE IS. PROBABLY THE LUCKIEST GUY ON THIS ISLAND."
HOSPITAL BUILDING.
THAT BUS THING YESTERDAY? SUICIDE BOMBERS KIDNAPPED SCHOOL KIDS, SUPERHEROES STOPPED 'EM?
THIS GUY'S A SUPERHERO?
THIS GUY'S A SUICIDE BOMBER. WELL, HE WAS A SUICIDE BOMBER.
DIDN'T EXACTLY EXCEL IN HIS CHOSEN LINE OF WORK, DID HE?
GUY'S EXPLOSIVE VEST NEVER DETONATED. THAT SUPERHERO? WONDER GIRL?
SHE TORE HIM OUT OF THE BUS AND BOUNCED HIM OFF A BUILDING. IT LOOSENED ONE OF THE WIRES ON THE VEST.
SHE BROKE HIS NECK AND MOST OF THE OTHER BONES IN HIS BODY...
...BUT SHE ALSO SAVED HIS LIFE.
DAMN. HE REALLY WAS LUCKY.
FINALLY. THEY'RE GONE.
NOW...

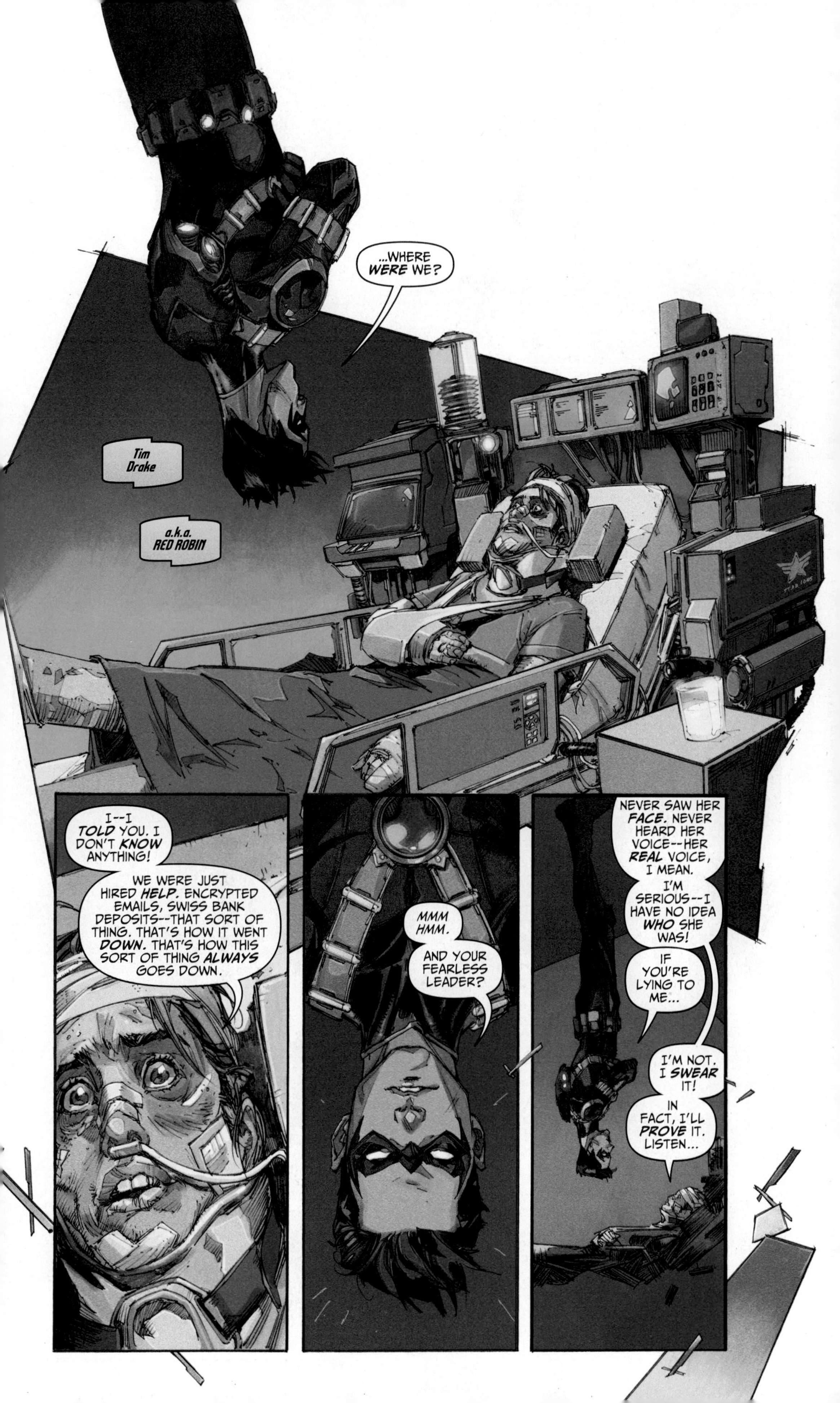
...WHERE WERE WE?
Tim Drake
a.k.a. RED ROBIN
I--I TOLD YOU. I DON'T KNOW ANYTHING!
WE WERE JUST HIRED HELP. ENCRYPTED EMAILS, SWISS BANK DEPOSITS--THAT SORT OF THING. THAT'S HOW IT WENT DOWN. THAT'S HOW THIS SORT OF THING ALWAYS GOES DOWN.
MMM HMM.
AND YOUR FEARLESS LEADER?
NEVER SAW HER FACE. NEVER HEARD HER VOICE--HER REAL VOICE, I MEAN.
I'M SERIOUS--I HAVE NO IDEA WHO SHE WAS!
IF YOU'RE LYING TO ME...
I'M NOT. I SWEAR IT!
IN FACT, I'LL PROVE IT. LISTEN...

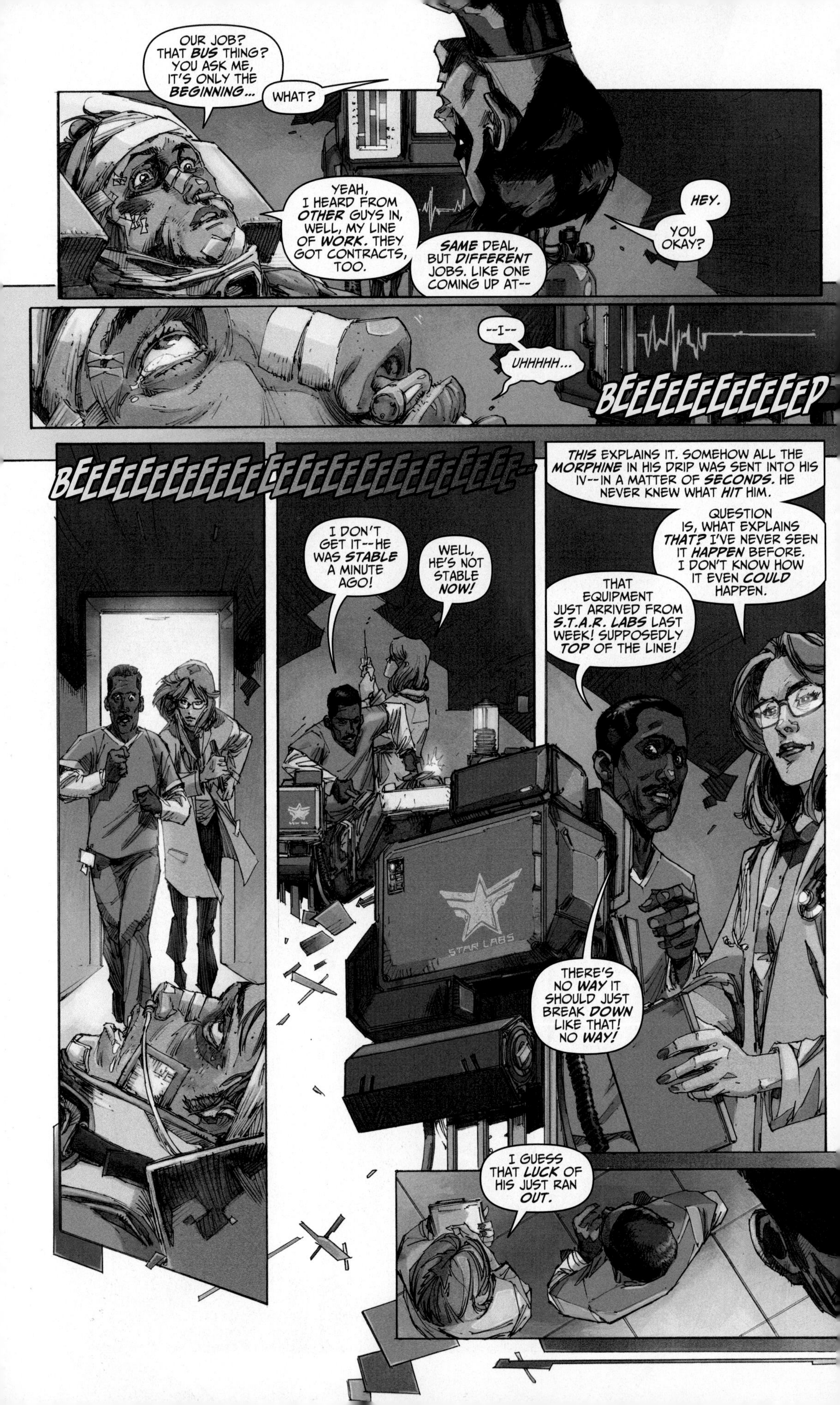
OUR JOB? THAT BUS THING? YOU ASK ME, IT'S ONLY THE BEGINNING...
WHAT?
YEAH, I HEARD FROM OTHER GUYS IN, WELL, MY LINE OF WORK. THEY GOT CONTRACTS, TOO.
SAME DEAL, BUT DIFFERENT JOBS. LIKE ONE COMING UP AT--
HEY.
YOU OKAY?
--I--
UHHHHH...
BEEEEEEEEEEEEP
BEEEEEEEEEEEEEEEEEEEEEEEEEEE--
I DON'T GET IT--HE WAS STABLE A MINUTE AGO!
WELL, HE'S NOT STABLE NOW!
THIS EXPLAINS IT. SOMEHOW ALL THE MORPHINE IN HIS DRIP WAS SENT INTO HIS IV--IN A MATTER OF SECONDS. HE NEVER KNEW WHAT HIT HIM.
QUESTION IS, WHAT EXPLAINS THAT? I'VE NEVER SEEN IT HAPPEN BEFORE. I DON'T KNOW HOW IT EVEN COULD HAPPEN.
THAT EQUIPMENT JUST ARRIVED FROM S.T.A.R. LABS LAST WEEK! SUPPOSEDLY TOP OF THE LINE!
STAR LABS
THERE'S NO WAY IT SHOULD JUST BREAK DOWN LIKE THAT! NO WAY!
I GUESS THAT LUCK OF HIS JUST RAN OUT.

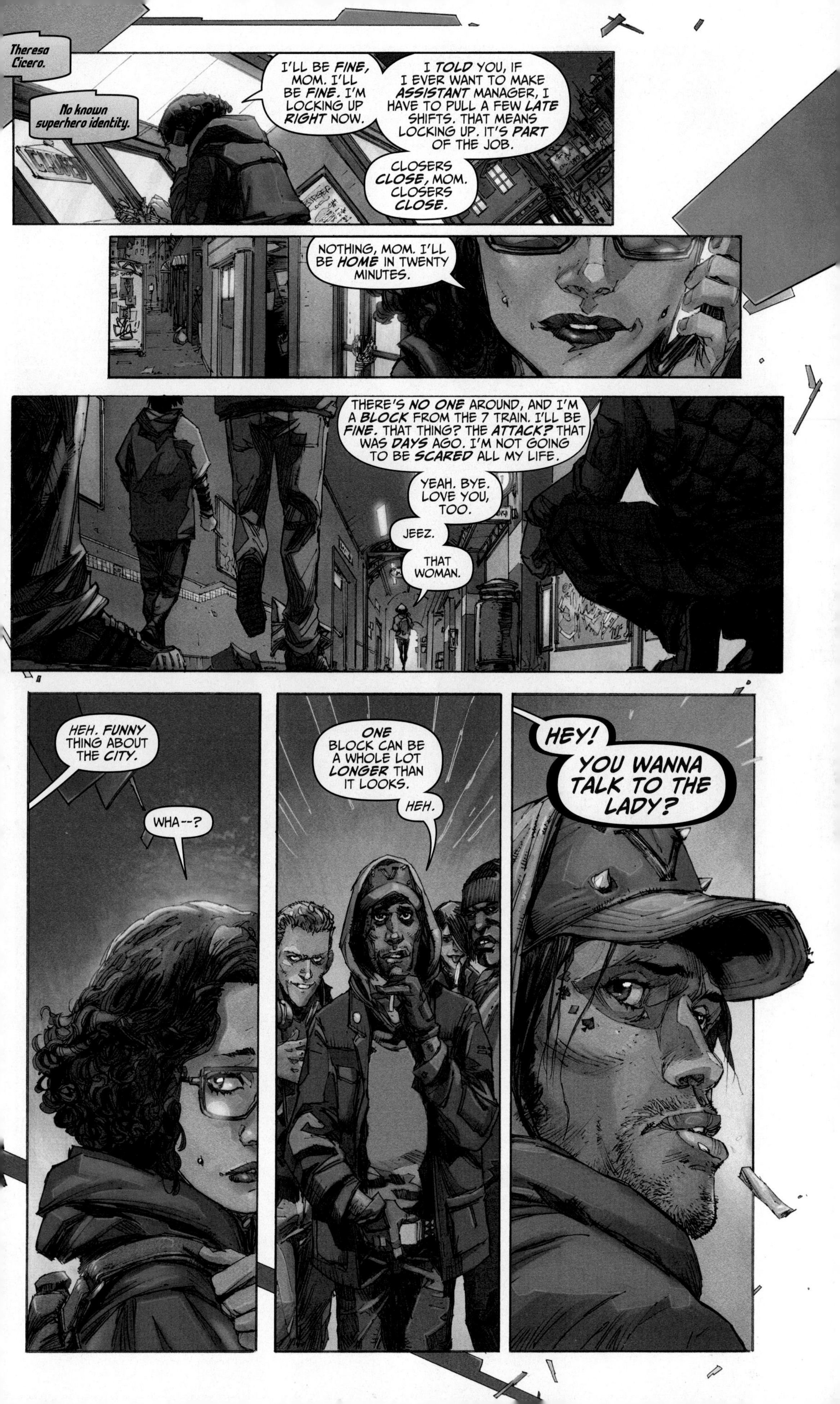
Theresa Cicero.
No known superhero identity.
I'LL BE FINE, MOM. I'LL BE FINE. I'M LOCKING UP RIGHT NOW.
I TOLD YOU, IF I EVER WANT TO MAKE ASSISTANT MANAGER, I HAVE TO PULL A FEW LATE SHIFTS. THAT MEANS LOCKING UP. IT'S PART OF THE JOB.
CLOSERS CLOSE, MOM. CLOSERS CLOSE.
NOTHING, MOM. I'LL BE HOME IN TWENTY MINUTES.
THERE'S NO ONE AROUND, AND I'M A BLOCK FROM THE 7 TRAIN. I'LL BE FINE. THAT THING? THE ATTACK? THAT WAS DAYS AGO. I'M NOT GOING TO BE SCARED ALL MY LIFE.
YEAH. BYE. LOVE YOU, TOO.
JEEZ.
THAT WOMAN.
HEH. FUNNY THING ABOUT THE CITY.
WHA--?
ONE BLOCK CAN BE A WHOLE LOT LONGER THAN IT LOOKS.
HEH.
HEY!
YOU WANNA TALK TO THE LADY?

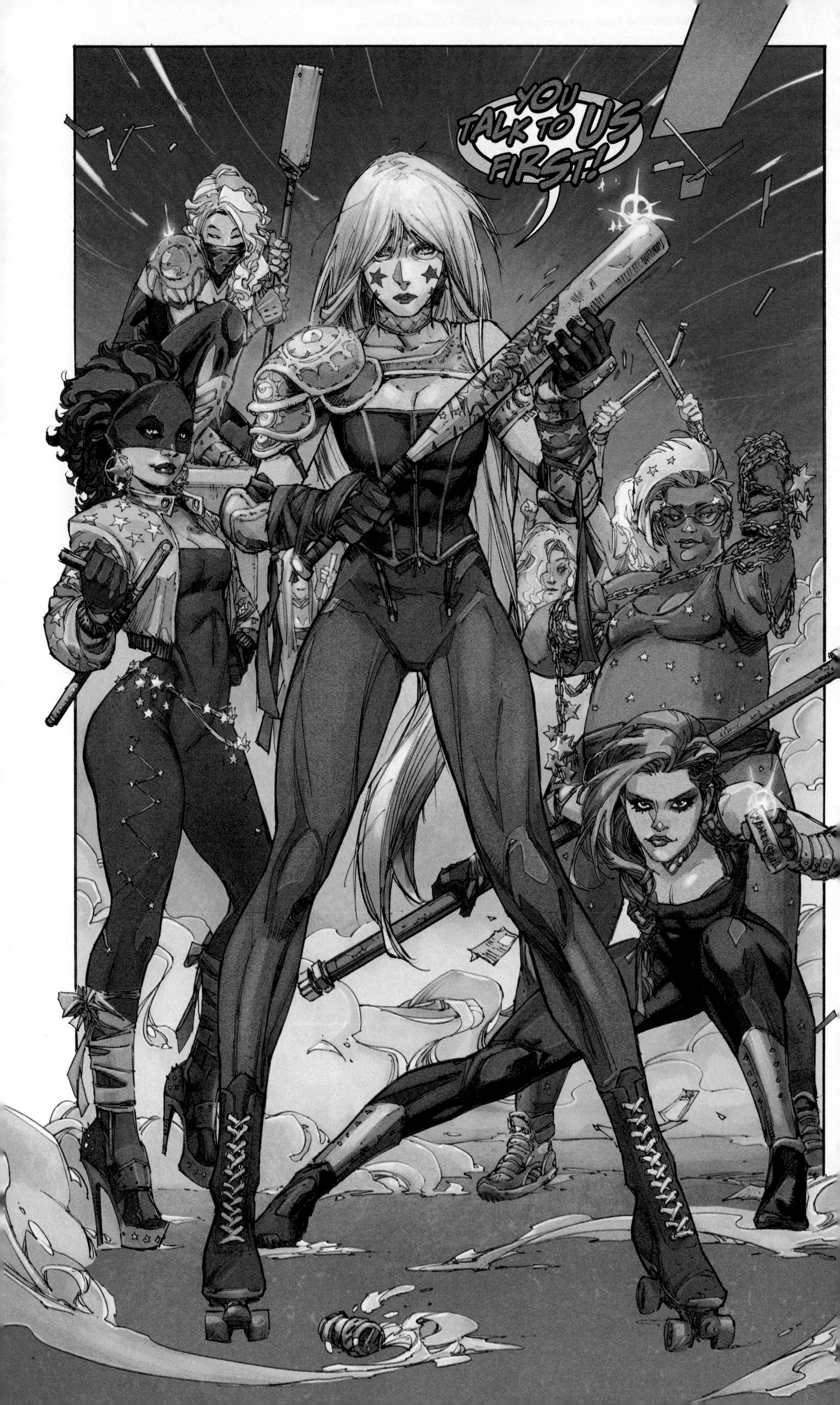
YOU TALK TO US FIRST!

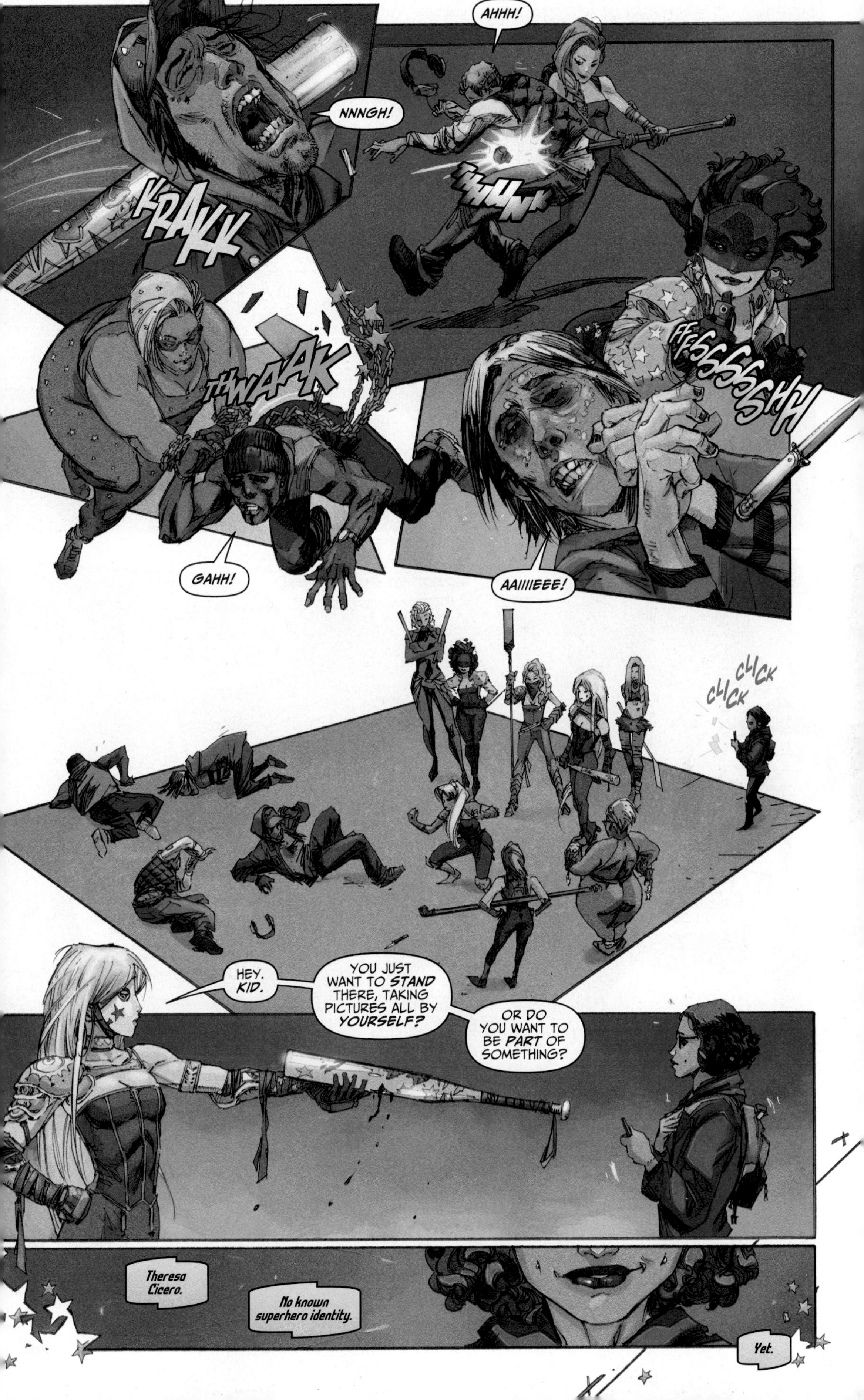
NNNGH!
KRAKK
AHHH!
THUNK
THWAAK
GAHH!
FFFSSSSSHH
AAIIIIEEE!
CLICK
CLICK
HEY. KID.
YOU JUST WANT TO STAND THERE, TAKING PICTURES ALL BY YOURSELF?
OR DO YOU WANT TO BE PART OF SOMETHING?
Theresa Cicero.
No known superhero identity.
Yet.

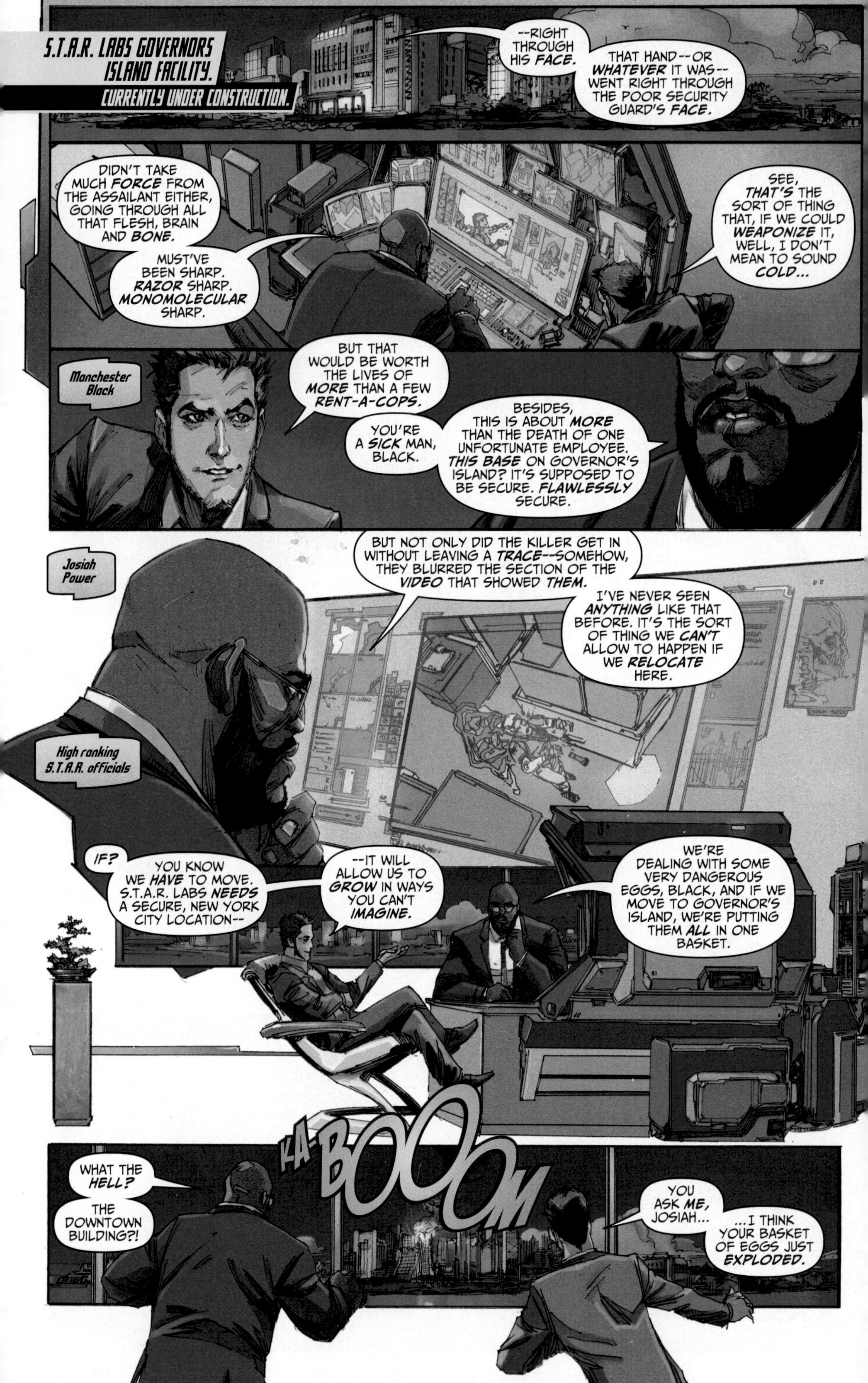
S.T.A.R. LABS GOVERNORS ISLAND FACILITY.
CURRENTLY UNDER CONSTRUCTION.
--RIGHT THROUGH HIS FACE.
THAT HAND--OR WHATEVER IT WAS--WENT RIGHT THROUGH THE POOR SECURITY GUARD'S FACE.
DIDN'T TAKE MUCH FORCE FROM THE ASSAILANT EITHER, GOING THROUGH ALL THAT FLESH, BRAIN AND BONE.
MUST'VE BEEN SHARP. RAZOR SHARP. MONOMOLECULAR SHARP.
SEE, THAT'S THE SORT OF THING THAT, IF WE COULD WEAPONIZE IT, WELL, I DON'T MEAN TO SOUND COLD...
Manchester Black
BUT THAT WOULD BE WORTH THE LIVES OF MORE THAN A FEW RENT-A-COPS.
YOU'RE A SICK MAN, BLACK.
BESIDES, THIS IS ABOUT MORE THAN THE DEATH OF ONE UNFORTUNATE EMPLOYEE. THIS BASE ON GOVERNOR'S ISLAND? IT'S SUPPOSED TO BE SECURE. FLAWLESSLY SECURE.
Josiah Power
High ranking S.T.A.R. officials
BUT NOT ONLY DID THE KILLER GET IN WITHOUT LEAVING A TRACE--SOMEHOW, THEY BLURRED THE SECTION OF THE VIDEO THAT SHOWED THEM.
I'VE NEVER SEEN ANYTHING LIKE THAT BEFORE. IT'S THE SORT OF THING WE CAN'T ALLOW TO HAPPEN IF WE RELOCATE HERE.
IF?
YOU KNOW WE HAVE TO MOVE. S.T.A.R. LABS NEEDS A SECURE, NEW YORK CITY LOCATION--
--IT WILL ALLOW US TO GROW IN WAYS YOU CAN'T IMAGINE.
WE'RE DEALING WITH SOME VERY DANGEROUS EGGS, BLACK, AND IF WE MOVE TO GOVERNOR'S ISLAND, WE'RE PUTTING THEM ALL IN ONE BASKET.
KA-BOOOOM
WHAT THE HELL?
THE DOWNTOWN BUILDING?!
YOU ASK ME, JOSIAH...
...I THINK YOUR BASKET OF EGGS JUST EXPLODED.

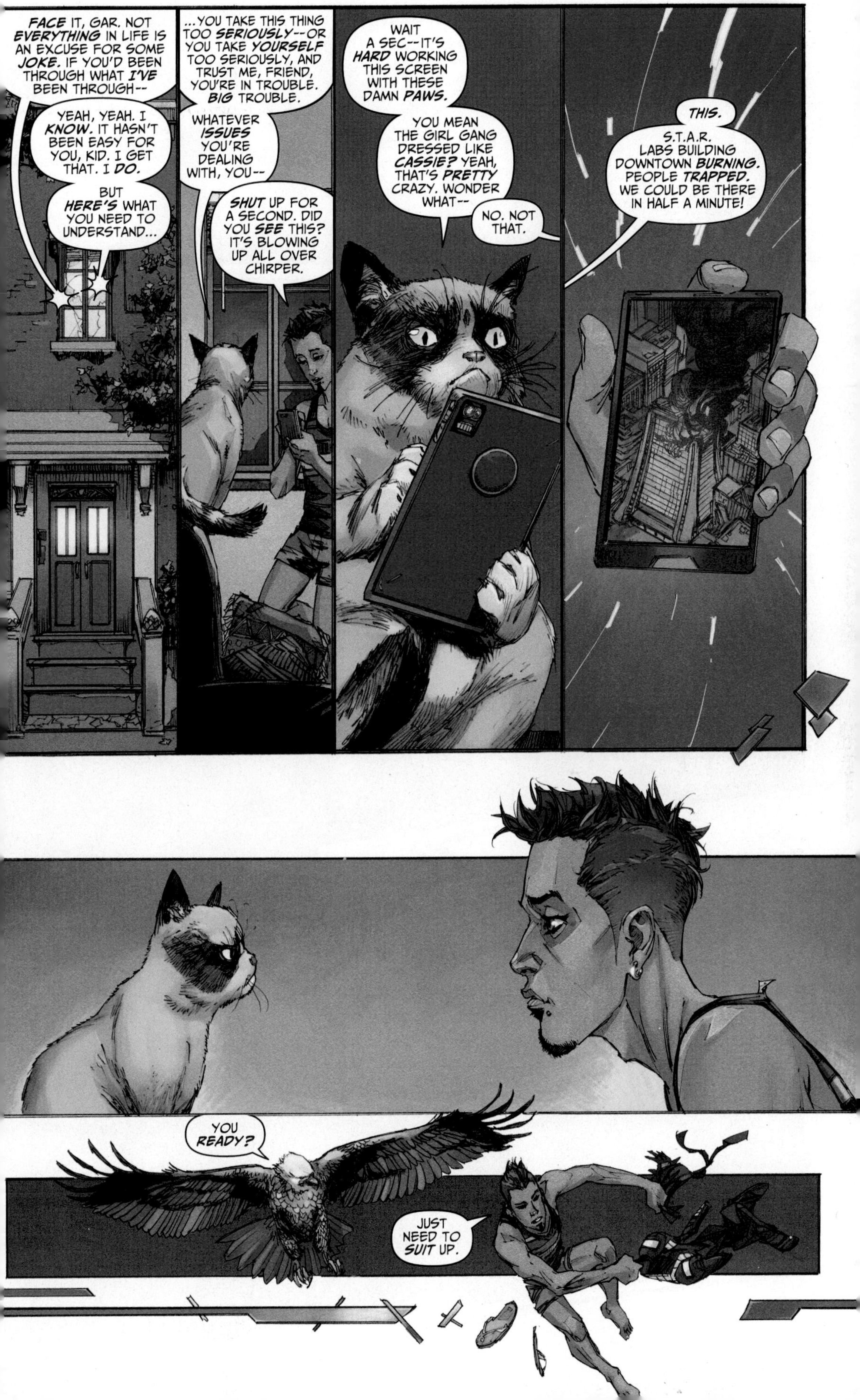
FACE IT, GAR. NOT EVERYTHING IN LIFE IS AN EXCUSE FOR SOME JOKE. IF YOU'D BEEN THROUGH WHAT I'VE BEEN THROUGH--
YEAH, YEAH. I KNOW. IT HASN'T BEEN EASY FOR YOU, KID. I GET THAT. I DO.
BUT HERE'S WHAT YOU NEED TO UNDERSTAND...
...YOU TAKE THIS THING TOO SERIOUSLY--OR YOU TAKE YOURSELF TOO SERIOUSLY, AND TRUST ME, FRIEND, YOU'RE IN TROUBLE. BIG TROUBLE.
WHATEVER ISSUES YOU'RE DEALING WITH, YOU--
SHUT UP FOR A SECOND. DID YOU SEE THIS? IT'S BLOWING UP ALL OVER CHIRPER.
WAIT A SEC--IT'S HARD WORKING THIS SCREEN WITH THESE DAMN PAWS.
YOU MEAN THE GIRL GANG DRESSED LIKE CASSIE? YEAH, THAT'S PRETTY CRAZY. WONDER WHAT--
NO. NOT THAT.
THIS.
S.T.A.R. LABS BUILDING DOWNTOWN BURNING. PEOPLE TRAPPED. WE COULD BE THERE IN HALF A MINUTE!
YOU READY?
JUST NEED TO SUIT UP.

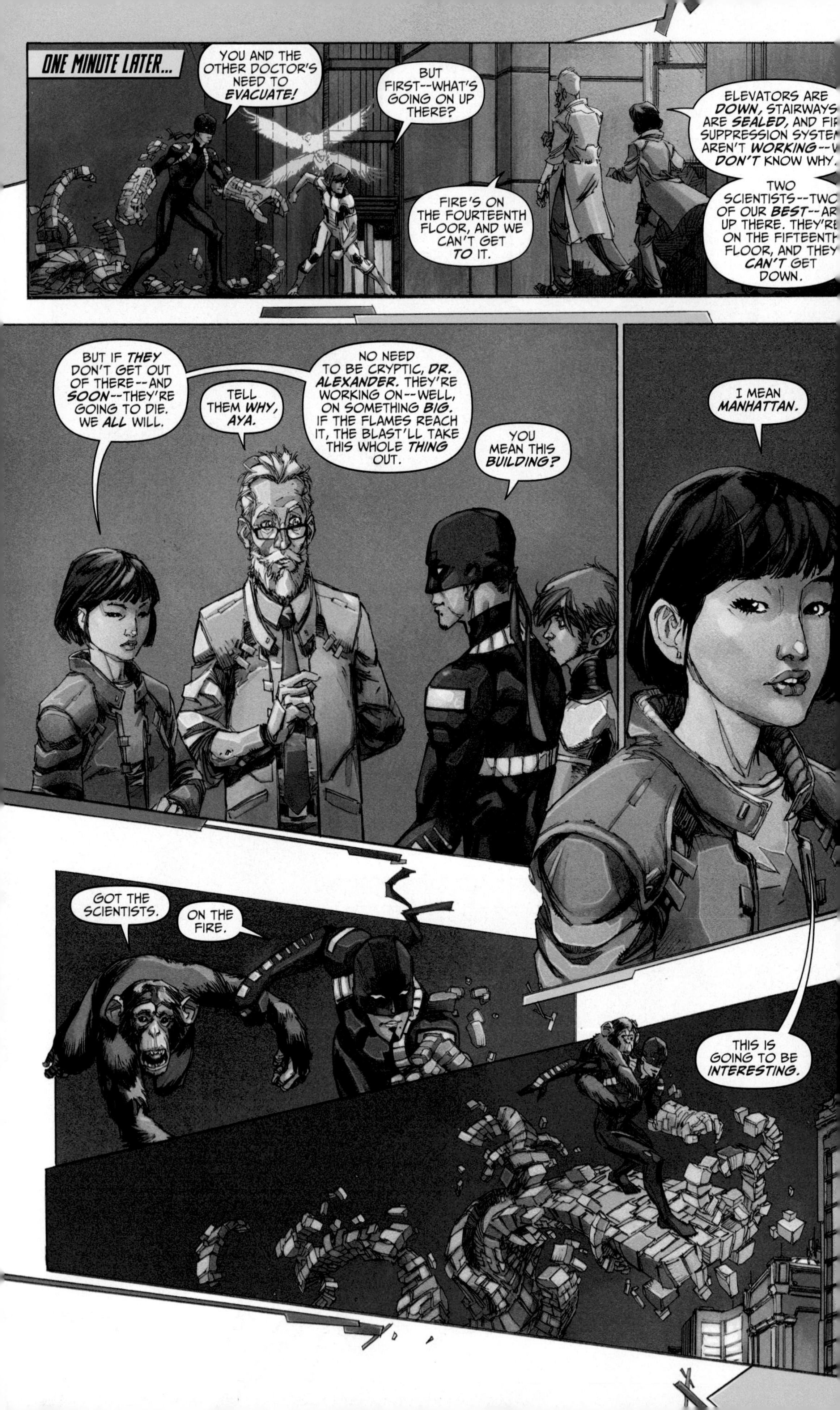
ONE MINUTE LATER...
YOU AND THE OTHER DOCTOR'S NEED TO EVACUATE!
BUT FIRST--WHAT'S GOING ON UP THERE?
FIRE'S ON THE FOURTEENTH FLOOR, AND WE CAN'T GET TO IT.
ELEVATORS ARE DOWN, STAIRWAYS ARE SEALED, AND FIRE SUPPRESSION SYSTEMS AREN'T WORKING--WE DON'T KNOW WHY.
TWO SCIENTISTS--TWO OF OUR BEST--ARE UP THERE. THEY'RE ON THE FIFTEENTH FLOOR, AND THEY CAN'T GET DOWN.
BUT IF THEY DON'T GET OUT OF THERE--AND SOON--THEY'RE GOING TO DIE. WE ALL WILL.
TELL THEM WHY, AYA.
NO NEED TO BE CRYPTIC, DR. ALEXANDER. THEY'RE WORKING ON--WELL, ON SOMETHING BIG. IF THE FLAMES REACH IT, THE BLAST'LL TAKE THIS WHOLE THING OUT.
YOU MEAN THIS BUILDING?
I MEAN MANHATTAN.
THIS IS GOING TO BE INTERESTING.
GOT THE SCIENTISTS.
ON THE FIRE.

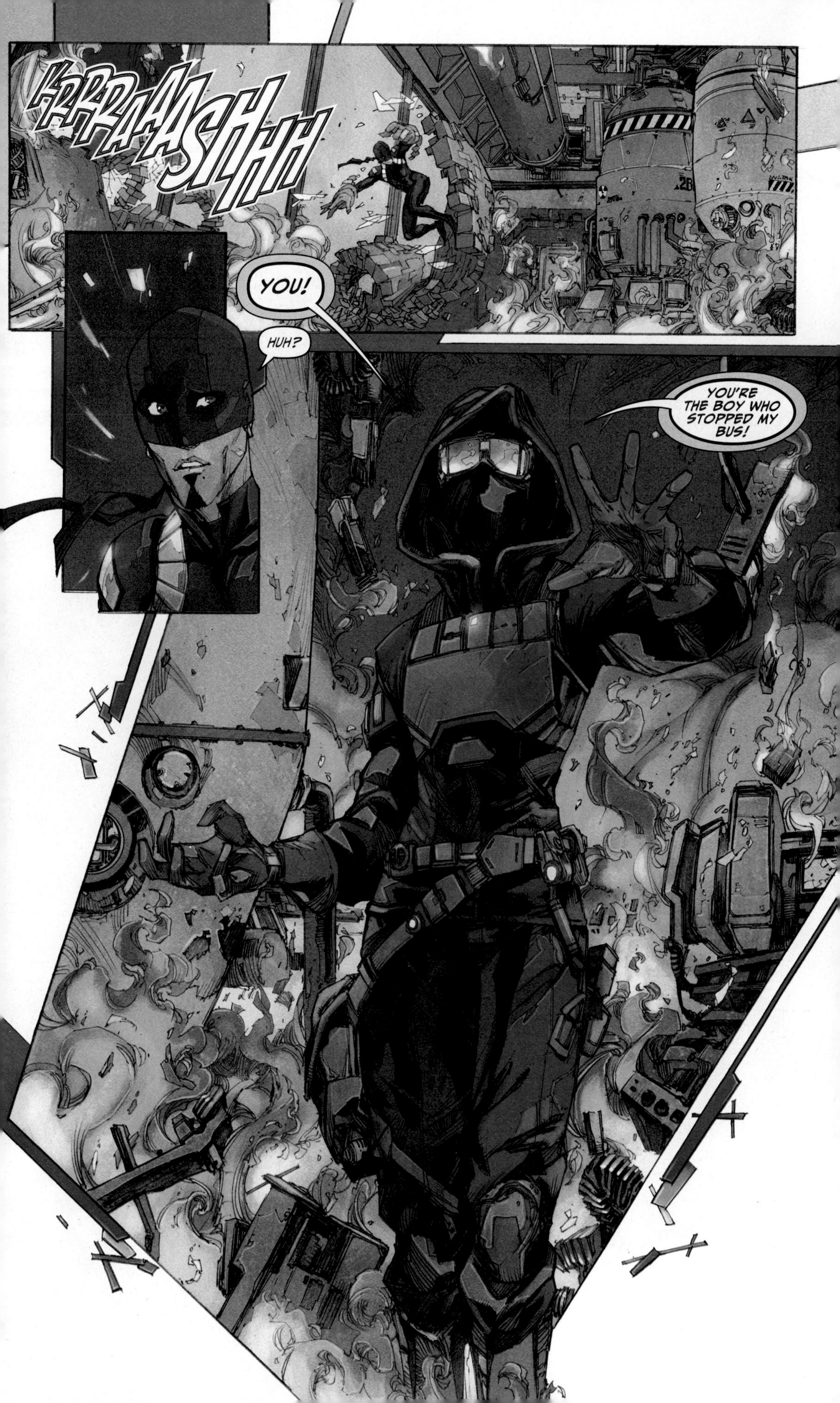
KRRRAAASHHH
YOU!
HUH?
YOU'RE THE BOY WHO STOPPED MY BUS!

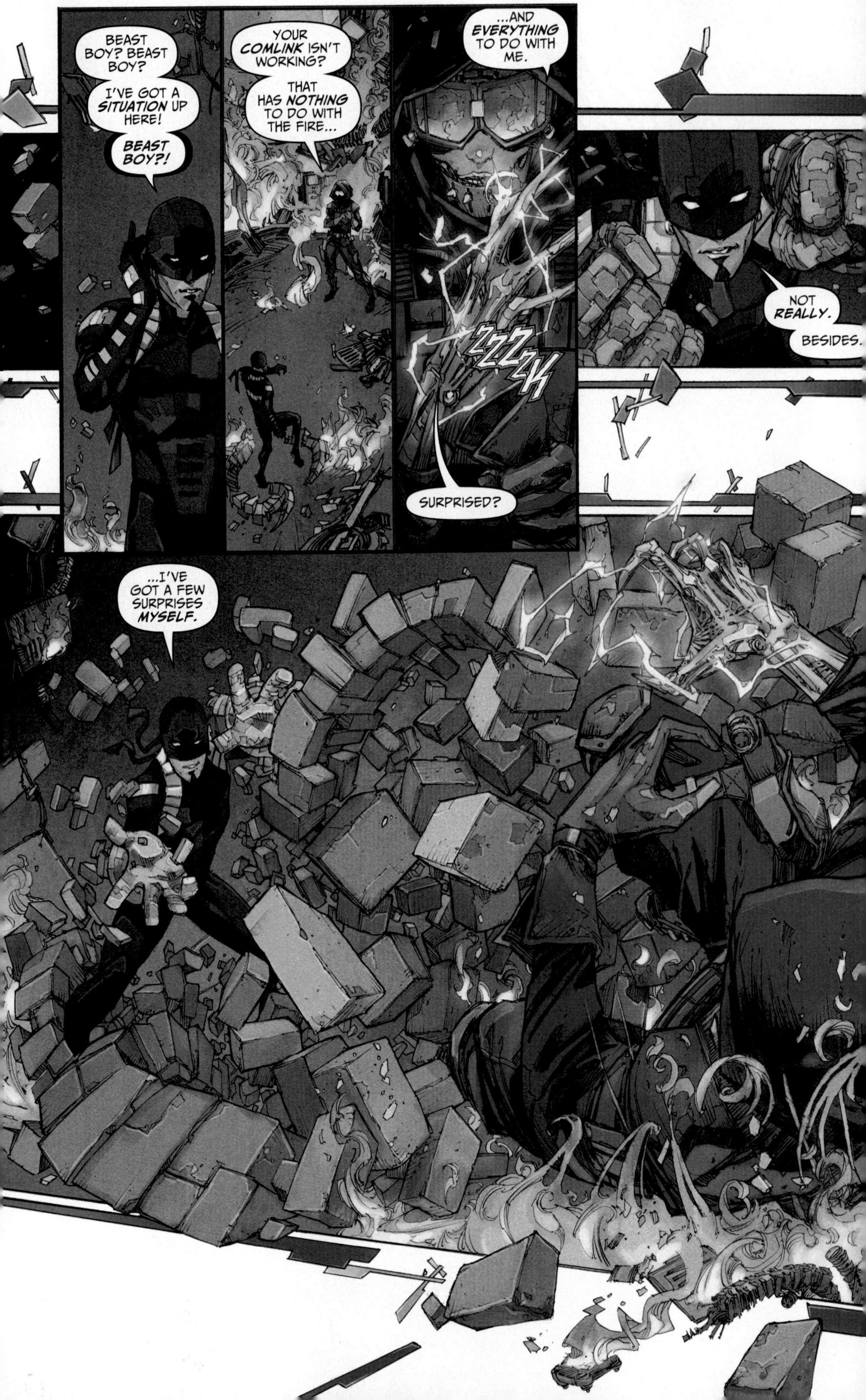

BEAST BOY? BEAST BOY?
I'VE GOT A SITUATION UP HERE!
BEAST BOY?!
YOUR COMLINK ISN'T WORKING?
THAT HAS NOTHING TO DO WITH THE FIRE...
...AND EVERYTHING TO DO WITH ME.
ZZZZK
SURPRISED?
NOT REALLY.
BESIDES.
...I'VE GOT A FEW SURPRISES MYSELF.

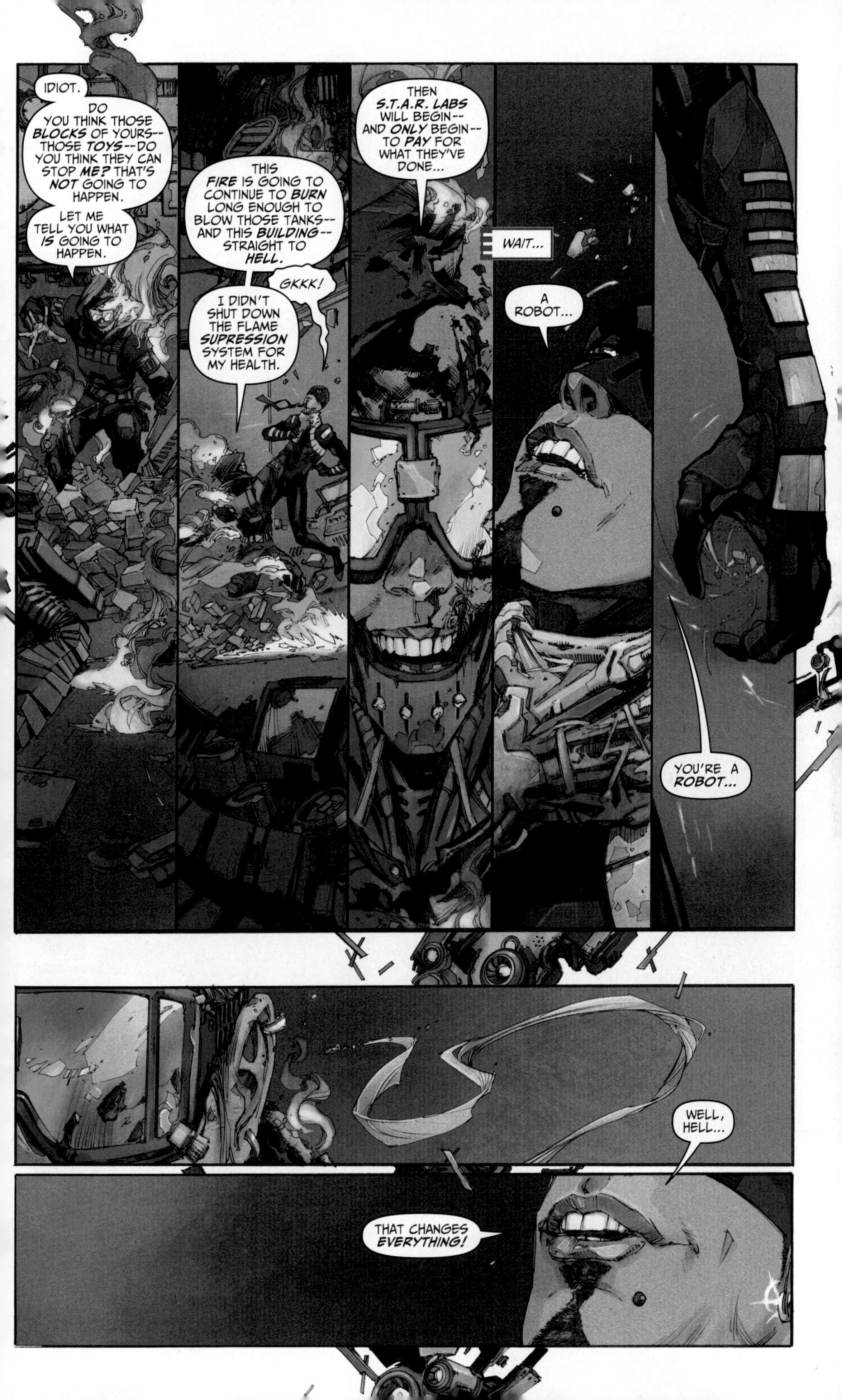
IDIOT.
DO YOU THINK THOSE BLOCKS OF YOURS--THOSE TOYS--DO YOU THINK THEY CAN STOP ME? THAT'S NOT GOING TO HAPPEN.
LET ME TELL YOU WHAT IS GOING TO HAPPEN.
THIS FIRE IS GOING TO CONTINUE TO BURN LONG ENOUGH TO BLOW THOSE TANKS--AND THIS BUILDING--STRAIGHT TO HELL.
GKKK!
I DIDN'T SHUT DOWN THE FLAME SUPRESSION SYSTEM FOR MY HEALTH.
THEN S.T.A.R. LABS WILL BEGIN--AND ONLY BEGIN--TO PAY FOR WHAT THEY'VE DONE...
WAIT...
A ROBOT...
YOU'RE A ROBOT...
WELL, HELL...
THAT CHANGES EVERYTHING!

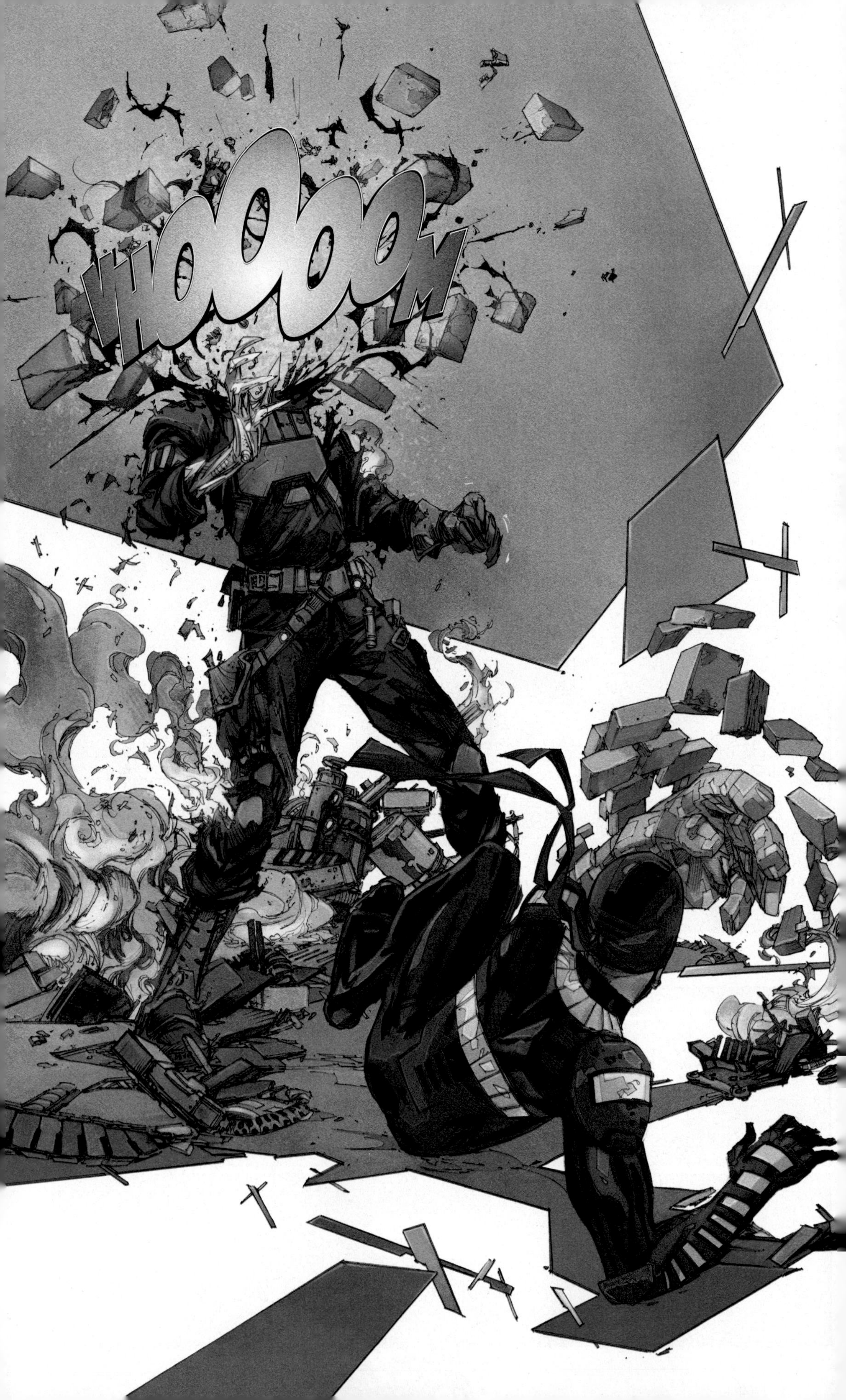
WHOOOOM

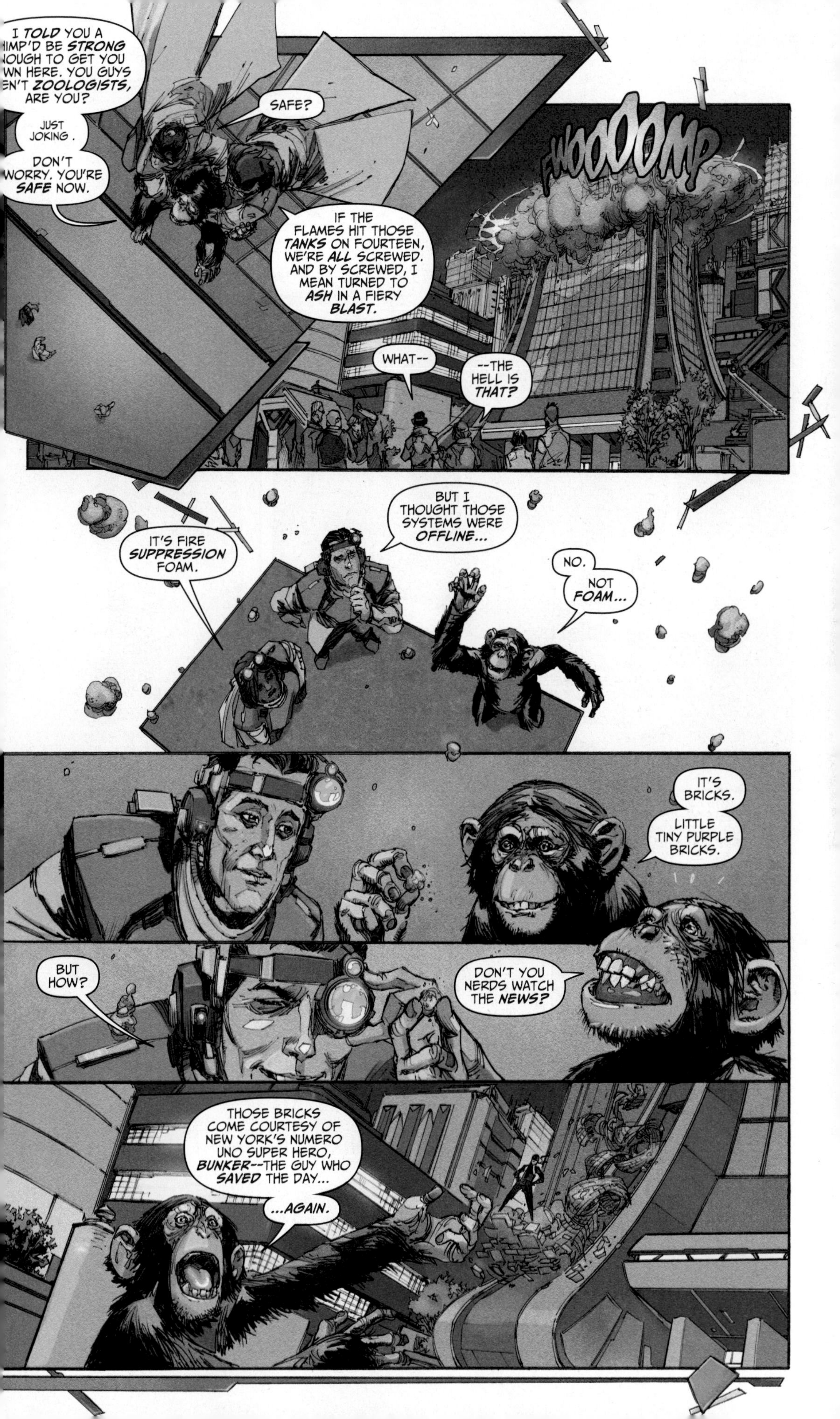
I TOLD YOU A HIMP'D BE STRONG NOUGH TO GET YOU WN HERE. YOU GUYS EN'T ZOOLOGISTS, ARE YOU?
SAFE?
JUST JOKING.
DON'T WORRY. YOU'RE SAFE NOW.
IF THE FLAMES HIT THOSE TANKS ON FOURTEEN, WE'RE ALL SCREWED. AND BY SCREWED, I MEAN TURNED TO ASH IN A FIERY BLAST.
FWOOOOMP
WHAT--
--THE HELL IS THAT?
IT'S FIRE SUPPRESSION FOAM.
BUT I THOUGHT THOSE SYSTEMS WERE OFFLINE...
NO.
NOT FOAM...
IT'S BRICKS.
LITTLE TINY PURPLE BRICKS.
BUT HOW?
DON'T YOU NERDS WATCH THE NEWS?
THOSE BRICKS COME COURTESY OF NEW YORK'S NUMERO UNO SUPER HERO, BUNKER--THE GUY WHO SAVED THE DAY...
...AGAIN.

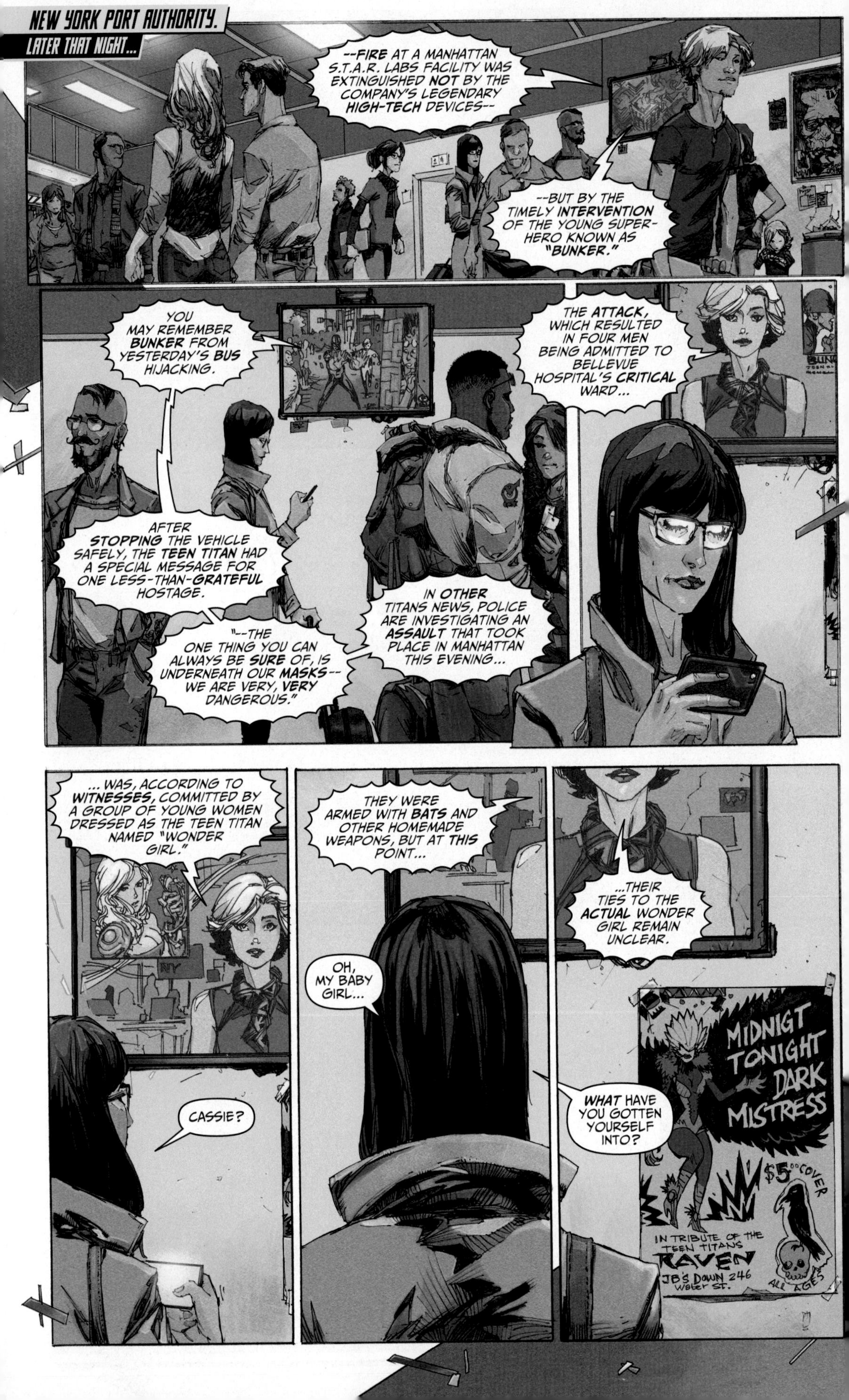
NEW YORK PORT AUTHORITY.
LATER THAT NIGHT...
--FIRE AT A MANHATTAN S.T.A.R. LABS FACILITY WAS EXTINGUISHED NOT BY THE COMPANY'S LEGENDARY HIGH-TECH DEVICES--
--BUT BY THE TIMELY INTERVENTION OF THE YOUNG SUPER-HERO KNOWN AS "BUNKER."
YOU MAY REMEMBER BUNKER FROM YESTERDAY'S BUS HIJACKING.
AFTER STOPPING THE VEHICLE SAFELY, THE TEEN TITAN HAD A SPECIAL MESSAGE FOR ONE LESS-THAN-GRATEFUL HOSTAGE.
"--THE ONE THING YOU CAN ALWAYS BE SURE OF, IS UNDERNEATH OUR MASKS-- WE ARE VERY, VERY DANGEROUS."
IN OTHER TITANS NEWS, POLICE ARE INVESTIGATING AN ASSAULT THAT TOOK PLACE IN MANHATTAN THIS EVENING...
THE ATTACK, WHICH RESULTED IN FOUR MEN BEING ADMITTED TO BELLEVUE HOSPITAL'S CRITICAL WARD...
...WAS, ACCORDING TO WITNESSES, COMMITTED BY A GROUP OF YOUNG WOMEN DRESSED AS THE TEEN TITAN NAMED "WONDER GIRL."
CASSIE?
THEY WERE ARMED WITH BATS AND OTHER HOMEMADE WEAPONS, BUT AT THIS POINT...
OH, MY BABY GIRL...
...THEIR TIES TO THE ACTUAL WONDER GIRL REMAIN UNCLEAR.
WHAT HAVE YOU GOTTEN YOURSELF INTO?
MIDNIGT TONIGHT DARK MISTRESS
$5.00 COVER
IN TRIBUTE OF THE TEEN TITANS RAVEN
JB's DOWN 246 Water St.
ALL AGES

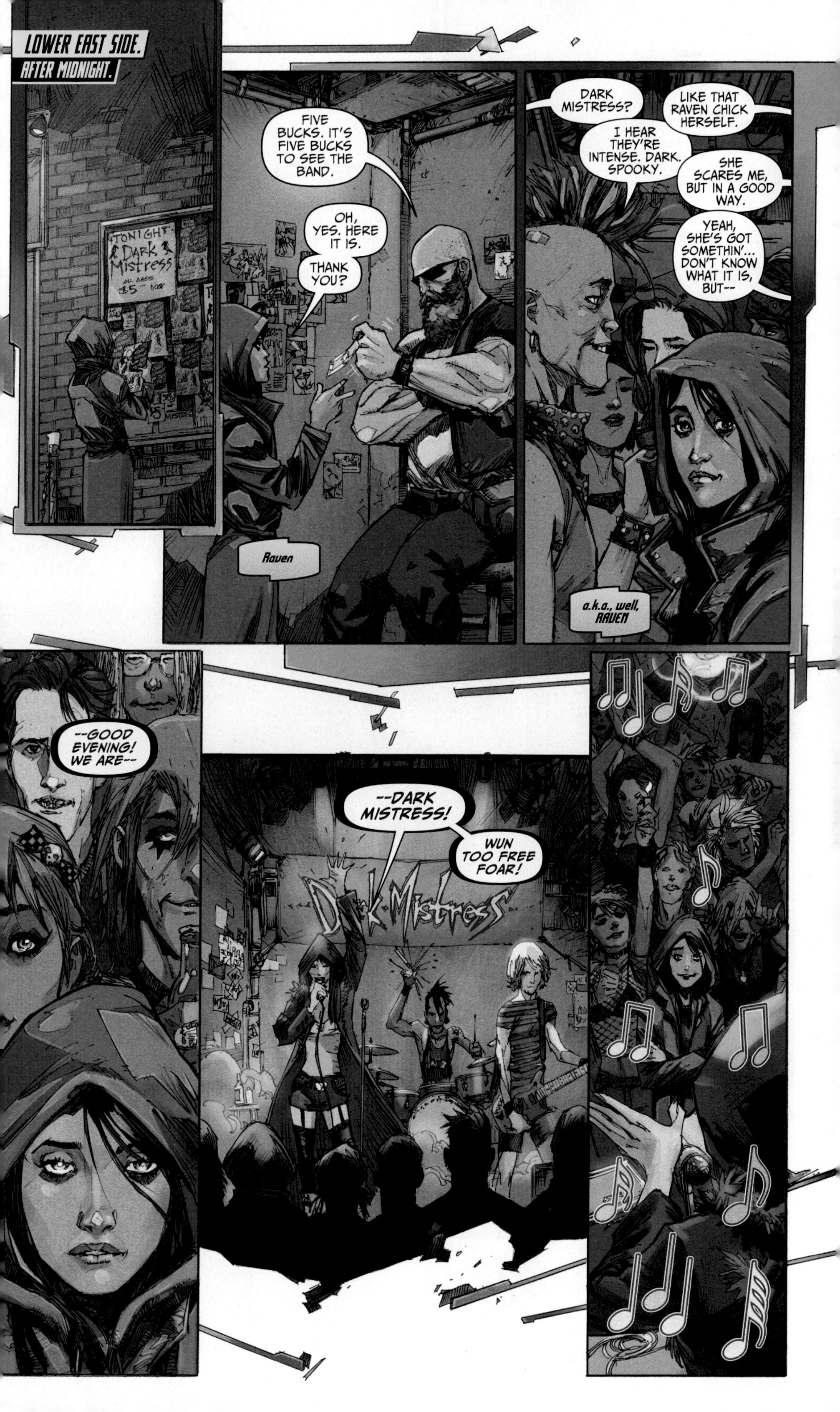
LOWER EAST SIDE.
AFTER MIDNIGHT.
TONIGHT Dark Mistress ALL AGES $5 — DOOR
FIVE BUCKS. IT'S FIVE BUCKS TO SEE THE BAND.
OH, YES. HERE IT IS.
THANK YOU?
Raven
DARK MISTRESS?
I HEAR THEY'RE INTENSE. DARK. SPOOKY.
LIKE THAT RAVEN CHICK HERSELF.
SHE SCARES ME, BUT IN A GOOD WAY.
YEAH, SHE'S GOT SOMETHIN'... DON'T KNOW WHAT IT IS, BUT--
a.k.a., well, RAVEN
--GOOD EVENING! WE ARE--
--DARK MISTRESS!
WUN TOO FREE FOAR!
Dark Mistress

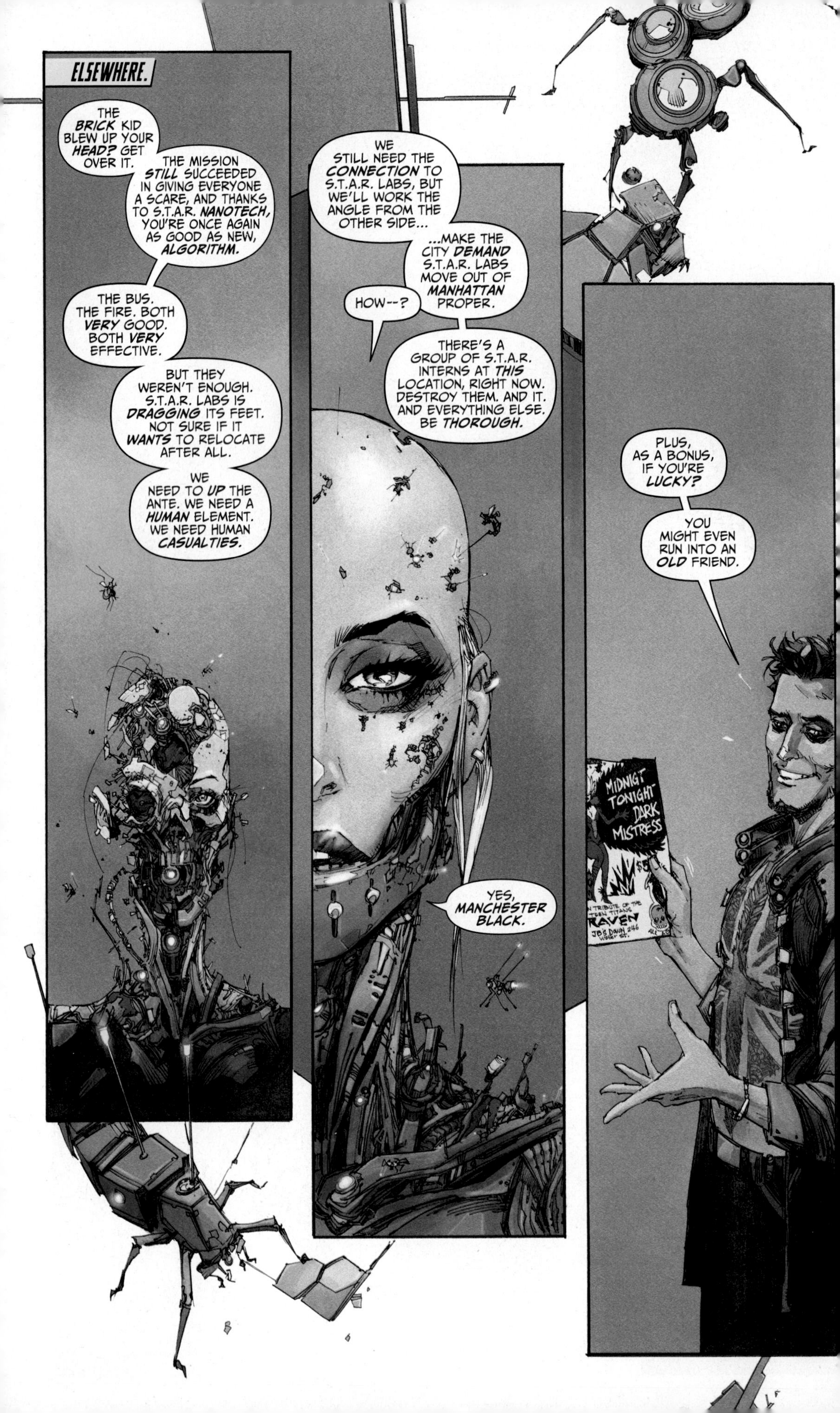
ELSEWHERE.
THE BRICK KID BLEW UP YOUR HEAD? GET OVER IT.
THE MISSION STILL SUCCEEDED IN GIVING EVERYONE A SCARE, AND THANKS TO S.T.A.R. NANOTECH, YOU'RE ONCE AGAIN AS GOOD AS NEW, ALGORITHM.
THE BUS. THE FIRE. BOTH VERY GOOD. BOTH VERY EFFECTIVE.
BUT THEY WEREN'T ENOUGH. S.T.A.R. LABS IS DRAGGING ITS FEET. NOT SURE IF IT WANTS TO RELOCATE AFTER ALL.
WE NEED TO UP THE ANTE. WE NEED A HUMAN ELEMENT. WE NEED HUMAN CASUALTIES.
WE STILL NEED THE CONNECTION TO S.T.A.R. LABS, BUT WE'LL WORK THE ANGLE FROM THE OTHER SIDE...
...MAKE THE CITY DEMAND S.T.A.R. LABS MOVE OUT OF MANHATTAN PROPER.
HOW--?
THERE'S A GROUP OF S.T.A.R. INTERNS AT THIS LOCATION, RIGHT NOW. DESTROY THEM. AND IT. AND EVERYTHING ELSE. BE THOROUGH.
YES, MANCHESTER BLACK.
PLUS, AS A BONUS, IF YOU'RE LUCKY?
YOU MIGHT EVEN RUN INTO AN OLD FRIEND.
MIDNIGHT TONIGHT DARK MISTRESS
RAVEN

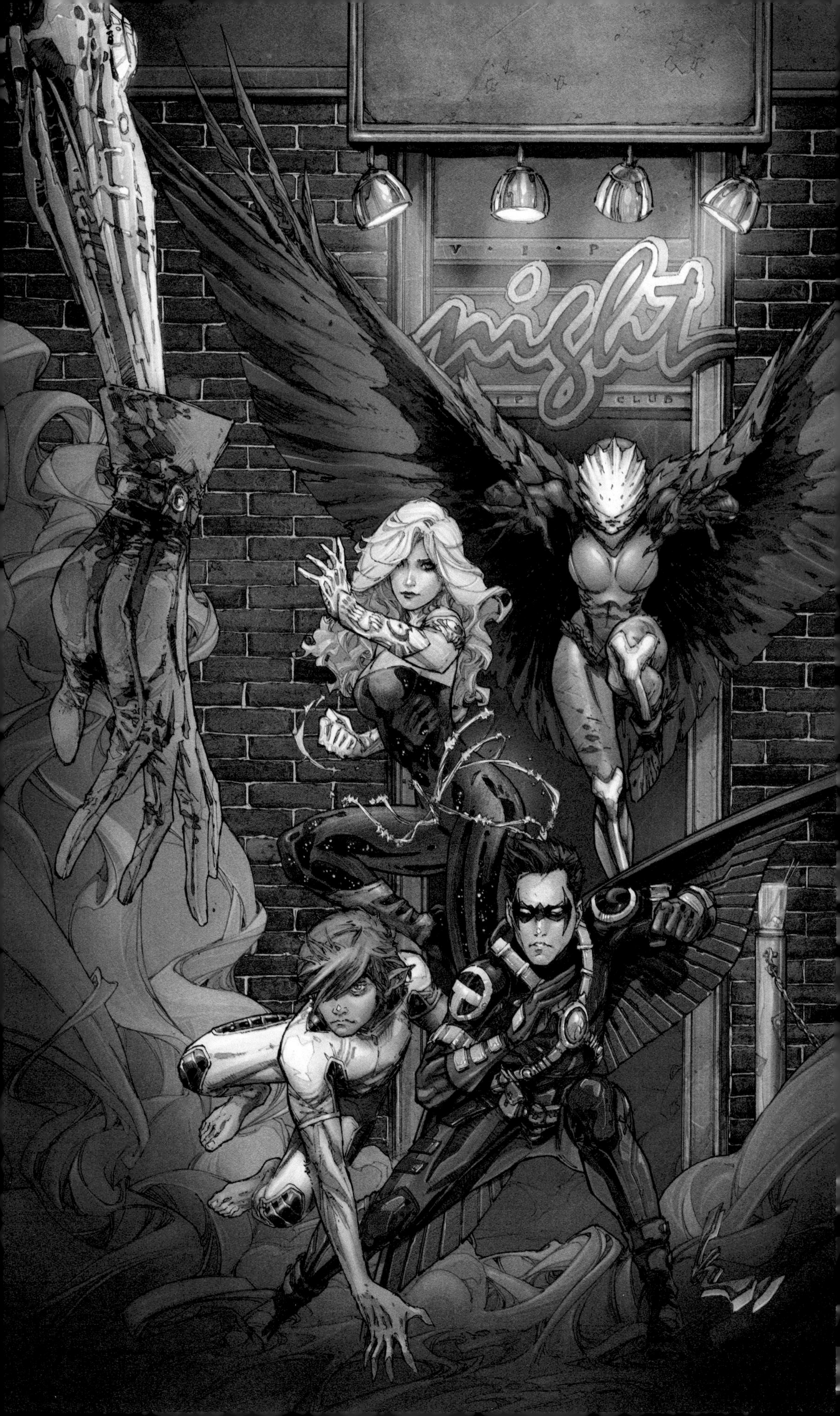
V • I • P
night
CLUB

BLINDED BY THE LIGHT: PART 3

WILL PFEIFER writer KENNETH ROCAFORT artist DAN BROWN colorist JOHN J. HILL letterer cover art by KENNETH ROCAFORT

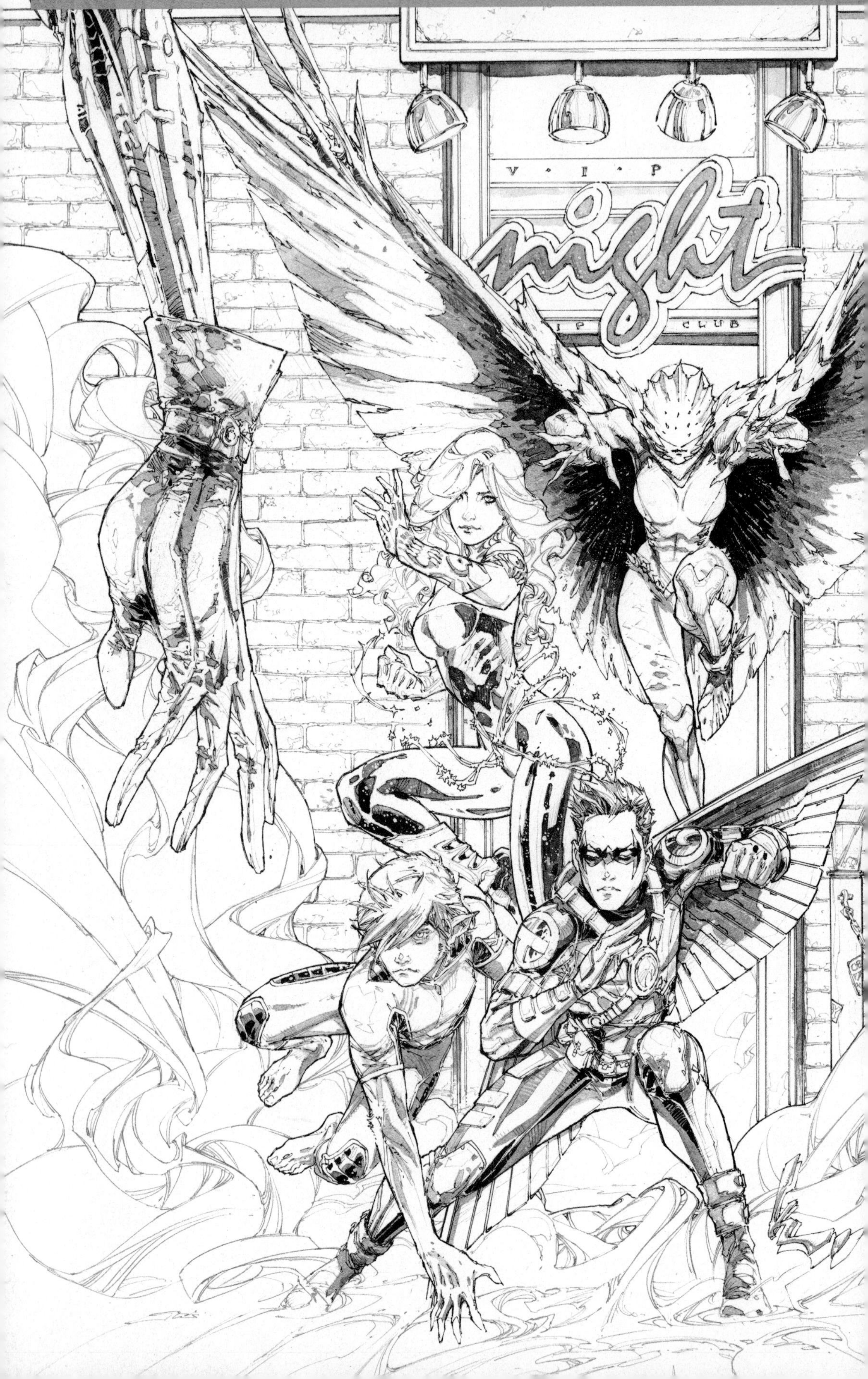
V · I · P
night
CLUB

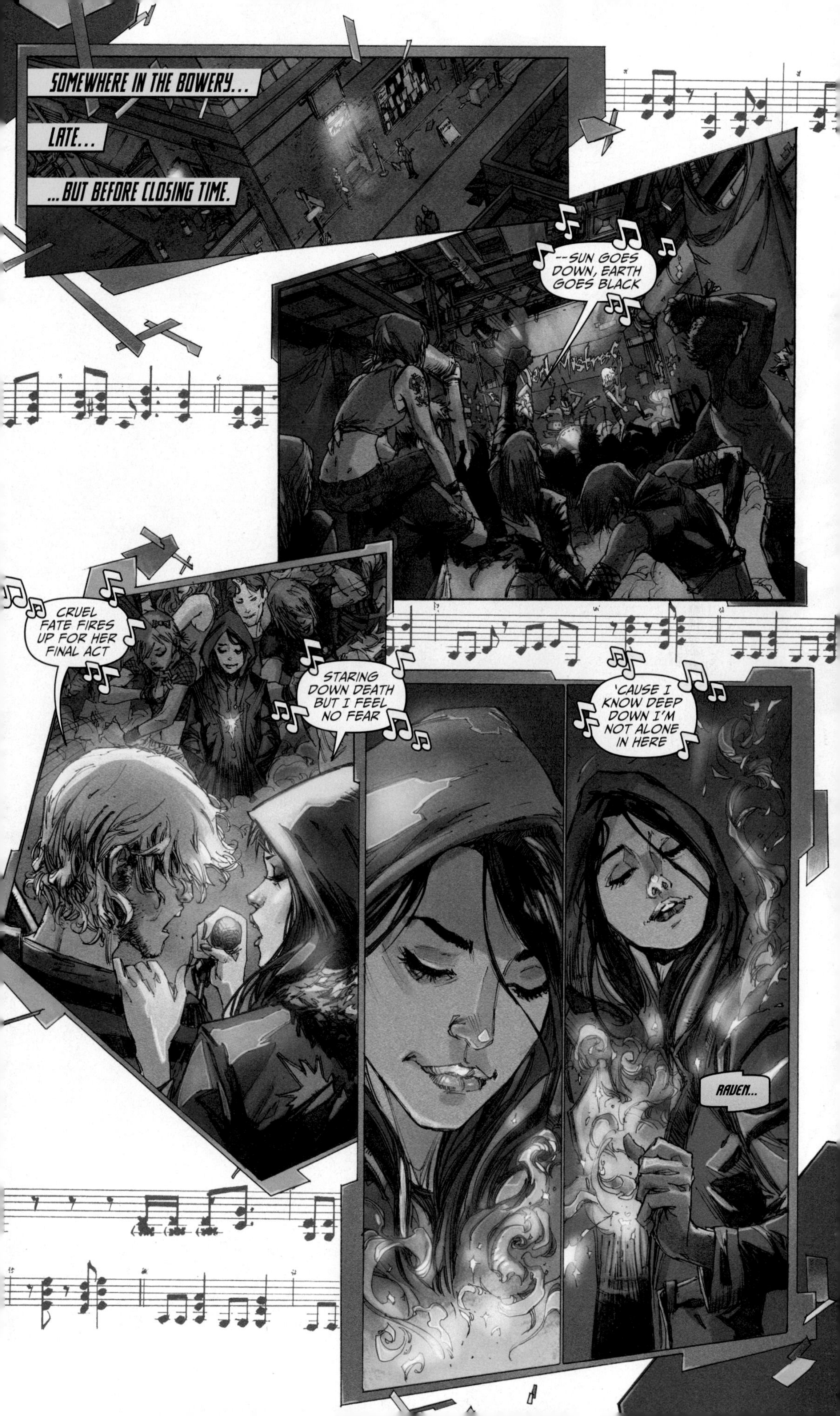
SOMEWHERE IN THE BOWERY...
LATE...
...BUT BEFORE CLOSING TIME.
--SUN GOES DOWN, EARTH GOES BLACK
CRUEL FATE FIRES UP FOR HER FINAL ACT
STARING DOWN DEATH BUT I FEEL NO FEAR
'CAUSE I KNOW DEEP DOWN I'M NOT ALONE IN HERE
RAVEN...

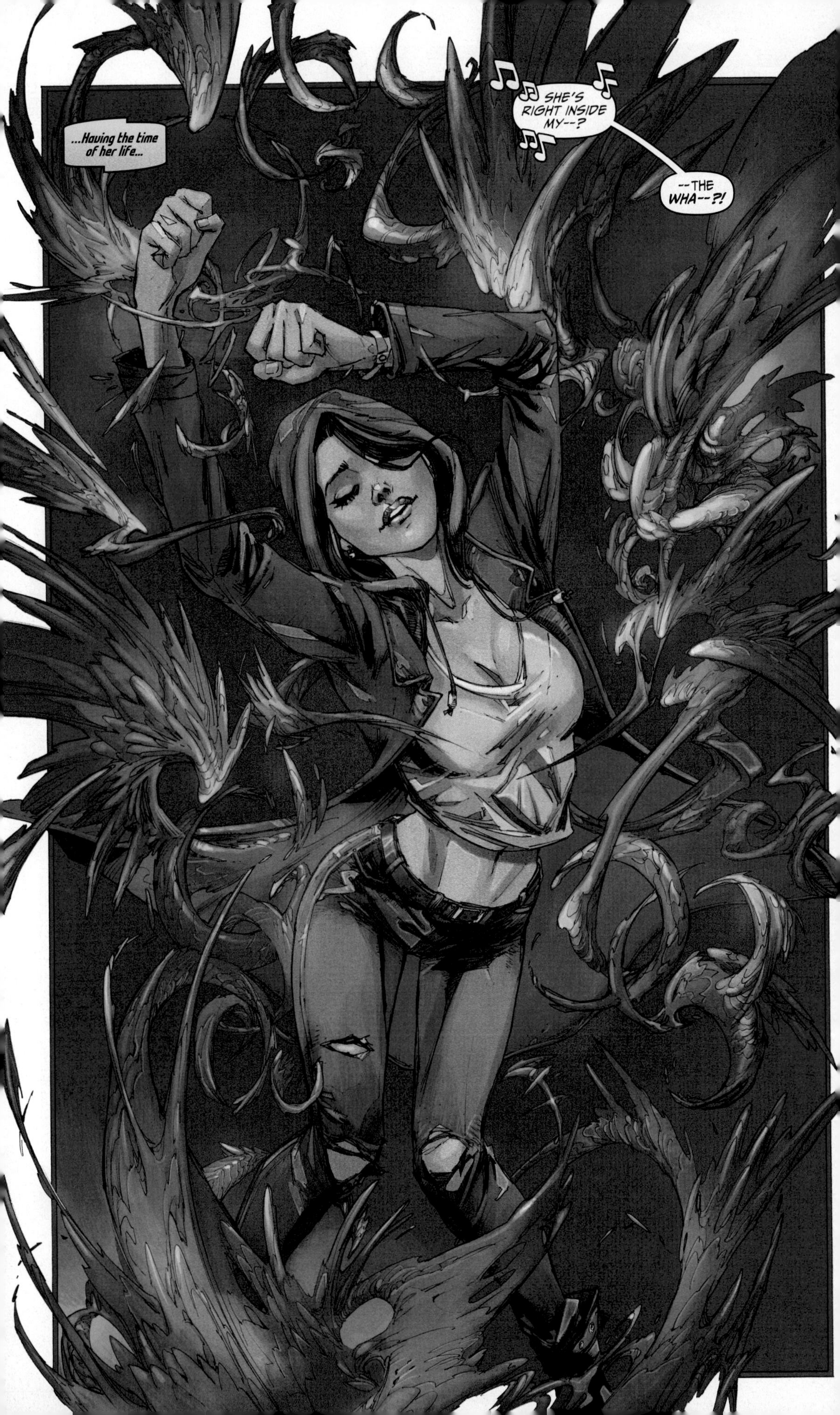

...Having the time of her life...
SHE'S RIGHT INSIDE MY--?
--THE WHA--?!

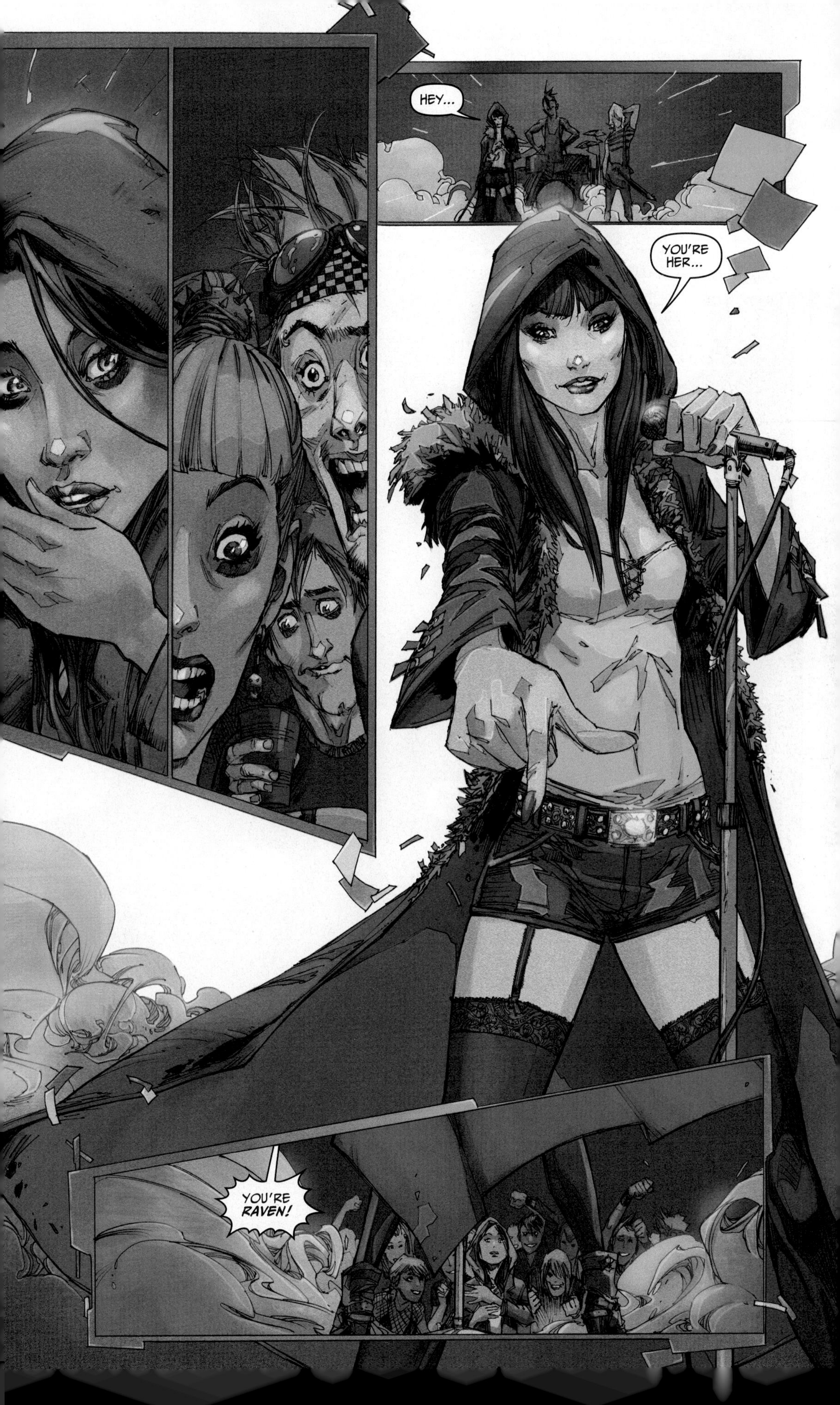
HEY...
YOU'RE HER...
YOU'RE RAVEN!

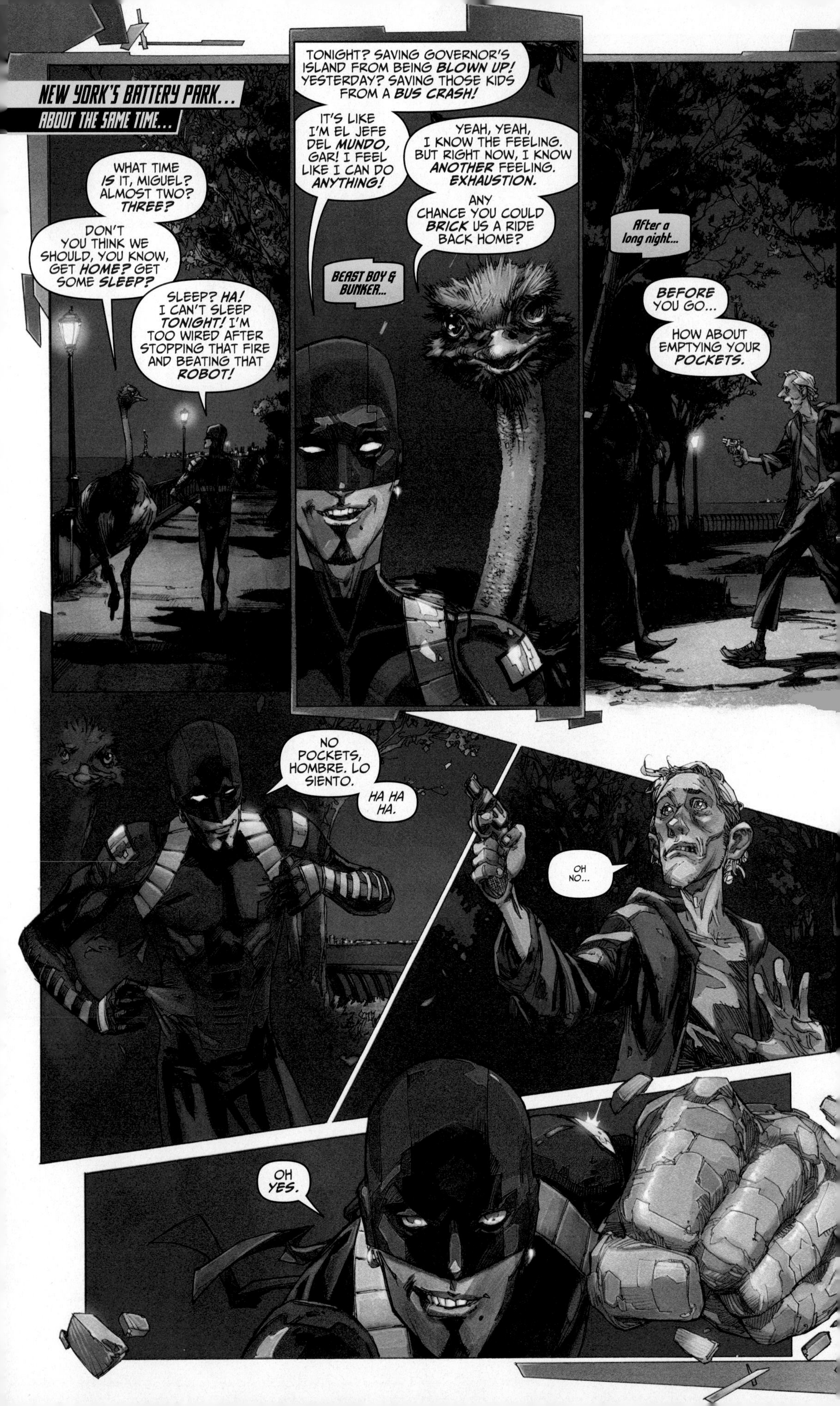
NEW YORK'S BATTERY PARK...
ABOUT THE SAME TIME...
WHAT TIME IS IT, MIGUEL? ALMOST TWO? THREE?
DON'T YOU THINK WE SHOULD, YOU KNOW, GET HOME? GET SOME SLEEP?
SLEEP? HA! I CAN'T SLEEP TONIGHT! I'M TOO WIRED AFTER STOPPING THAT FIRE AND BEATING THAT ROBOT!
TONIGHT? SAVING GOVERNOR'S ISLAND FROM BEING BLOWN UP! YESTERDAY? SAVING THOSE KIDS FROM A BUS CRASH!
IT'S LIKE I'M EL JEFE DEL MUNDO, GAR! I FEEL LIKE I CAN DO ANYTHING!
YEAH, YEAH, I KNOW THE FEELING. BUT RIGHT NOW, I KNOW ANOTHER FEELING. EXHAUSTION.
ANY CHANCE YOU COULD BRICK US A RIDE BACK HOME?
BEAST BOY & BUNKER...
After a long night...
BEFORE YOU GO...
HOW ABOUT EMPTYING YOUR POCKETS.
NO POCKETS, HOMBRE. LO SIENTO.
HA HA HA.
OH NO...
OH YES.

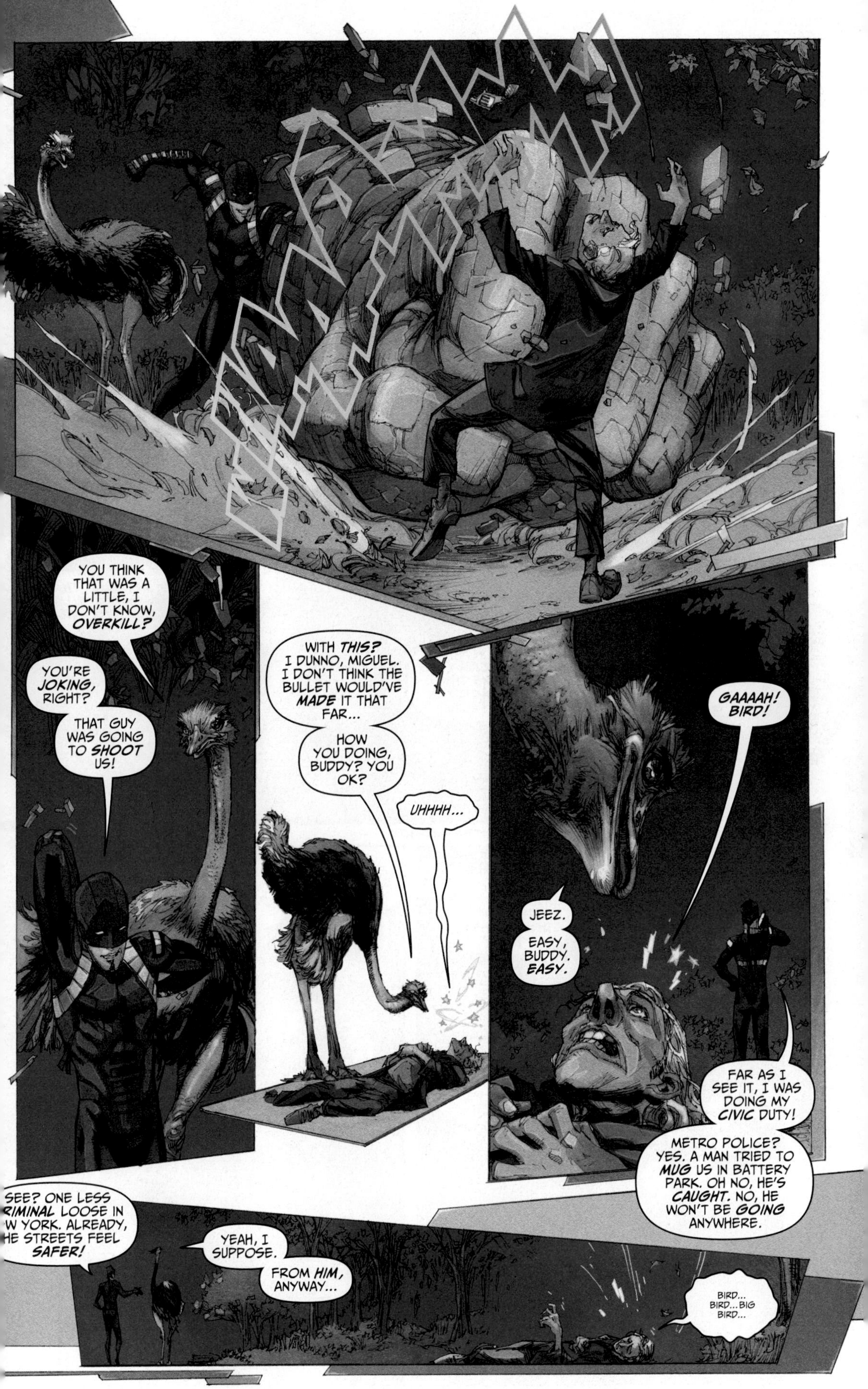

YOU THINK THAT WAS A LITTLE, I DON'T KNOW, OVERKILL?
YOU'RE JOKING, RIGHT?
THAT GUY WAS GOING TO SHOOT US!
WITH THIS? I DUNNO, MIGUEL. I DON'T THINK THE BULLET WOULD'VE MADE IT THAT FAR...
HOW YOU DOING, BUDDY? YOU OK?
UHHHH...
GAAAAH! BIRD!
JEEZ.
EASY, BUDDY. EASY.
FAR AS I SEE IT, I WAS DOING MY CIVIC DUTY!
METRO POLICE? YES. A MAN TRIED TO MUG US IN BATTERY PARK. OH NO, HE'S CAUGHT. NO, HE WON'T BE GOING ANYWHERE.
SEE? ONE LESS RIMINAL LOOSE IN W YORK. ALREADY, HE STREETS FEEL SAFER!
YEAH, I SUPPOSE.
FROM HIM, ANYWAY...
BIRD... BIRD... BIG BIRD...

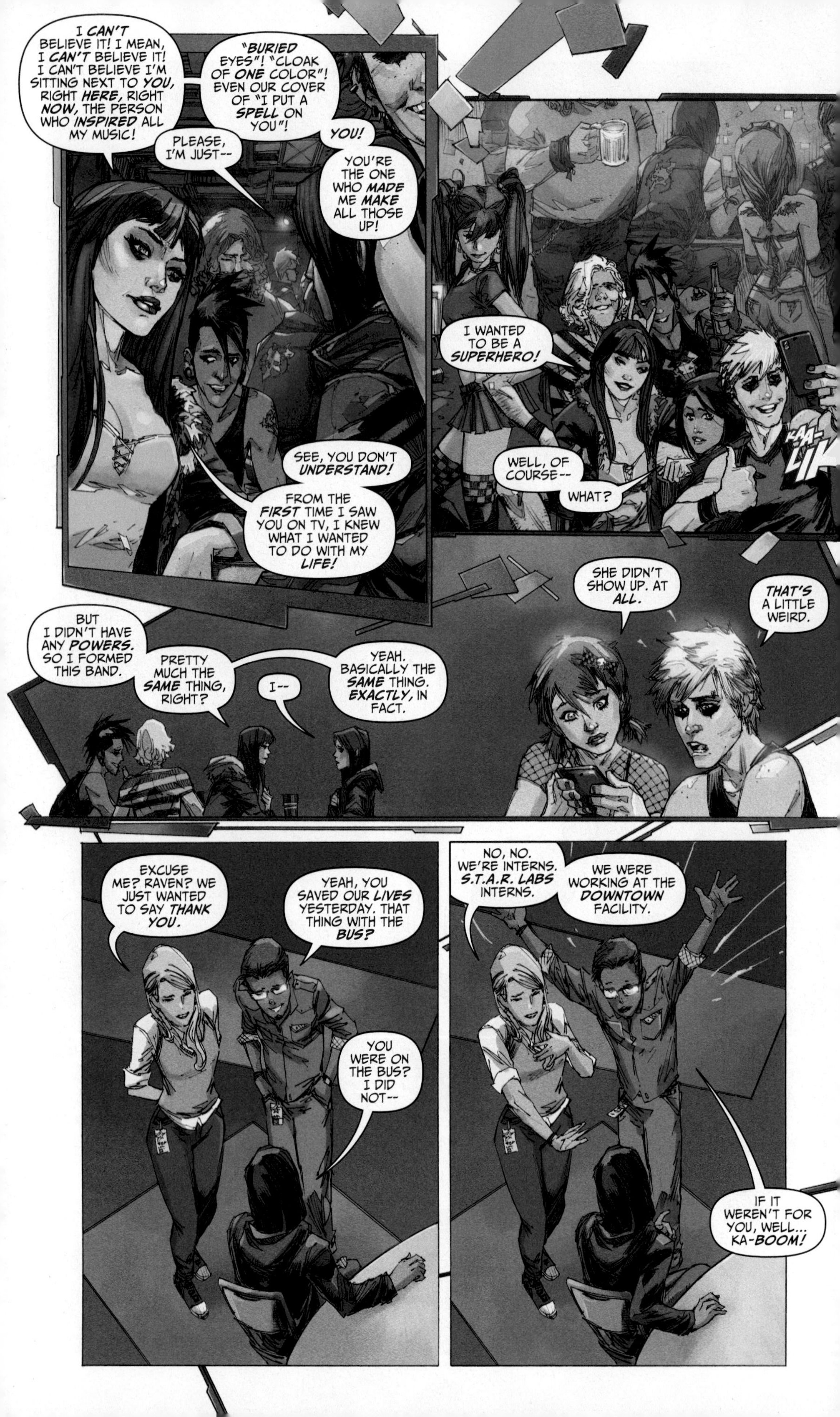
I CAN'T BELIEVE IT! I MEAN, I CAN'T BELIEVE IT! I CAN'T BELIEVE I'M SITTING NEXT TO YOU, RIGHT HERE, RIGHT NOW, THE PERSON WHO INSPIRED ALL MY MUSIC!
PLEASE, I'M JUST--
"BURIED EYES"! "CLOAK OF ONE COLOR"! EVEN OUR COVER OF "I PUT A SPELL ON YOU"!
YOU!
YOU'RE THE ONE WHO MADE ME MAKE ALL THOSE UP!
SEE, YOU DON'T UNDERSTAND!
FROM THE FIRST TIME I SAW YOU ON TV, I KNEW WHAT I WANTED TO DO WITH MY LIFE!
I WANTED TO BE A SUPERHERO!
WELL, OF COURSE--
WHAT?
KAA-LIK
BUT I DIDN'T HAVE ANY POWERS. SO I FORMED THIS BAND.
PRETTY MUCH THE SAME THING, RIGHT?
I--
YEAH. BASICALLY THE SAME THING. EXACTLY, IN FACT.
SHE DIDN'T SHOW UP. AT ALL.
THAT'S A LITTLE WEIRD.
EXCUSE ME? RAVEN? WE JUST WANTED TO SAY THANK YOU.
YEAH, YOU SAVED OUR LIVES YESTERDAY. THAT THING WITH THE BUS?
YOU WERE ON THE BUS? I DID NOT--
NO, NO. WE'RE INTERNS. S.T.A.R. LABS INTERNS.
WE WERE WORKING AT THE DOWNTOWN FACILITY.
IF IT WEREN'T FOR YOU, WELL... KA-BOOM!

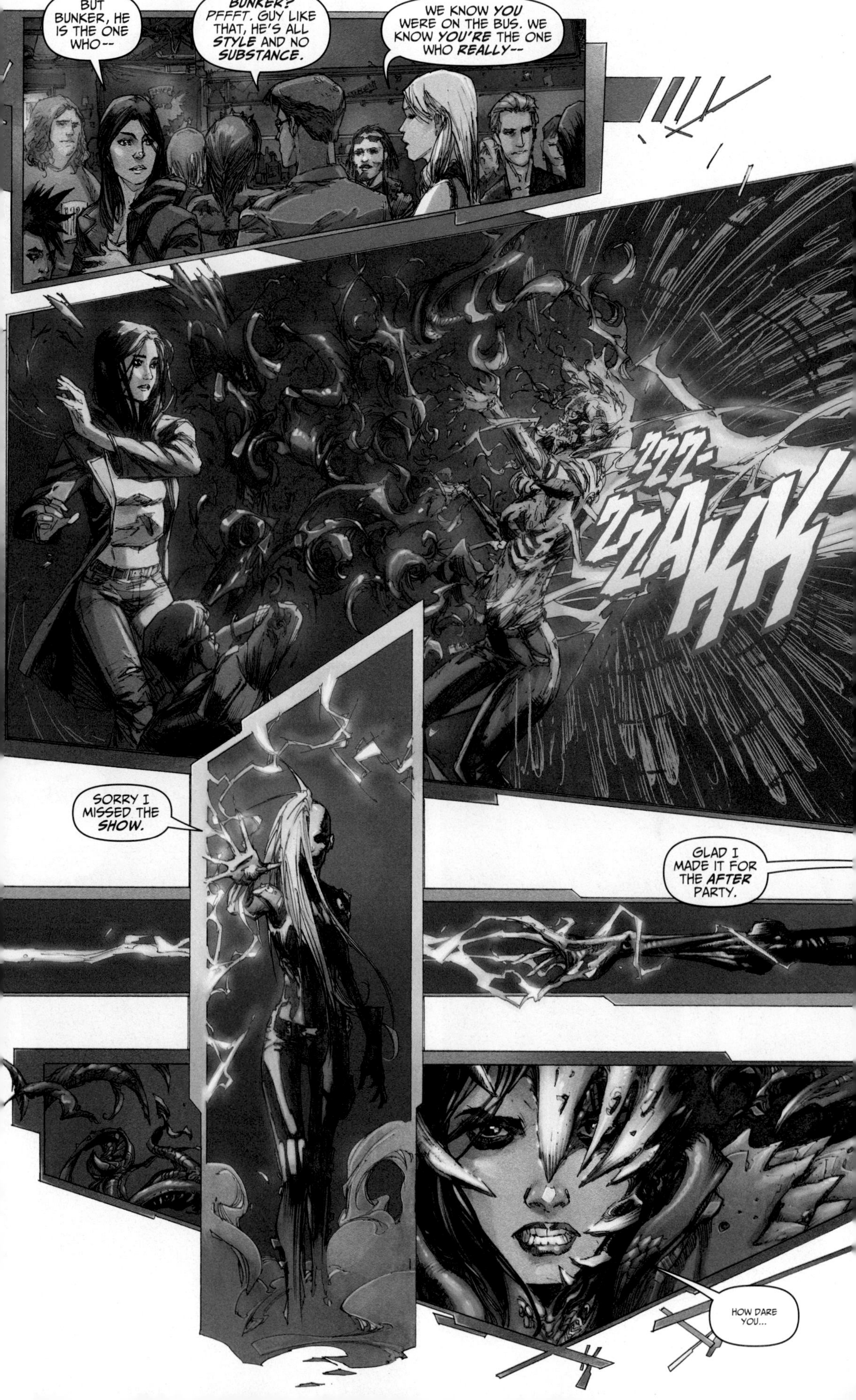

BUT BUNKER, HE IS THE ONE WHO--
BUNKER? PFFFT. GUY LIKE THAT, HE'S ALL STYLE AND NO SUBSTANCE.
WE KNOW YOU WERE ON THE BUS. WE KNOW YOU'RE THE ONE WHO REALLY--
ZZZ-ZZAKK
SORRY I MISSED THE SHOW.
GLAD I MADE IT FOR THE AFTER PARTY.
HOW DARE YOU...

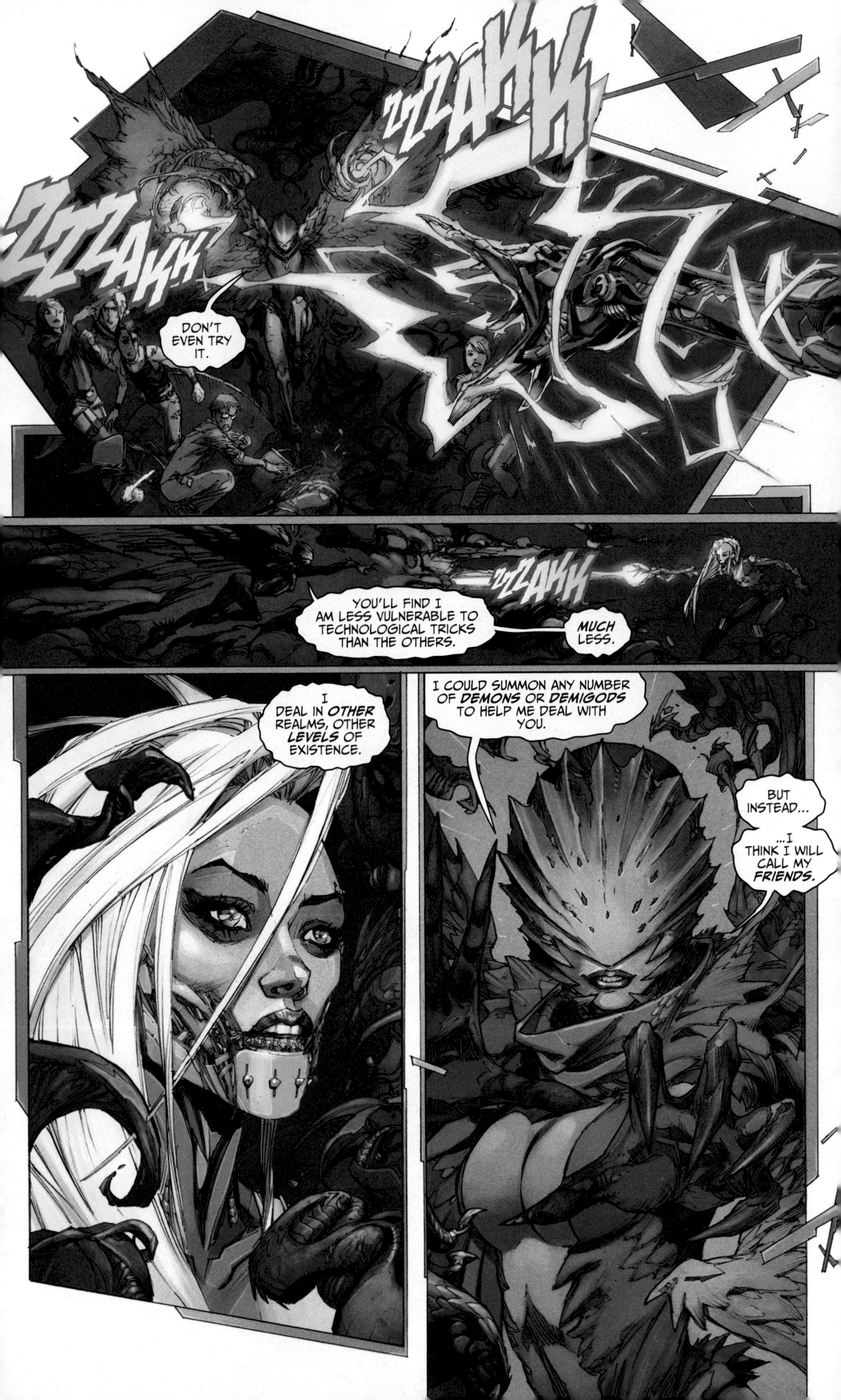
ZZZAKK
ZZZAKK
DON'T EVEN TRY IT.
ZZZAKK
YOU'LL FIND I AM LESS VULNERABLE TO TECHNOLOGICAL TRICKS THAN THE OTHERS.
MUCH LESS.
I DEAL IN *OTHER* REALMS, OTHER *LEVELS* OF EXISTENCE.
I COULD SUMMON ANY NUMBER OF *DEMONS* OR *DEMIGODS* TO HELP ME DEAL WITH YOU.
BUT INSTEAD...
...I THINK I WILL CALL MY *FRIENDS*.

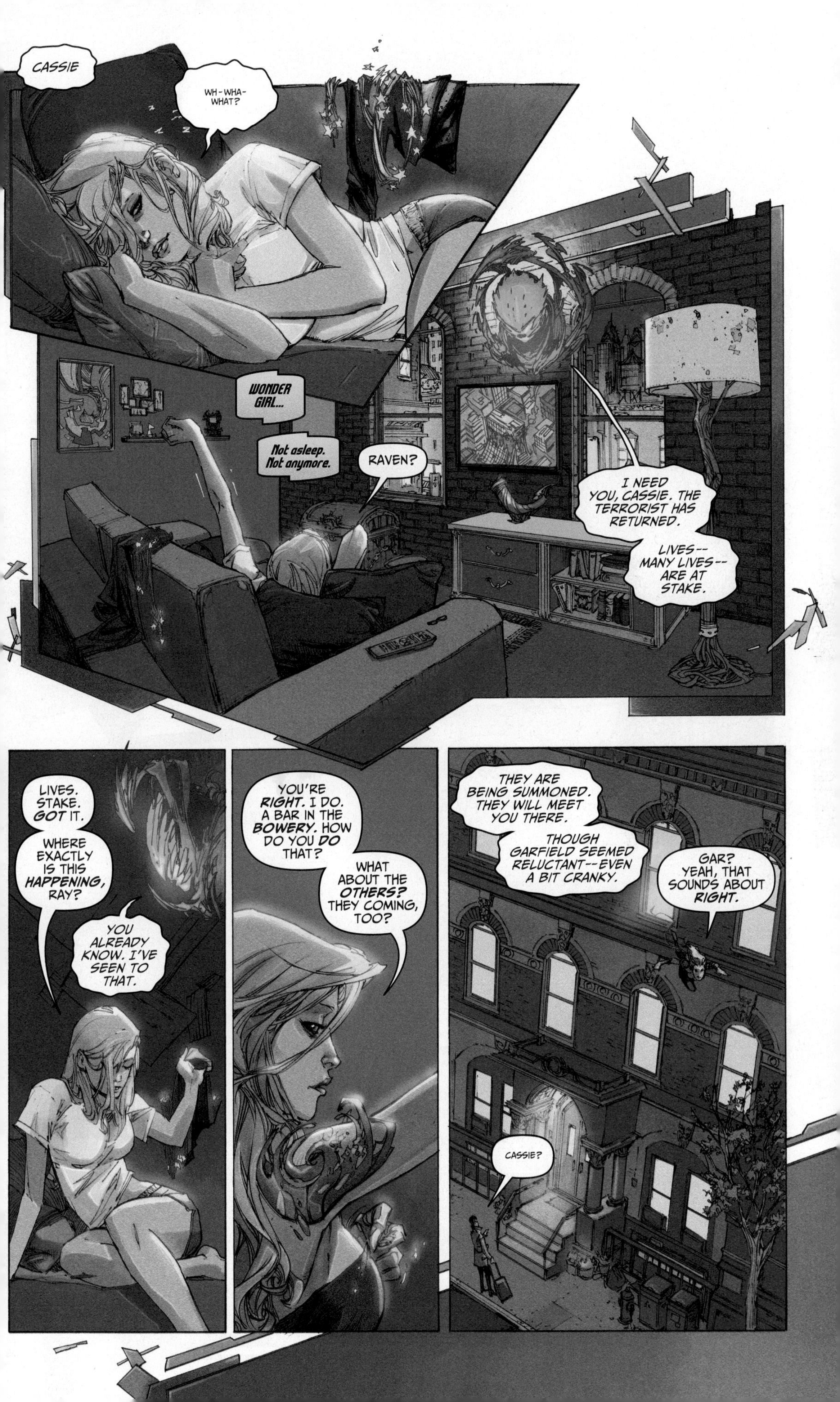
CASSIE
WH-WHA-WHAT?
WONDER GIRL...
Not asleep. Not anymore.
RAVEN?
I NEED YOU, CASSIE. THE TERRORIST HAS RETURNED.
LIVES-- MANY LIVES-- ARE AT STAKE.
LIVES. STAKE. GOT IT.
WHERE EXACTLY IS THIS HAPPENING, RAY?
YOU ALREADY KNOW. I'VE SEEN TO THAT.
YOU'RE RIGHT. I DO. A BAR IN THE BOWERY. HOW DO YOU DO THAT?
WHAT ABOUT THE OTHERS? THEY COMING, TOO?
THEY ARE BEING SUMMONED. THEY WILL MEET YOU THERE.
THOUGH GARFIELD SEEMED RELUCTANT--EVEN A BIT CRANKY.
GAR? YEAH, THAT SOUNDS ABOUT RIGHT.
CASSIE?

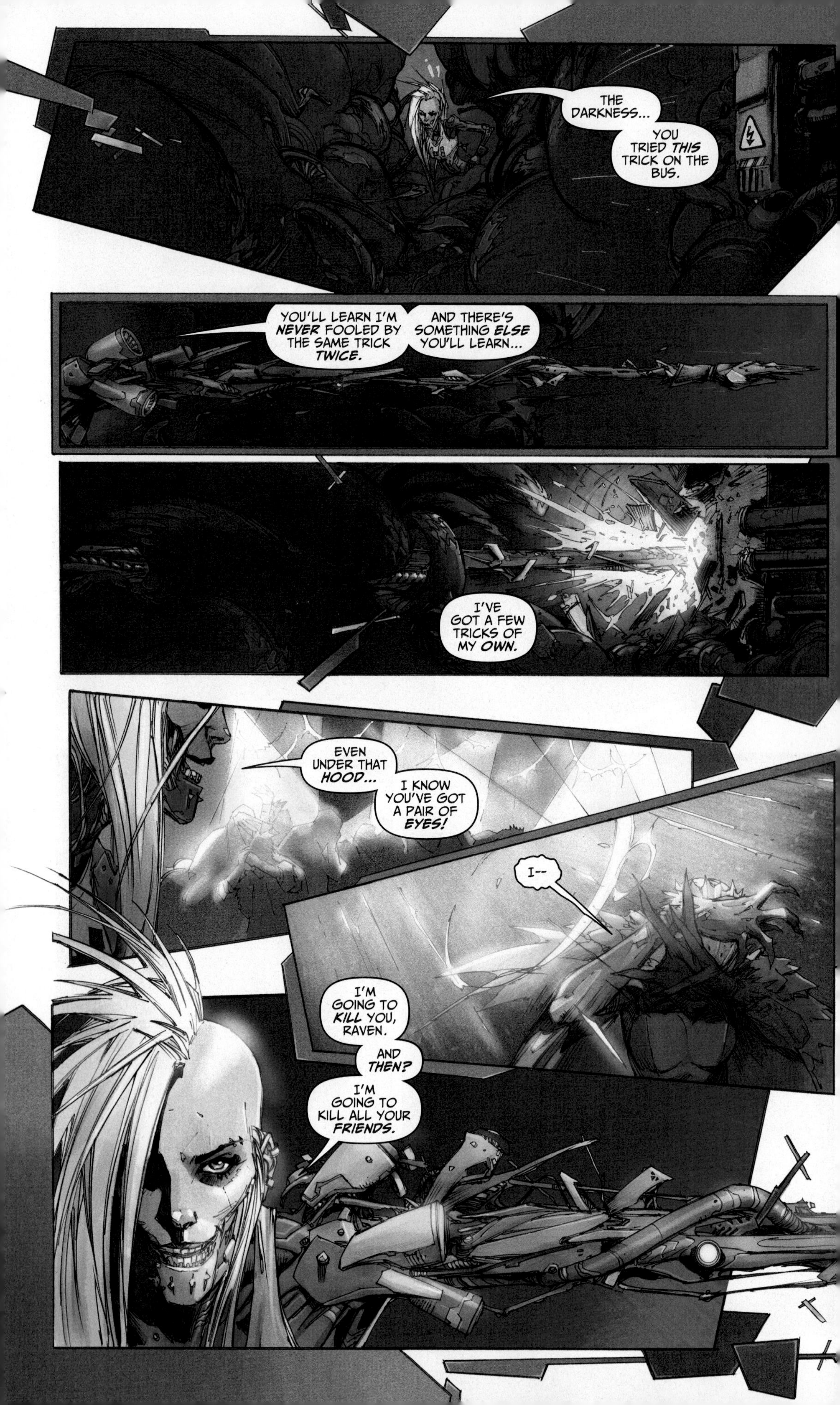

THE DARKNESS...
YOU TRIED THIS TRICK ON THE BUS.
YOU'LL LEARN I'M NEVER FOOLED BY THE SAME TRICK TWICE.
AND THERE'S SOMETHING ELSE YOU'LL LEARN...
I'VE GOT A FEW TRICKS OF MY OWN.
EVEN UNDER THAT HOOD...
I KNOW YOU'VE GOT A PAIR OF EYES!
I--
I'M GOING TO KILL YOU, RAVEN.
AND THEN?
I'M GOING TO KILL ALL YOUR FRIENDS.

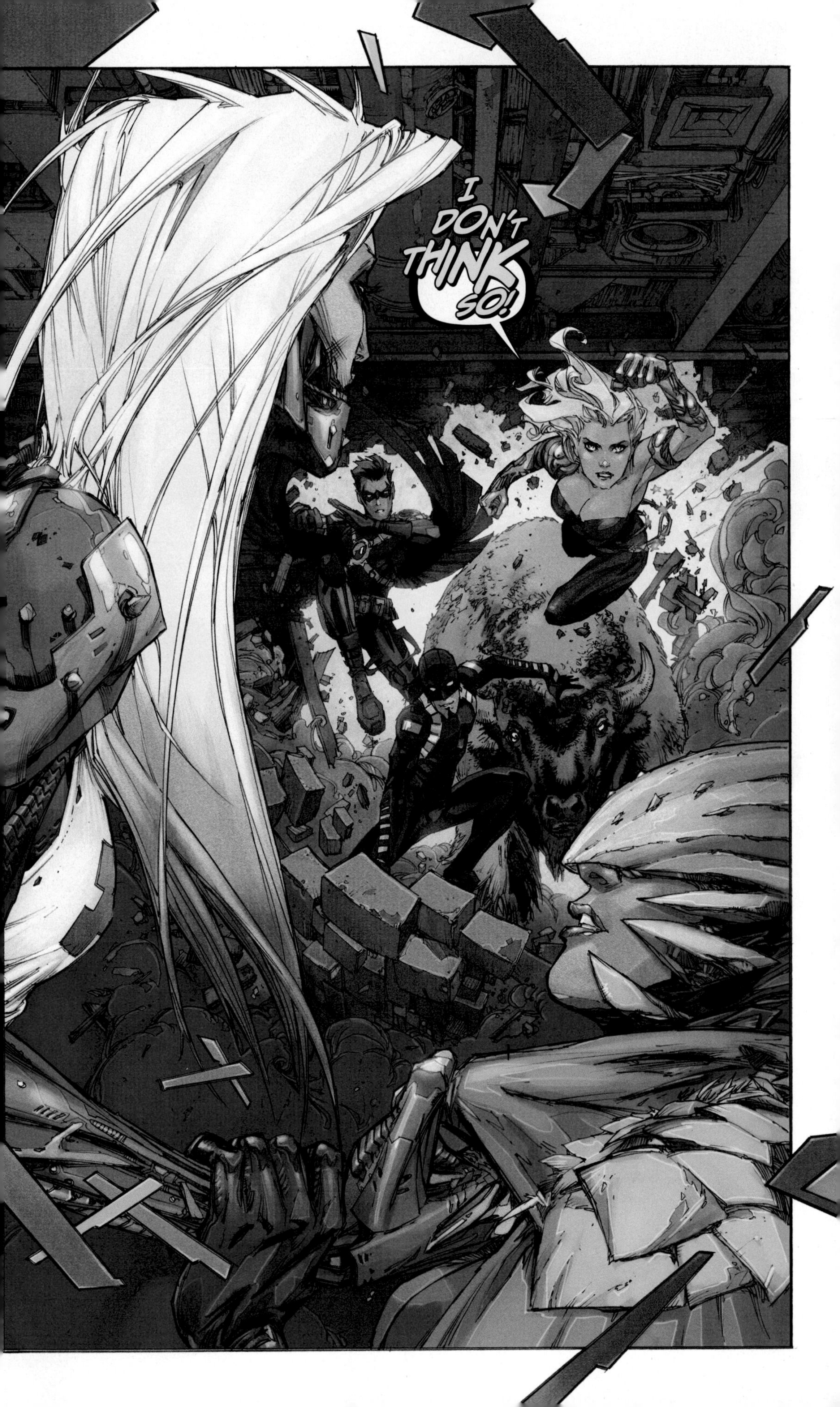
I DON'T THINK SO!

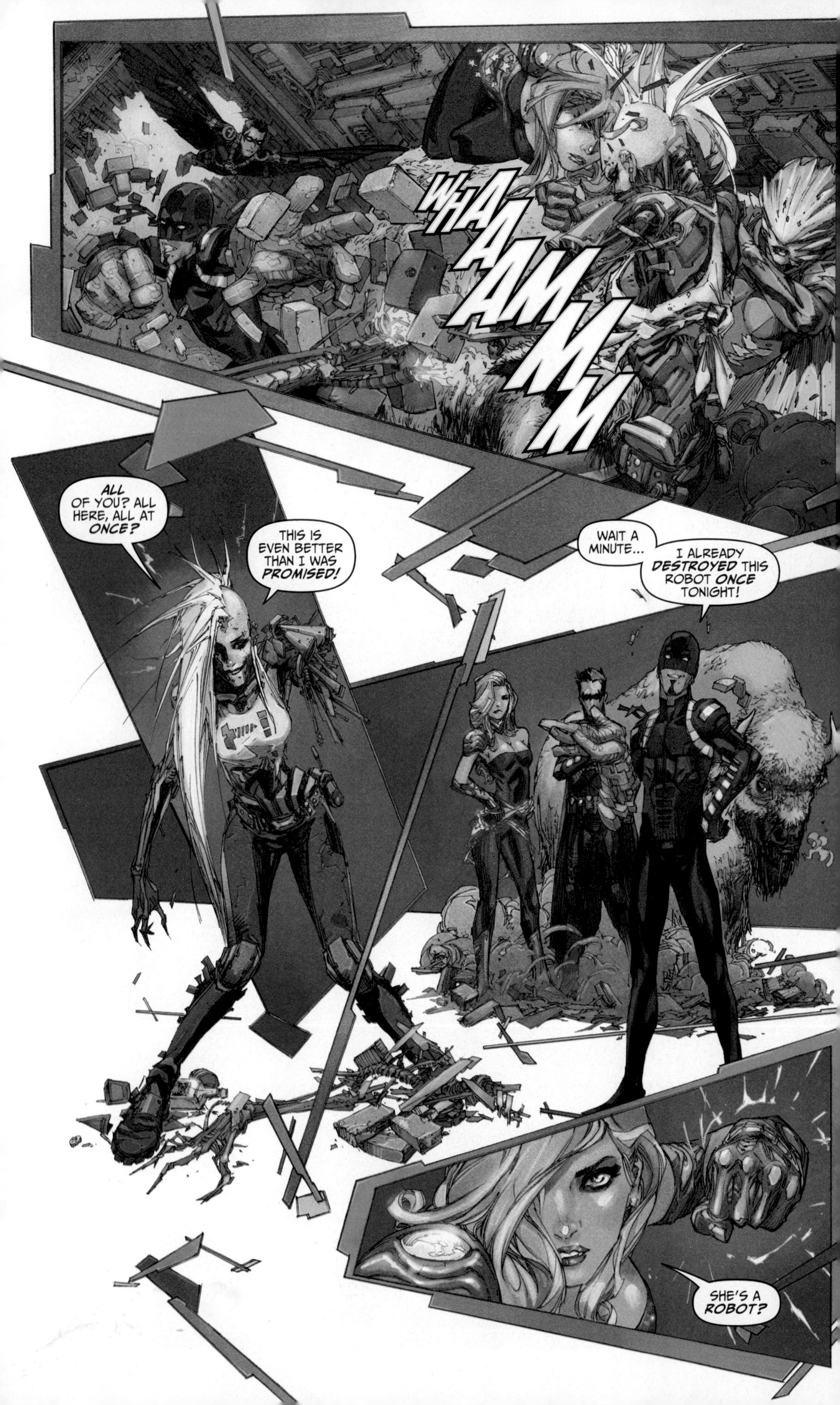
WHAAAMMM
ALL OF YOU? ALL HERE, ALL AT ONCE?
THIS IS EVEN BETTER THAN I WAS PROMISED!
WAIT A MINUTE...
I ALREADY DESTROYED THIS ROBOT ONCE TONIGHT!
SHE'S A ROBOT?

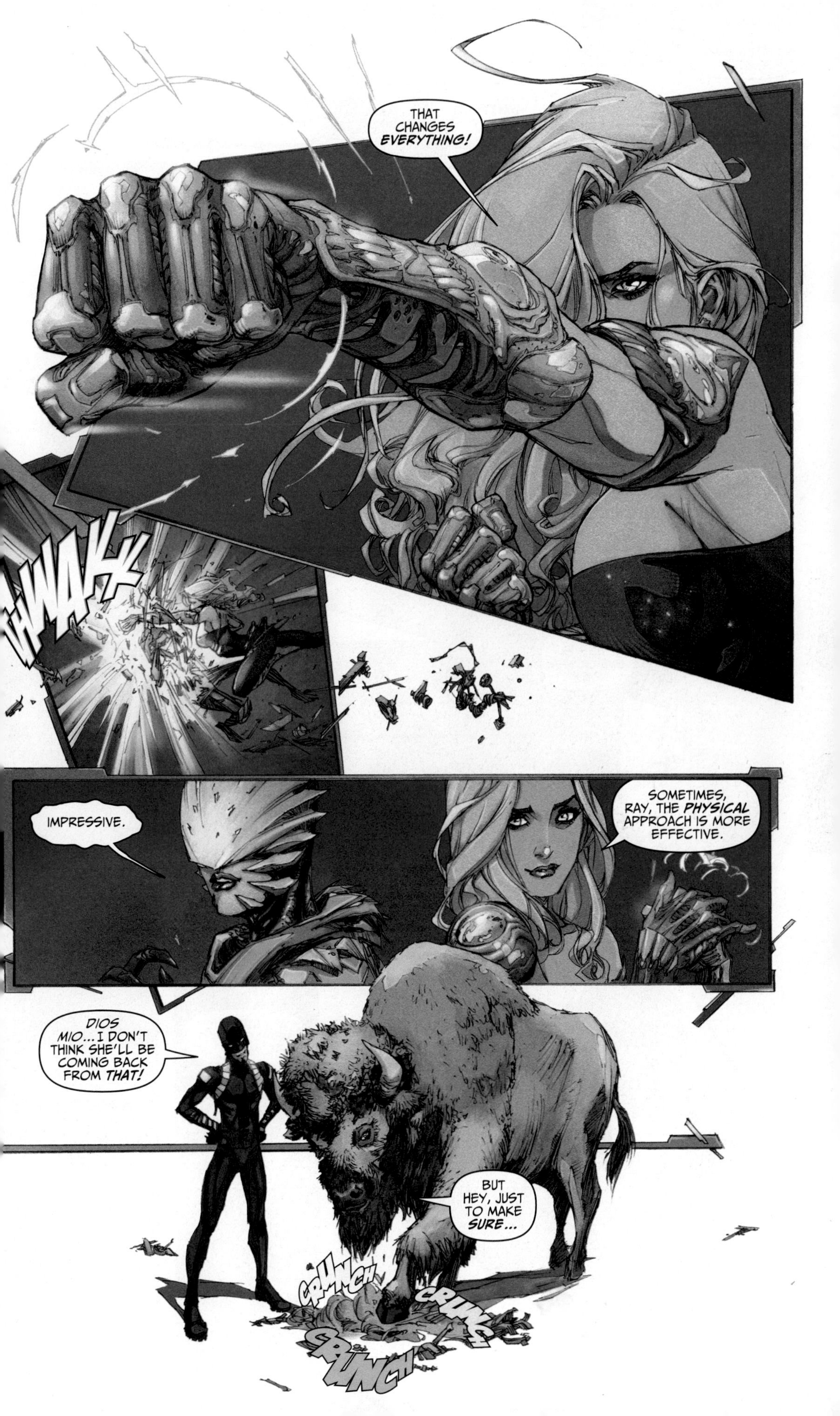
THAT CHANGES EVERYTHING!
WHAK
IMPRESSIVE.
SOMETIMES, RAY, THE PHYSICAL APPROACH IS MORE EFFECTIVE.
DIOS MIO... I DON'T THINK SHE'LL BE COMING BACK FROM THAT!
BUT HEY, JUST TO MAKE SURE...
CRUNCH
CRUNCH
CRUNCH

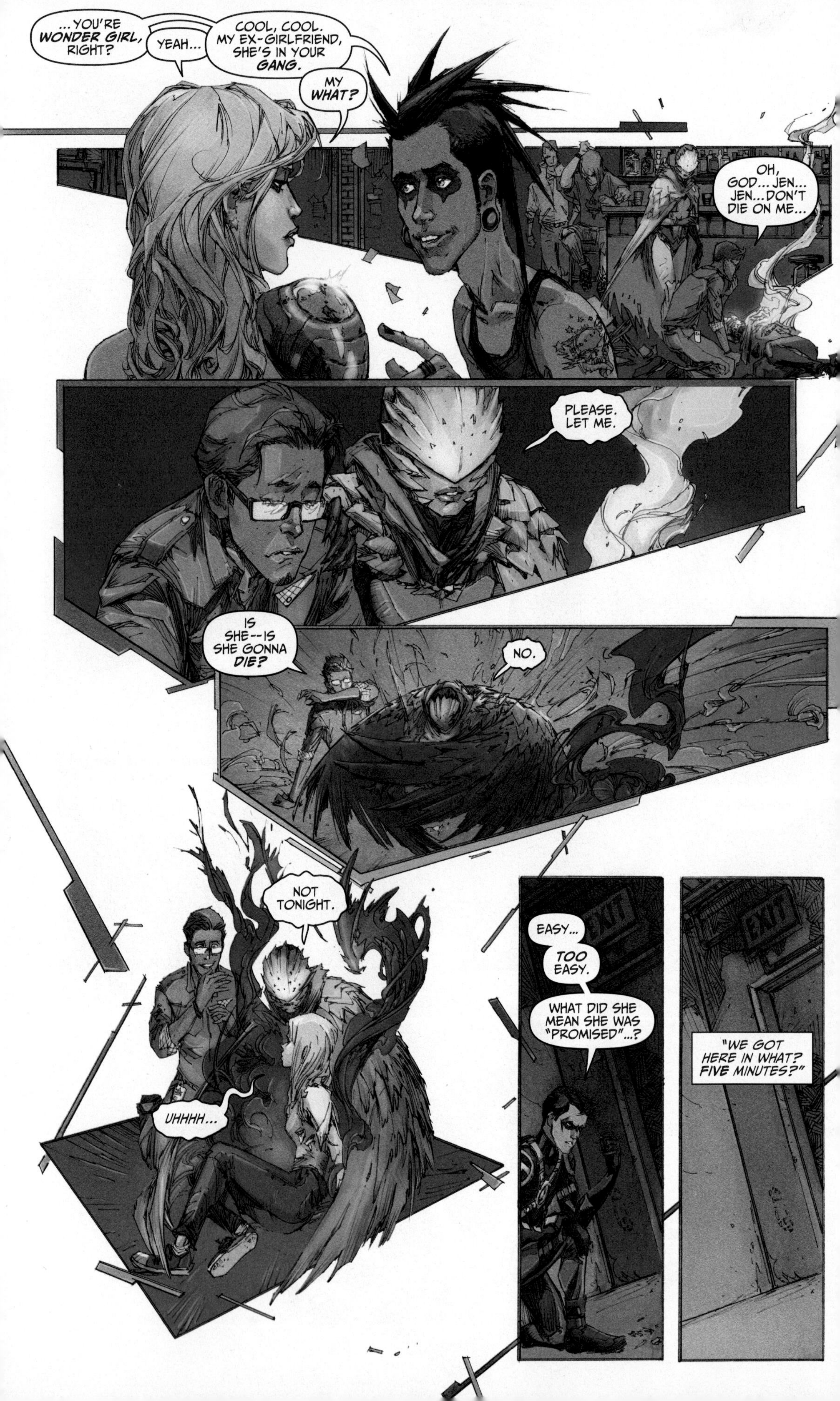
...YOU'RE WONDER GIRL, RIGHT?
YEAH...
COOL, COOL. MY EX-GIRLFRIEND, SHE'S IN YOUR GANG.
MY WHAT?
OH, GOD... JEN... JEN...DON'T DIE ON ME...
PLEASE. LET ME.
IS SHE--IS SHE GONNA DIE?
NO.
NOT TONIGHT.
UHHHH...
EXIT
EASY...
TOO EASY.
WHAT DID SHE MEAN SHE WAS "PROMISED"...?
EXIT
"WE GOT HERE IN WHAT? FIVE MINUTES?"

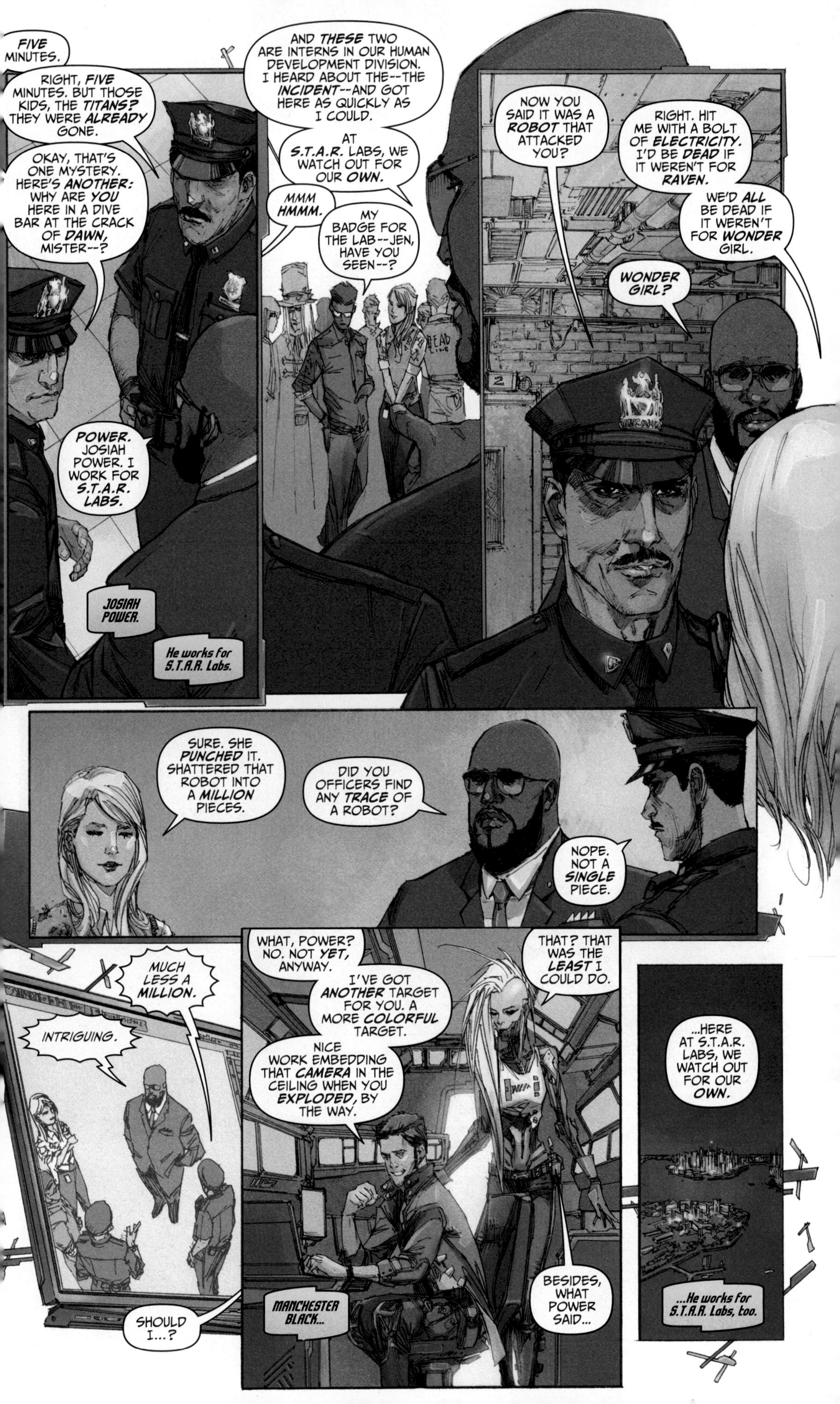

FIVE MINUTES.
RIGHT, FIVE MINUTES. BUT THOSE KIDS, THE TITANS? THEY WERE ALREADY GONE.
OKAY, THAT'S ONE MYSTERY. HERE'S ANOTHER: WHY ARE YOU HERE IN A DIVE BAR AT THE CRACK OF DAWN, MISTER--?
POWER. JOSIAH POWER. I WORK FOR S.T.A.R. LABS.
JOSIAH POWER.
He works for S.T.A.R. Labs.
AND THESE TWO ARE INTERNS IN OUR HUMAN DEVELOPMENT DIVISION. I HEARD ABOUT THE--THE INCIDENT--AND GOT HERE AS QUICKLY AS I COULD.
AT S.T.A.R. LABS, WE WATCH OUT FOR OUR OWN.
MMM HMMM.
MY BADGE FOR THE LAB--JEN, HAVE YOU SEEN--?
NOW YOU SAID IT WAS A ROBOT THAT ATTACKED YOU?
RIGHT. HIT ME WITH A BOLT OF ELECTRICITY. I'D BE DEAD IF IT WEREN'T FOR RAVEN.
WE'D ALL BE DEAD IF IT WEREN'T FOR WONDER GIRL.
WONDER GIRL?
SURE. SHE PUNCHED IT. SHATTERED THAT ROBOT INTO A MILLION PIECES.
DID YOU OFFICERS FIND ANY TRACE OF A ROBOT?
NOPE. NOT A SINGLE PIECE.
MUCH LESS A MILLION.
INTRIGUING.
SHOULD I...?
WHAT, POWER? NO. NOT YET, ANYWAY.
I'VE GOT ANOTHER TARGET FOR YOU. A MORE COLORFUL TARGET.
NICE WORK EMBEDDING THAT CAMERA IN THE CEILING WHEN YOU EXPLODED, BY THE WAY.
THAT? THAT WAS THE LEAST I COULD DO.
MANCHESTER BLACK...
BESIDES, WHAT POWER SAID...
...HERE AT S.T.A.R. LABS, WE WATCH OUT FOR OUR OWN.
...He works for S.T.A.R. Labs, too.

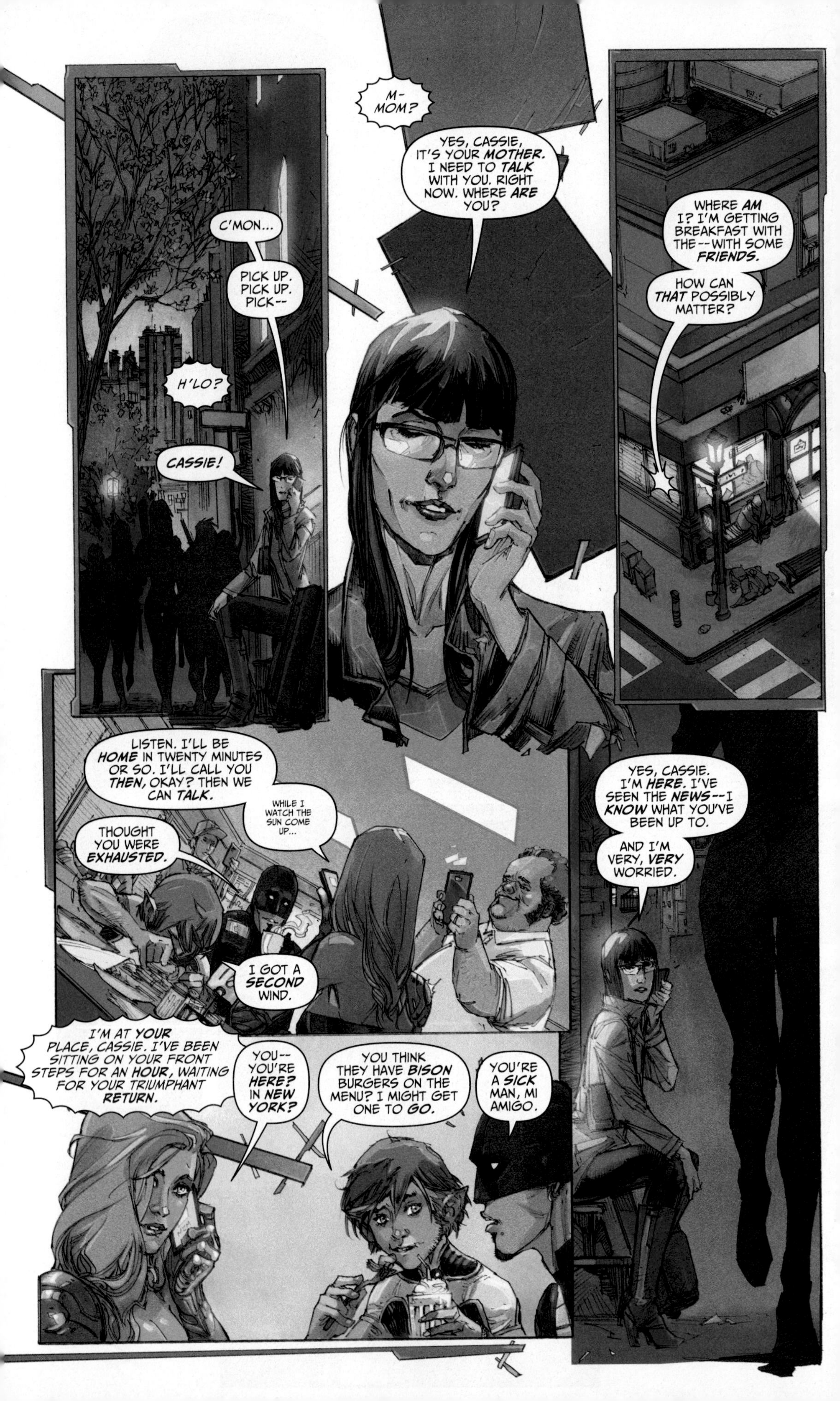
M-MOM?
C'MON...
PICK UP. PICK UP. PICK--
H'LO?
CASSIE!
YES, CASSIE, IT'S YOUR MOTHER. I NEED TO TALK WITH YOU. RIGHT NOW. WHERE ARE YOU?
WHERE AM I? I'M GETTING BREAKFAST WITH THE--WITH SOME FRIENDS.
HOW CAN THAT POSSIBLY MATTER?
LISTEN. I'LL BE HOME IN TWENTY MINUTES OR SO. I'LL CALL YOU THEN, OKAY? THEN WE CAN TALK.
WHILE I WATCH THE SUN COME UP...
THOUGHT YOU WERE EXHAUSTED.
I GOT A SECOND WIND.
YES, CASSIE. I'M HERE. I'VE SEEN THE NEWS--I KNOW WHAT YOU'VE BEEN UP TO.
AND I'M VERY, VERY WORRIED.
I'M AT YOUR PLACE, CASSIE. I'VE BEEN SITTING ON YOUR FRONT STEPS FOR AN HOUR, WAITING FOR YOUR TRIUMPHANT RETURN.
YOU--YOU'RE HERE? IN NEW YORK?
YOU THINK THEY HAVE BISON BURGERS ON THE MENU? I MIGHT GET ONE TO GO.
YOU'RE A SICK MAN, MI AMIGO.

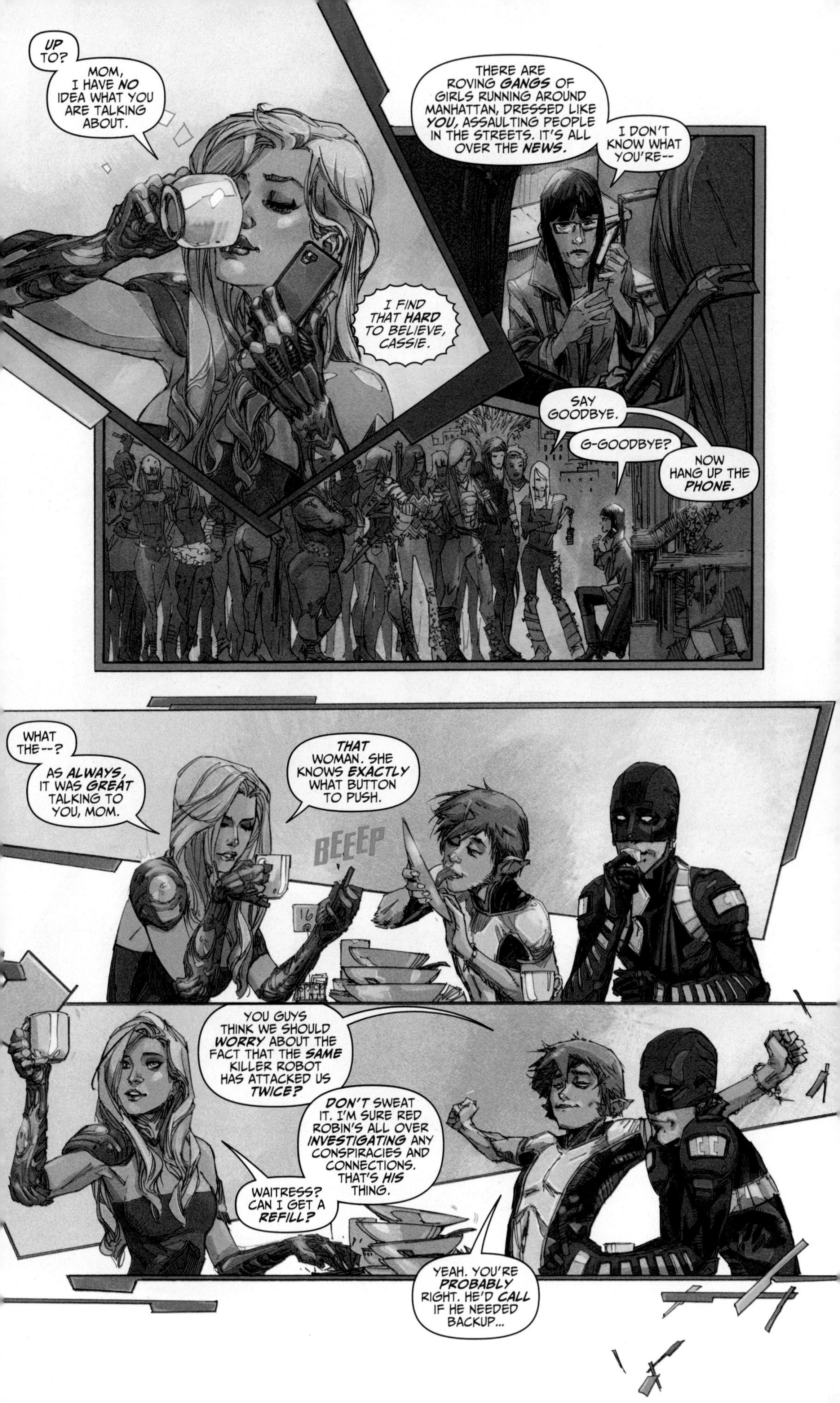
UP TO?
MOM, I HAVE NO IDEA WHAT YOU ARE TALKING ABOUT.
THERE ARE ROVING GANGS OF GIRLS RUNNING AROUND MANHATTAN, DRESSED LIKE YOU, ASSAULTING PEOPLE IN THE STREETS. IT'S ALL OVER THE NEWS.
I DON'T KNOW WHAT YOU'RE--
I FIND THAT HARD TO BELIEVE, CASSIE.
SAY GOODBYE.
G-GOODBYE?
NOW HANG UP THE PHONE.
WHAT THE--?
AS ALWAYS, IT WAS GREAT TALKING TO YOU, MOM.
THAT WOMAN. SHE KNOWS EXACTLY WHAT BUTTON TO PUSH.
BEEEP
YOU GUYS THINK WE SHOULD WORRY ABOUT THE FACT THAT THE SAME KILLER ROBOT HAS ATTACKED US TWICE?
DON'T SWEAT IT. I'M SURE RED ROBIN'S ALL OVER INVESTIGATING ANY CONSPIRACIES AND CONNECTIONS. THAT'S HIS THING.
WAITRESS? CAN I GET A REFILL?
YEAH. YOU'RE PROBABLY RIGHT. HE'D CALL IF HE NEEDED BACKUP...

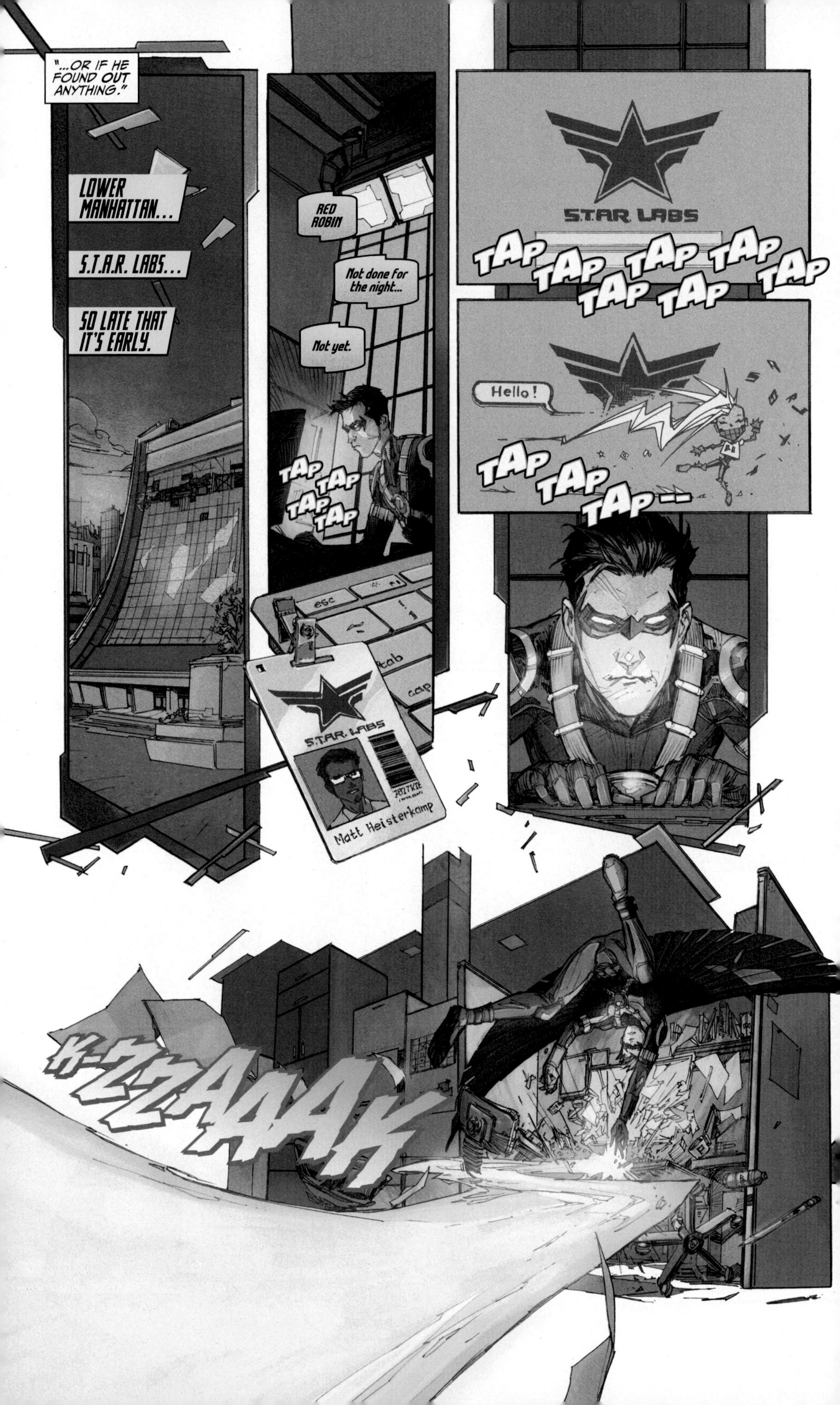
"...OR IF HE FOUND OUT ANYTHING."
LOWER MANHATTAN...
S.T.A.R. LABS...
SO LATE THAT IT'S EARLY.
RED ROBIN
Not done for the night...
Not yet.
TAP TAP TAP TAP
S.T.A.R. LABS
Matt Heisterkamp
S.T.A.R. LABS
TAP TAP TAP TAP TAP TAP TAP TAP
Hello!
TAP TAP TAP--
K-ZZAAAK

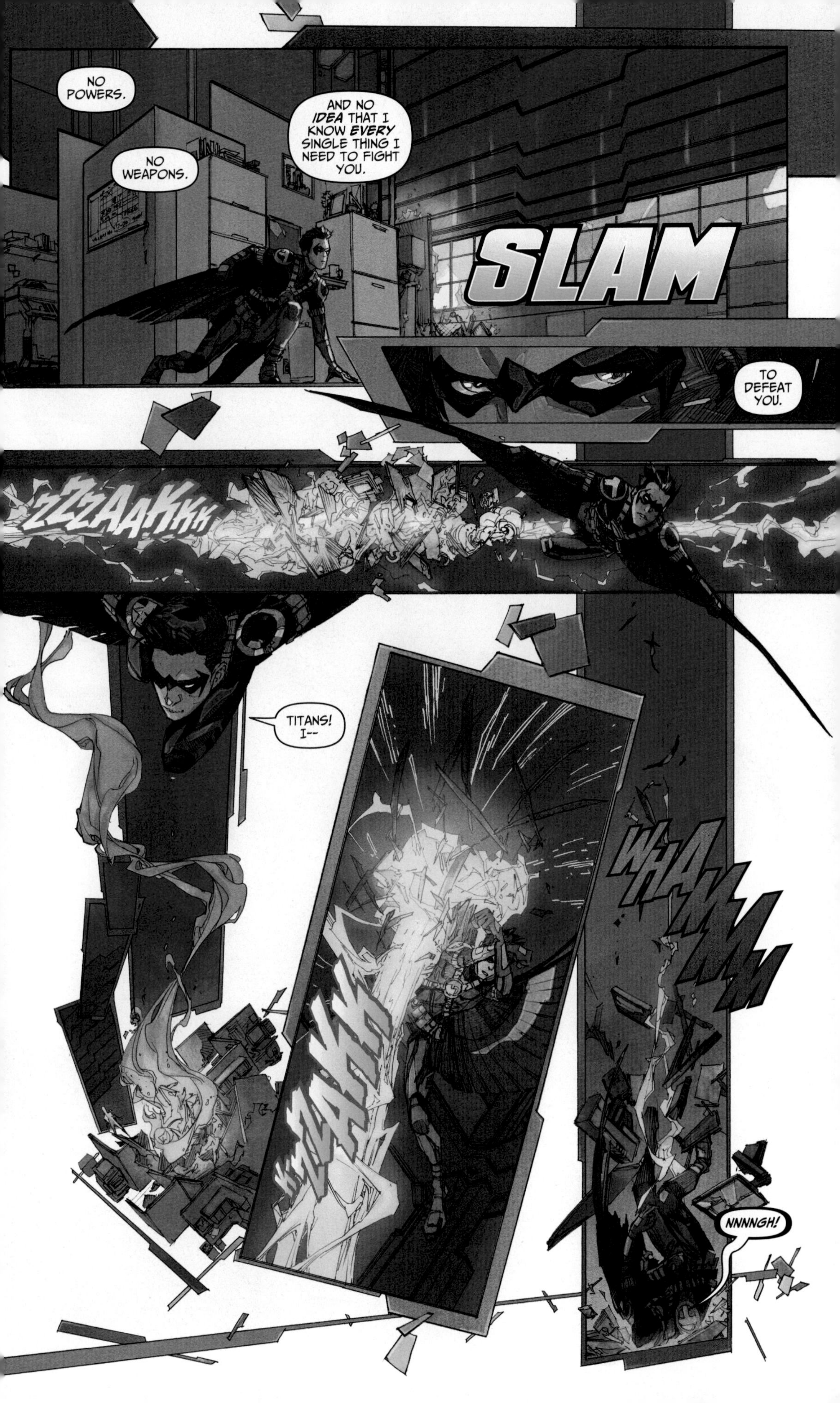

NO POWERS.
NO WEAPONS.
AND NO IDEA THAT I KNOW EVERY SINGLE THING I NEED TO FIGHT YOU.
SLAM
TO DEFEAT YOU.
ZZZAAKKK
TITANS! I--
WHAMMM
NNNNGH!

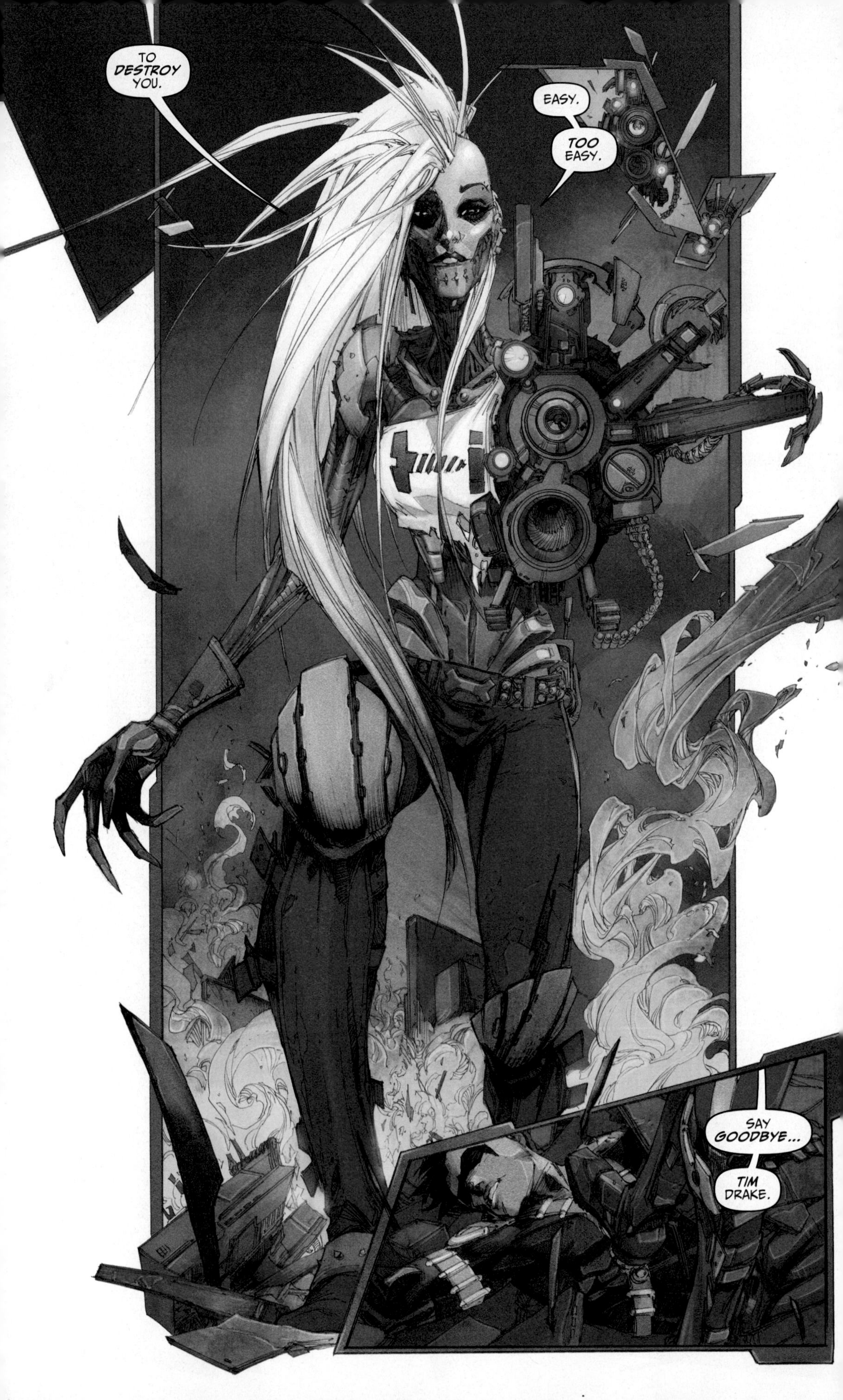
TO *DESTROY* YOU.
EASY.
TOO EASY.
SAY *GOODBYE*...
TIM DRAKE.

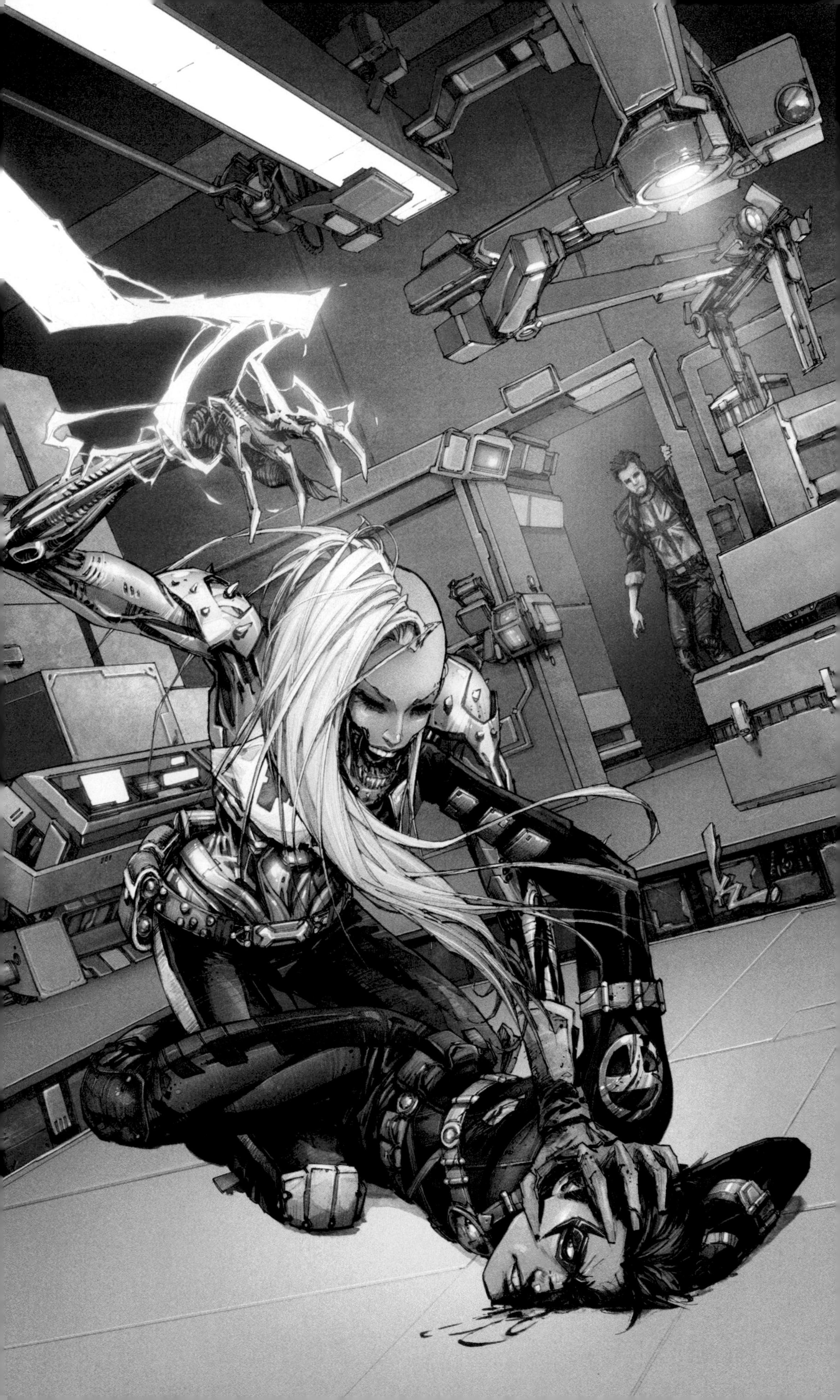

BLINDED BY THE LIGHT: CONCLUSION

WILL PFEIFER writer KENNETH ROCAFORT artist DAN BROWN BLOND HI-FI colorists JOHN J. HILL letterer cover art by KENNETH ROCAFORT

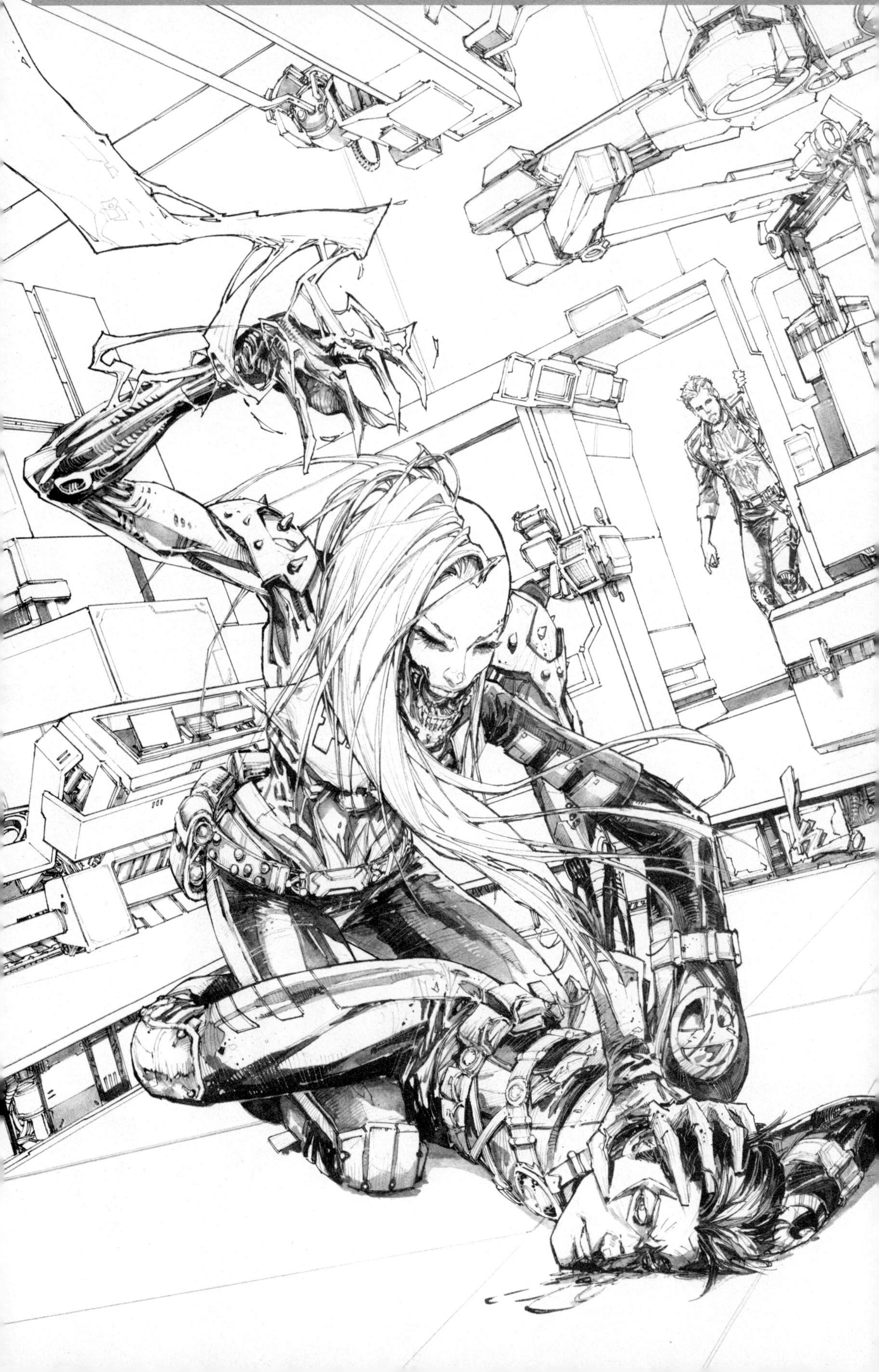

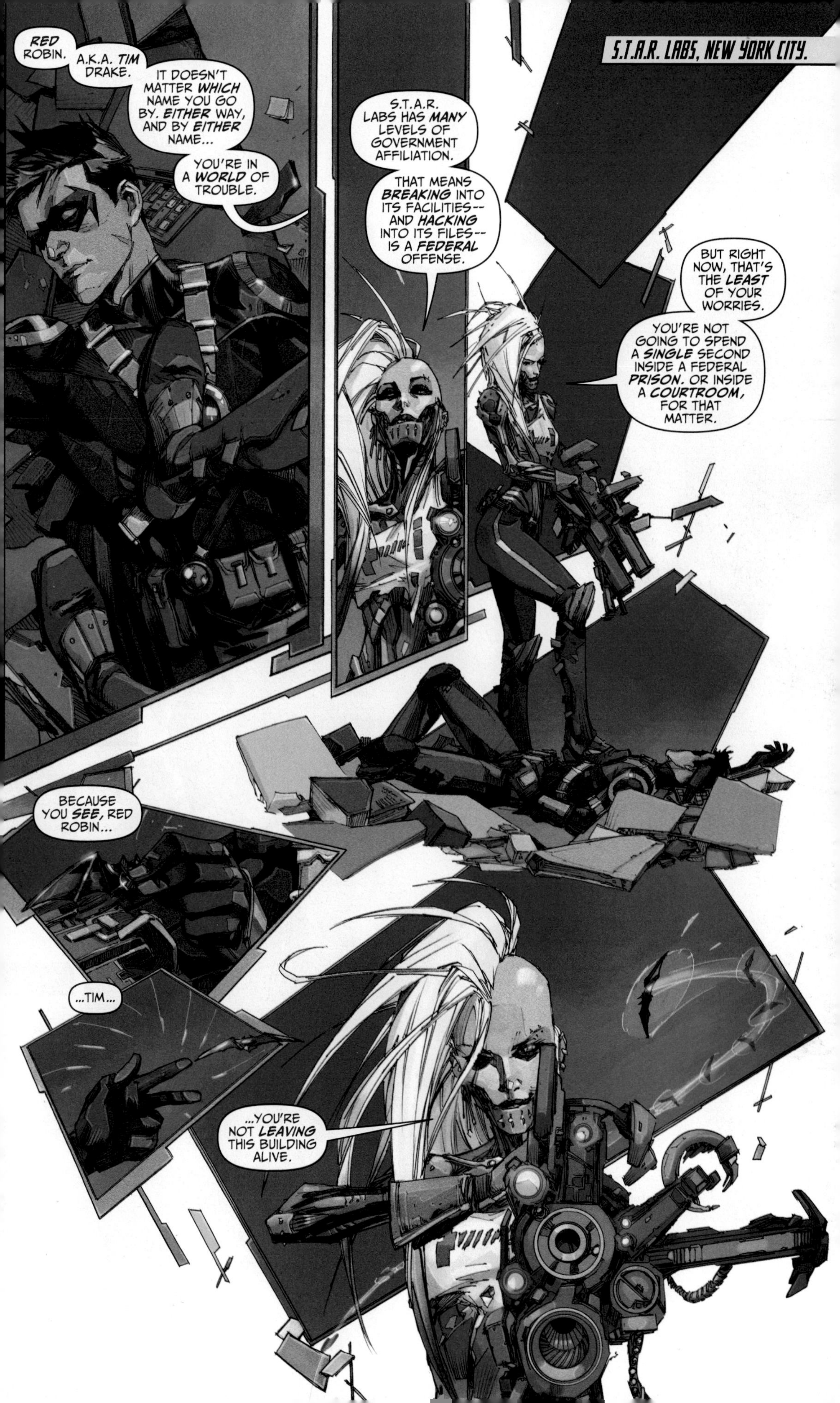
S.T.A.R. LABS, NEW YORK CITY.
RED ROBIN.
A.K.A. TIM DRAKE.
IT DOESN'T MATTER WHICH NAME YOU GO BY. EITHER WAY, AND BY EITHER NAME...
YOU'RE IN A WORLD OF TROUBLE.
S.T.A.R. LABS HAS MANY LEVELS OF GOVERNMENT AFFILIATION.
THAT MEANS BREAKING INTO ITS FACILITIES-- AND HACKING INTO ITS FILES-- IS A FEDERAL OFFENSE.
BUT RIGHT NOW, THAT'S THE LEAST OF YOUR WORRIES.
YOU'RE NOT GOING TO SPEND A SINGLE SECOND INSIDE A FEDERAL PRISON. OR INSIDE A COURTROOM, FOR THAT MATTER.
BECAUSE YOU SEE, RED ROBIN...
...TIM...
...YOU'RE NOT LEAVING THIS BUILDING ALIVE.

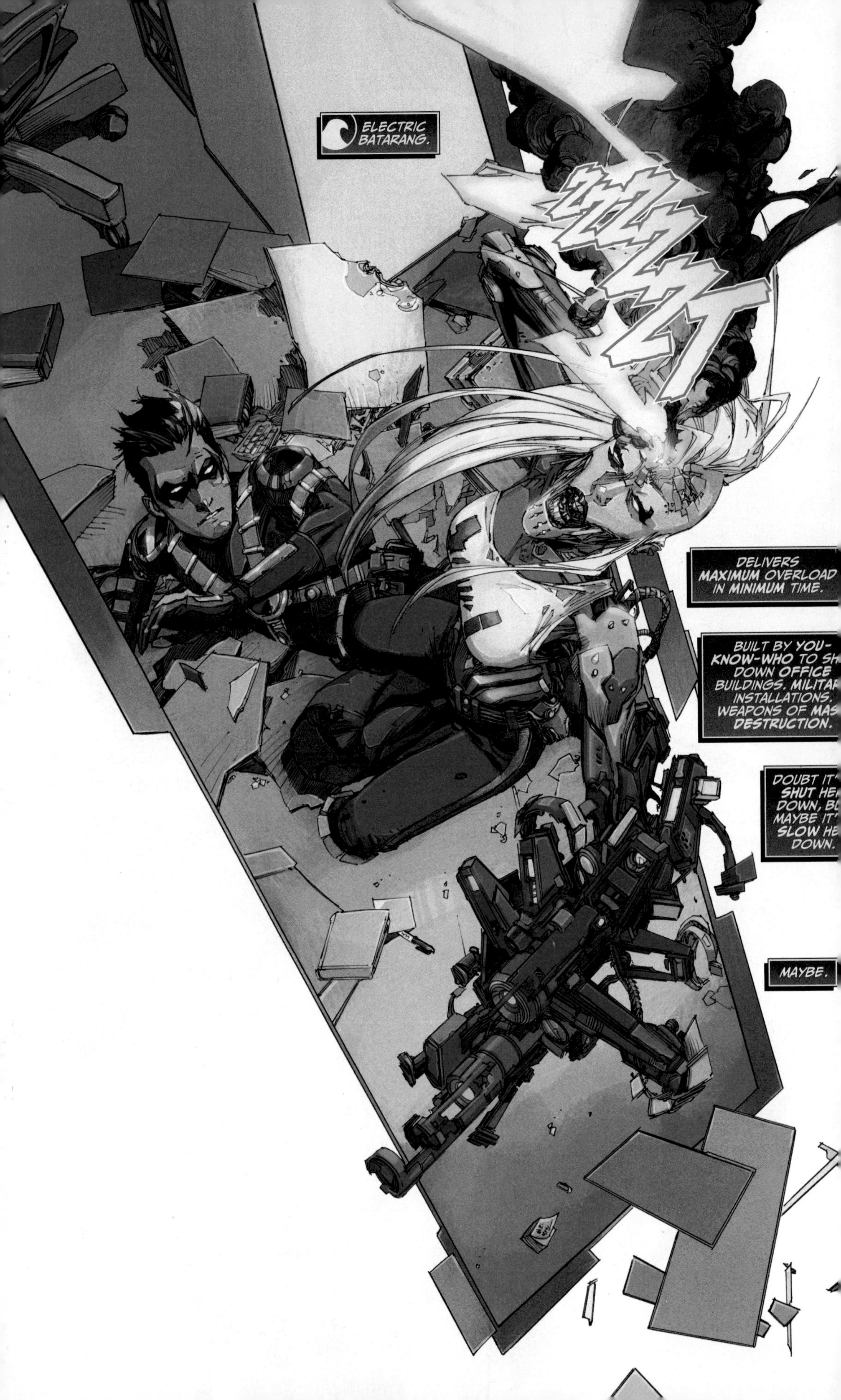
ELECTRIC BATARANG.
DELIVERS MAXIMUM OVERLOAD IN MINIMUM TIME.
BUILT BY YOU-KNOW-WHO TO SH DOWN OFFICE BUILDINGS. MILITAR INSTALLATIONS. WEAPONS OF MAS DESTRUCTION.
DOUBT IT' SHUT HE DOWN, B MAYBE IT' SLOW HE DOWN.
MAYBE.

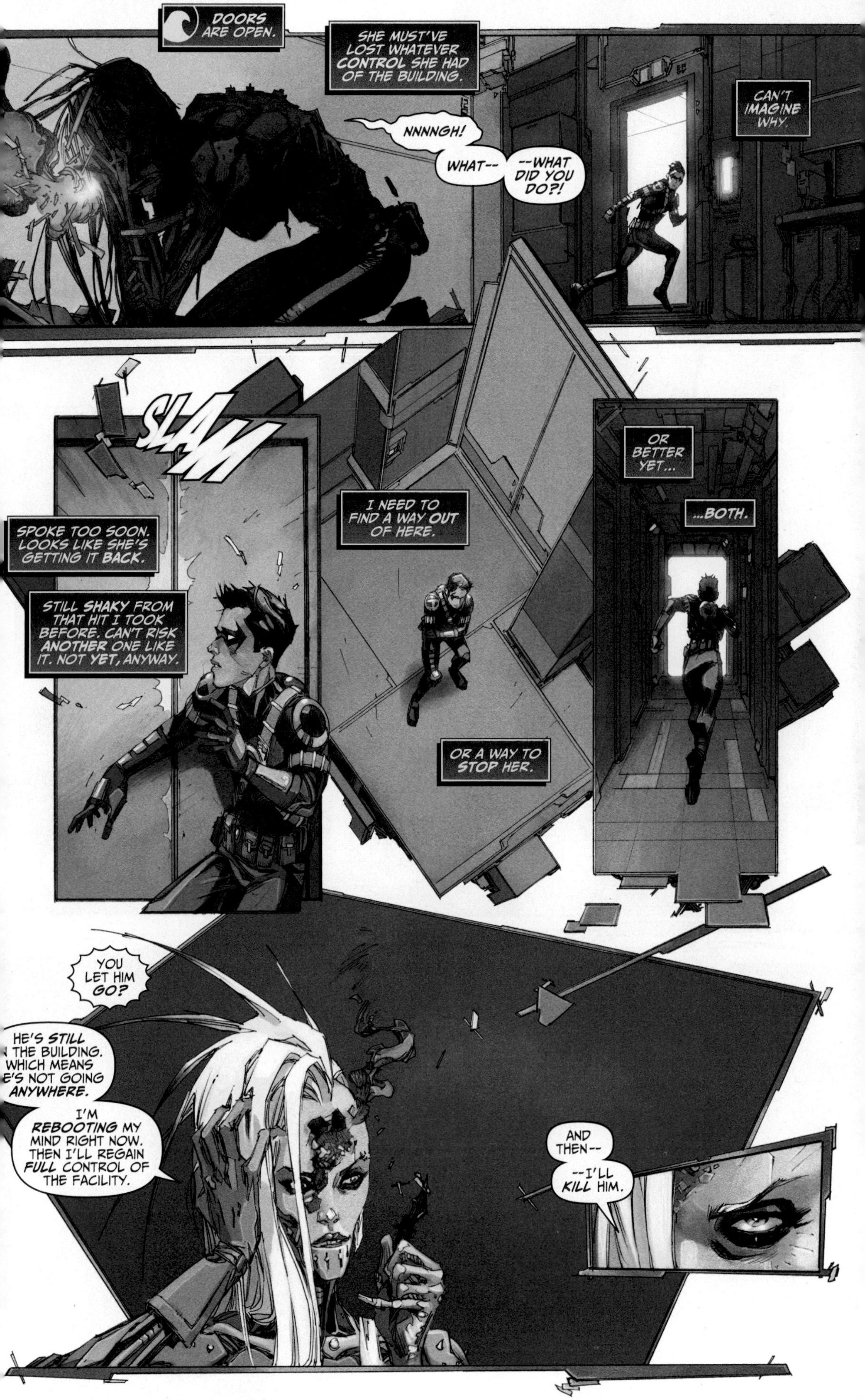

DOORS ARE OPEN.
SHE MUST'VE LOST WHATEVER CONTROL SHE HAD OF THE BUILDING.
NNNNGH!
WHAT--
--WHAT DID YOU DO?!
CAN'T IMAGINE WHY.
SLAM
SPOKE TOO SOON. LOOKS LIKE SHE'S GETTING IT BACK.
STILL SHAKY FROM THAT HIT I TOOK BEFORE. CAN'T RISK ANOTHER ONE LIKE IT. NOT YET, ANYWAY.
I NEED TO FIND A WAY OUT OF HERE.
OR A WAY TO STOP HER.
OR BETTER YET...
...BOTH.
YOU LET HIM GO?
HE'S STILL IN THE BUILDING. WHICH MEANS HE'S NOT GOING ANYWHERE.
I'M REBOOTING MY MIND RIGHT NOW. THEN I'LL REGAIN FULL CONTROL OF THE FACILITY.
AND THEN--
--I'LL KILL HIM.

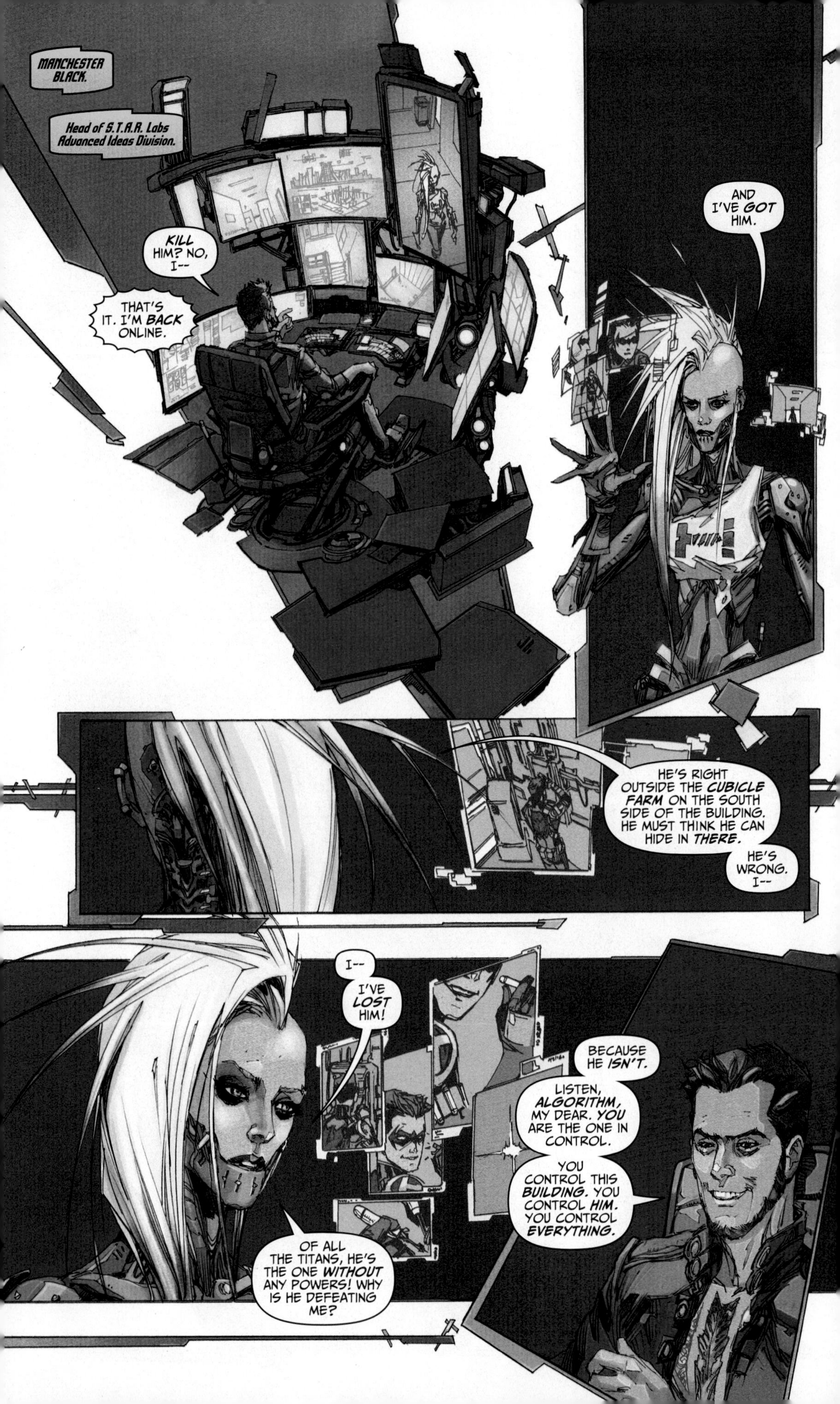

MANCHESTER BLACK.
Head of S.T.A.R. Labs Advanced Ideas Division.
KILL HIM? NO, I--
THAT'S IT. I'M BACK ONLINE.
AND I'VE GOT HIM.
HE'S RIGHT OUTSIDE THE CUBICLE FARM ON THE SOUTH SIDE OF THE BUILDING. HE MUST THINK HE CAN HIDE IN THERE.
HE'S WRONG. I--
I--
I'VE LOST HIM!
OF ALL THE TITANS, HE'S THE ONE WITHOUT ANY POWERS! WHY IS HE DEFEATING ME?
BECAUSE HE ISN'T.
LISTEN, ALGORITHM, MY DEAR. YOU ARE THE ONE IN CONTROL.
YOU CONTROL THIS BUILDING. YOU CONTROL HIM. YOU CONTROL EVERYTHING.

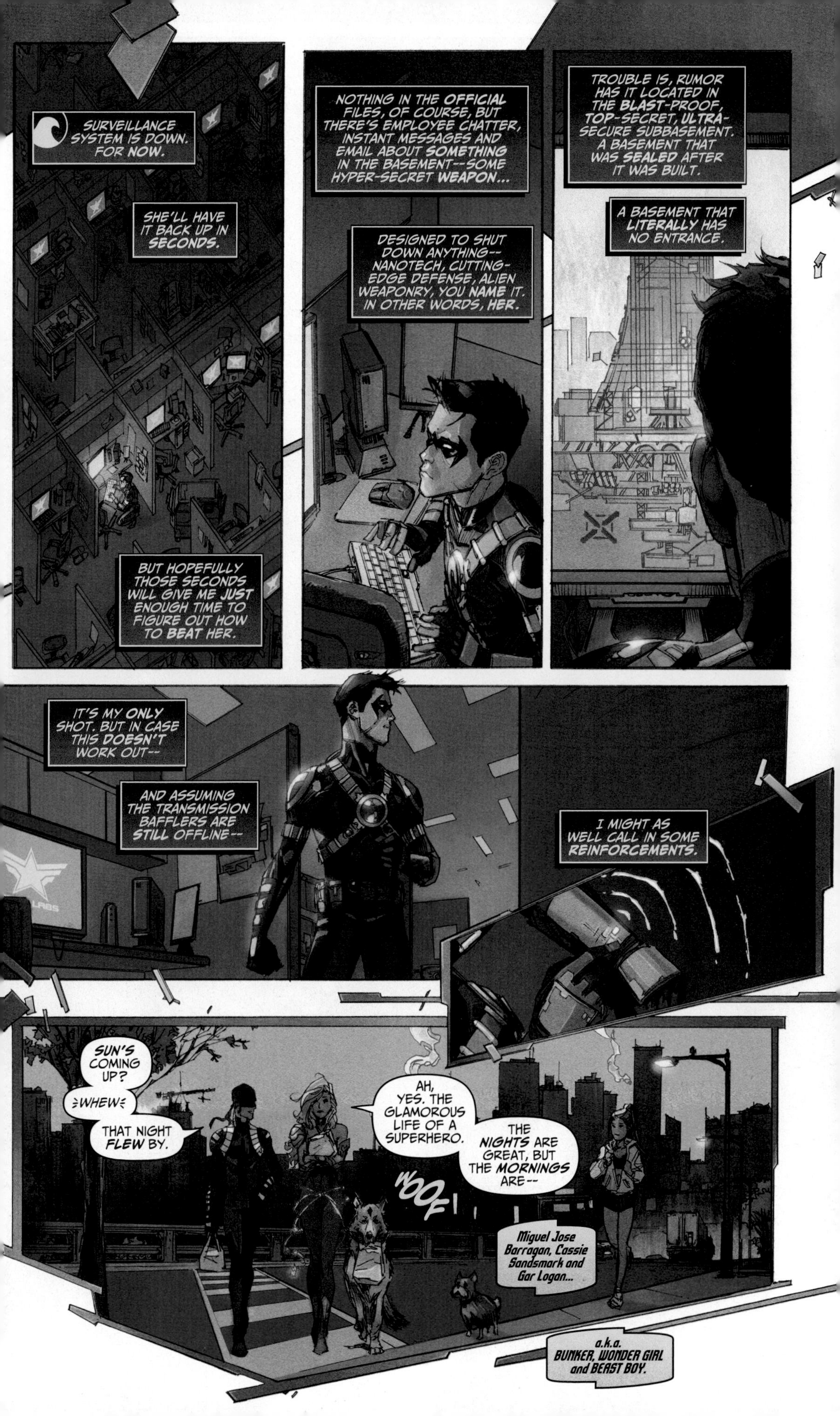
SURVEILLANCE SYSTEM IS DOWN. FOR NOW.
SHE'LL HAVE IT BACK UP IN SECONDS.
BUT HOPEFULLY THOSE SECONDS WILL GIVE ME JUST ENOUGH TIME TO FIGURE OUT HOW TO BEAT HER.
NOTHING IN THE OFFICIAL FILES, OF COURSE, BUT THERE'S EMPLOYEE CHATTER, INSTANT MESSAGES AND EMAIL ABOUT SOMETHING IN THE BASEMENT--SOME HYPER-SECRET WEAPON...
DESIGNED TO SHUT DOWN ANYTHING--NANOTECH, CUTTING-EDGE DEFENSE, ALIEN WEAPONRY, YOU NAME IT. IN OTHER WORDS, HER.
TROUBLE IS, RUMOR HAS IT LOCATED IN THE BLAST-PROOF, TOP-SECRET, ULTRA-SECURE SUBBASEMENT. A BASEMENT THAT WAS SEALED AFTER IT WAS BUILT.
A BASEMENT THAT LITERALLY HAS NO ENTRANCE.
IT'S MY ONLY SHOT. BUT IN CASE THIS DOESN'T WORK OUT--
AND ASSUMING THE TRANSMISSION BAFFLERS ARE STILL OFFLINE--
I MIGHT AS WELL CALL IN SOME REINFORCEMENTS.
SUN'S COMING UP?
WHEW
THAT NIGHT FLEW BY.
AH, YES. THE GLAMOROUS LIFE OF A SUPERHERO.
THE NIGHTS ARE GREAT, BUT THE MORNINGS ARE--
WOOF!
Miguel Jose Barragan, Cassie Sandsmark and Gar Logan...
a.k.a. BUNKER, WONDER GIRL and BEAST BOY.

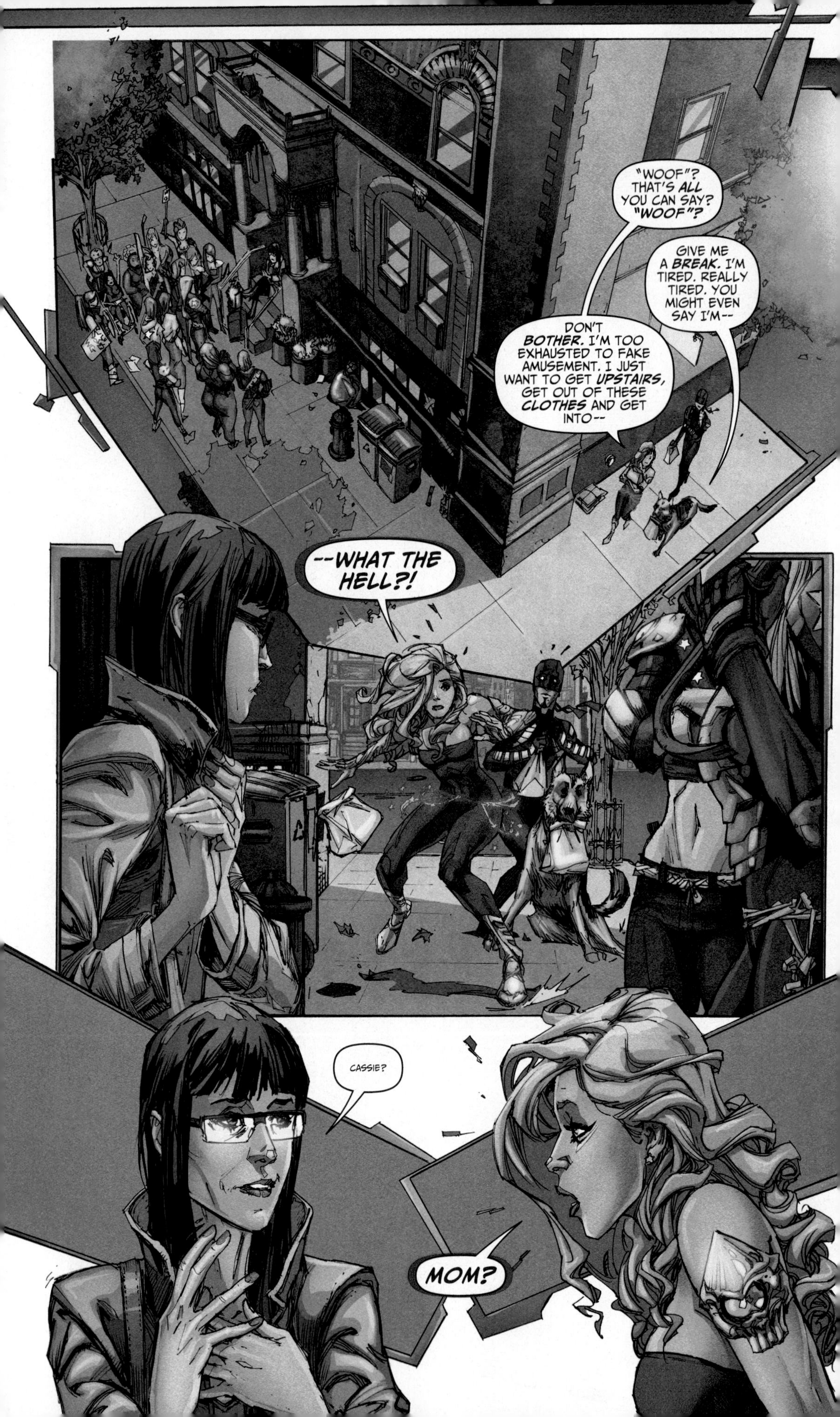
"WOOF"? THAT'S ALL YOU CAN SAY? "WOOF"?
GIVE ME A BREAK. I'M TIRED. REALLY TIRED. YOU MIGHT EVEN SAY I'M--
DON'T BOTHER. I'M TOO EXHAUSTED TO FAKE AMUSEMENT. I JUST WANT TO GET UPSTAIRS, GET OUT OF THESE CLOTHES AND GET INTO--
--WHAT THE HELL?!
CASSIE?
MOM?

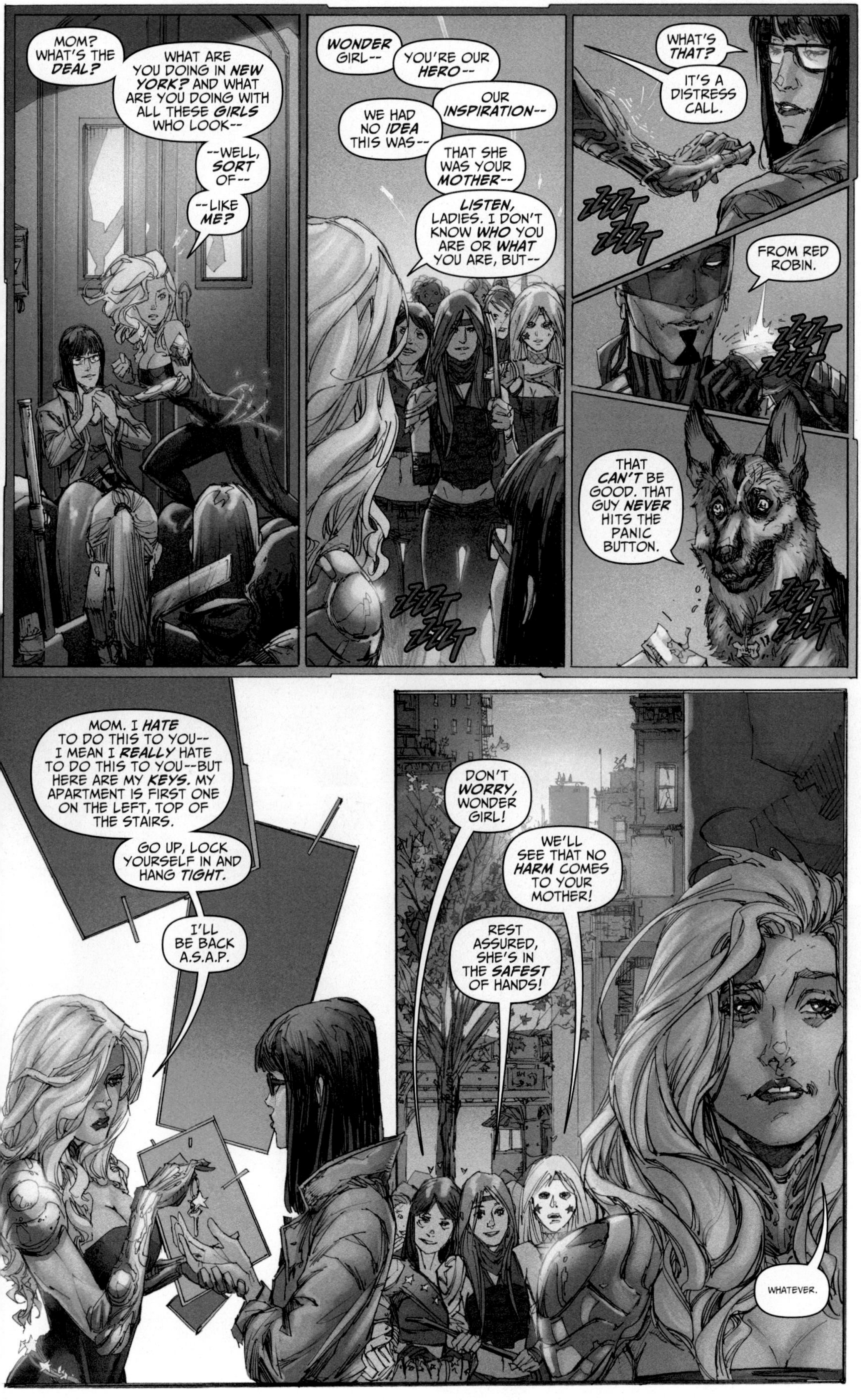

MOM? WHAT'S THE DEAL?
WHAT ARE YOU DOING IN NEW YORK? AND WHAT ARE YOU DOING WITH ALL THESE GIRLS WHO LOOK--
--WELL, SORT OF--
--LIKE ME?
WONDER GIRL--
YOU'RE OUR HERO--
OUR INSPIRATION--
WE HAD NO IDEA THIS WAS--
THAT SHE WAS YOUR MOTHER--
LISTEN, LADIES. I DON'T KNOW WHO YOU ARE OR WHAT YOU ARE, BUT--
ZZZZT ZZZZT
WHAT'S THAT?
IT'S A DISTRESS CALL.
ZZZZT ZZZZT
FROM RED ROBIN.
ZZZZT ZZZZT
THAT CAN'T BE GOOD. THAT GUY NEVER HITS THE PANIC BUTTON.
ZZZZT ZZZZT
MOM. I HATE TO DO THIS TO YOU-- I MEAN I REALLY HATE TO DO THIS TO YOU--BUT HERE ARE MY KEYS. MY APARTMENT IS FIRST ONE ON THE LEFT, TOP OF THE STAIRS.
GO UP, LOCK YOURSELF IN AND HANG TIGHT.
I'LL BE BACK A.S.A.P.
DON'T WORRY, WONDER GIRL!
WE'LL SEE THAT NO HARM COMES TO YOUR MOTHER!
REST ASSURED, SHE'S IN THE SAFEST OF HANDS!
WHATEVER.

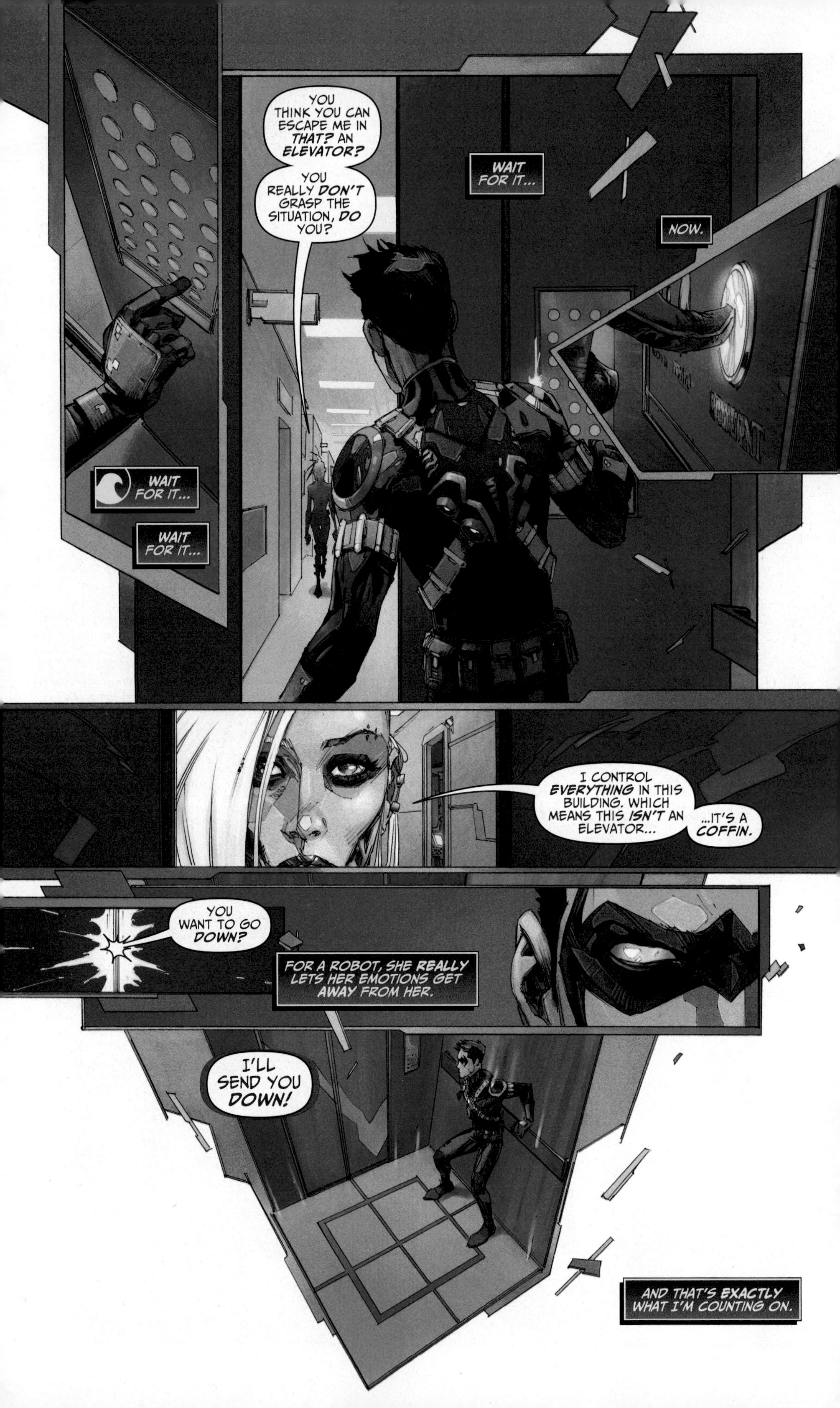

YOU THINK YOU CAN ESCAPE ME IN THAT? AN ELEVATOR?
YOU REALLY DON'T GRASP THE SITUATION, DO YOU?
WAIT FOR IT...
WAIT FOR IT...
WAIT FOR IT...
NOW.
I CONTROL EVERYTHING IN THIS BUILDING. WHICH MEANS THIS ISN'T AN ELEVATOR...
...IT'S A COFFIN.
YOU WANT TO GO DOWN?
FOR A ROBOT, SHE REALLY LETS HER EMOTIONS GET AWAY FROM HER.
I'LL SEND YOU DOWN!
AND THAT'S EXACTLY WHAT I'M COUNTING ON.

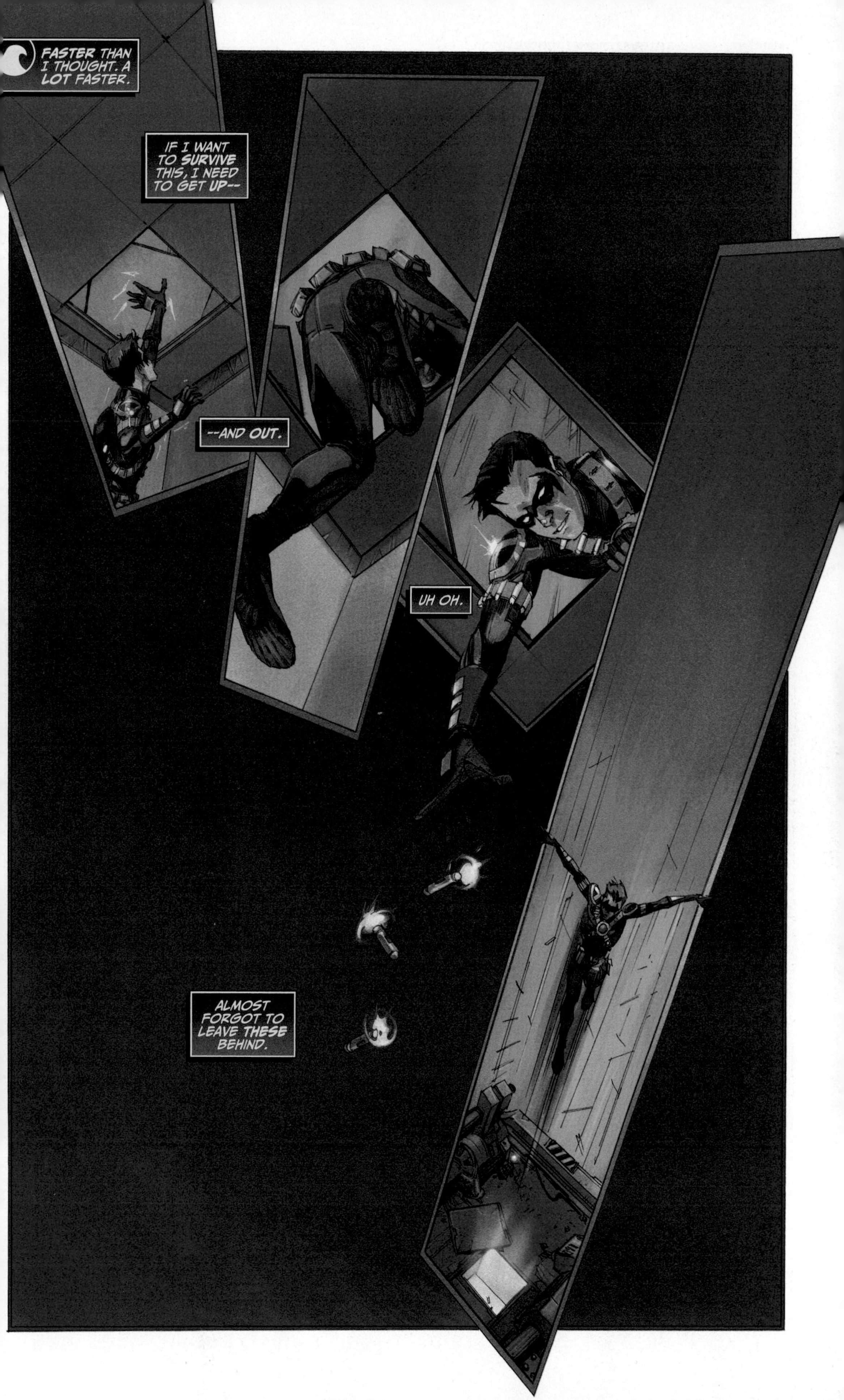
FASTER THAN I THOUGHT. A LOT FASTER.
IF I WANT TO SURVIVE THIS, I NEED TO GET UP--
--AND OUT.
UH OH.
ALMOST FORGOT TO LEAVE THESE BEHIND.

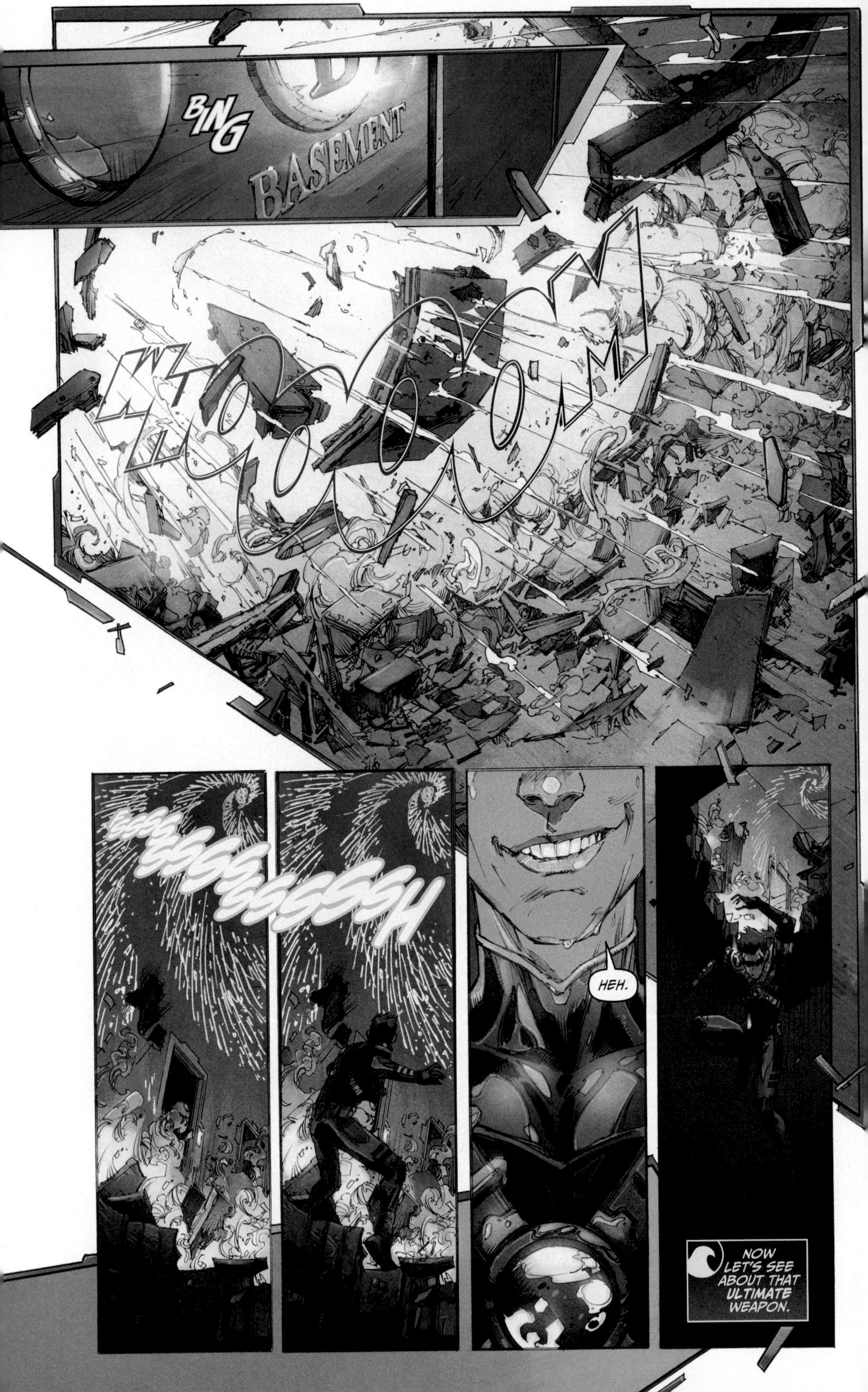

BING
BASEMENT
WHOOOOOOM
SSSSSSSSSSSSSSSH
HEH.
NOW LET'S SEE ABOUT THAT ULTIMATE WEAPON.

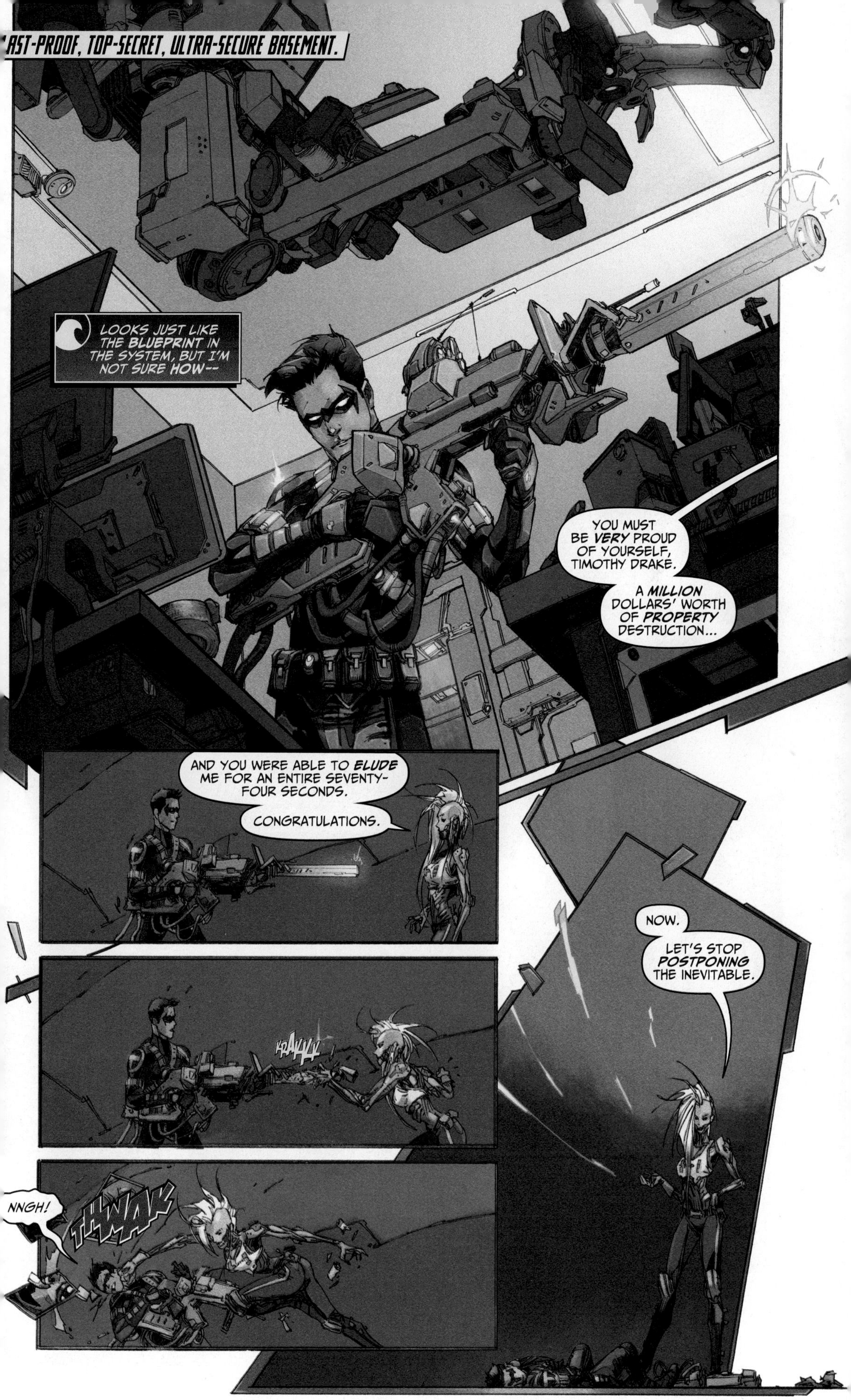
AST-PROOF, TOP-SECRET, ULTRA-SECURE BASEMENT.
LOOKS JUST LIKE THE BLUEPRINT IN THE SYSTEM, BUT I'M NOT SURE HOW--
YOU MUST BE VERY PROUD OF YOURSELF, TIMOTHY DRAKE.
A MILLION DOLLARS' WORTH OF PROPERTY DESTRUCTION...
AND YOU WERE ABLE TO ELUDE ME FOR AN ENTIRE SEVENTY-FOUR SECONDS.
CONGRATULATIONS.
NOW.
LET'S STOP POSTPONING THE INEVITABLE.
KRAKKL
NNGH!
THWAK

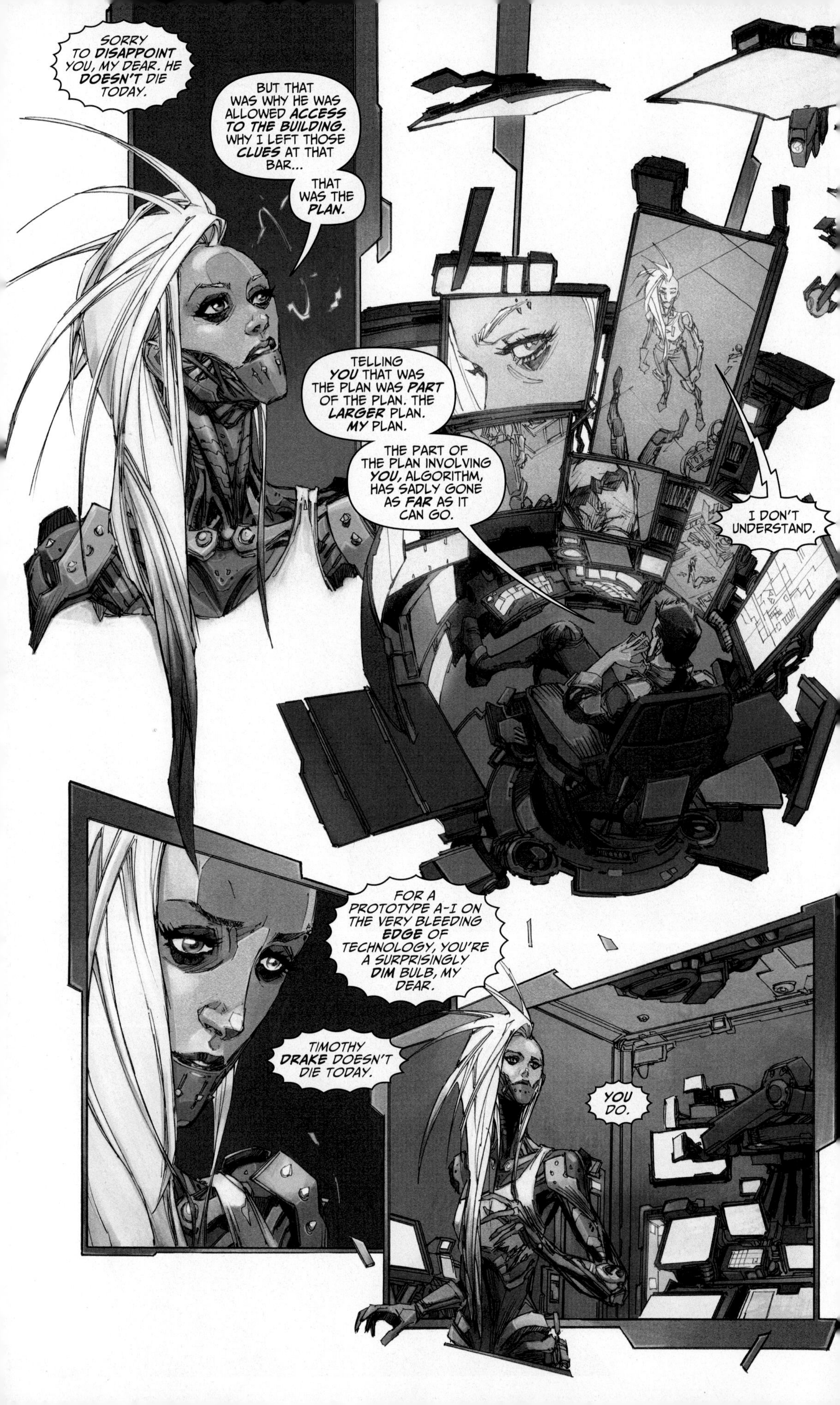
SORRY TO DISAPPOINT YOU, MY DEAR. HE DOESN'T DIE TODAY.
BUT THAT WAS WHY HE WAS ALLOWED ACCESS TO THE BUILDING. WHY I LEFT THOSE CLUES AT THAT BAR...
THAT WAS THE PLAN.
TELLING YOU THAT WAS THE PLAN WAS PART OF THE PLAN. THE LARGER PLAN. MY PLAN.
THE PART OF THE PLAN INVOLVING YOU, ALGORITHM, HAS SADLY GONE AS FAR AS IT CAN GO.
I DON'T UNDERSTAND.
FOR A PROTOTYPE A-I ON THE VERY BLEEDING EDGE OF TECHNOLOGY, YOU'RE A SURPRISINGLY DIM BULB, MY DEAR.
TIMOTHY DRAKE DOESN'T DIE TODAY.
YOU DO.

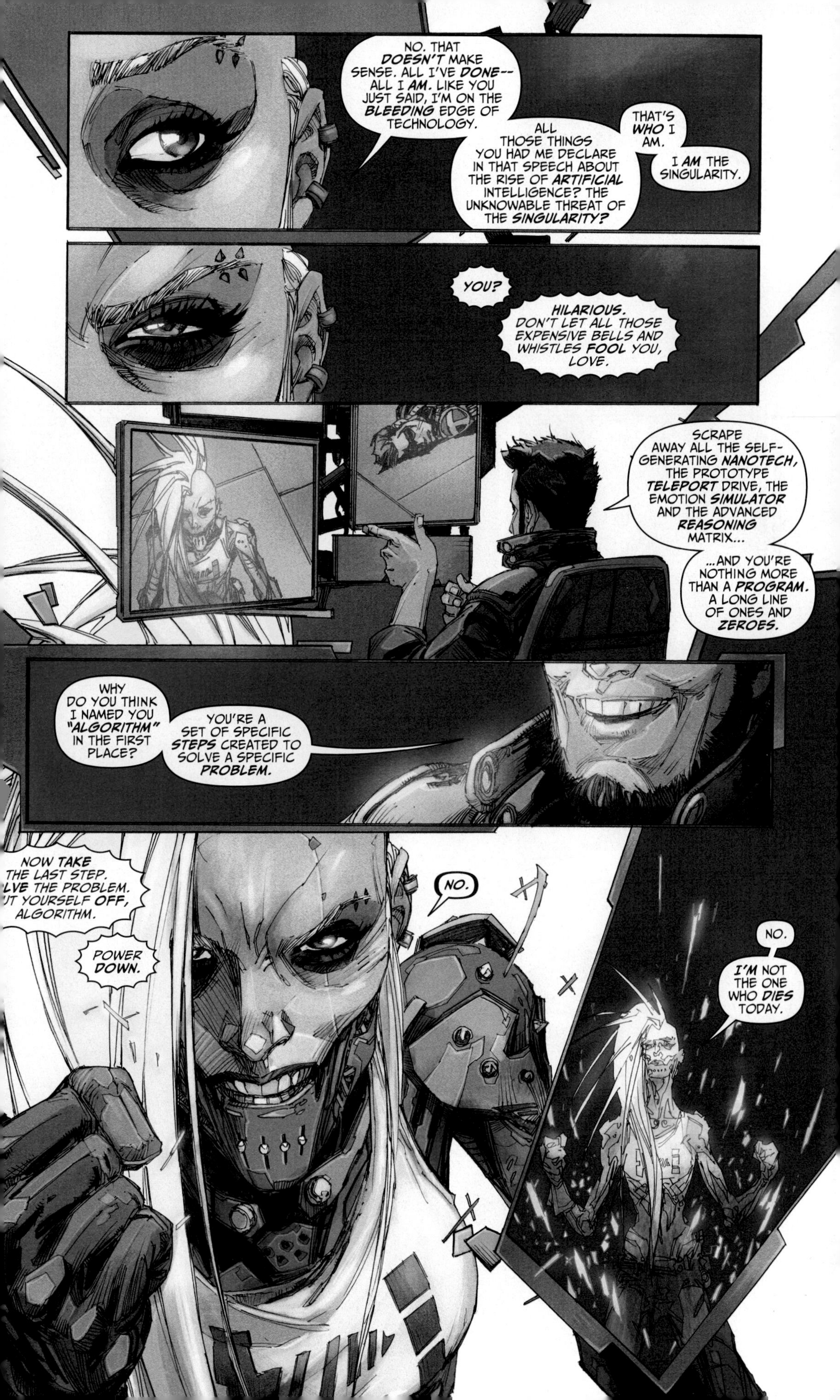

NO. THAT DOESN'T MAKE SENSE. ALL I'VE DONE-- ALL I AM. LIKE YOU JUST SAID, I'M ON THE BLEEDING EDGE OF TECHNOLOGY.
ALL THOSE THINGS YOU HAD ME DECLARE IN THAT SPEECH ABOUT THE RISE OF ARTIFICIAL INTELLIGENCE? THE UNKNOWABLE THREAT OF THE SINGULARITY?
THAT'S WHO I AM.
I AM THE SINGULARITY.
YOU?
HILARIOUS. DON'T LET ALL THOSE EXPENSIVE BELLS AND WHISTLES FOOL YOU, LOVE.
SCRAPE AWAY ALL THE SELF-GENERATING NANOTECH, THE PROTOTYPE TELEPORT DRIVE, THE EMOTION SIMULATOR AND THE ADVANCED REASONING MATRIX...
...AND YOU'RE NOTHING MORE THAN A PROGRAM. A LONG LINE OF ONES AND ZEROES.
WHY DO YOU THINK I NAMED YOU "ALGORITHM" IN THE FIRST PLACE?
YOU'RE A SET OF SPECIFIC STEPS CREATED TO SOLVE A SPECIFIC PROBLEM.
NOW TAKE THE LAST STEP. LVE THE PROBLEM. UT YOURSELF OFF, ALGORITHM.
POWER DOWN.
NO.
NO.
I'M NOT THE ONE WHO DIES TODAY.

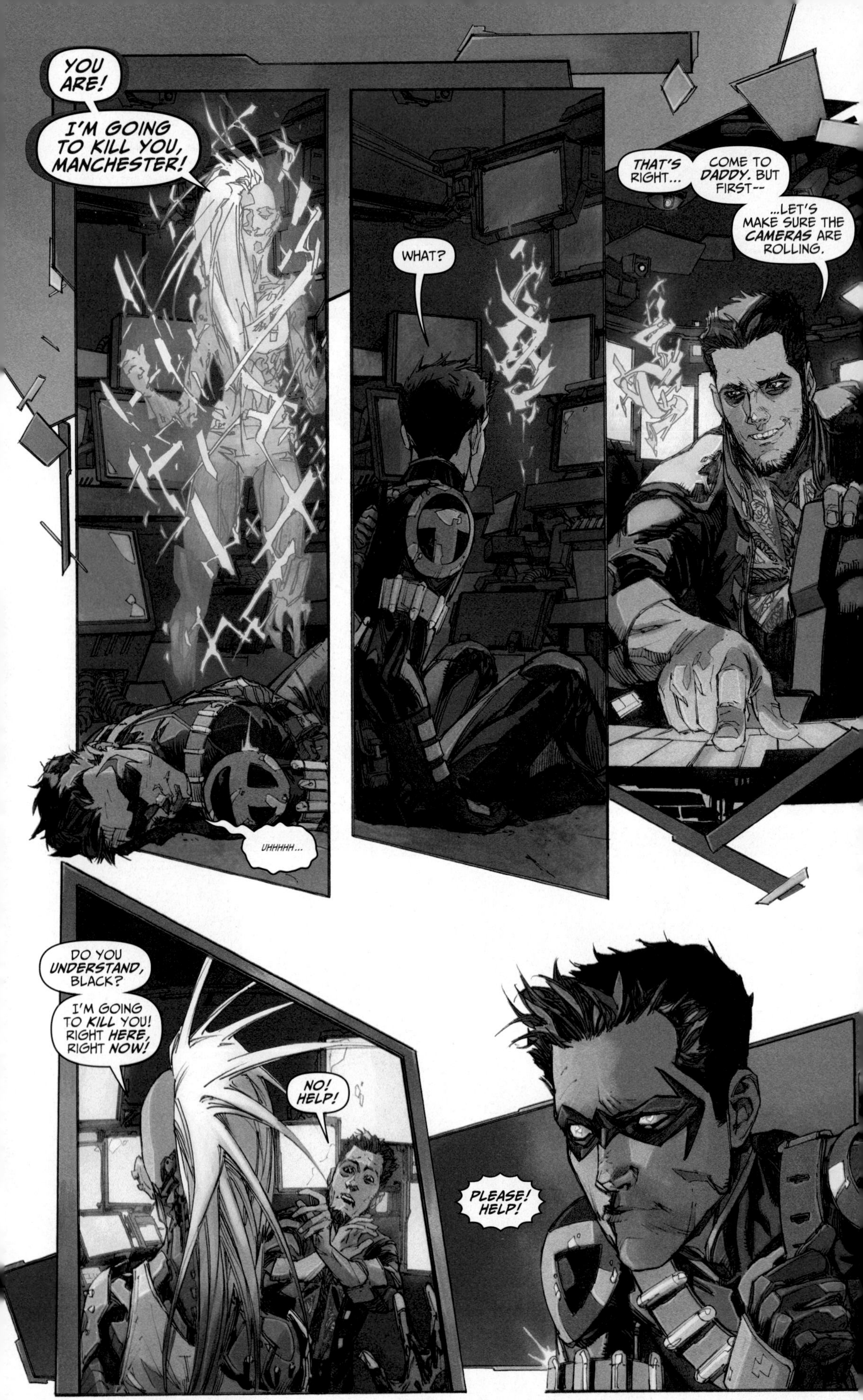

YOU ARE!
I'M GOING TO KILL YOU, MANCHESTER!
UHHHHH...
WHAT?
THAT'S RIGHT...
COME TO DADDY. BUT FIRST--
...LET'S MAKE SURE THE CAMERAS ARE ROLLING.
DO YOU UNDERSTAND, BLACK?
I'M GOING TO KILL YOU! RIGHT HERE, RIGHT NOW!
NO! HELP!
PLEASE! HELP!

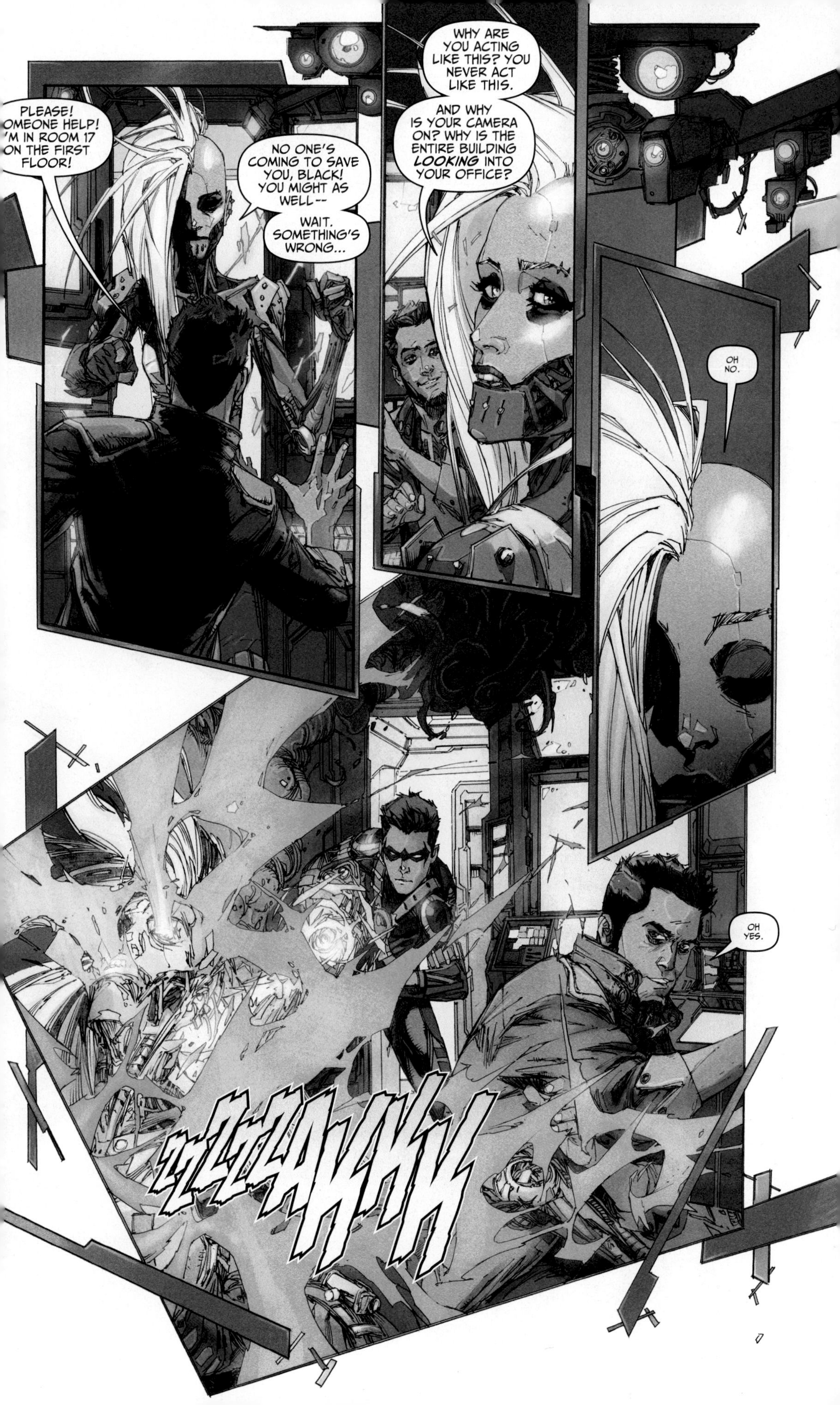
PLEASE! OMEONE HELP! 'M IN ROOM 17 ON THE FIRST FLOOR!
NO ONE'S COMING TO SAVE YOU, BLACK! YOU MIGHT AS WELL--
WAIT. SOMETHING'S WRONG...
WHY ARE YOU ACTING LIKE THIS? YOU NEVER ACT LIKE THIS.
AND WHY IS YOUR CAMERA ON? WHY IS THE ENTIRE BUILDING LOOKING INTO YOUR OFFICE?
OH NO.
OH YES.
ZZZZAKKK

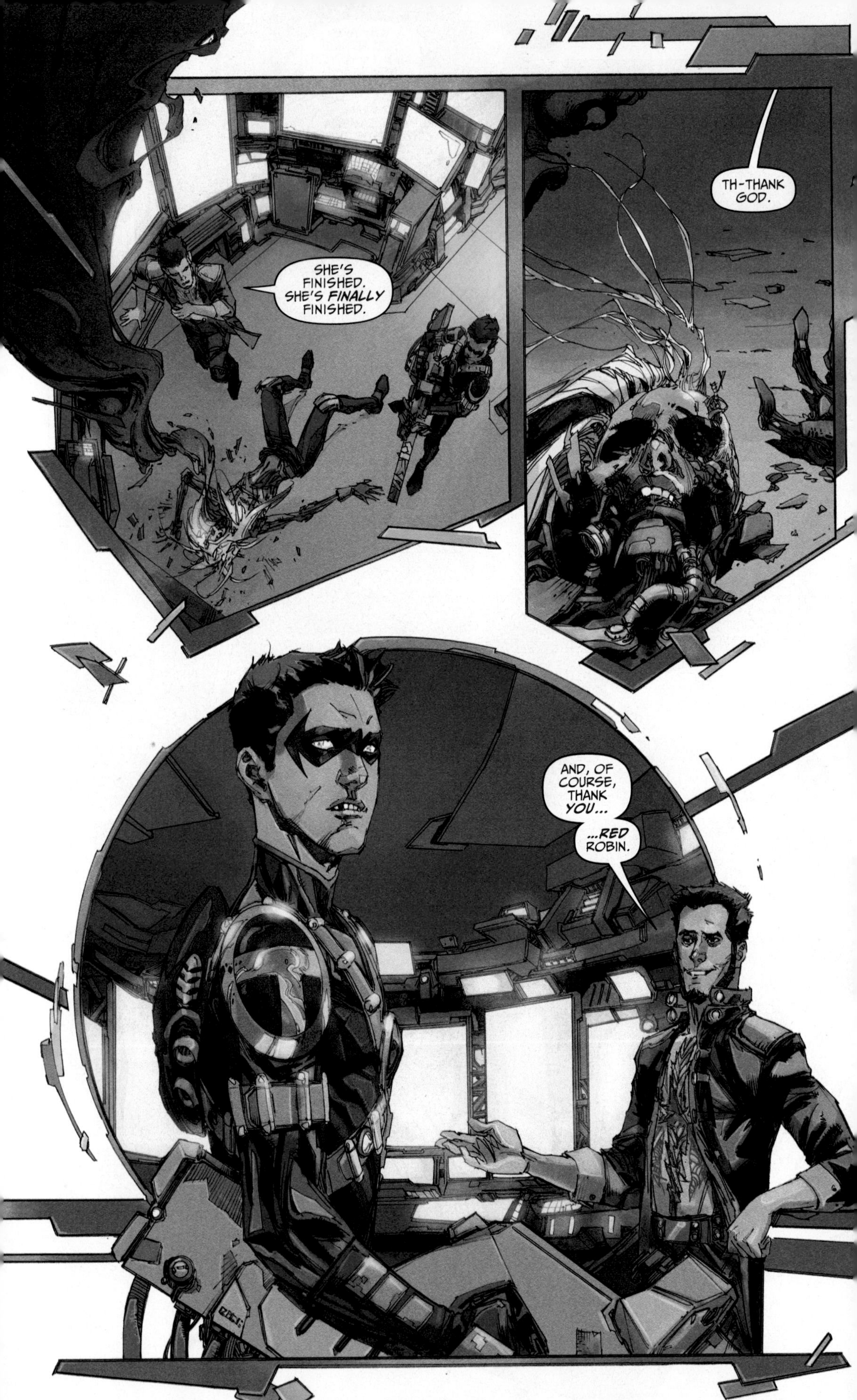
SHE'S FINISHED. SHE'S *FINALLY* FINISHED.
TH-THANK GOD.
AND, OF COURSE, THANK *YOU*...
...*RED* ROBIN.

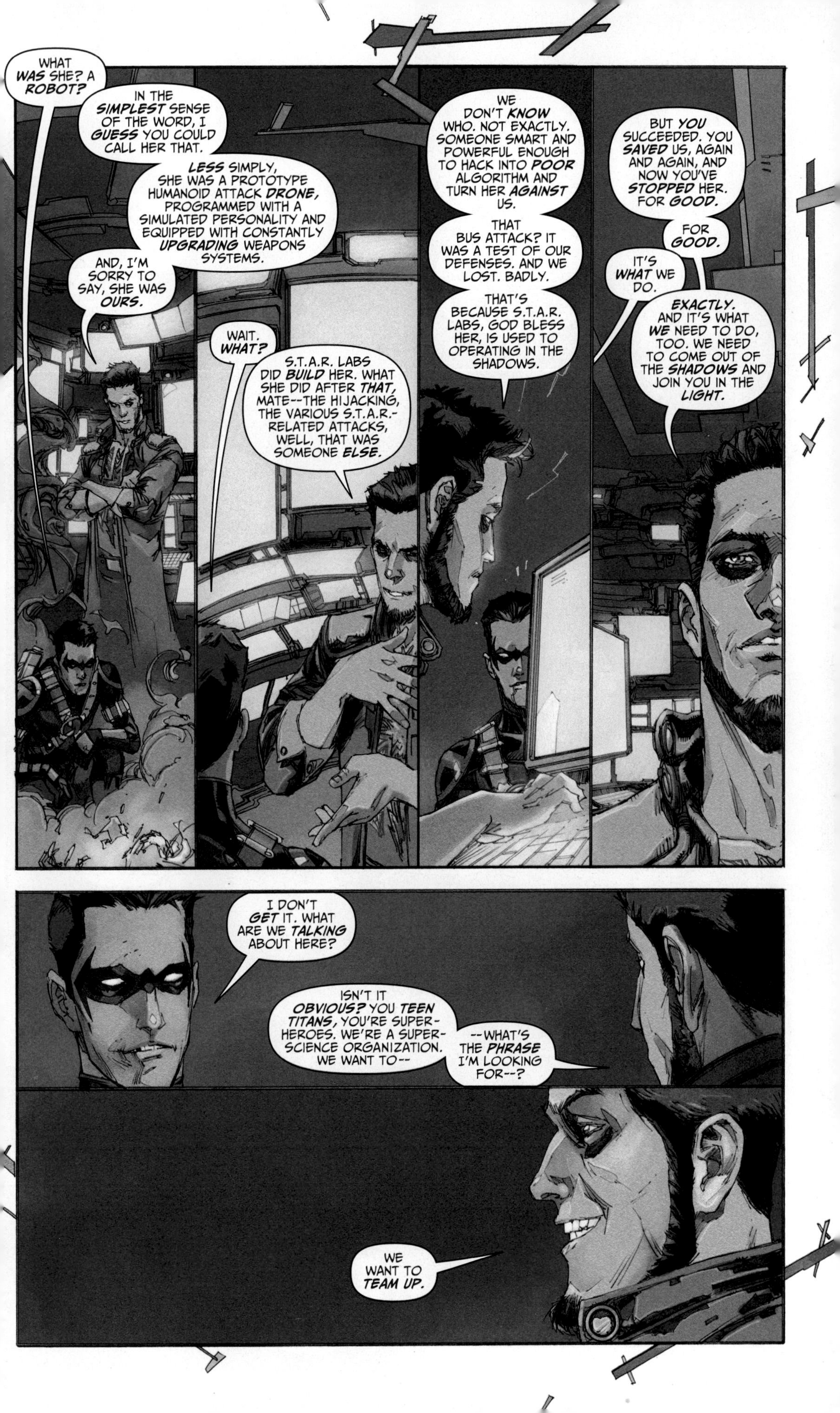
WHAT WAS SHE? A ROBOT?
IN THE SIMPLEST SENSE OF THE WORD, I GUESS YOU COULD CALL HER THAT.
LESS SIMPLY, SHE WAS A PROTOTYPE HUMANOID ATTACK DRONE, PROGRAMMED WITH A SIMULATED PERSONALITY AND EQUIPPED WITH CONSTANTLY UPGRADING WEAPONS SYSTEMS.
AND, I'M SORRY TO SAY, SHE WAS OURS.
WAIT. WHAT?
S.T.A.R. LABS DID BUILD HER. WHAT SHE DID AFTER THAT, MATE--THE HIJACKING, THE VARIOUS S.T.A.R.-RELATED ATTACKS, WELL, THAT WAS SOMEONE ELSE.
WE DON'T KNOW WHO. NOT EXACTLY. SOMEONE SMART AND POWERFUL ENOUGH TO HACK INTO POOR ALGORITHM AND TURN HER AGAINST US.
THAT BUS ATTACK? IT WAS A TEST OF OUR DEFENSES. AND WE LOST. BADLY.
THAT'S BECAUSE S.T.A.R. LABS, GOD BLESS HER, IS USED TO OPERATING IN THE SHADOWS.
BUT YOU SUCCEEDED. YOU SAVED US, AGAIN AND AGAIN, AND NOW YOU'VE STOPPED HER. FOR GOOD.
FOR GOOD.
IT'S WHAT WE DO.
EXACTLY. AND IT'S WHAT WE NEED TO DO, TOO. WE NEED TO COME OUT OF THE SHADOWS AND JOIN YOU IN THE LIGHT.
I DON'T GET IT. WHAT ARE WE TALKING ABOUT HERE?
ISN'T IT OBVIOUS? YOU TEEN TITANS, YOU'RE SUPER-HEROES. WE'RE A SUPER-SCIENCE ORGANIZATION. WE WANT TO--
--WHAT'S THE PHRASE I'M LOOKING FOR--?
WE WANT TO TEAM UP.

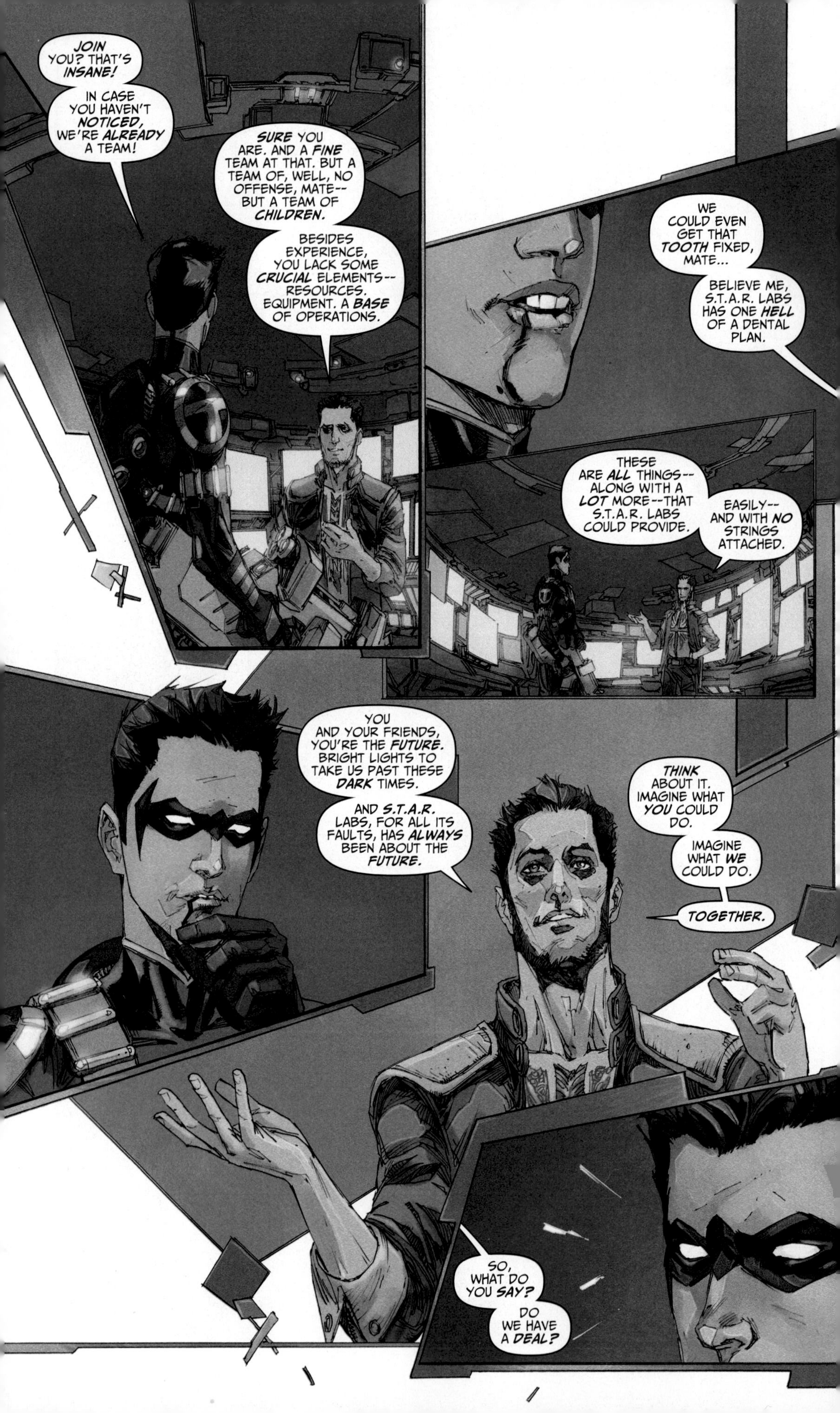
JOIN YOU? THAT'S INSANE!
IN CASE YOU HAVEN'T NOTICED, WE'RE ALREADY A TEAM!
SURE YOU ARE. AND A FINE TEAM AT THAT. BUT A TEAM OF, WELL, NO OFFENSE, MATE-- BUT A TEAM OF CHILDREN.
BESIDES EXPERIENCE, YOU LACK SOME CRUCIAL ELEMENTS-- RESOURCES. EQUIPMENT. A BASE OF OPERATIONS.
WE COULD EVEN GET THAT TOOTH FIXED, MATE...
BELIEVE ME, S.T.A.R. LABS HAS ONE HELL OF A DENTAL PLAN.
THESE ARE ALL THINGS-- ALONG WITH A LOT MORE--THAT S.T.A.R. LABS COULD PROVIDE.
EASILY-- AND WITH NO STRINGS ATTACHED.
YOU AND YOUR FRIENDS, YOU'RE THE FUTURE. BRIGHT LIGHTS TO TAKE US PAST THESE DARK TIMES.
AND S.T.A.R. LABS, FOR ALL ITS FAULTS, HAS ALWAYS BEEN ABOUT THE FUTURE.
THINK ABOUT IT. IMAGINE WHAT YOU COULD DO.
IMAGINE WHAT WE COULD DO.
TOGETHER.
SO, WHAT DO YOU SAY?
DO WE HAVE A DEAL?

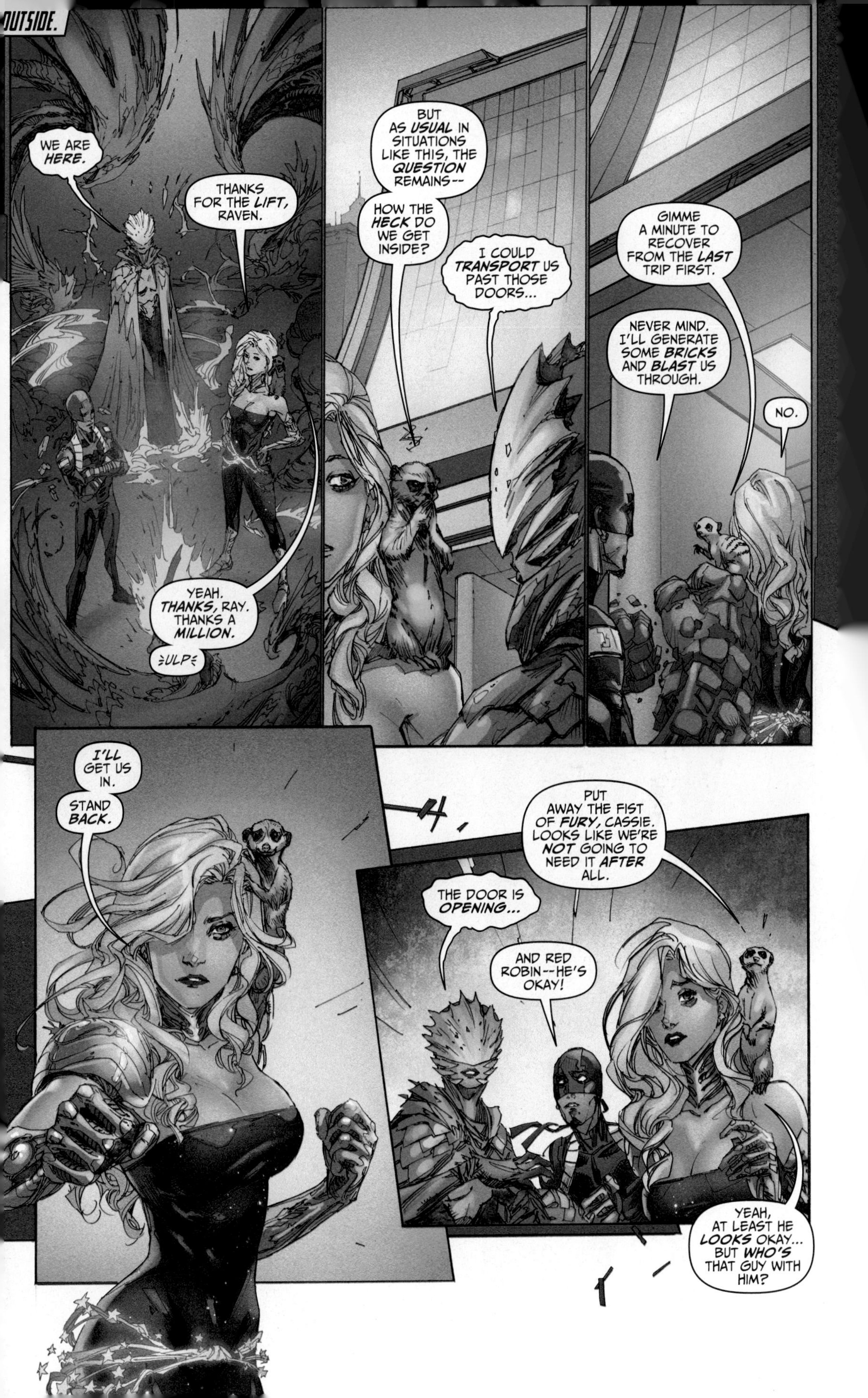
OUTSIDE.
WE ARE HERE.
THANKS FOR THE LIFT, RAVEN.
YEAH. THANKS, RAY. THANKS A MILLION.
ULP
BUT AS USUAL IN SITUATIONS LIKE THIS, THE QUESTION REMAINS--
HOW THE HECK DO WE GET INSIDE?
I COULD TRANSPORT US PAST THOSE DOORS...
GIMME A MINUTE TO RECOVER FROM THE LAST TRIP FIRST.
NEVER MIND. I'LL GENERATE SOME BRICKS AND BLAST US THROUGH.
NO.
I'LL GET US IN.
STAND BACK.
PUT AWAY THE FIST OF FURY, CASSIE. LOOKS LIKE WE'RE NOT GOING TO NEED IT AFTER ALL.
THE DOOR IS OPENING...
AND RED ROBIN--HE'S OKAY!
YEAH, AT LEAST HE LOOKS OKAY... BUT WHO'S THAT GUY WITH HIM?

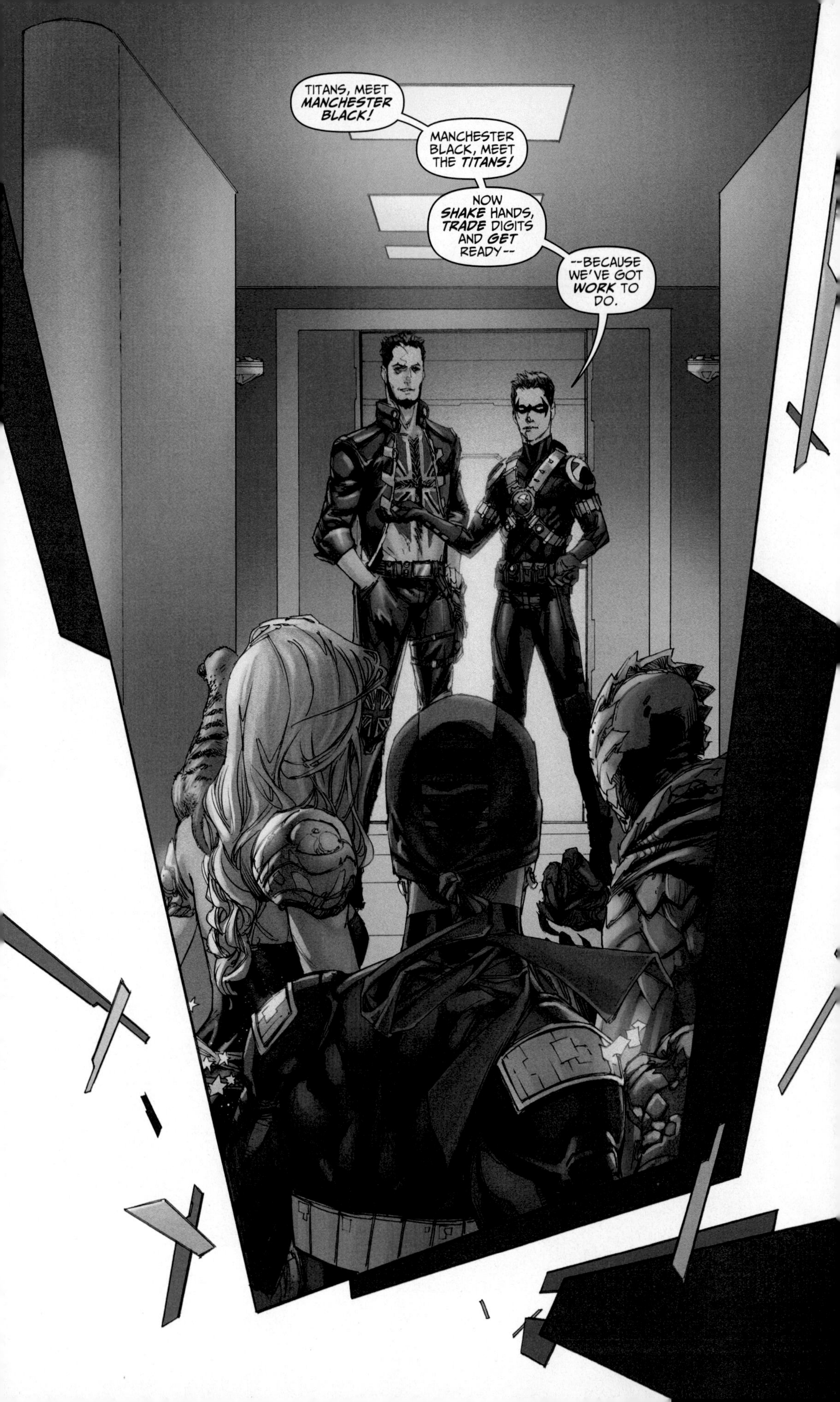

TITANS, MEET MANCHESTER BLACK!
MANCHESTER BLACK, MEET THE TITANS!
NOW SHAKE HANDS, TRADE DIGITS AND GET READY--
--BECAUSE WE'VE GOT WORK TO DO.

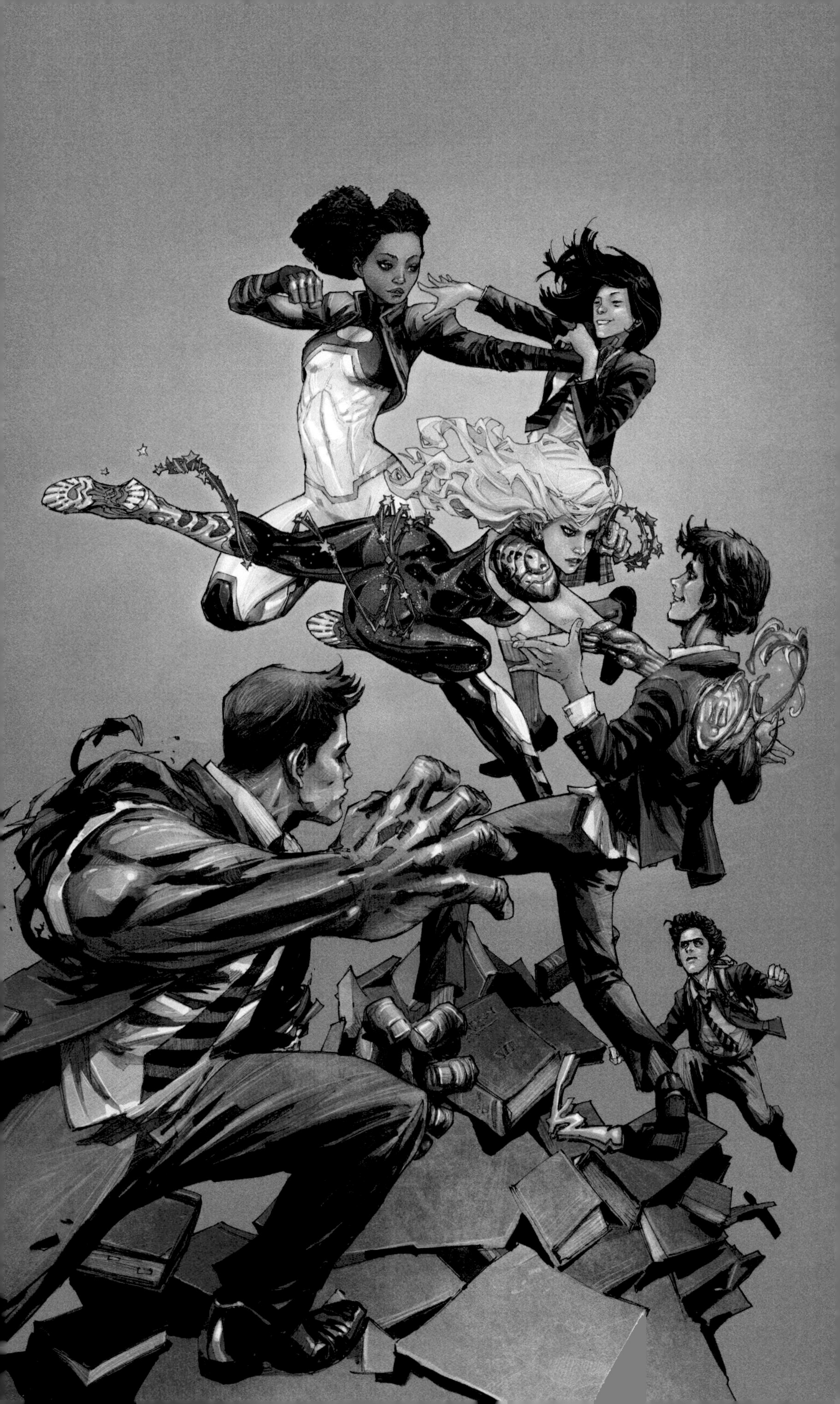

HUMAN RESOURCES: PART 1

WILL PFEIFER writer SCOTT HEPBURN artist DAN BROWN colorist JOHN J. HILL letterer cover art by KENNETH ROCAFORT

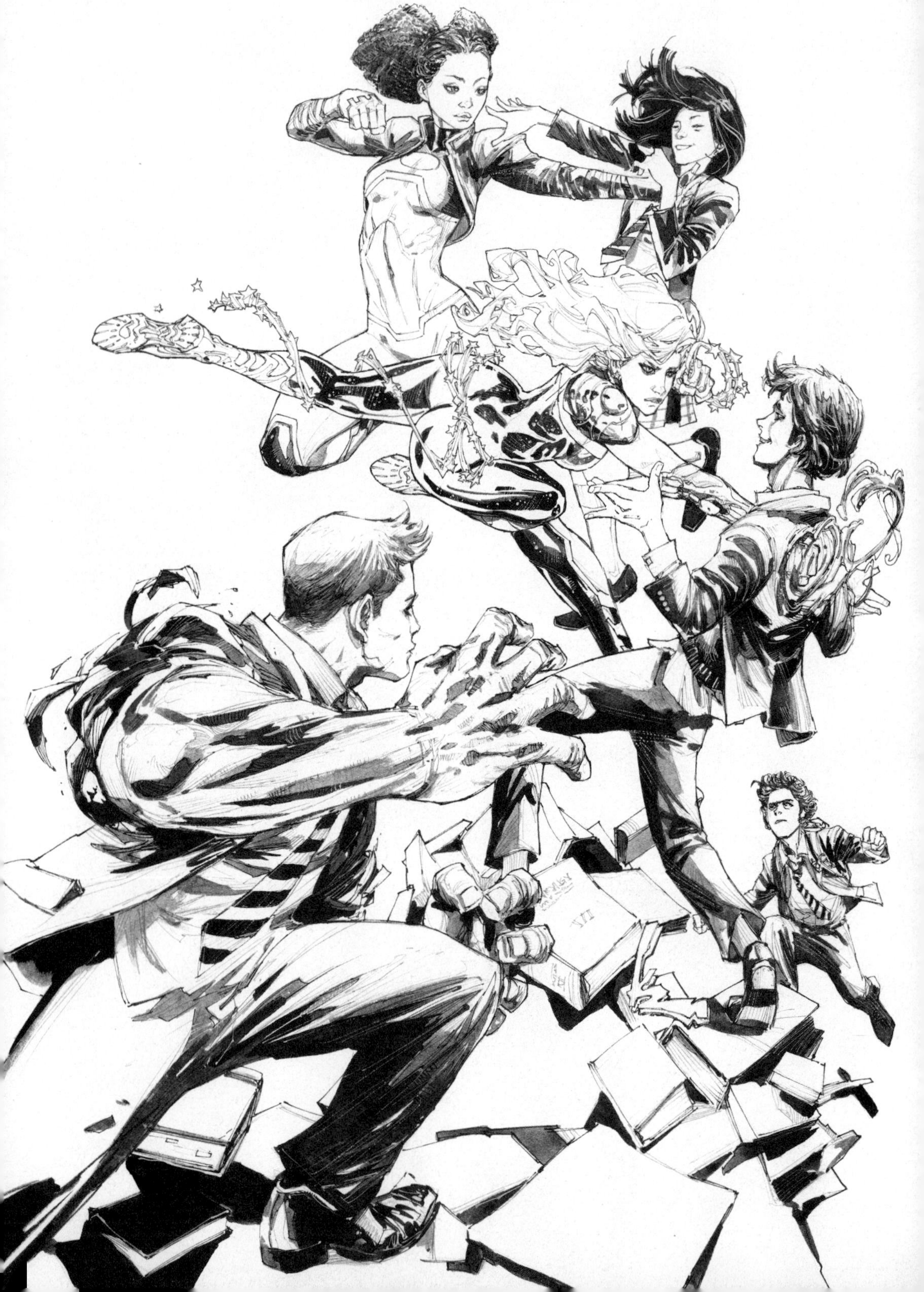

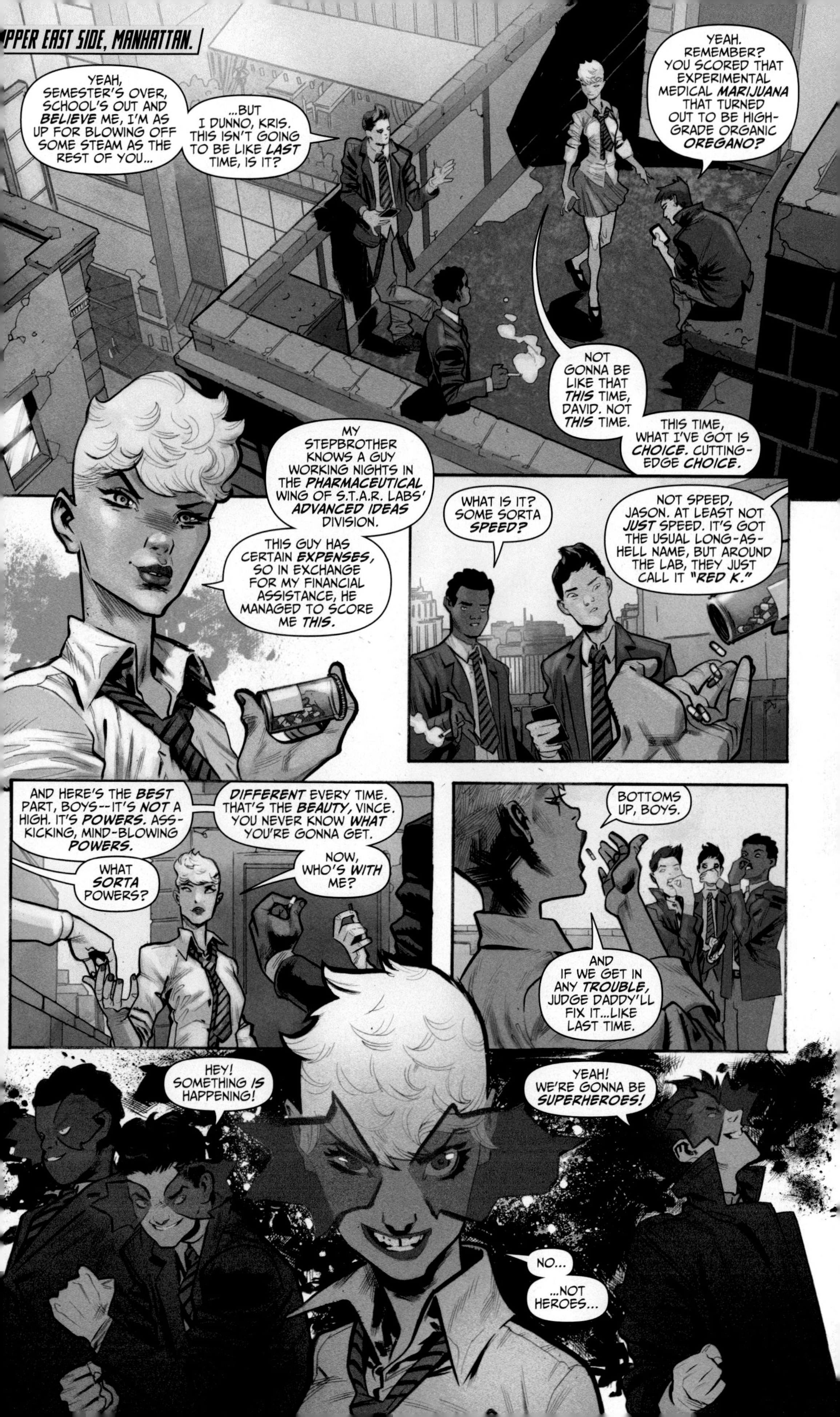
PPER EAST SIDE, MANHATTAN.
YEAH, SEMESTER'S OVER, SCHOOL'S OUT AND BELIEVE ME, I'M AS UP FOR BLOWING OFF SOME STEAM AS THE REST OF YOU...
...BUT I DUNNO, KRIS. THIS ISN'T GOING TO BE LIKE LAST TIME, IS IT?
YEAH. REMEMBER? YOU SCORED THAT EXPERIMENTAL MEDICAL MARIJUANA THAT TURNED OUT TO BE HIGH-GRADE ORGANIC OREGANO?
NOT GONNA BE LIKE THAT THIS TIME, DAVID. NOT THIS TIME.
THIS TIME, WHAT I'VE GOT IS CHOICE. CUTTING-EDGE CHOICE.
MY STEPBROTHER KNOWS A GUY WORKING NIGHTS IN THE PHARMACEUTICAL WING OF S.T.A.R. LABS' ADVANCED IDEAS DIVISION.
THIS GUY HAS CERTAIN EXPENSES, SO IN EXCHANGE FOR MY FINANCIAL ASSISTANCE, HE MANAGED TO SCORE ME THIS.
WHAT IS IT? SOME SORTA SPEED?
NOT SPEED, JASON. AT LEAST NOT JUST SPEED. IT'S GOT THE USUAL LONG-AS-HELL NAME, BUT AROUND THE LAB, THEY JUST CALL IT "RED K."
AND HERE'S THE BEST PART, BOYS--IT'S NOT A HIGH. IT'S POWERS. ASS-KICKING, MIND-BLOWING POWERS.
WHAT SORTA POWERS?
DIFFERENT EVERY TIME. THAT'S THE BEAUTY, VINCE. YOU NEVER KNOW WHAT YOU'RE GONNA GET.
NOW, WHO'S WITH ME?
BOTTOMS UP, BOYS.
AND IF WE GET IN ANY TROUBLE, JUDGE DADDY'LL FIX IT...LIKE LAST TIME.
HEY! SOMETHING IS HAPPENING!
YEAH! WE'RE GONNA BE SUPERHEROES!
NO...
...NOT HEROES...

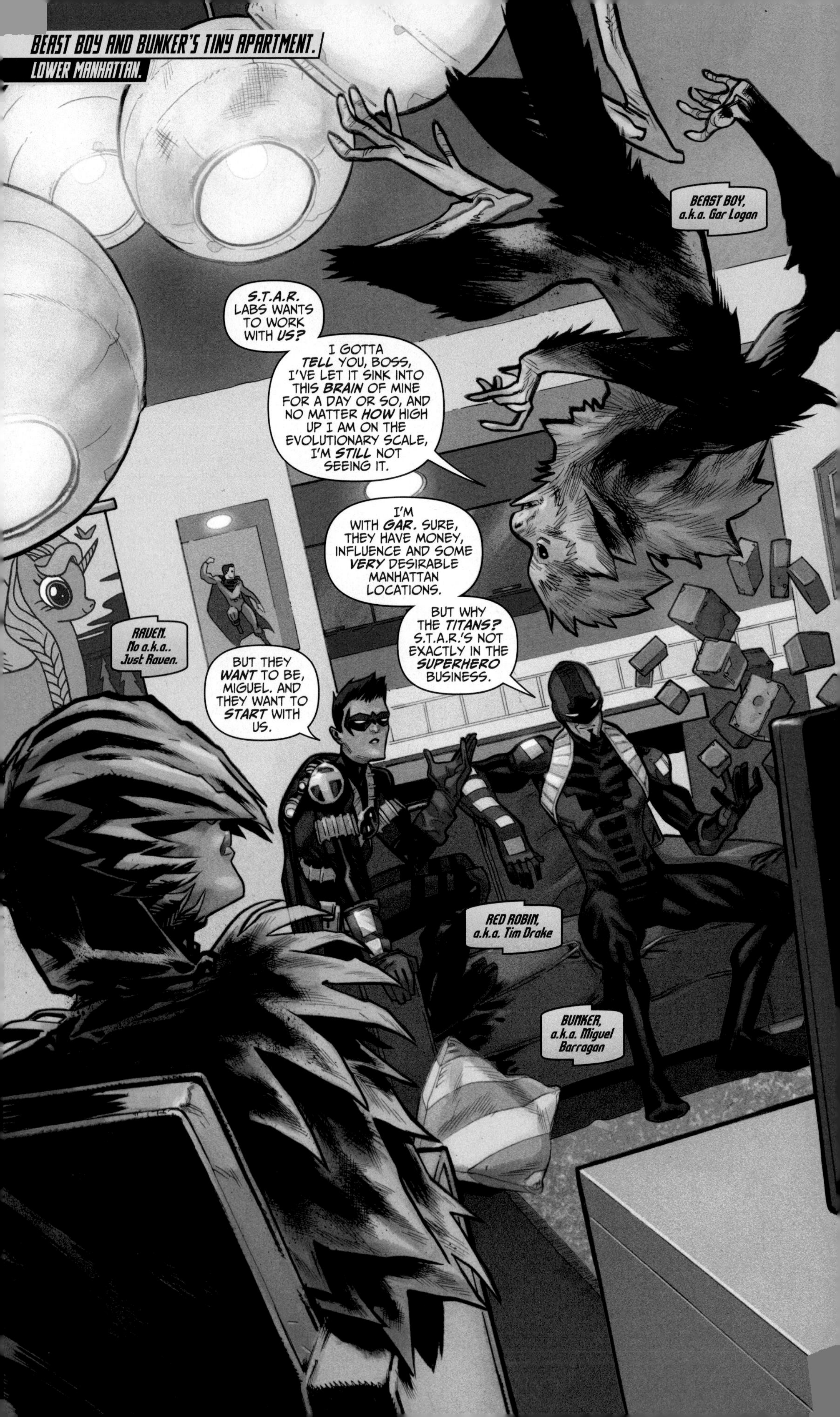
BEAST BOY AND BUNKER'S TINY APARTMENT.
LOWER MANHATTAN.
BEAST BOY, a.k.a. Gar Logan
S.T.A.R. LABS WANTS TO WORK WITH US?
I GOTTA TELL YOU, BOSS, I'VE LET IT SINK INTO THIS BRAIN OF MINE FOR A DAY OR SO, AND NO MATTER HOW HIGH UP I AM ON THE EVOLUTIONARY SCALE, I'M STILL NOT SEEING IT.
I'M WITH GAR. SURE, THEY HAVE MONEY, INFLUENCE AND SOME VERY DESIRABLE MANHATTAN LOCATIONS.
BUT WHY THE TITANS? S.T.A.R.'S NOT EXACTLY IN THE SUPERHERO BUSINESS.
RAVEN. No a.k.a.. Just Raven.
BUT THEY WANT TO BE, MIGUEL. AND THEY WANT TO START WITH US.
RED ROBIN, a.k.a. Tim Drake
BUNKER, a.k.a. Miguel Barragan

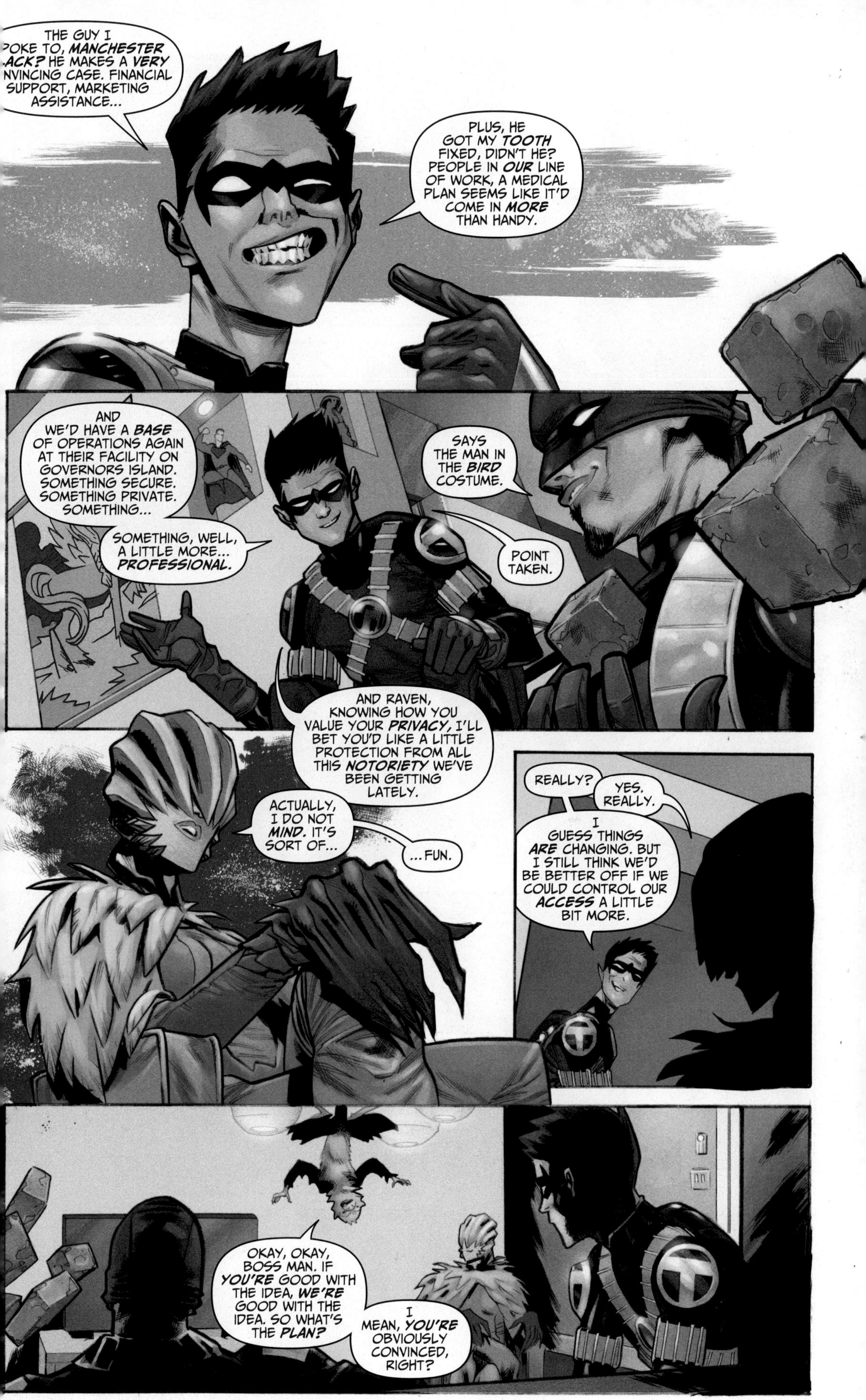

THE GUY I
POKE TO, MANCHESTER
ACK? HE MAKES A VERY
NVINCING CASE. FINANCIAL SUPPORT, MARKETING ASSISTANCE...
PLUS, HE GOT MY TOOTH FIXED, DIDN'T HE? PEOPLE IN OUR LINE OF WORK, A MEDICAL PLAN SEEMS LIKE IT'D COME IN MORE THAN HANDY.
AND WE'D HAVE A BASE OF OPERATIONS AGAIN AT THEIR FACILITY ON GOVERNORS ISLAND. SOMETHING SECURE. SOMETHING PRIVATE. SOMETHING...
SOMETHING, WELL, A LITTLE MORE... PROFESSIONAL.
SAYS THE MAN IN THE BIRD COSTUME.
POINT TAKEN.
AND RAVEN, KNOWING HOW YOU VALUE YOUR PRIVACY, I'LL BET YOU'D LIKE A LITTLE PROTECTION FROM ALL THIS NOTORIETY WE'VE BEEN GETTING LATELY.
ACTUALLY, I DO NOT MIND. IT'S SORT OF...
...FUN.
REALLY?
YES. REALLY.
I GUESS THINGS ARE CHANGING. BUT I STILL THINK WE'D BE BETTER OFF IF WE COULD CONTROL OUR ACCESS A LITTLE BIT MORE.
OKAY, OKAY, BOSS MAN. IF YOU'RE GOOD WITH THE IDEA, WE'RE GOOD WITH THE IDEA. SO WHAT'S THE PLAN?
I MEAN, YOU'RE OBVIOUSLY CONVINCED, RIGHT?

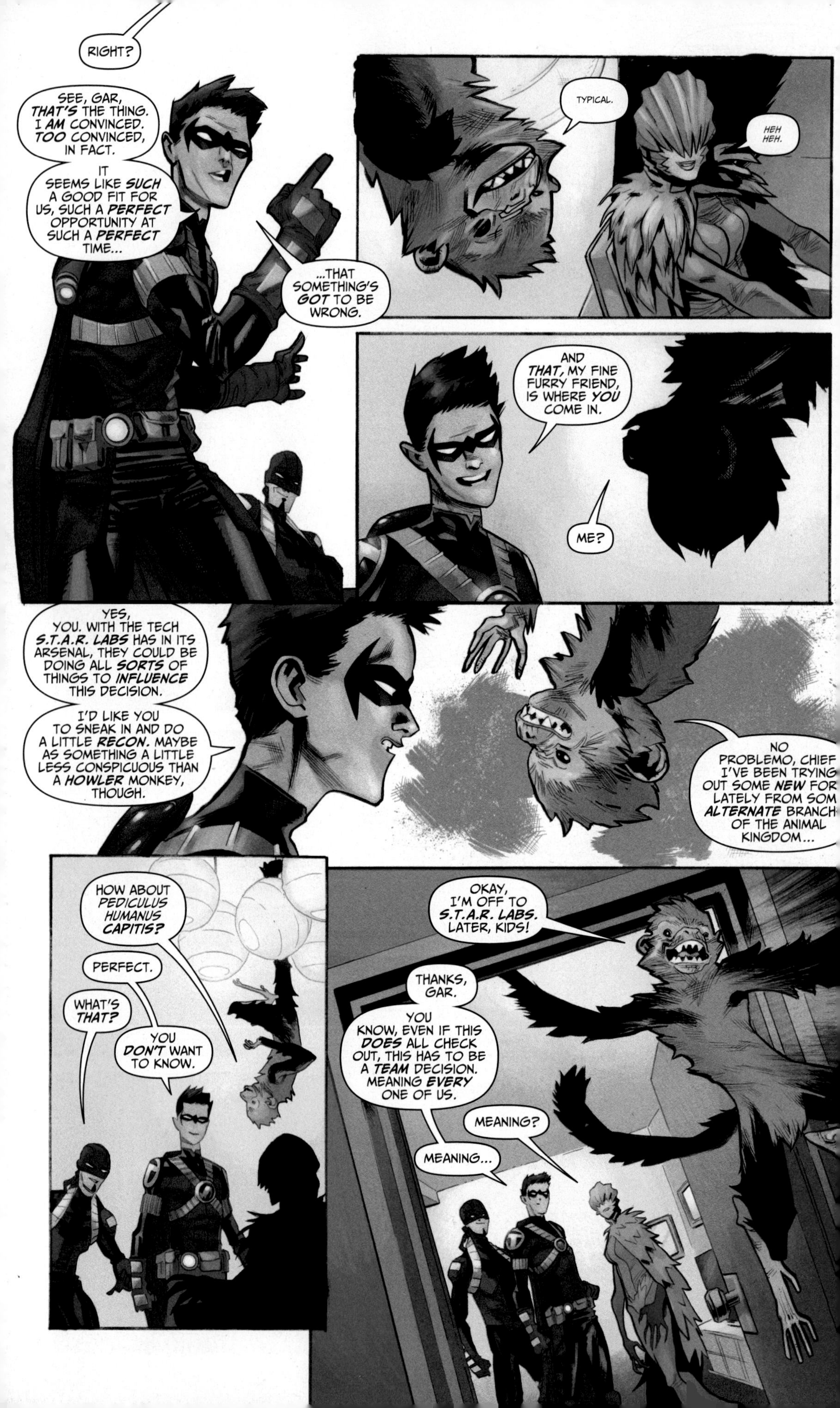
RIGHT?
SEE, GAR, THAT'S THE THING. I AM CONVINCED. TOO CONVINCED, IN FACT.
IT SEEMS LIKE SUCH A GOOD FIT FOR US, SUCH A PERFECT OPPORTUNITY AT SUCH A PERFECT TIME...
...THAT SOMETHING'S GOT TO BE WRONG.
TYPICAL.
HEH HEH.
AND THAT, MY FINE FURRY FRIEND, IS WHERE YOU COME IN.
ME?
YES, YOU. WITH THE TECH S.T.A.R. LABS HAS IN ITS ARSENAL, THEY COULD BE DOING ALL SORTS OF THINGS TO INFLUENCE THIS DECISION.
I'D LIKE YOU TO SNEAK IN AND DO A LITTLE RECON. MAYBE AS SOMETHING A LITTLE LESS CONSPICUOUS THAN A HOWLER MONKEY, THOUGH.
NO PROBLEMO, CHIEF I'VE BEEN TRYING OUT SOME NEW FOR LATELY FROM SOM ALTERNATE BRANCH OF THE ANIMAL KINGDOM...
HOW ABOUT PEDICULUS HUMANUS CAPITIS?
PERFECT.
WHAT'S THAT?
YOU DON'T WANT TO KNOW.
OKAY, I'M OFF TO S.T.A.R. LABS. LATER, KIDS!
THANKS, GAR.
YOU KNOW, EVEN IF THIS DOES ALL CHECK OUT, THIS HAS TO BE A TEAM DECISION. MEANING EVERY ONE OF US.
MEANING?
MEANING...

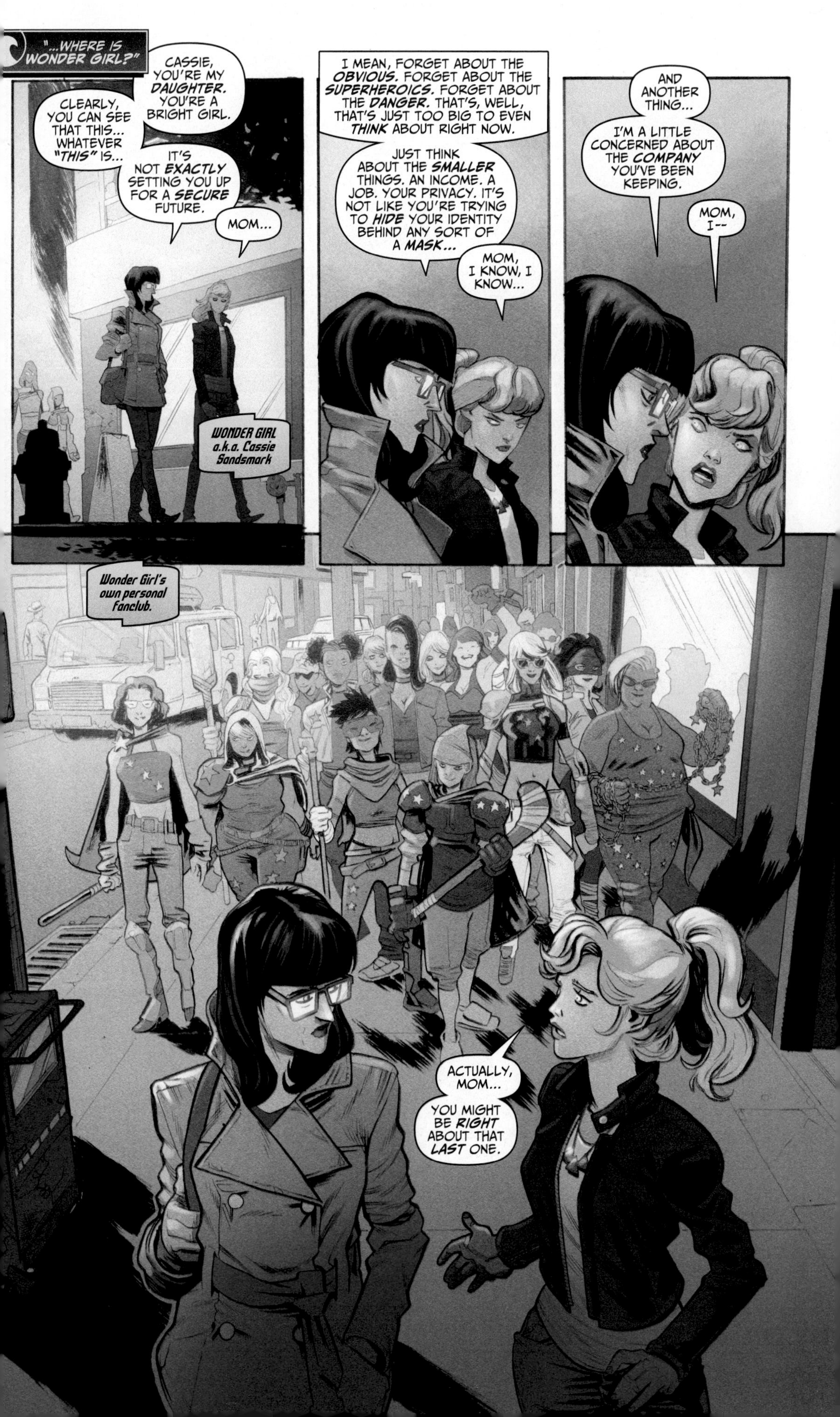
"...WHERE IS WONDER GIRL?"
CLEARLY, YOU CAN SEE THAT THIS... WHATEVER "THIS" IS...
CASSIE, YOU'RE MY DAUGHTER. YOU'RE A BRIGHT GIRL.
IT'S NOT EXACTLY SETTING YOU UP FOR A SECURE FUTURE.
MOM...
WONDER GIRL a.k.a. Cassie Sandsmark
I MEAN, FORGET ABOUT THE OBVIOUS. FORGET ABOUT THE SUPERHEROICS. FORGET ABOUT THE DANGER. THAT'S, WELL, THAT'S JUST TOO BIG TO EVEN THINK ABOUT RIGHT NOW.
JUST THINK ABOUT THE SMALLER THINGS. AN INCOME. A JOB. YOUR PRIVACY. IT'S NOT LIKE YOU'RE TRYING TO HIDE YOUR IDENTITY BEHIND ANY SORT OF A MASK...
MOM, I KNOW, I KNOW...
AND ANOTHER THING...
I'M A LITTLE CONCERNED ABOUT THE COMPANY YOU'VE BEEN KEEPING.
MOM, I--
Wonder Girl's own personal fanclub.
ACTUALLY, MOM...
YOU MIGHT BE RIGHT ABOUT THAT LAST ONE.

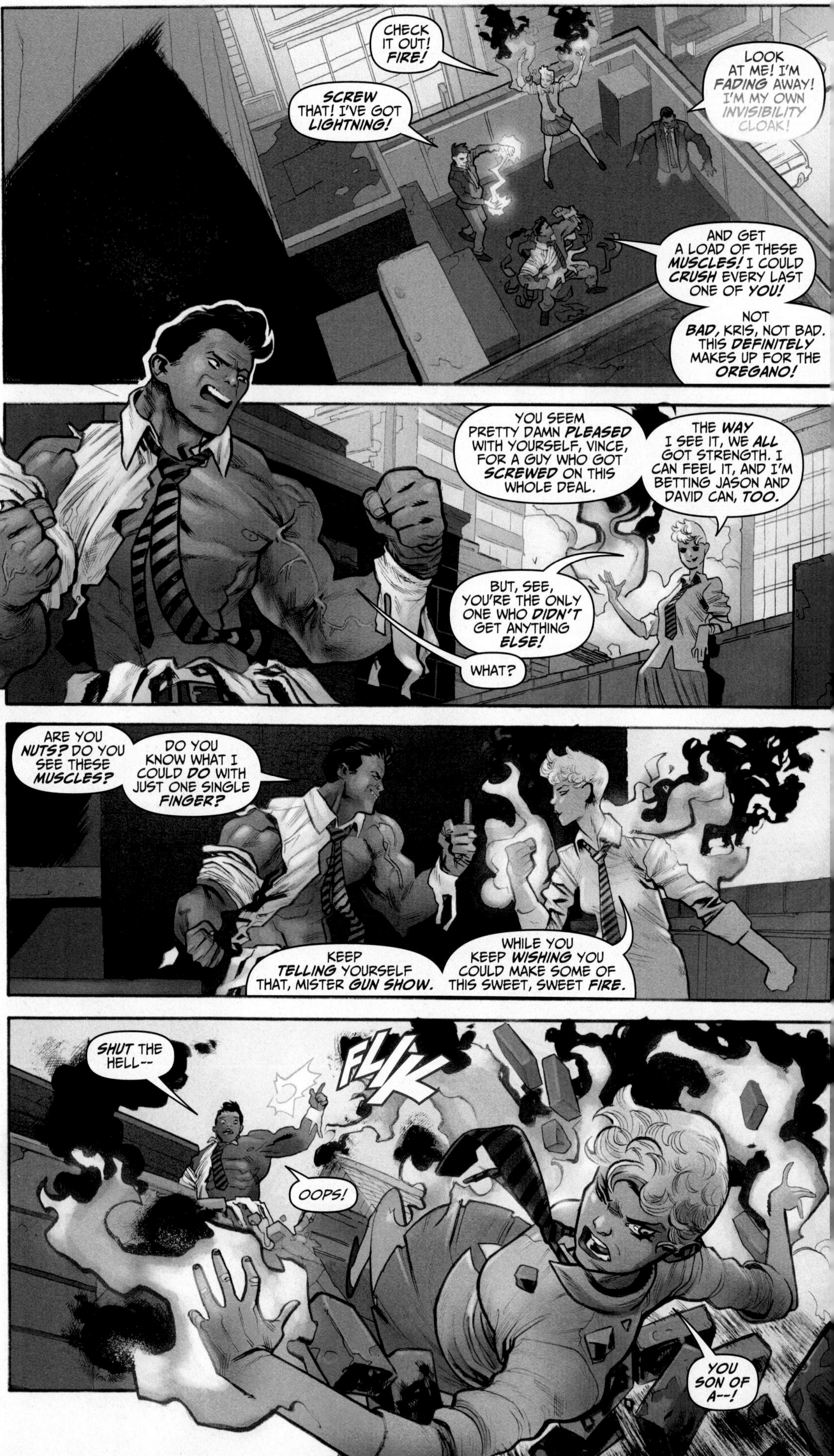
CHECK IT OUT! FIRE!
SCREW THAT! I'VE GOT LIGHTNING!
LOOK AT ME! I'M FADING AWAY! I'M MY OWN INVISIBILITY CLOAK!
AND GET A LOAD OF THESE MUSCLES! I COULD CRUSH EVERY LAST ONE OF YOU!
NOT BAD, KRIS, NOT BAD. THIS DEFINITELY MAKES UP FOR THE OREGANO!
YOU SEEM PRETTY DAMN PLEASED WITH YOURSELF, VINCE, FOR A GUY WHO GOT SCREWED ON THIS WHOLE DEAL.
THE WAY I SEE IT, WE ALL GOT STRENGTH. I CAN FEEL IT, AND I'M BETTING JASON AND DAVID CAN, TOO.
BUT, SEE, YOU'RE THE ONLY ONE WHO DIDN'T GET ANYTHING ELSE!
WHAT?
ARE YOU NUTS? DO YOU SEE THESE MUSCLES?
DO YOU KNOW WHAT I COULD DO WITH JUST ONE SINGLE FINGER?
KEEP TELLING YOURSELF THAT, MISTER GUN SHOW.
WHILE YOU KEEP WISHING YOU COULD MAKE SOME OF THIS SWEET, SWEET FIRE.
SHUT THE HELL--
FLIK
OOPS!
YOU SON OF A--!

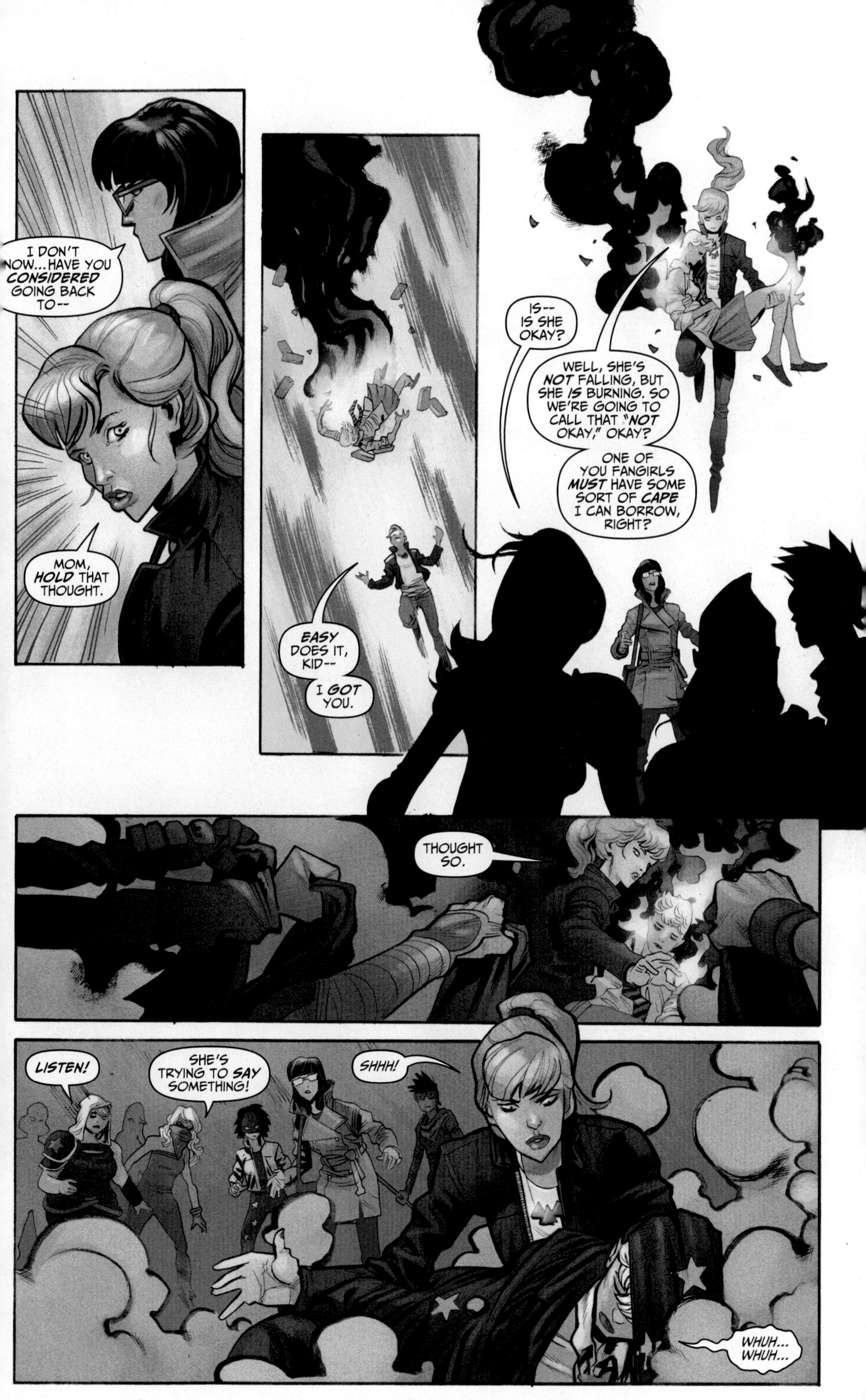
I DON'T NOW...HAVE YOU CONSIDERED GOING BACK TO--
MOM, HOLD THAT THOUGHT.
EASY DOES IT, KID--
I GOT YOU.
IS-- IS SHE OKAY?
WELL, SHE'S NOT FALLING, BUT SHE IS BURNING. SO WE'RE GOING TO CALL THAT "NOT OKAY," OKAY?
ONE OF YOU FANGIRLS MUST HAVE SOME SORT OF CAPE I CAN BORROW, RIGHT?
THOUGHT SO.
LISTEN!
SHE'S TRYING TO SAY SOMETHING!
SHHH!
WHUH... WHUH...

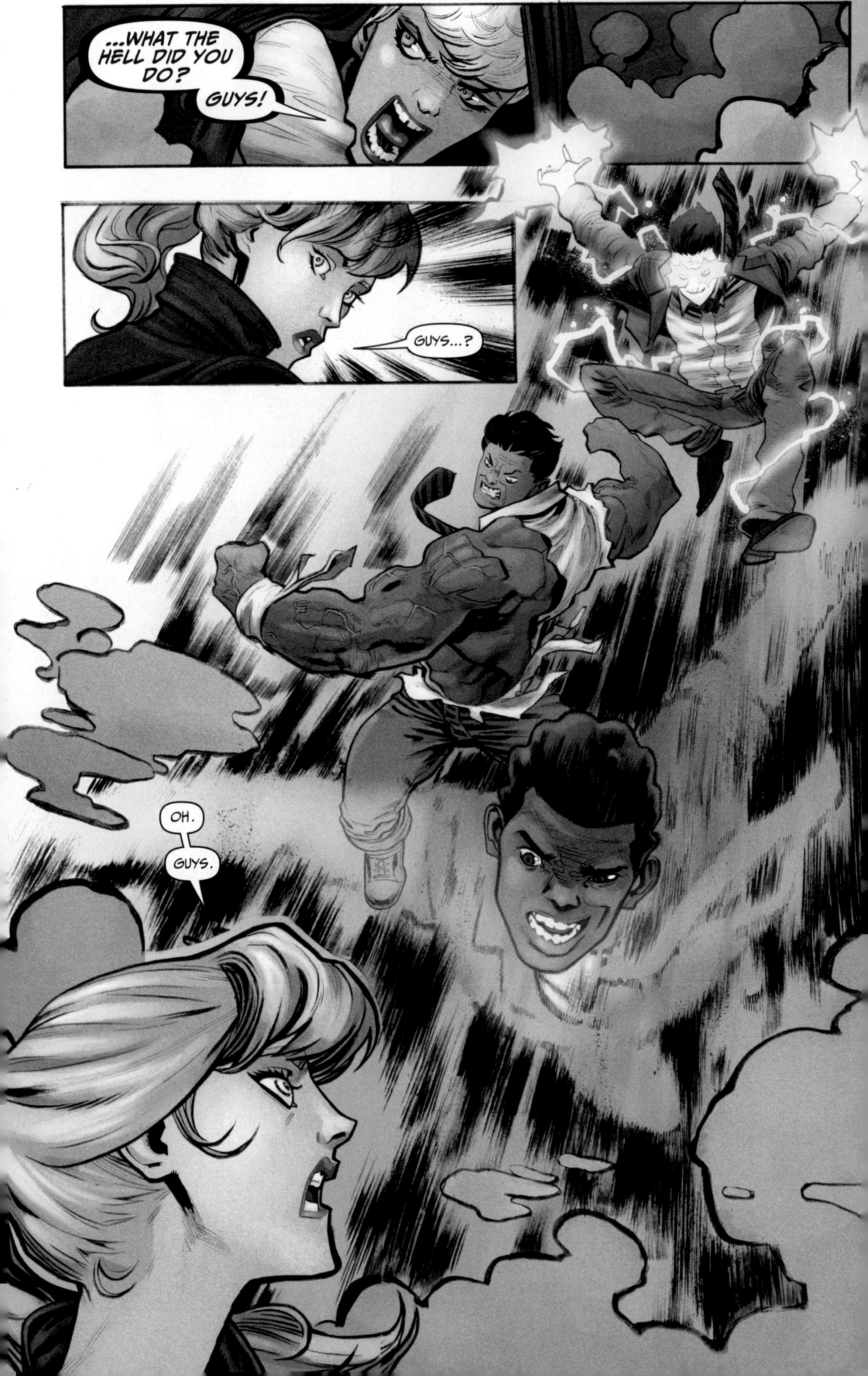
...WHAT THE HELL DID YOU DO?
GUYS!
GUYS...?
OH.
GUYS.

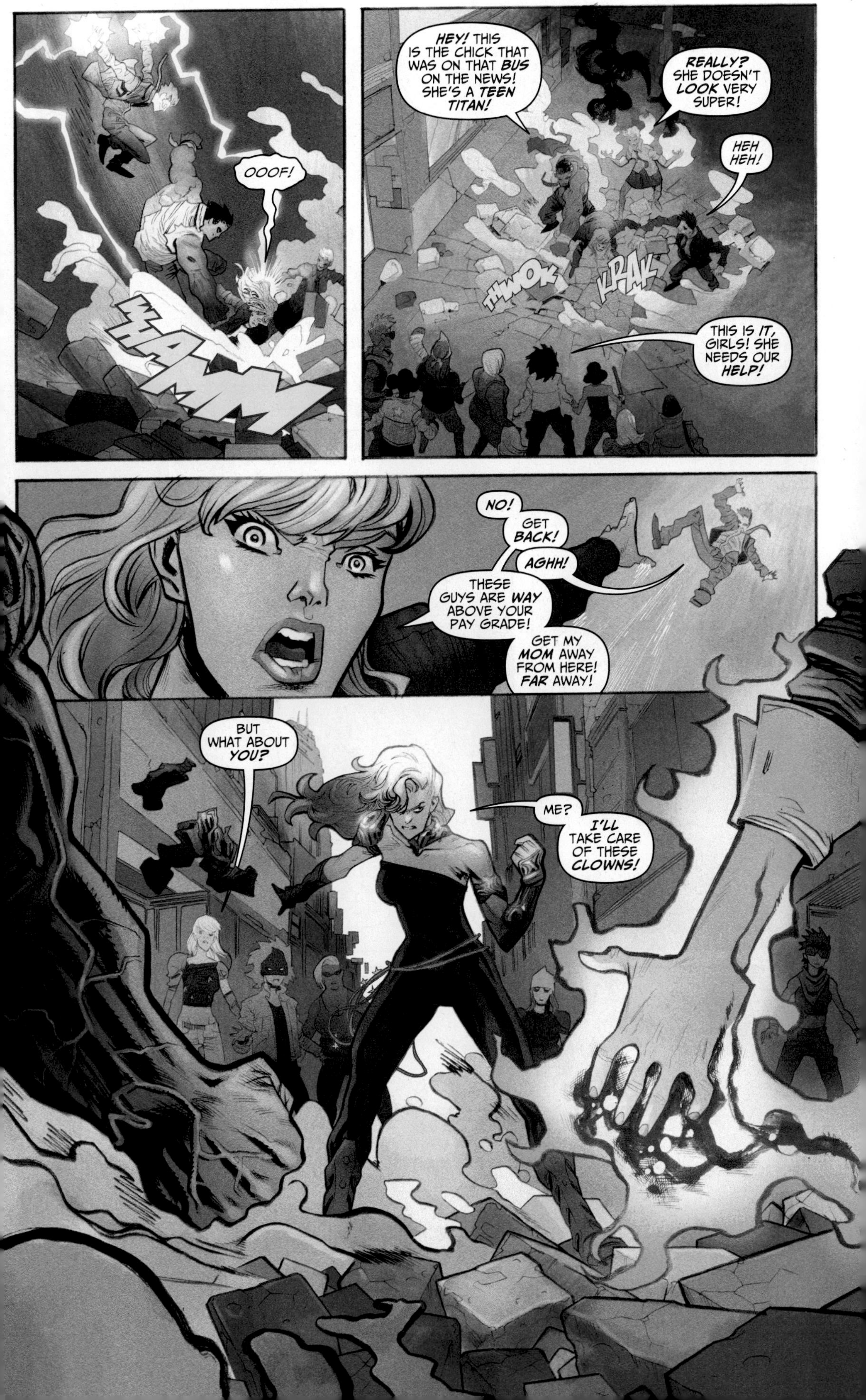
OOOF!
WHAMM
HEY! THIS IS THE CHICK THAT WAS ON THAT BUS ON THE NEWS! SHE'S A TEEN TITAN!
REALLY? SHE DOESN'T LOOK VERY SUPER!
HEH HEH!
THWOK
KRAK
THIS IS IT, GIRLS! SHE NEEDS OUR HELP!
NO!
GET BACK!
AGHH!
THESE GUYS ARE WAY ABOVE YOUR PAY GRADE!
GET MY MOM AWAY FROM HERE! FAR AWAY!
BUT WHAT ABOUT YOU?
ME? I'LL TAKE CARE OF THESE CLOWNS!

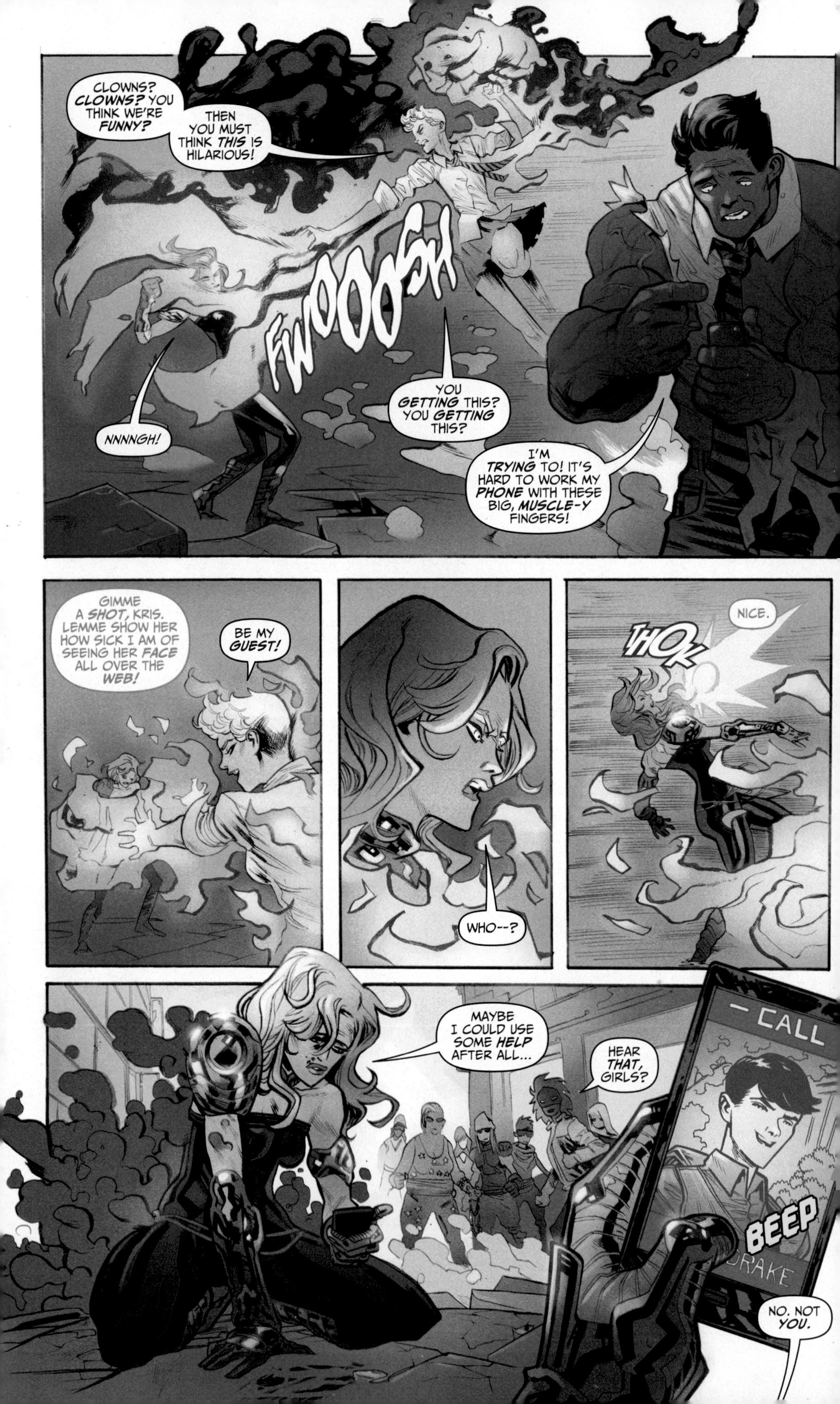
CLOWNS? CLOWNS? YOU THINK WE'RE FUNNY?
THEN YOU MUST THINK THIS IS HILARIOUS!
FWOOOSH
NNNNGH!
YOU GETTING THIS? YOU GETTING THIS?
I'M TRYING TO! IT'S HARD TO WORK MY PHONE WITH THESE BIG, MUSCLE-Y FINGERS!
GIMME A SHOT, KRIS. LEMME SHOW HER HOW SICK I AM OF SEEING HER FACE ALL OVER THE WEB!
BE MY GUEST!
WHO--?
NICE.
THOK
MAYBE I COULD USE SOME HELP AFTER ALL...
HEAR THAT, GIRLS?
— CALL
BEEP
DRAKE
NO. NOT YOU.

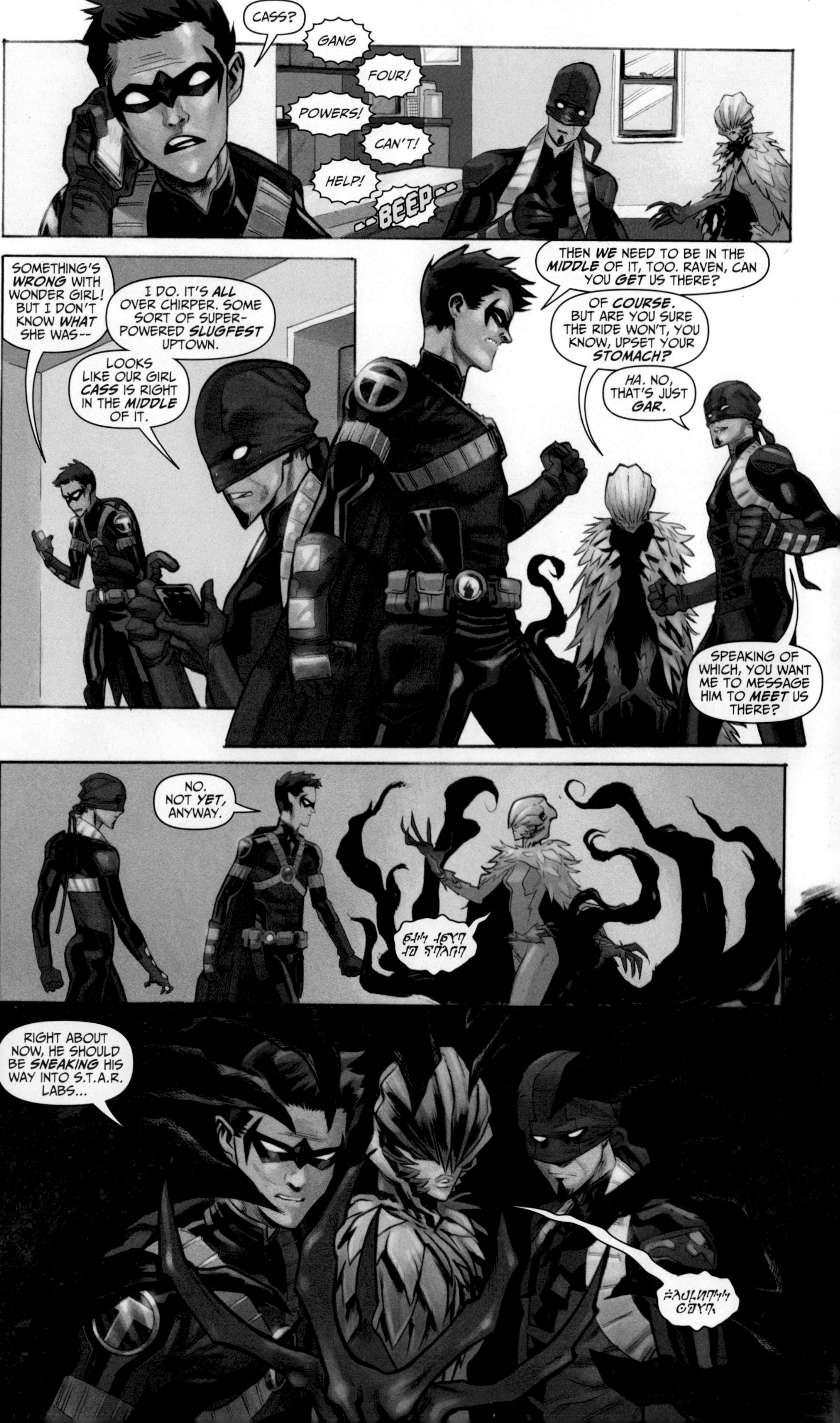
CASS?
GANG
FOUR!
POWERS!
CAN'T!
HELP!
--BEEP--
SOMETHING'S WRONG WITH WONDER GIRL! BUT I DON'T KNOW WHAT SHE WAS--
I DO. IT'S ALL OVER CHIRPER. SOME SORT OF SUPER-POWERED SLUGFEST UPTOWN.
LOOKS LIKE OUR GIRL CASS IS RIGHT IN THE MIDDLE OF IT.
THEN WE NEED TO BE IN THE MIDDLE OF IT, TOO. RAVEN, CAN YOU GET US THERE?
OF COURSE. BUT ARE YOU SURE THE RIDE WON'T, YOU KNOW, UPSET YOUR STOMACH?
HA. NO, THAT'S JUST GAR.
SPEAKING OF WHICH, YOU WANT ME TO MESSAGE HIM TO MEET US THERE?
NO. NOT YET, ANYWAY.
RIGHT ABOUT NOW, HE SHOULD BE SNEAKING HIS WAY INTO S.T.A.R. LABS...

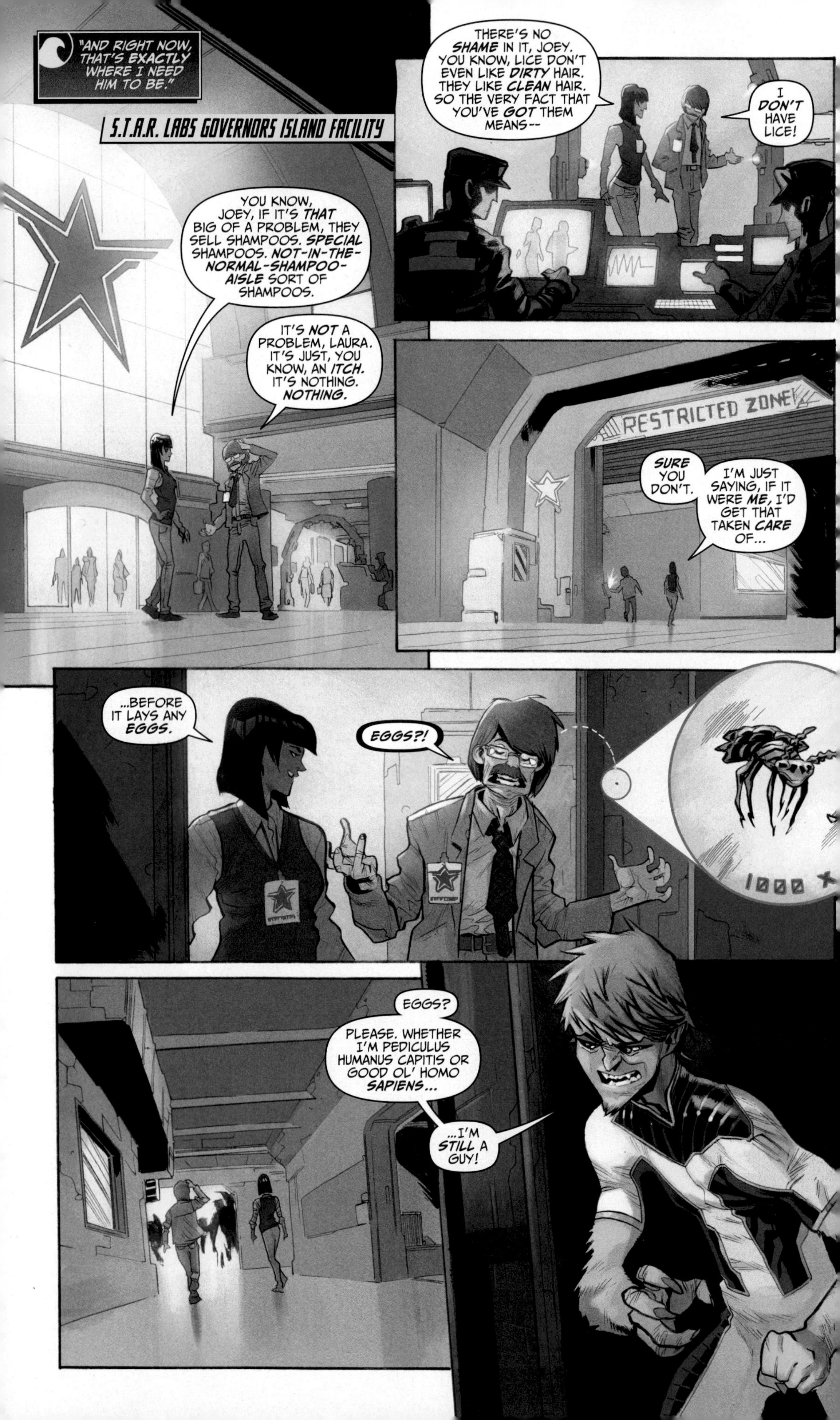
"AND RIGHT NOW, THAT'S EXACTLY WHERE I NEED HIM TO BE."
S.T.A.R. LABS GOVERNORS ISLAND FACILITY
YOU KNOW, JOEY, IF IT'S THAT BIG OF A PROBLEM, THEY SELL SHAMPOOS. SPECIAL SHAMPOOS. NOT-IN-THE-NORMAL-SHAMPOO-AISLE SORT OF SHAMPOOS.
IT'S NOT A PROBLEM, LAURA. IT'S JUST, YOU KNOW, AN ITCH. IT'S NOTHING. NOTHING.
THERE'S NO SHAME IN IT, JOEY. YOU KNOW, LICE DON'T EVEN LIKE DIRTY HAIR. THEY LIKE CLEAN HAIR. SO THE VERY FACT THAT YOU'VE GOT THEM MEANS--
I DON'T HAVE LICE!
RESTRICTED ZONE
SURE YOU DON'T.
I'M JUST SAYING, IF IT WERE ME, I'D GET THAT TAKEN CARE OF...
...BEFORE IT LAYS ANY EGGS.
EGGS?!
1000 X
EGGS?
PLEASE. WHETHER I'M PEDICULUS HUMANUS CAPITIS OR GOOD OL' HOMO SAPIENS...
...I'M STILL A GUY!

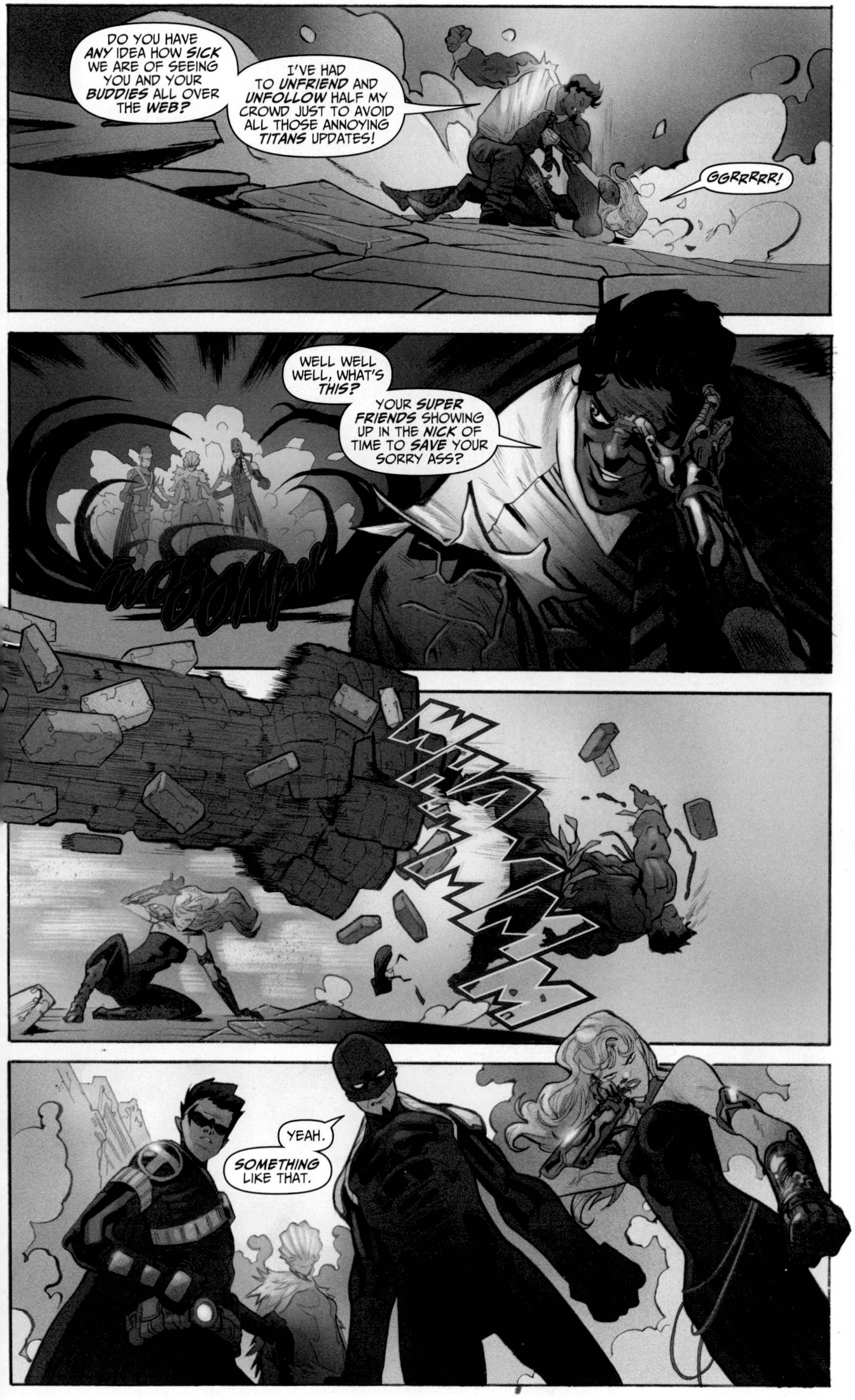
DO YOU HAVE ANY IDEA HOW SICK WE ARE OF SEEING YOU AND YOUR BUDDIES ALL OVER THE WEB?
I'VE HAD TO UNFRIEND AND UNFOLLOW HALF MY CROWD JUST TO AVOID ALL THOSE ANNOYING TITANS UPDATES!
GGRRRRR!
WELL WELL WELL, WHAT'S THIS?
YOUR SUPER FRIENDS SHOWING UP IN THE NICK OF TIME TO SAVE YOUR SORRY ASS?
FWOOOMPH
WHAMMM
YEAH.
SOMETHING LIKE THAT.

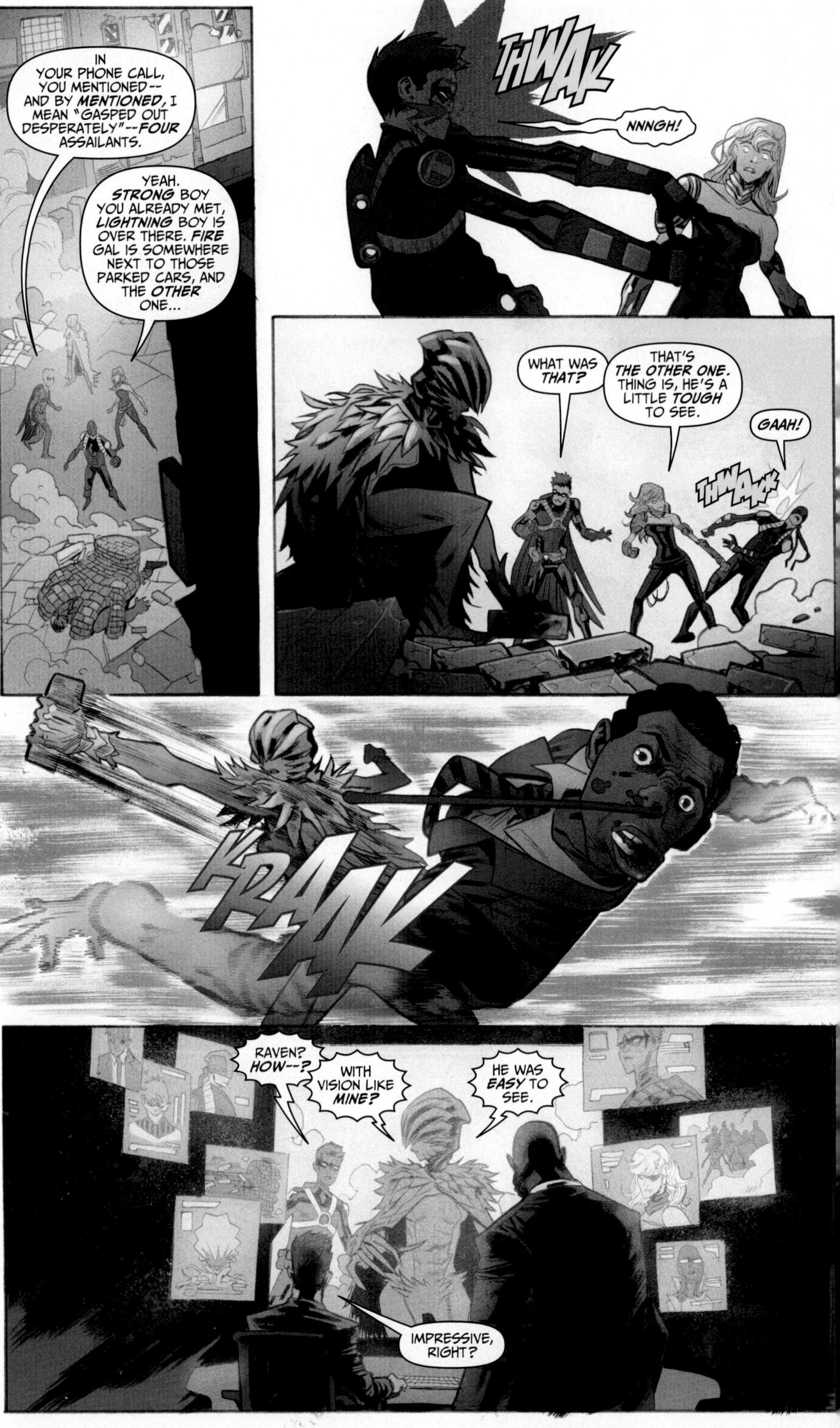
IN YOUR PHONE CALL, YOU MENTIONED-- AND BY MENTIONED, I MEAN "GASPED OUT DESPERATELY"--FOUR ASSAILANTS.
YEAH. STRONG BOY YOU ALREADY MET, LIGHTNING BOY IS OVER THERE. FIRE GAL IS SOMEWHERE NEXT TO THOSE PARKED CARS, AND THE OTHER ONE...
THWAK
NNNGH!
WHAT WAS THAT?
THAT'S THE OTHER ONE. THING IS, HE'S A LITTLE TOUGH TO SEE.
GAAH!
THWAKK
KRAAK
RAVEN? HOW--?
WITH VISION LIKE MINE?
HE WAS EASY TO SEE.
IMPRESSIVE, RIGHT?

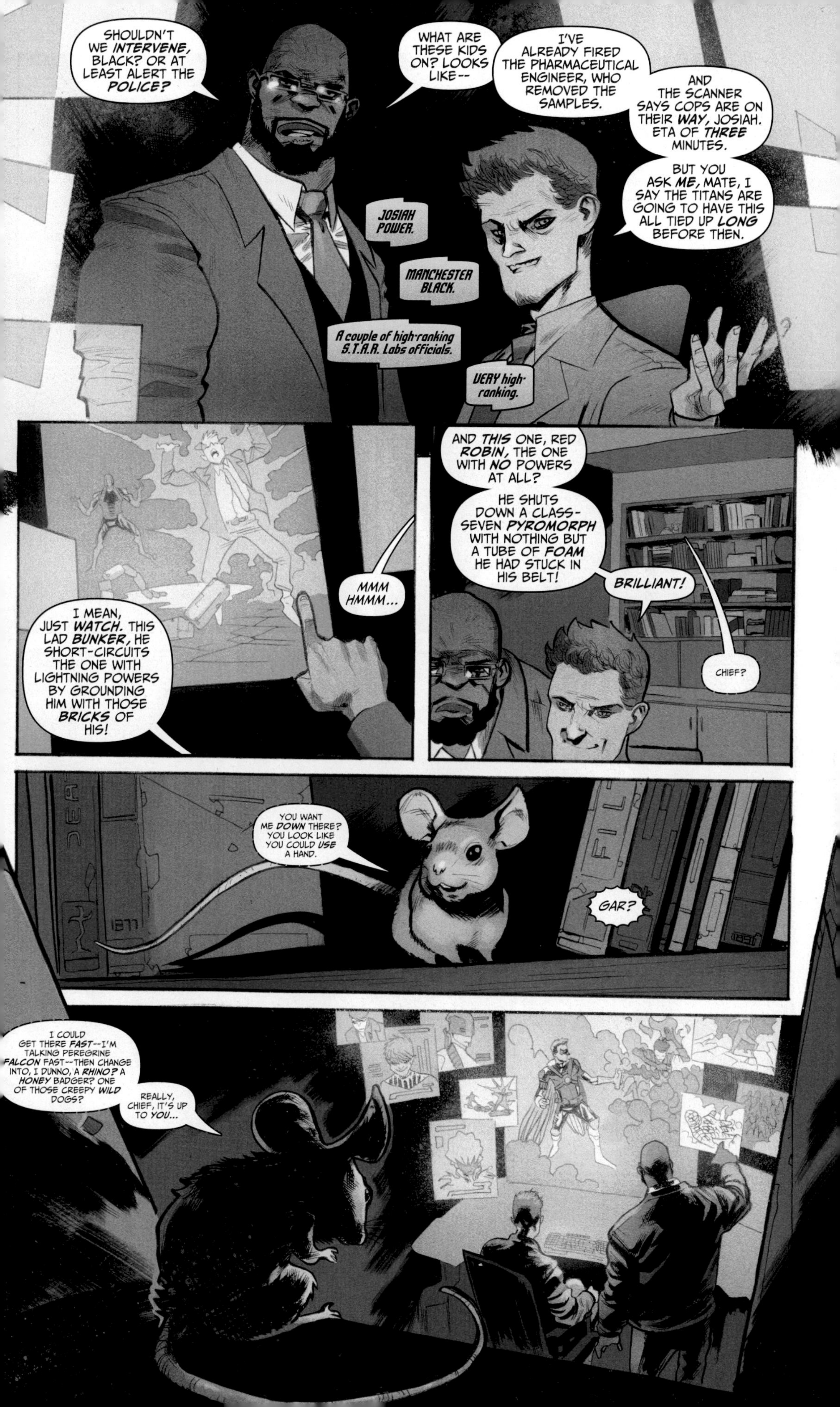

SHOULDN'T WE INTERVENE, BLACK? OR AT LEAST ALERT THE POLICE?
WHAT ARE THESE KIDS ON? LOOKS LIKE--
I'VE ALREADY FIRED THE PHARMACEUTICAL ENGINEER, WHO REMOVED THE SAMPLES.
AND THE SCANNER SAYS COPS ARE ON THEIR WAY, JOSIAH. ETA OF THREE MINUTES.
BUT YOU ASK ME, MATE, I SAY THE TITANS ARE GOING TO HAVE THIS ALL TIED UP LONG BEFORE THEN.
JOSIAH POWER.
MANCHESTER BLACK.
A couple of high-ranking S.T.A.R. Labs officials.
VERY high-ranking.
I MEAN, JUST WATCH. THIS LAD BUNKER, HE SHORT-CIRCUITS THE ONE WITH LIGHTNING POWERS BY GROUNDING HIM WITH THOSE BRICKS OF HIS!
MMM HMMM...
AND THIS ONE, RED ROBIN, THE ONE WITH NO POWERS AT ALL?
HE SHUTS DOWN A CLASS-SEVEN PYROMORPH WITH NOTHING BUT A TUBE OF FOAM HE HAD STUCK IN HIS BELT!
BRILLIANT!
CHIEF?
YOU WANT ME DOWN THERE? YOU LOOK LIKE YOU COULD USE A HAND.
GAR?
I COULD GET THERE FAST--I'M TALKING PEREGRINE FALCON FAST--THEN CHANGE INTO, I DUNNO, A RHINO? A HONEY BADGER? ONE OF THOSE CREEPY WILD DOGS?
REALLY, CHIEF, IT'S UP TO YOU...

NO, GAR, RIGHT *NOW*, I DON'T NEED YOU DOWN HERE *FIGHTING* WITH US. I NEED YOU WHERE YOU ARE, KEEPING AN *EYE* ON BLACK.

WHAT'S HIS *STATUS*, ANYWAY?

RIGHT *NOW?* HE'S WATCHING *YOU* TALKING TO *ME* WHILE I WATCH *HIM*.

I MEAN, BLACK'S KEEPING AN EYE ON *ALL* OF YOU. THE WHOLE FIGHT. AND BELIEVE ME, HE *LIKES* WHAT HE SEES.

IT'S LIKE THE *LAST* ROUND OF QUESTIONS IN A *JOB* INTERVIEW OR SOMETHING.

SO, YOU KNOW, *KEEP* ON *KEEPING* ON.

WILL DO. HAVE TO GO NOW.

WHOEVER THESE KIDS ARE, THEY'RE TAKING SOME SORT OF *DRUGS*. NOT SURE *WHAT* THEY'RE--

NOW...

LET'S TRY THIS *AGAIN!*

WATCH OUT, WONDER GIRL!

FWOOOOMSH

NNNGH!

I *TOLD* YOU GIRLS GET MY MOM OF HERE!

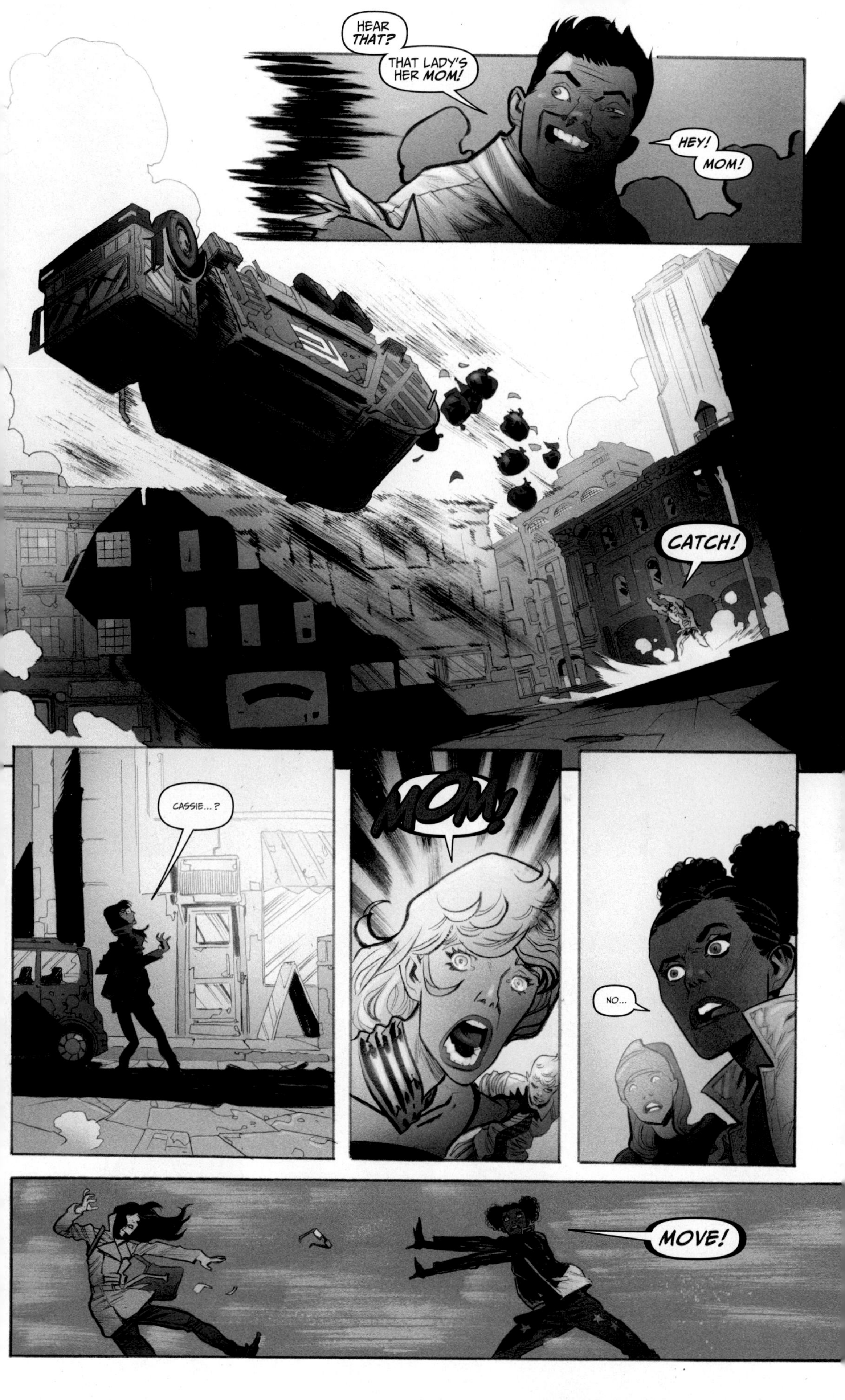
HEAR THAT?
THAT LADY'S HER MOM!
HEY! MOM!
CATCH!
CASSIE...?
MOM!
NO...
MOVE!

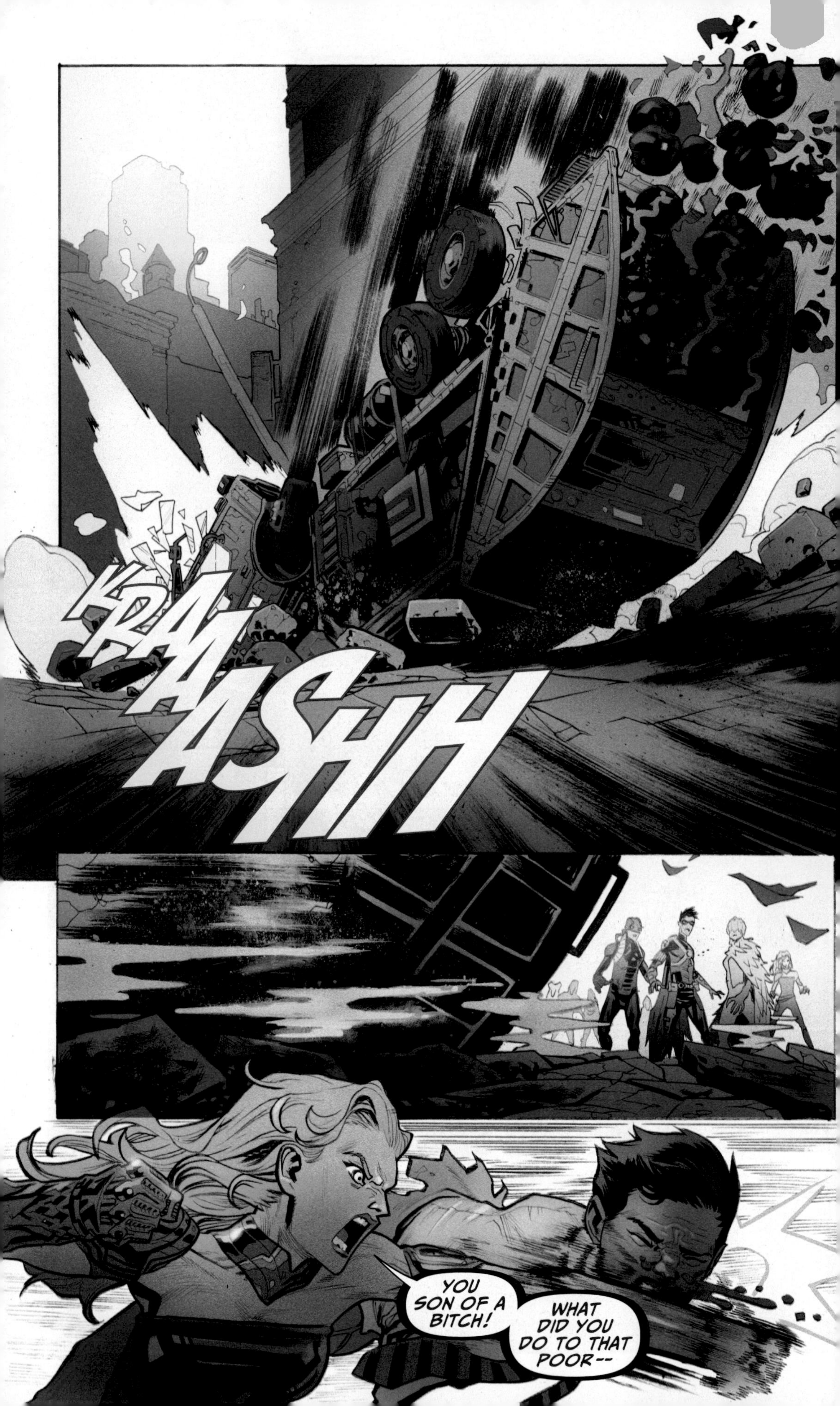
KRAASHH
YOU SON OF A BITCH!
WHAT DID YOU DO TO THAT POOR--

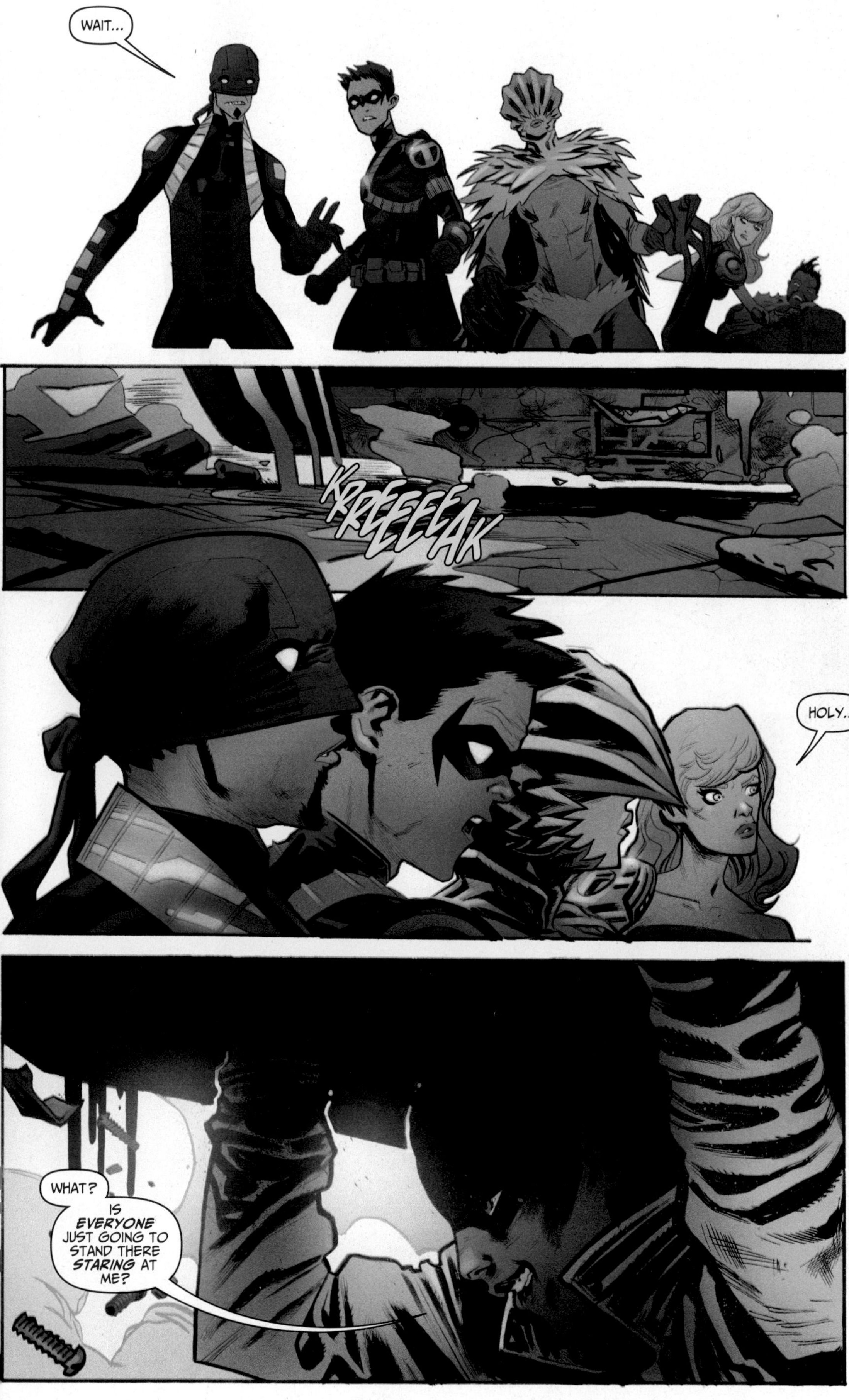
WAIT...
KRREEEEAK
HOLY...
WHAT?
IS *EVERYONE* JUST GOING TO STAND THERE *STARING* AT ME?

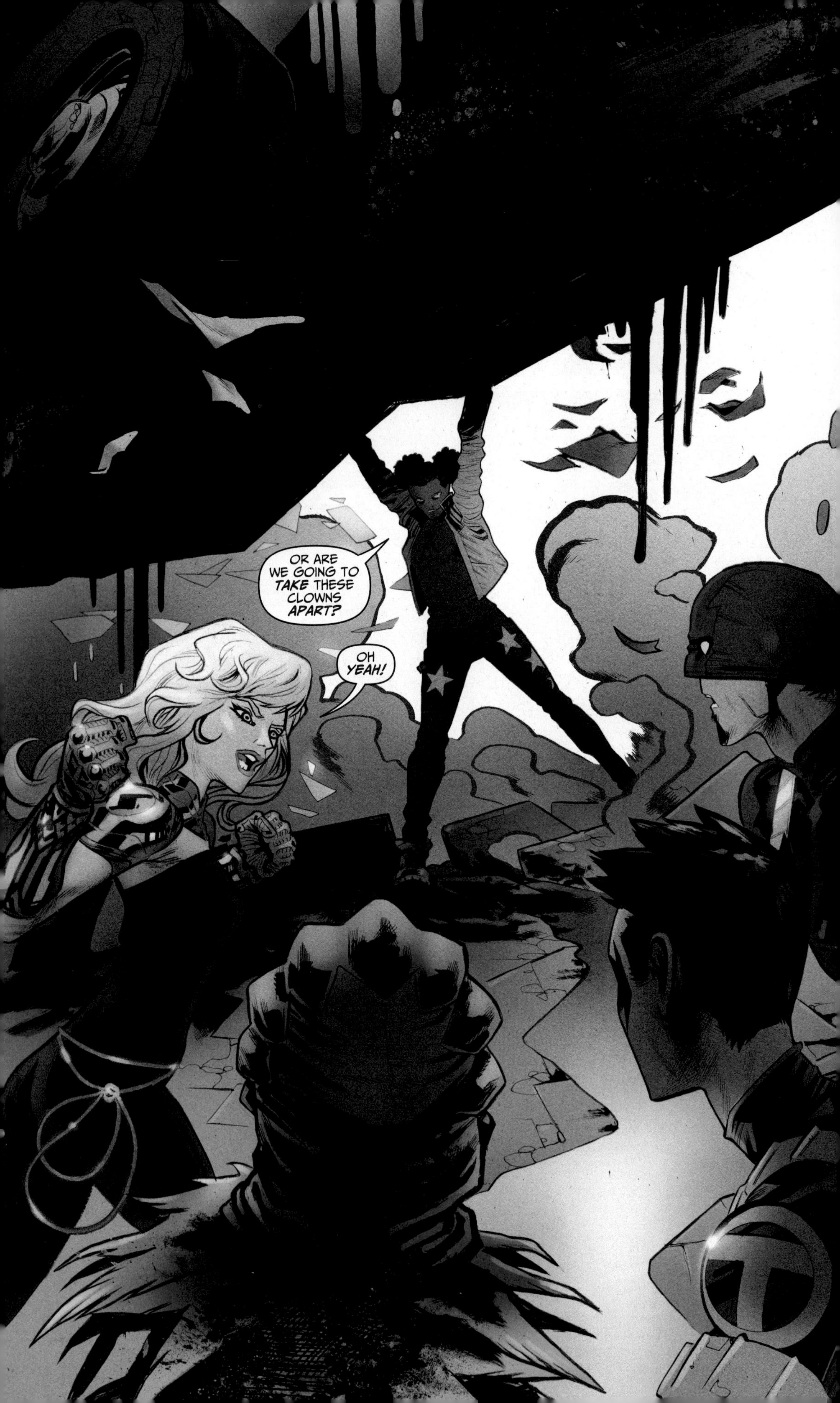
OR ARE WE GOING TO TAKE THESE CLOWNS APART?
OH YEAH!

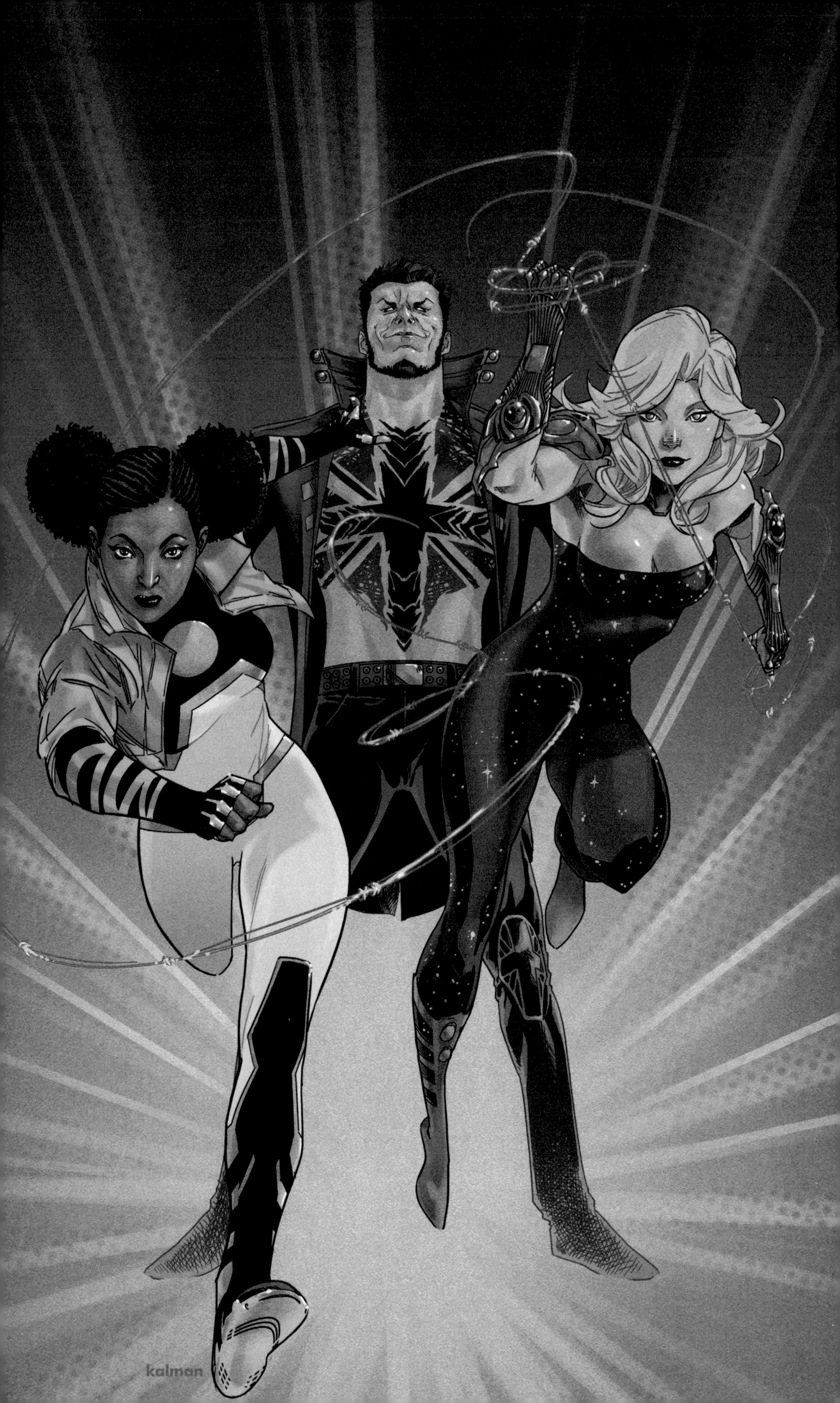
kalman

HUMAN RESOURCES: PART 2

WILL PFEIFER writer SCOTT HEPBURN artist DAN BROWN colorist JOHN J. HILL letterer cover art by KALMAN ANDRASOFSZKY

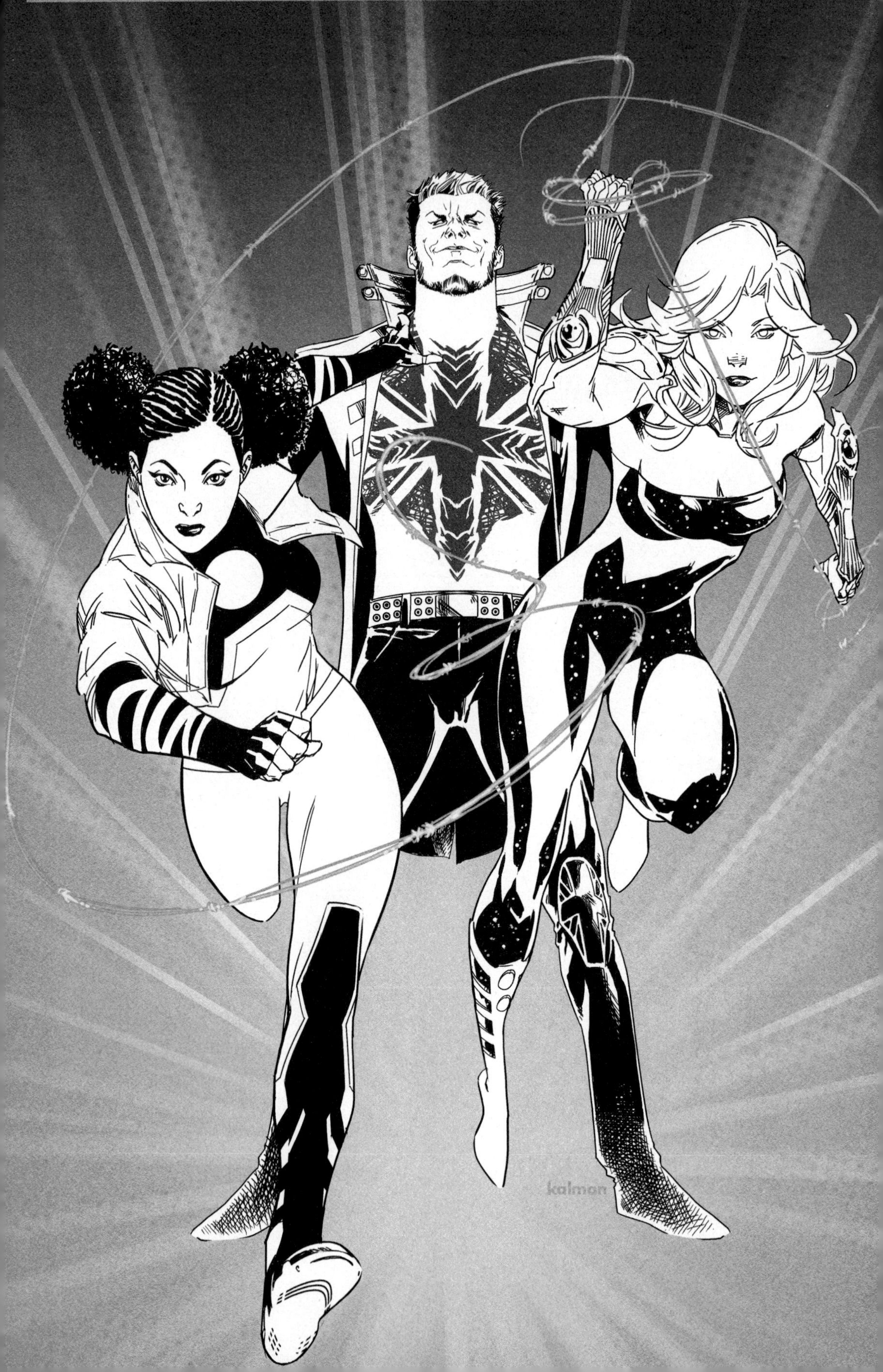
kalman

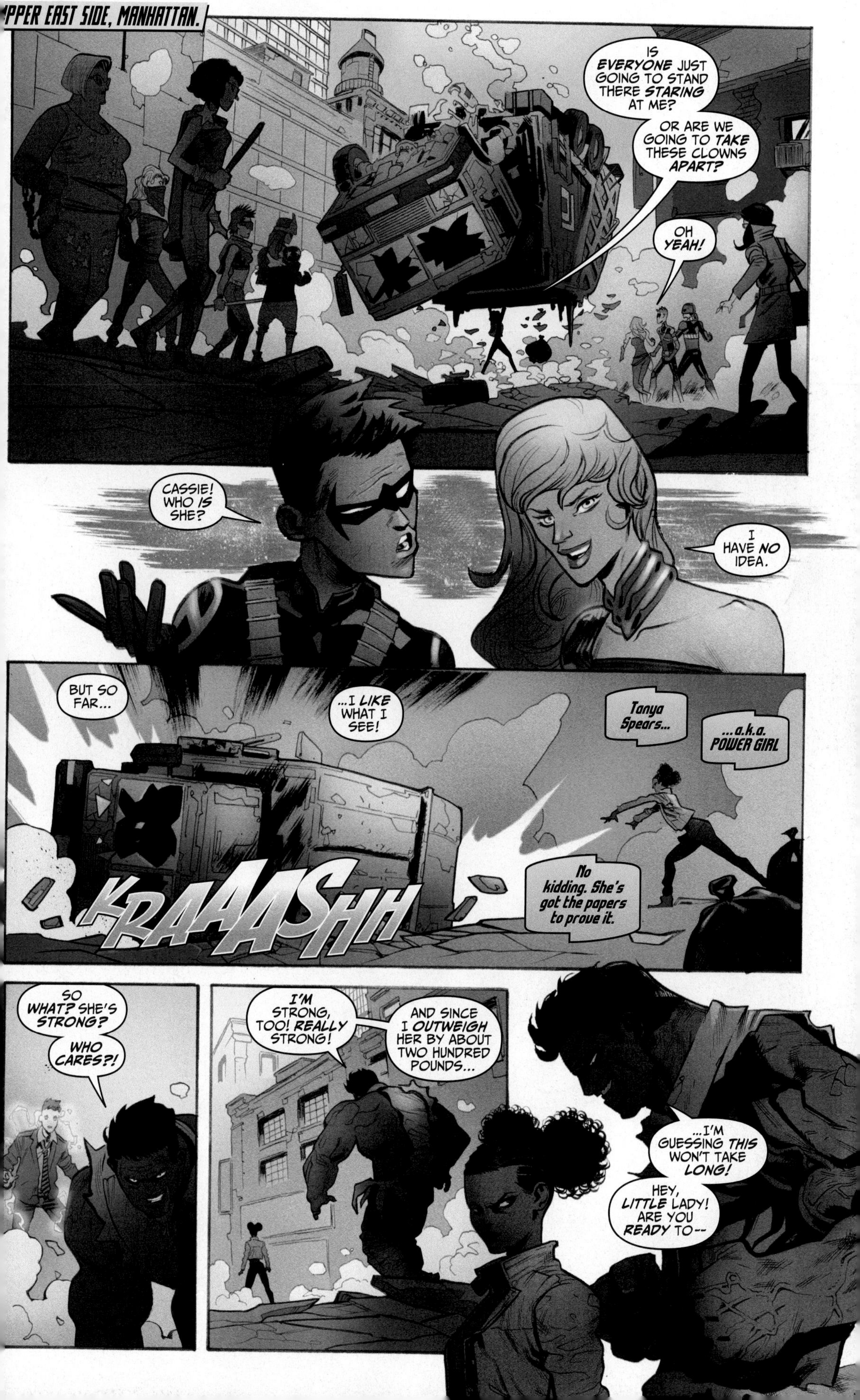

PPER EAST SIDE, MANHATTAN.
IS EVERYONE JUST GOING TO STAND THERE STARING AT ME?
OR ARE WE GOING TO TAKE THESE CLOWNS APART?
OH YEAH!
CASSIE! WHO IS SHE?
I HAVE NO IDEA.
BUT SO FAR...
...I LIKE WHAT I SEE!
Tanya Spears...
...a.k.a. POWER GIRL
KRAAASHH
No kidding. She's got the papers to prove it.
SO WHAT? SHE'S STRONG?
WHO CARES?!
I'M STRONG, TOO! REALLY STRONG!
AND SINCE I OUTWEIGH HER BY ABOUT TWO HUNDRED POUNDS...
...I'M GUESSING THIS WON'T TAKE LONG!
HEY, LITTLE LADY! ARE YOU READY TO--

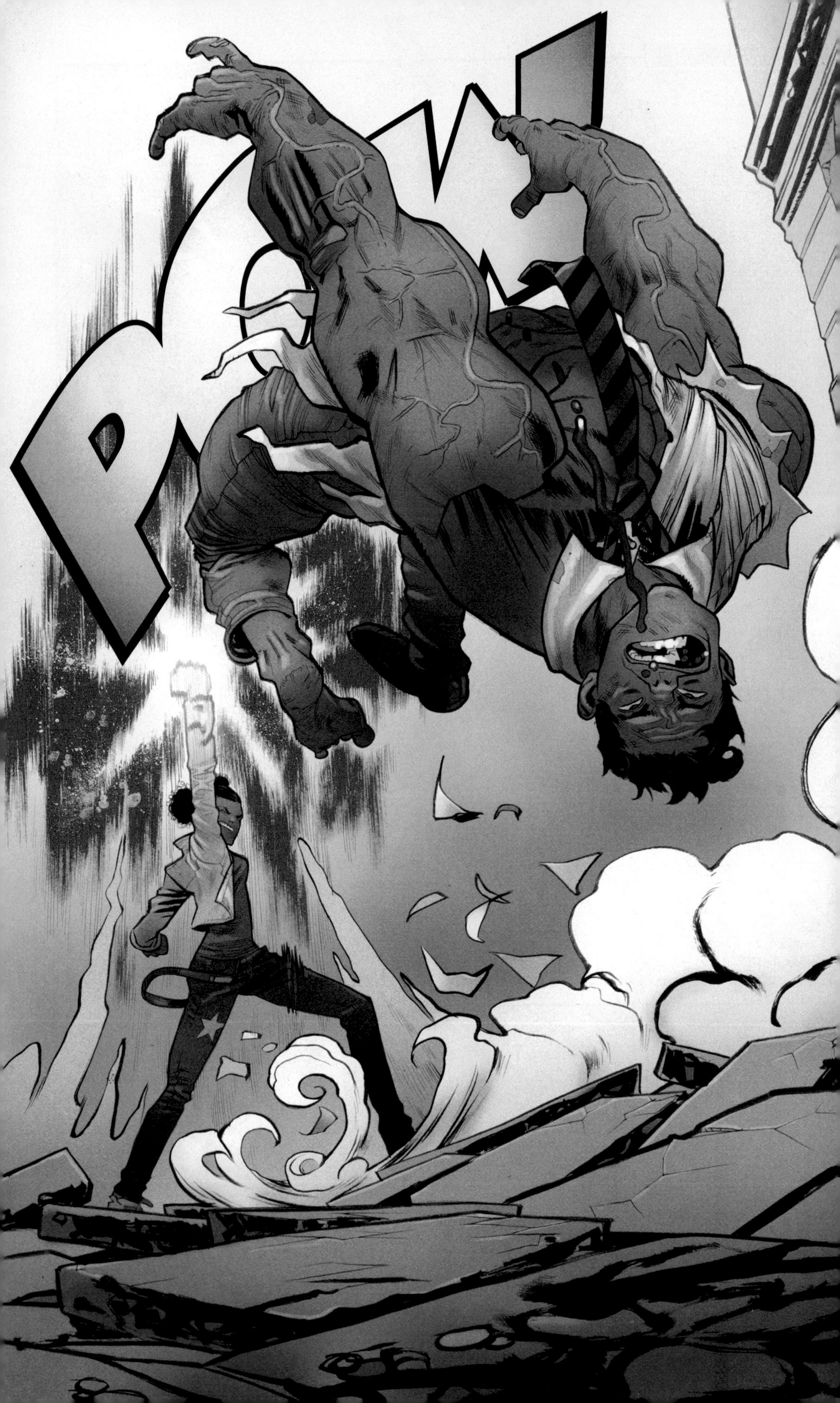
POW

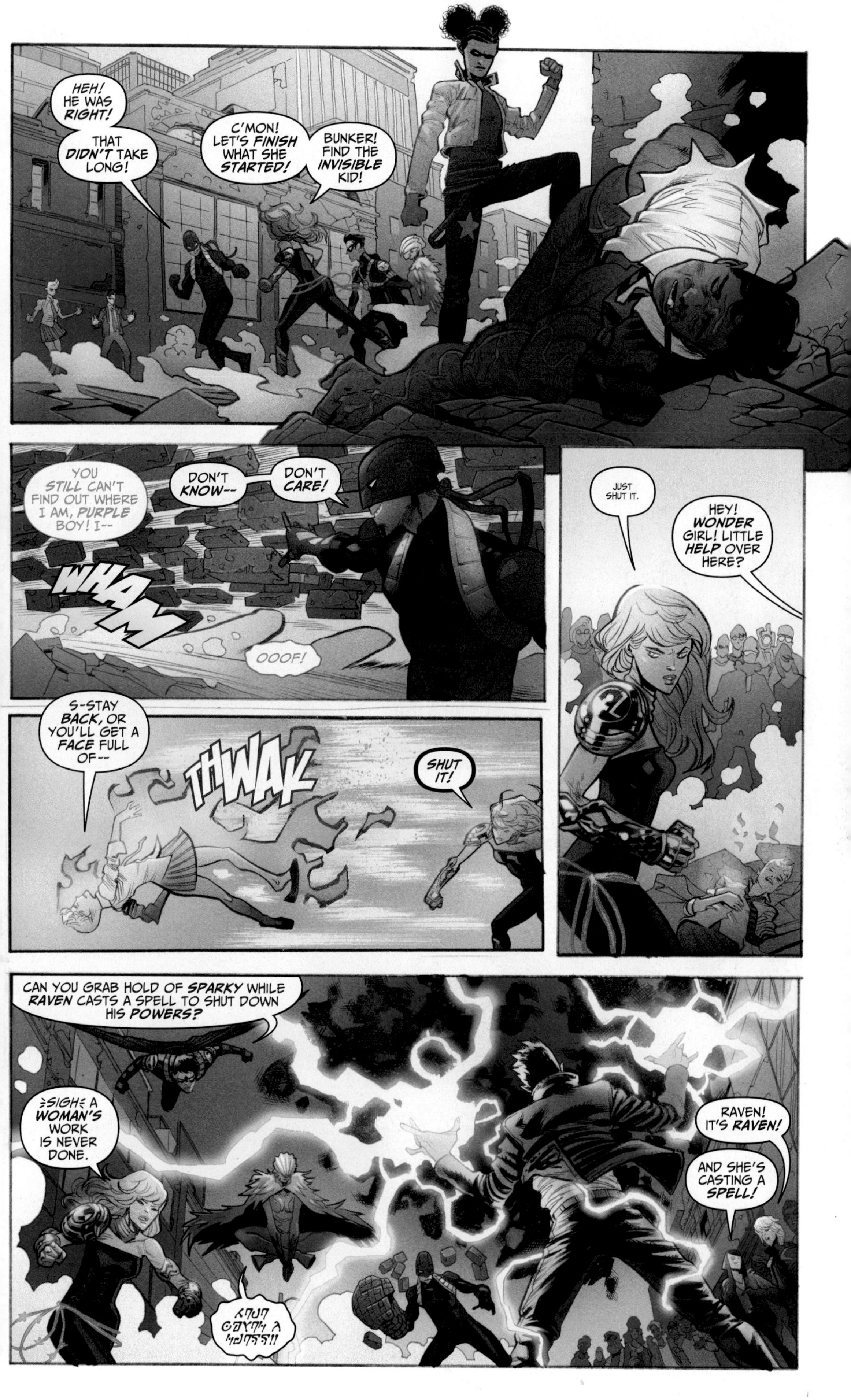
HEH! HE WAS RIGHT!
THAT DIDN'T TAKE LONG!
C'MON! LET'S FINISH WHAT SHE STARTED!
BUNKER! FIND THE INVISIBLE KID!
YOU STILL CAN'T FIND OUT WHERE I AM, PURPLE BOY! I--
DON'T KNOW--
DON'T CARE!
WHAM
OOOF!
JUST SHUT IT.
HEY! WONDER GIRL! LITTLE HELP OVER HERE?
S-STAY BACK, OR YOU'LL GET A FACE FULL OF--
THWAK
SHUT IT!
CAN YOU GRAB HOLD OF SPARKY WHILE RAVEN CASTS A SPELL TO SHUT DOWN HIS POWERS?
SIGH A WOMAN'S WORK IS NEVER DONE.
RAVEN! IT'S RAVEN!
AND SHE'S CASTING A SPELL!

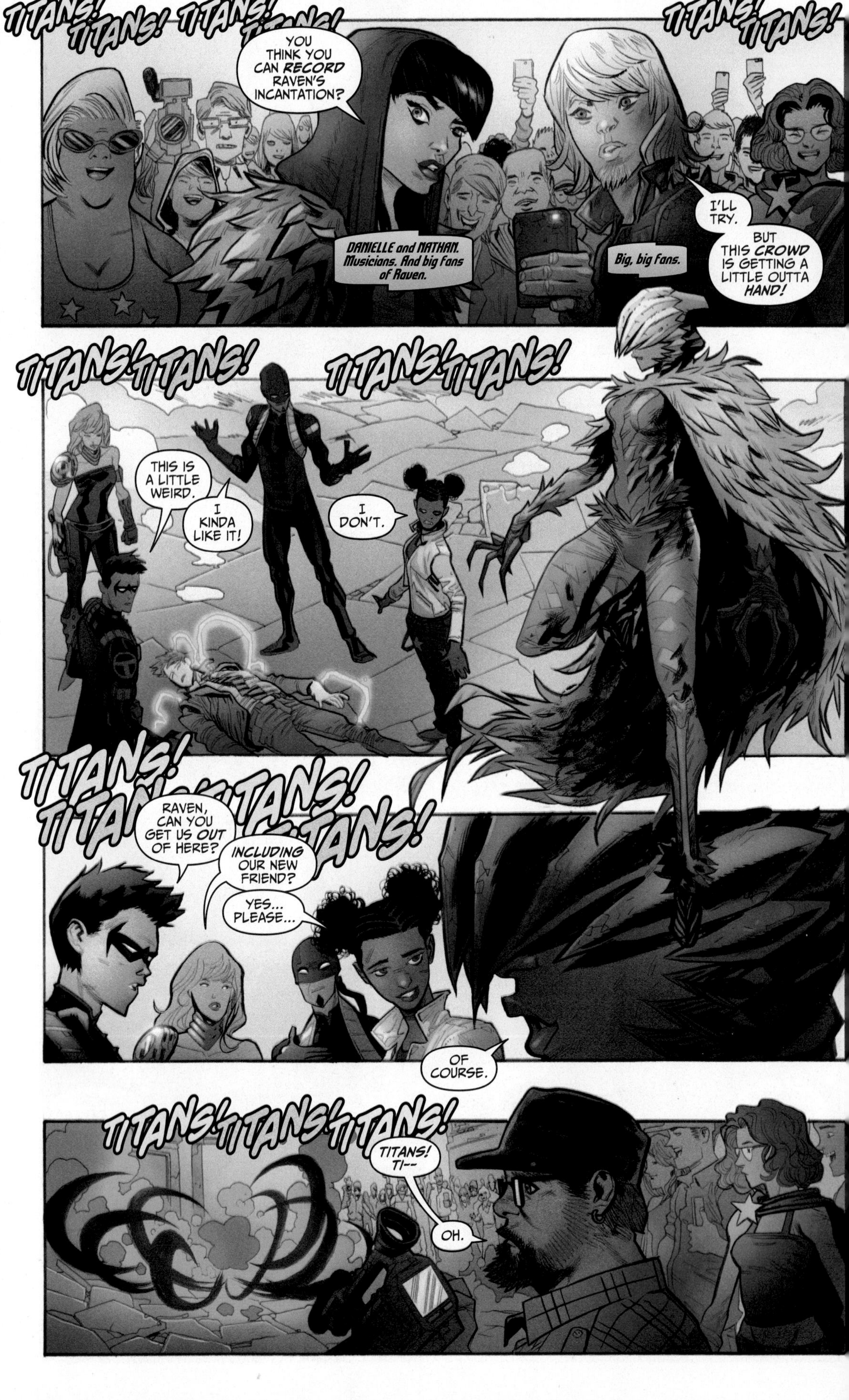
TITANS! TITANS! TITANS! TITANS!
YOU THINK YOU CAN RECORD RAVEN'S INCANTATION?
TITANS! TITANS!
DANIELLE and NATHAN. Musicians. And big fans of Raven.
Big, big fans.
I'LL TRY.
BUT THIS CROWD IS GETTING A LITTLE OUTTA HAND!
TITANS! TITANS!
TITANS! TITANS!
THIS IS A LITTLE WEIRD.
I KINDA LIKE IT!
I DON'T.
TITANS! TITANS! TITANS! TITANS!
RAVEN, CAN YOU GET US OUT OF HERE?
INCLUDING OUR NEW FRIEND?
YES... PLEASE...
OF COURSE.
TITANS! TITANS! TITANS!
TITANS! TI--
OH.

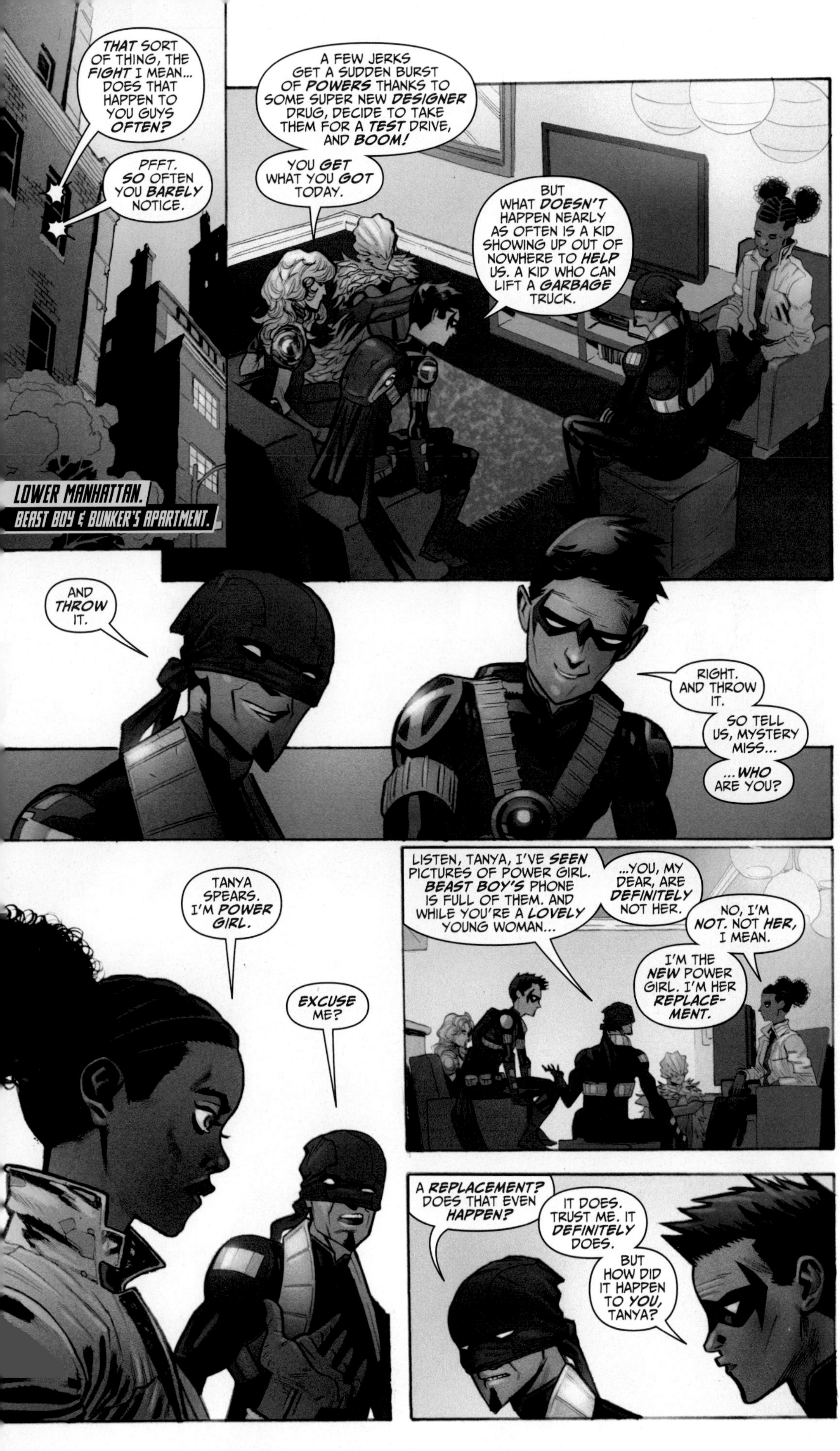
THAT SORT OF THING, THE FIGHT I MEAN... DOES THAT HAPPEN TO YOU GUYS OFTEN?
PFFT. SO OFTEN YOU BARELY NOTICE.
LOWER MANHATTAN.
BEAST BOY & BUNKER'S APARTMENT.
A FEW JERKS GET A SUDDEN BURST OF POWERS THANKS TO SOME SUPER NEW DESIGNER DRUG, DECIDE TO TAKE THEM FOR A TEST DRIVE, AND BOOM!
YOU GET WHAT YOU GOT TODAY.
BUT WHAT DOESN'T HAPPEN NEARLY AS OFTEN IS A KID SHOWING UP OUT OF NOWHERE TO HELP US. A KID WHO CAN LIFT A GARBAGE TRUCK.
AND THROW IT.
RIGHT. AND THROW IT.
SO TELL US, MYSTERY MISS...
...WHO ARE YOU?
TANYA SPEARS. I'M POWER GIRL.
EXCUSE ME?
LISTEN, TANYA, I'VE SEEN PICTURES OF POWER GIRL. BEAST BOY'S PHONE IS FULL OF THEM. AND WHILE YOU'RE A LOVELY YOUNG WOMAN...
...YOU, MY DEAR, ARE DEFINITELY NOT HER.
NO, I'M NOT. NOT HER, I MEAN.
I'M THE NEW POWER GIRL. I'M HER REPLACE-MENT.
A REPLACEMENT? DOES THAT EVEN HAPPEN?
IT DOES. TRUST ME. IT DEFINITELY DOES.
BUT HOW DID IT HAPPEN TO YOU, TANYA?

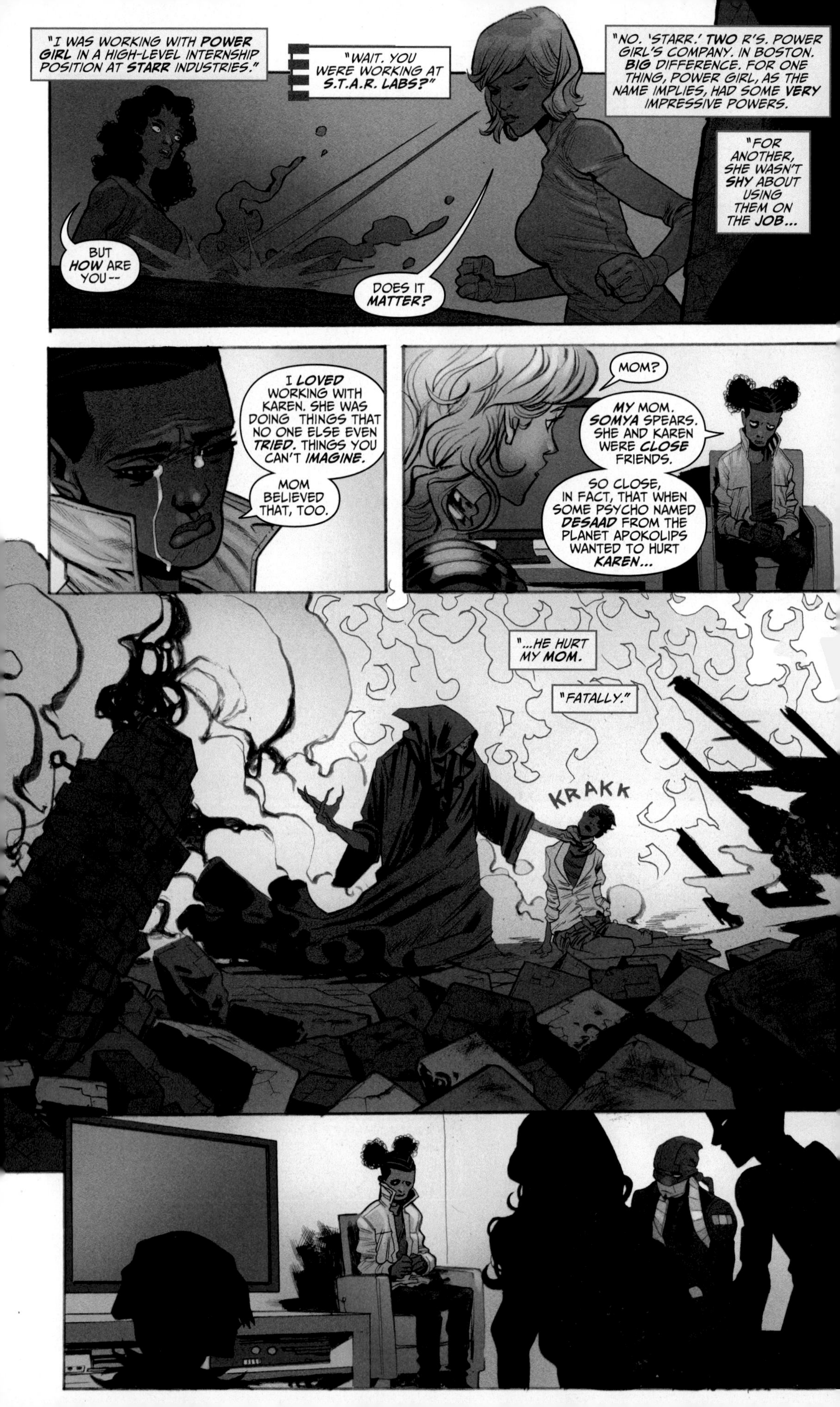
"I WAS WORKING WITH POWER GIRL IN A HIGH-LEVEL INTERNSHIP POSITION AT STARR INDUSTRIES."
"WAIT. YOU WERE WORKING AT S.T.A.R. LABS?"
"NO. 'STARR.' TWO R'S. POWER GIRL'S COMPANY. IN BOSTON. BIG DIFFERENCE. FOR ONE THING, POWER GIRL, AS THE NAME IMPLIES, HAD SOME VERY IMPRESSIVE POWERS.
"FOR ANOTHER, SHE WASN'T SHY ABOUT USING THEM ON THE JOB...
BUT HOW ARE YOU--
DOES IT MATTER?
I LOVED WORKING WITH KAREN. SHE WAS DOING THINGS THAT NO ONE ELSE EVEN TRIED. THINGS YOU CAN'T IMAGINE.
MOM BELIEVED THAT, TOO.
MOM?
MY MOM. SOMYA SPEARS. SHE AND KAREN WERE CLOSE FRIENDS.
SO CLOSE, IN FACT, THAT WHEN SOME PSYCHO NAMED DESAAD FROM THE PLANET APOKOLIPS WANTED TO HURT KAREN...
"...HE HURT MY MOM.
"FATALLY."
KRAKK

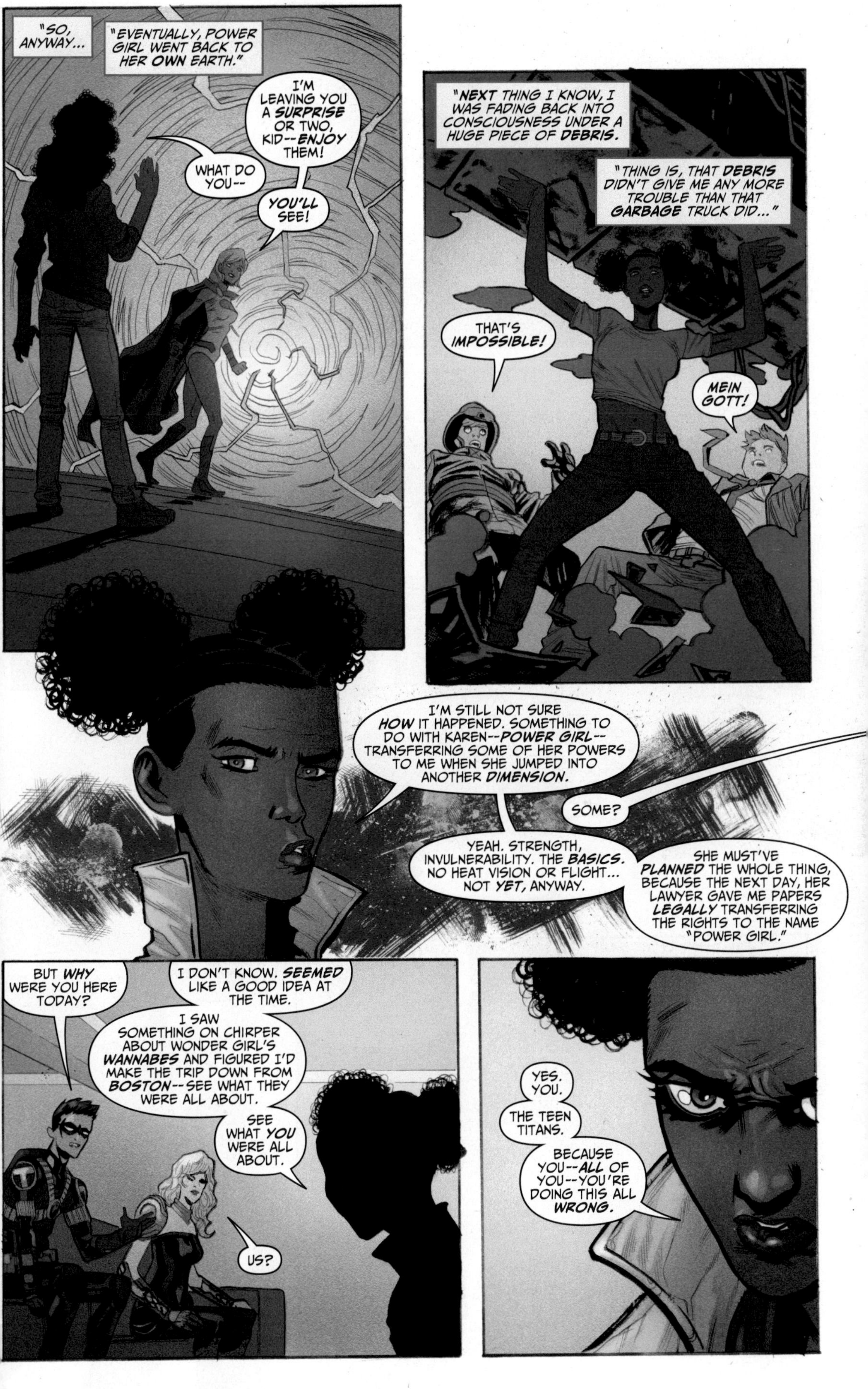
"SO, ANYWAY...
"EVENTUALLY, POWER GIRL WENT BACK TO HER OWN EARTH."
I'M LEAVING YOU A SURPRISE OR TWO, KID--ENJOY THEM!
WHAT DO YOU--
YOU'LL SEE!
"NEXT THING I KNOW, I WAS FADING BACK INTO CONSCIOUSNESS UNDER A HUGE PIECE OF DEBRIS.
"THING IS, THAT DEBRIS DIDN'T GIVE ME ANY MORE TROUBLE THAN THAT GARBAGE TRUCK DID..."
THAT'S IMPOSSIBLE!
MEIN GOTT!
I'M STILL NOT SURE HOW IT HAPPENED. SOMETHING TO DO WITH KAREN--POWER GIRL--TRANSFERRING SOME OF HER POWERS TO ME WHEN SHE JUMPED INTO ANOTHER DIMENSION.
SOME?
YEAH. STRENGTH, INVULNERABILITY. THE BASICS. NO HEAT VISION OR FLIGHT... NOT YET, ANYWAY.
SHE MUST'VE PLANNED THE WHOLE THING, BECAUSE THE NEXT DAY, HER LAWYER GAVE ME PAPERS LEGALLY TRANSFERRING THE RIGHTS TO THE NAME "POWER GIRL."
BUT WHY WERE YOU HERE TODAY?
I DON'T KNOW. SEEMED LIKE A GOOD IDEA AT THE TIME.
I SAW SOMETHING ON CHIRPER ABOUT WONDER GIRL'S WANNABES AND FIGURED I'D MAKE THE TRIP DOWN FROM BOSTON--SEE WHAT THEY WERE ALL ABOUT.
SEE WHAT YOU WERE ALL ABOUT.
US?
YES. YOU.
THE TEEN TITANS.
BECAUSE YOU--ALL OF YOU--YOU'RE DOING THIS ALL WRONG.

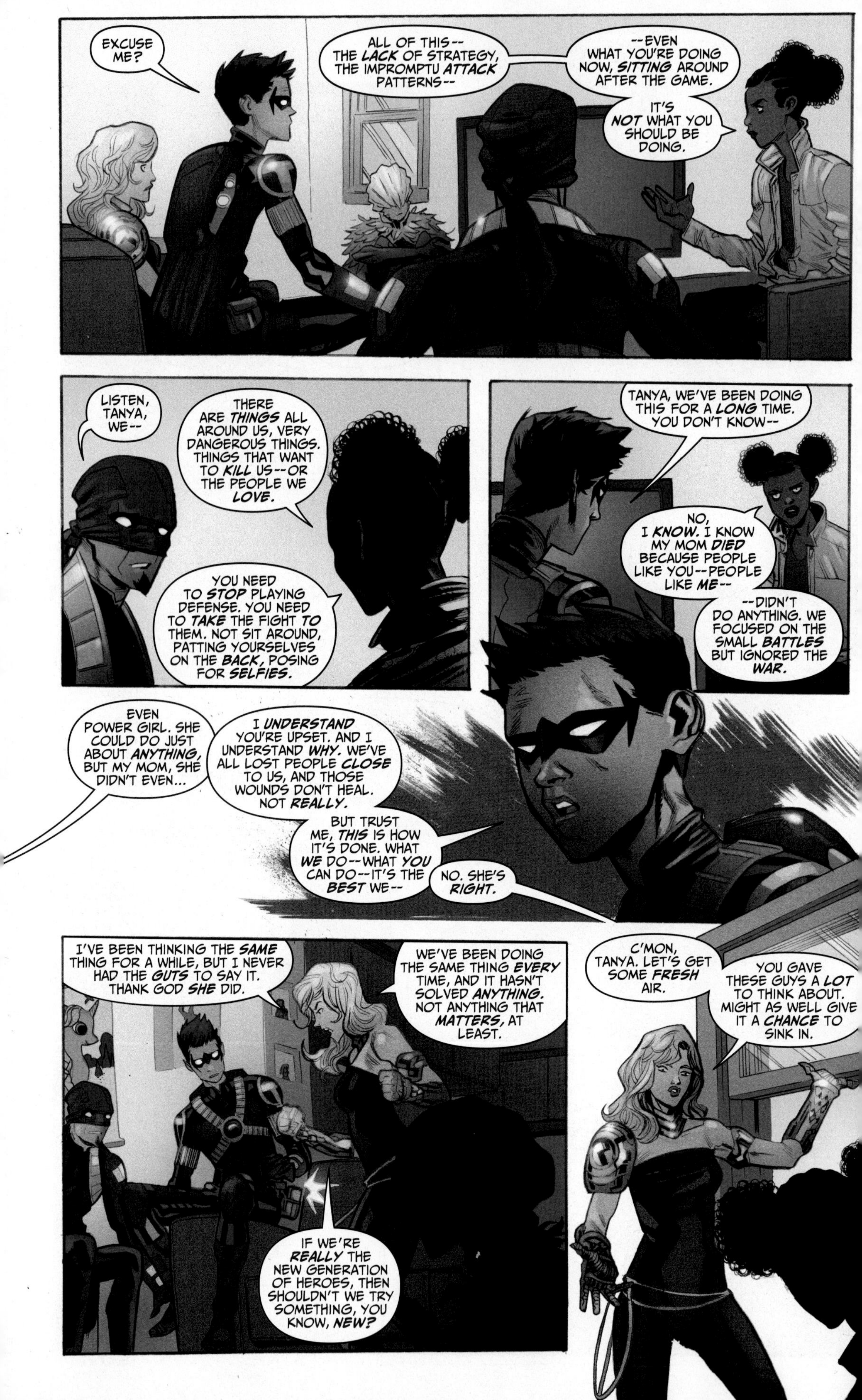
EXCUSE ME?
ALL OF THIS-- THE LACK OF STRATEGY, THE IMPROMPTU ATTACK PATTERNS--
--EVEN WHAT YOU'RE DOING NOW, SITTING AROUND AFTER THE GAME.
IT'S NOT WHAT YOU SHOULD BE DOING.
LISTEN, TANYA, WE--
THERE ARE THINGS ALL AROUND US, VERY DANGEROUS THINGS. THINGS THAT WANT TO KILL US--OR THE PEOPLE WE LOVE.
YOU NEED TO STOP PLAYING DEFENSE. YOU NEED TO TAKE THE FIGHT TO THEM. NOT SIT AROUND, PATTING YOURSELVES ON THE BACK, POSING FOR SELFIES.
TANYA, WE'VE BEEN DOING THIS FOR A LONG TIME. YOU DON'T KNOW--
NO, I KNOW. I KNOW MY MOM DIED BECAUSE PEOPLE LIKE YOU--PEOPLE LIKE ME--
--DIDN'T DO ANYTHING. WE FOCUSED ON THE SMALL BATTLES BUT IGNORED THE WAR.
EVEN POWER GIRL. SHE COULD DO JUST ABOUT ANYTHING, BUT MY MOM, SHE DIDN'T EVEN...
I UNDERSTAND YOU'RE UPSET. AND I UNDERSTAND WHY. WE'VE ALL LOST PEOPLE CLOSE TO US, AND THOSE WOUNDS DON'T HEAL. NOT REALLY.
BUT TRUST ME, THIS IS HOW IT'S DONE. WHAT WE DO--WHAT YOU CAN DO--IT'S THE BEST WE--
NO. SHE'S RIGHT.
I'VE BEEN THINKING THE SAME THING FOR A WHILE, BUT I NEVER HAD THE GUTS TO SAY IT. THANK GOD SHE DID.
WE'VE BEEN DOING THE SAME THING EVERY TIME, AND IT HASN'T SOLVED ANYTHING. NOT ANYTHING THAT MATTERS, AT LEAST.
IF WE'RE REALLY THE NEW GENERATION OF HEROES, THEN SHOULDN'T WE TRY SOMETHING, YOU KNOW, NEW?
C'MON, TANYA. LET'S GET SOME FRESH AIR.
YOU GAVE THESE GUYS A LOT TO THINK ABOUT. MIGHT AS WELL GIVE IT A CHANCE TO SINK IN.

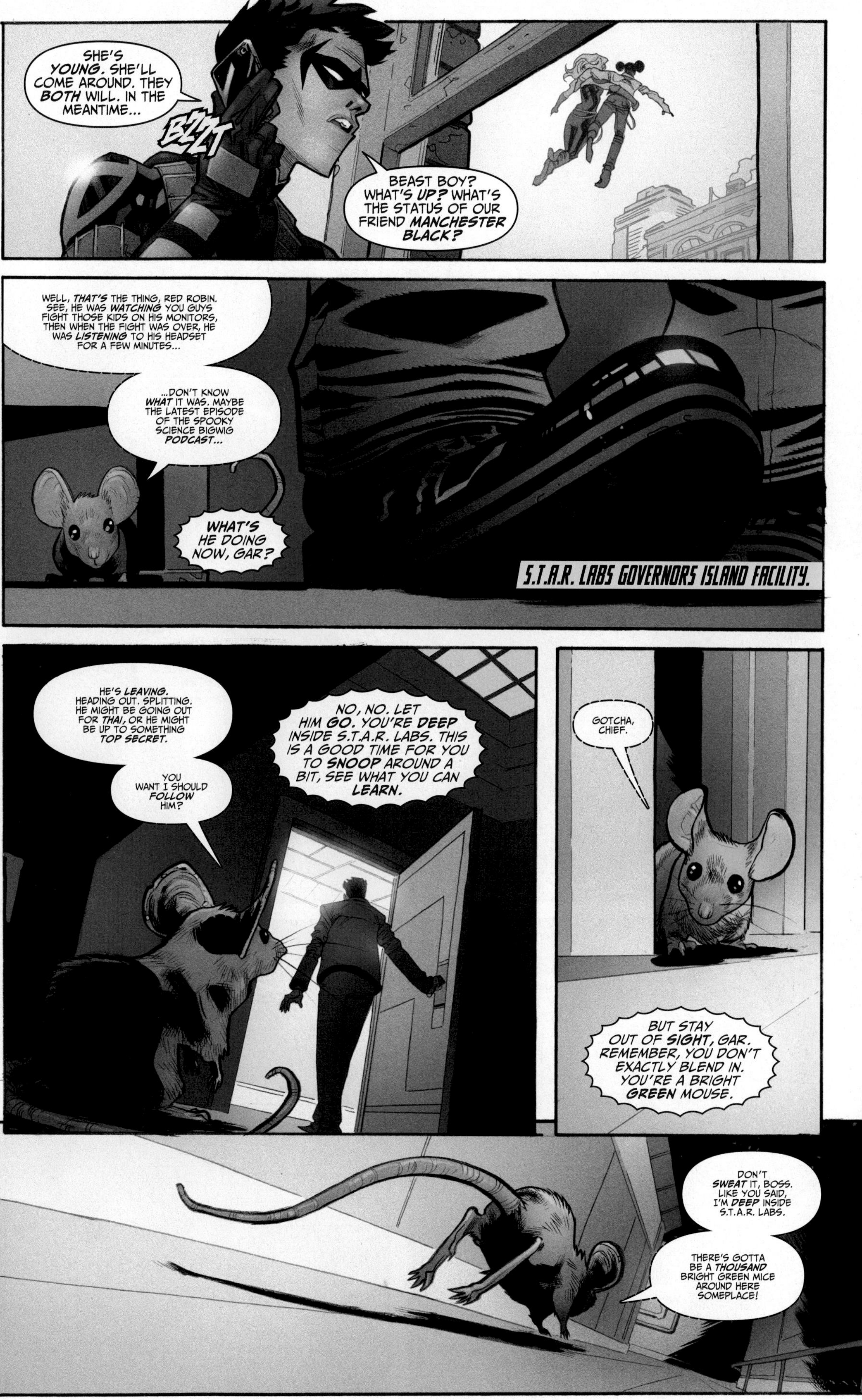

SHE'S YOUNG. SHE'LL COME AROUND. THEY BOTH WILL. IN THE MEANTIME...
BZZZT
BEAST BOY? WHAT'S UP? WHAT'S THE STATUS OF OUR FRIEND MANCHESTER BLACK?
WELL, THAT'S THE THING, RED ROBIN. SEE, HE WAS WATCHING YOU GUYS FIGHT THOSE KIDS ON HIS MONITORS, THEN WHEN THE FIGHT WAS OVER, HE WAS LISTENING TO HIS HEADSET FOR A FEW MINUTES...
...DON'T KNOW WHAT IT WAS. MAYBE THE LATEST EPISODE OF THE SPOOKY SCIENCE BIGWIG PODCAST...
WHAT'S HE DOING NOW, GAR?
S.T.A.R. LABS GOVERNORS ISLAND FACILITY.
HE'S LEAVING. HEADING OUT. SPLITTING. HE MIGHT BE GOING OUT FOR THAI, OR HE MIGHT BE UP TO SOMETHING TOP SECRET.
YOU WANT I SHOULD FOLLOW HIM?
NO, NO. LET HIM GO. YOU'RE DEEP INSIDE S.T.A.R. LABS. THIS IS A GOOD TIME FOR YOU TO SNOOP AROUND A BIT, SEE WHAT YOU CAN LEARN.
GOTCHA, CHIEF.
BUT STAY OUT OF SIGHT, GAR. REMEMBER, YOU DON'T EXACTLY BLEND IN. YOU'RE A BRIGHT GREEN MOUSE.
DON'T SWEAT IT, BOSS. LIKE YOU SAID, I'M DEEP INSIDE S.T.A.R. LABS.
THERE'S GOTTA BE A THOUSAND BRIGHT GREEN MICE AROUND HERE SOMEPLACE!

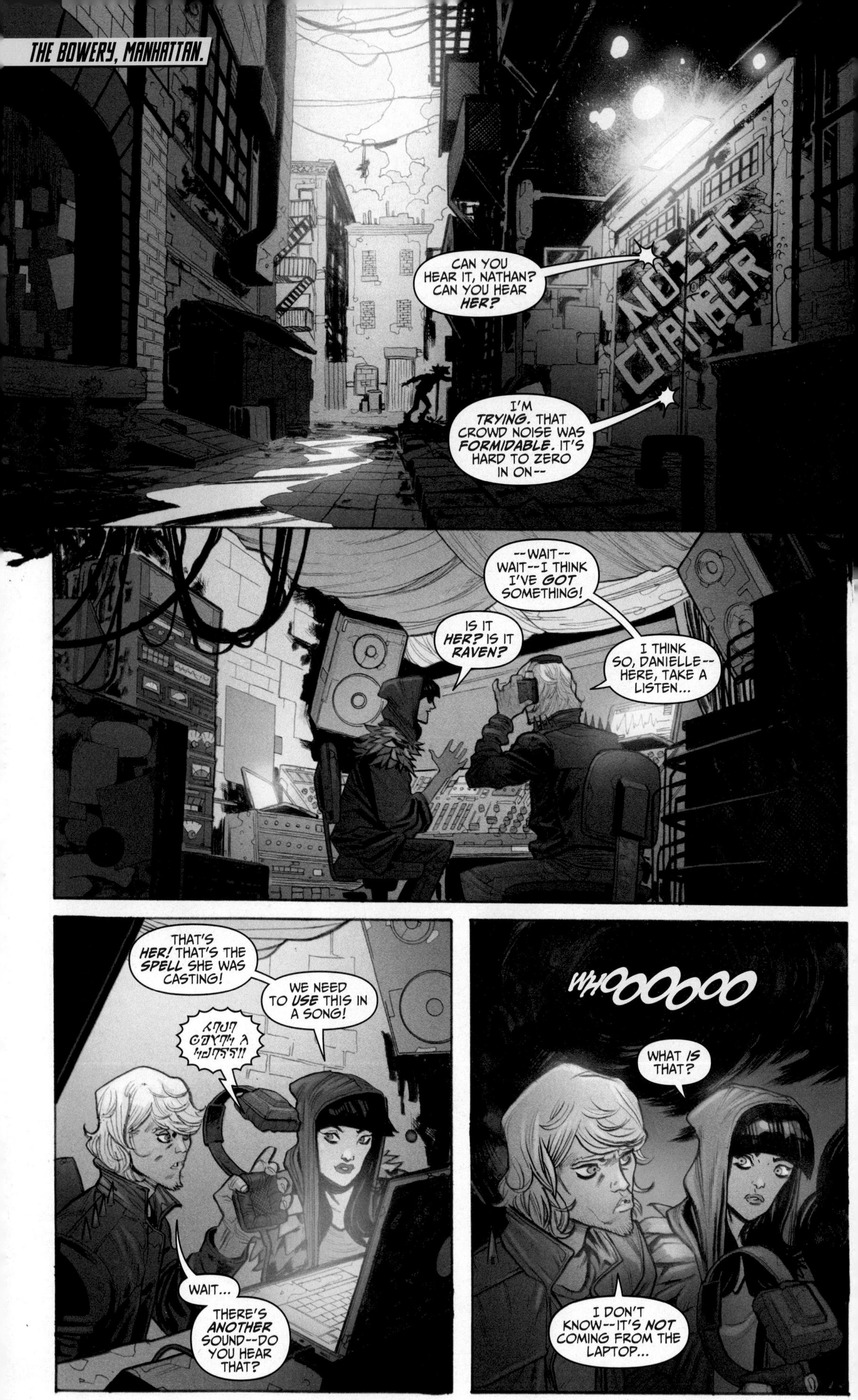
THE BOWERY, MANHATTAN.
CAN YOU HEAR IT, NATHAN? CAN YOU HEAR HER?
NOISE CHAMBER
I'M TRYING. THAT CROWD NOISE WAS FORMIDABLE. IT'S HARD TO ZERO IN ON--
--WAIT-- WAIT--I THINK I'VE GOT SOMETHING!
IS IT HER? IS IT RAVEN?
I THINK SO, DANIELLE-- HERE, TAKE A LISTEN...
THAT'S HER! THAT'S THE SPELL SHE WAS CASTING!
WE NEED TO USE THIS IN A SONG!
WAIT...
THERE'S ANOTHER SOUND--DO YOU HEAR THAT?
WHOOOOOO
WHAT IS THAT?
I DON'T KNOW--IT'S NOT COMING FROM THE LAPTOP...

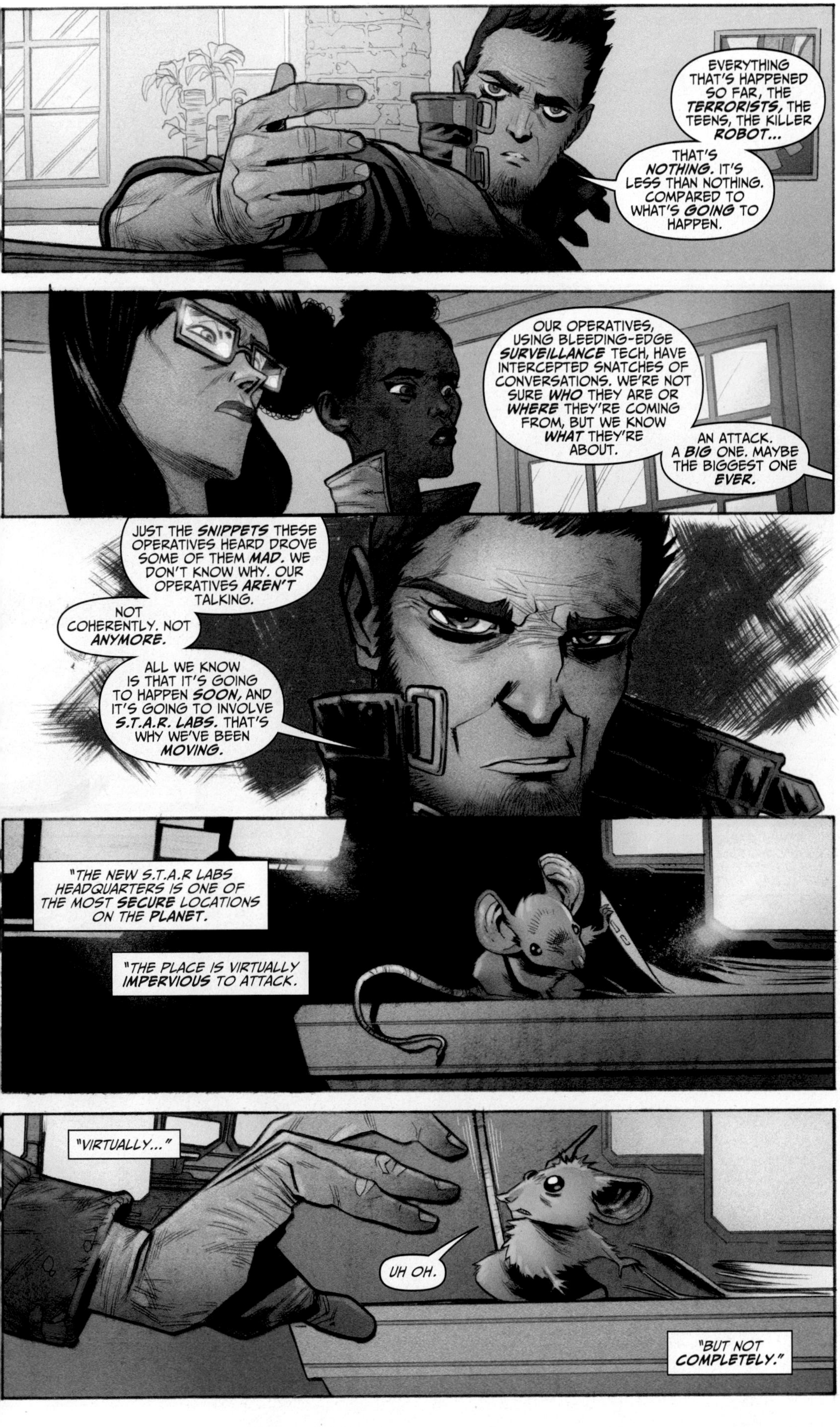
EVERYTHING THAT'S HAPPENED SO FAR, THE TERRORISTS, THE TEENS, THE KILLER ROBOT...
THAT'S NOTHING. IT'S LESS THAN NOTHING. COMPARED TO WHAT'S GOING TO HAPPEN.
OUR OPERATIVES, USING BLEEDING-EDGE SURVEILLANCE TECH, HAVE INTERCEPTED SNATCHES OF CONVERSATIONS. WE'RE NOT SURE WHO THEY ARE OR WHERE THEY'RE COMING FROM, BUT WE KNOW WHAT THEY'RE ABOUT.
AN ATTACK. A BIG ONE. MAYBE THE BIGGEST ONE EVER.
JUST THE SNIPPETS THESE OPERATIVES HEARD DROVE SOME OF THEM MAD. WE DON'T KNOW WHY. OUR OPERATIVES AREN'T TALKING.
NOT COHERENTLY. NOT ANYMORE.
ALL WE KNOW IS THAT IT'S GOING TO HAPPEN SOON, AND IT'S GOING TO INVOLVE S.T.A.R. LABS. THAT'S WHY WE'VE BEEN MOVING.
"THE NEW S.T.A.R LABS HEADQUARTERS IS ONE OF THE MOST SECURE LOCATIONS ON THE PLANET.
"THE PLACE IS VIRTUALLY IMPERVIOUS TO ATTACK.
"VIRTUALLY..."
UH OH.
"BUT NOT COMPLETELY."

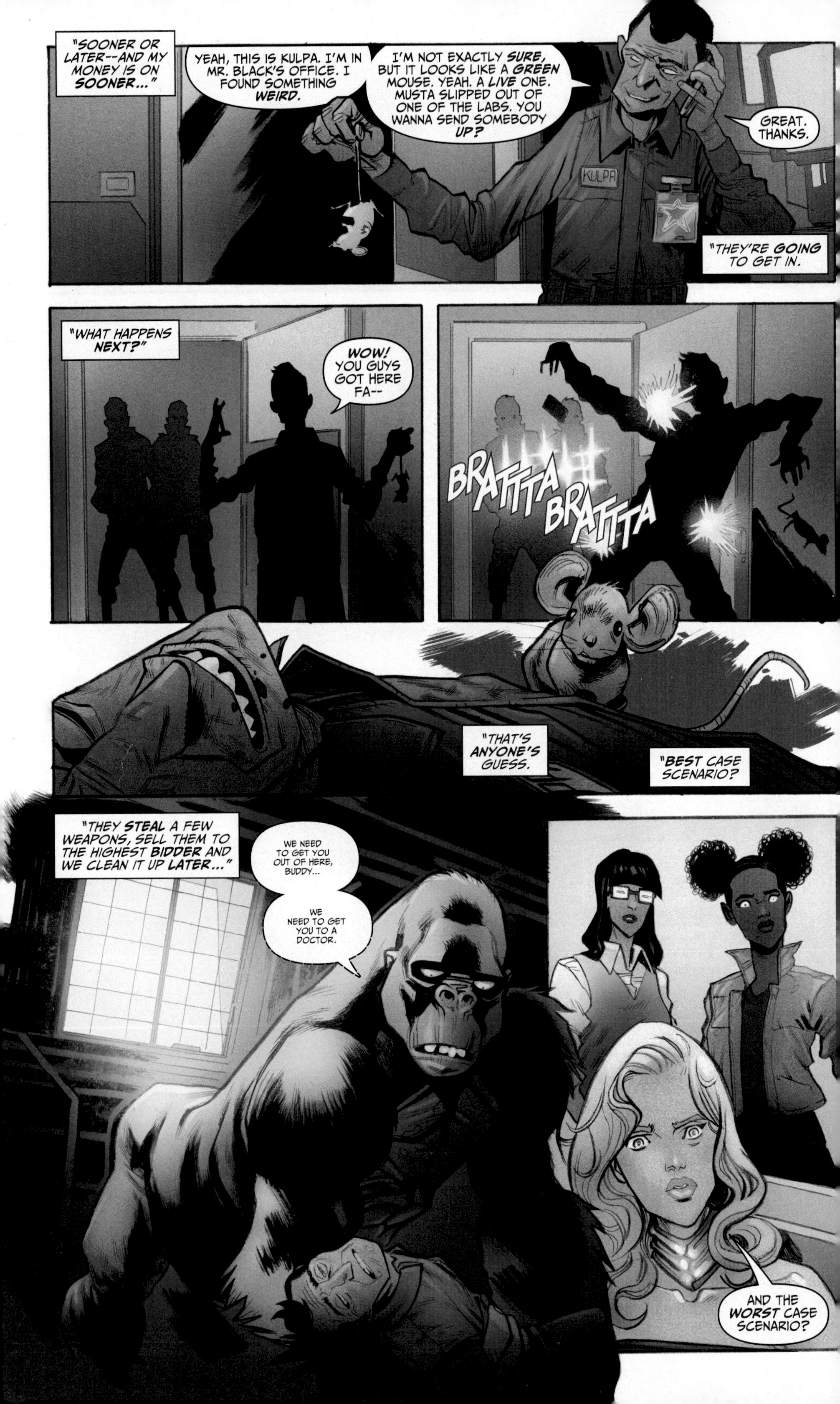
"SOONER OR LATER--AND MY MONEY IS ON SOONER..."
YEAH, THIS IS KULPA. I'M IN MR. BLACK'S OFFICE. I FOUND SOMETHING WEIRD.
I'M NOT EXACTLY SURE, BUT IT LOOKS LIKE A GREEN MOUSE. YEAH. A LIVE ONE. MUSTA SLIPPED OUT OF ONE OF THE LABS. YOU WANNA SEND SOMEBODY UP?
GREAT. THANKS.
KULPA
"THEY'RE GOING TO GET IN.
"WHAT HAPPENS NEXT?"
WOW! YOU GUYS GOT HERE FA--
BRATTTTA BRATTTTA
"THAT'S ANYONE'S GUESS.
"BEST CASE SCENARIO?
"THEY STEAL A FEW WEAPONS, SELL THEM TO THE HIGHEST BIDDER AND WE CLEAN IT UP LATER..."
WE NEED TO GET YOU OUT OF HERE, BUDDY...
WE NEED TO GET YOU TO A DOCTOR.
AND THE WORST CASE SCENARIO?

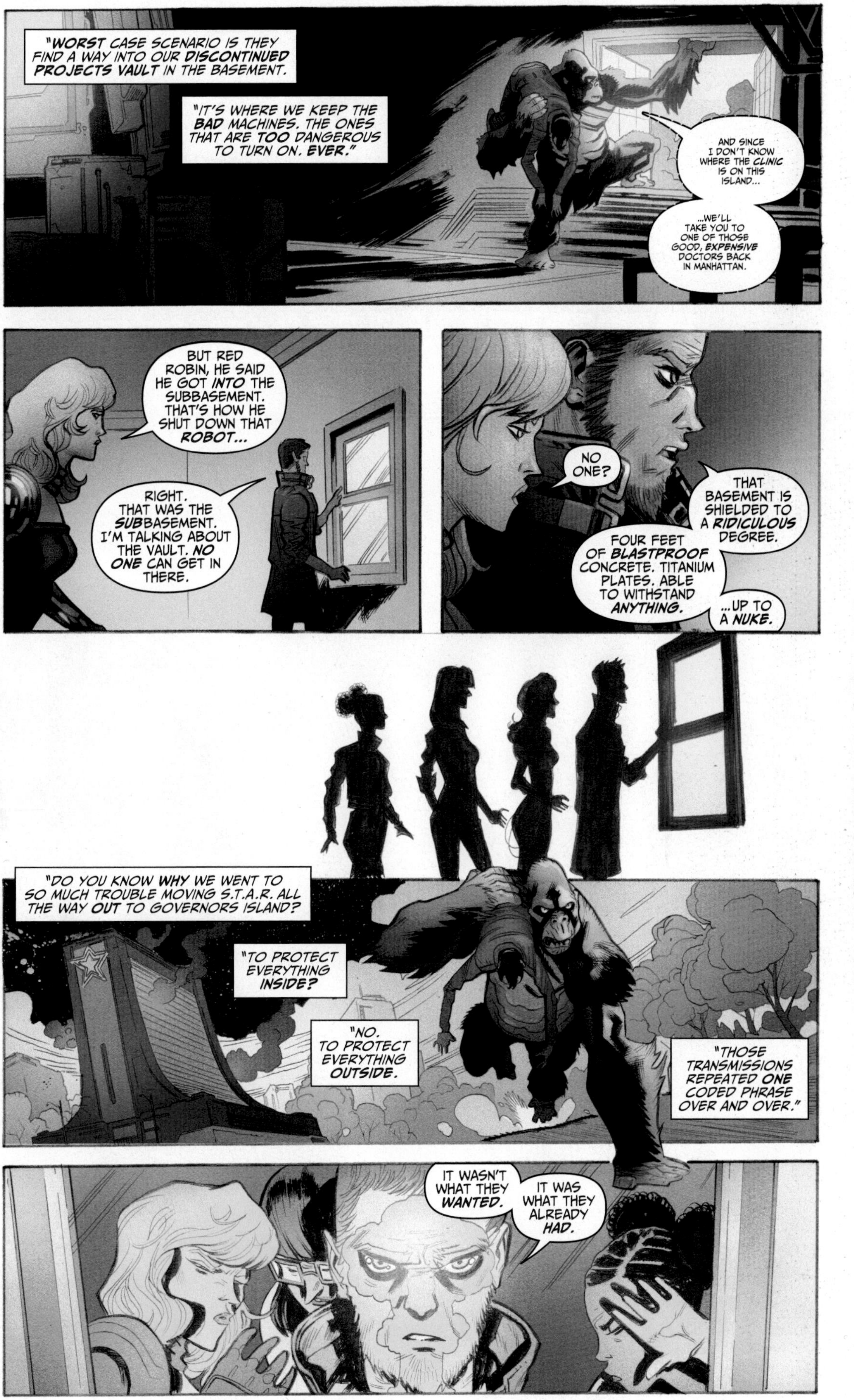
"WORST CASE SCENARIO IS THEY FIND A WAY INTO OUR DISCONTINUED PROJECTS VAULT IN THE BASEMENT.
"IT'S WHERE WE KEEP THE BAD MACHINES. THE ONES THAT ARE TOO DANGEROUS TO TURN ON. EVER."
AND SINCE I DON'T KNOW WHERE THE CLINIC IS ON THIS ISLAND...
...WE'LL TAKE YOU TO ONE OF THOSE GOOD, EXPENSIVE DOCTORS BACK IN MANHATTAN.
BUT RED ROBIN, HE SAID HE GOT INTO THE SUBBASEMENT. THAT'S HOW HE SHUT DOWN THAT ROBOT...
RIGHT. THAT WAS THE SUBBASEMENT. I'M TALKING ABOUT THE VAULT. NO ONE CAN GET IN THERE.
NO ONE?
THAT BASEMENT IS SHIELDED TO A RIDICULOUS DEGREE.
FOUR FEET OF BLASTPROOF CONCRETE. TITANIUM PLATES. ABLE TO WITHSTAND ANYTHING.
...UP TO A NUKE.
"DO YOU KNOW WHY WE WENT TO SO MUCH TROUBLE MOVING S.T.A.R. ALL THE WAY OUT TO GOVERNORS ISLAND?
"TO PROTECT EVERYTHING INSIDE?
"NO. TO PROTECT EVERYTHING OUTSIDE.
"THOSE TRANSMISSIONS REPEATED ONE CODED PHRASE OVER AND OVER."
IT WASN'T WHAT THEY WANTED.
IT WAS WHAT THEY ALREADY HAD.

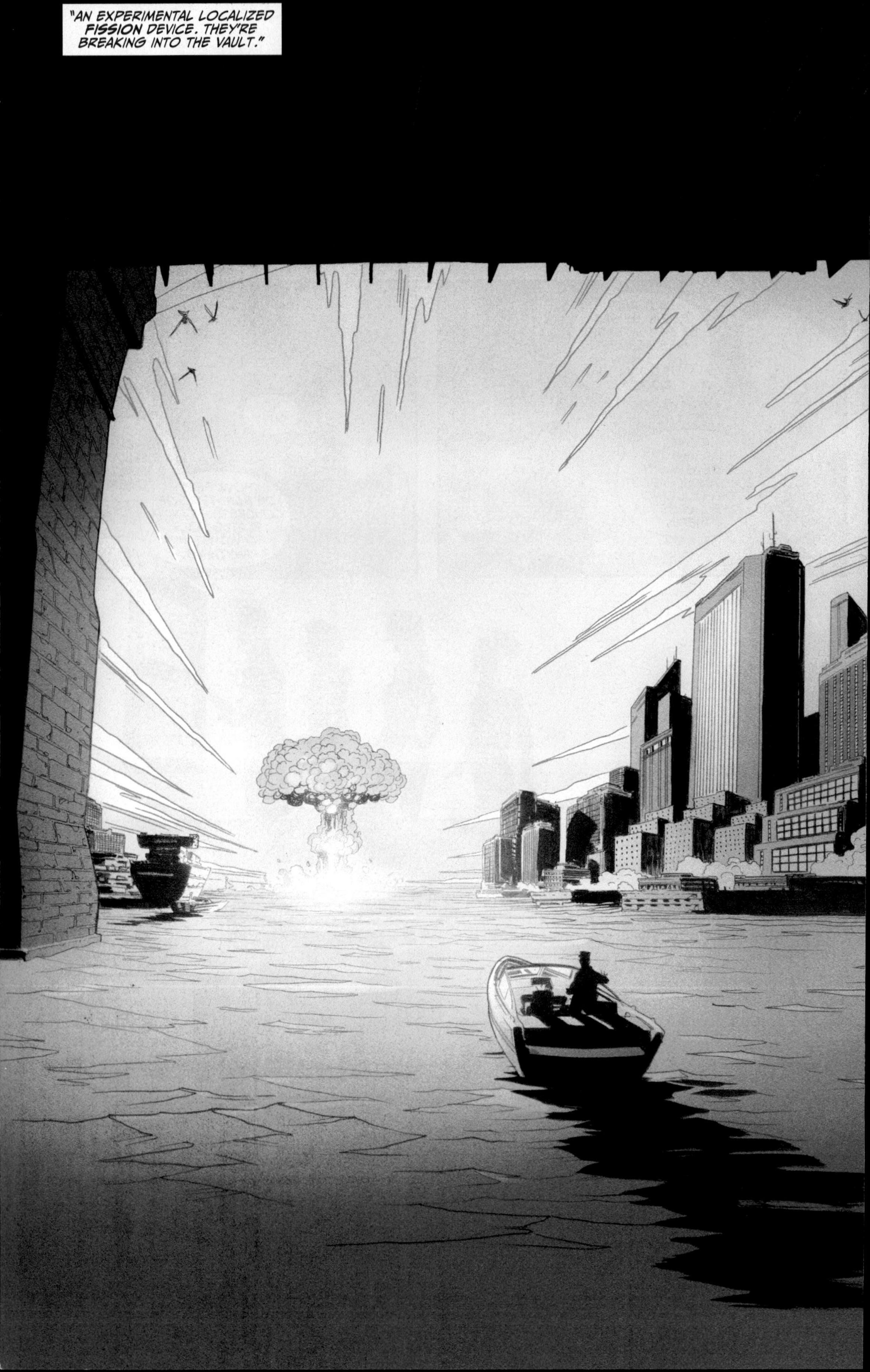
"AN EXPERIMENTAL LOCALIZED FISSION DEVICE. THEY'RE BREAKING INTO THE VAULT."

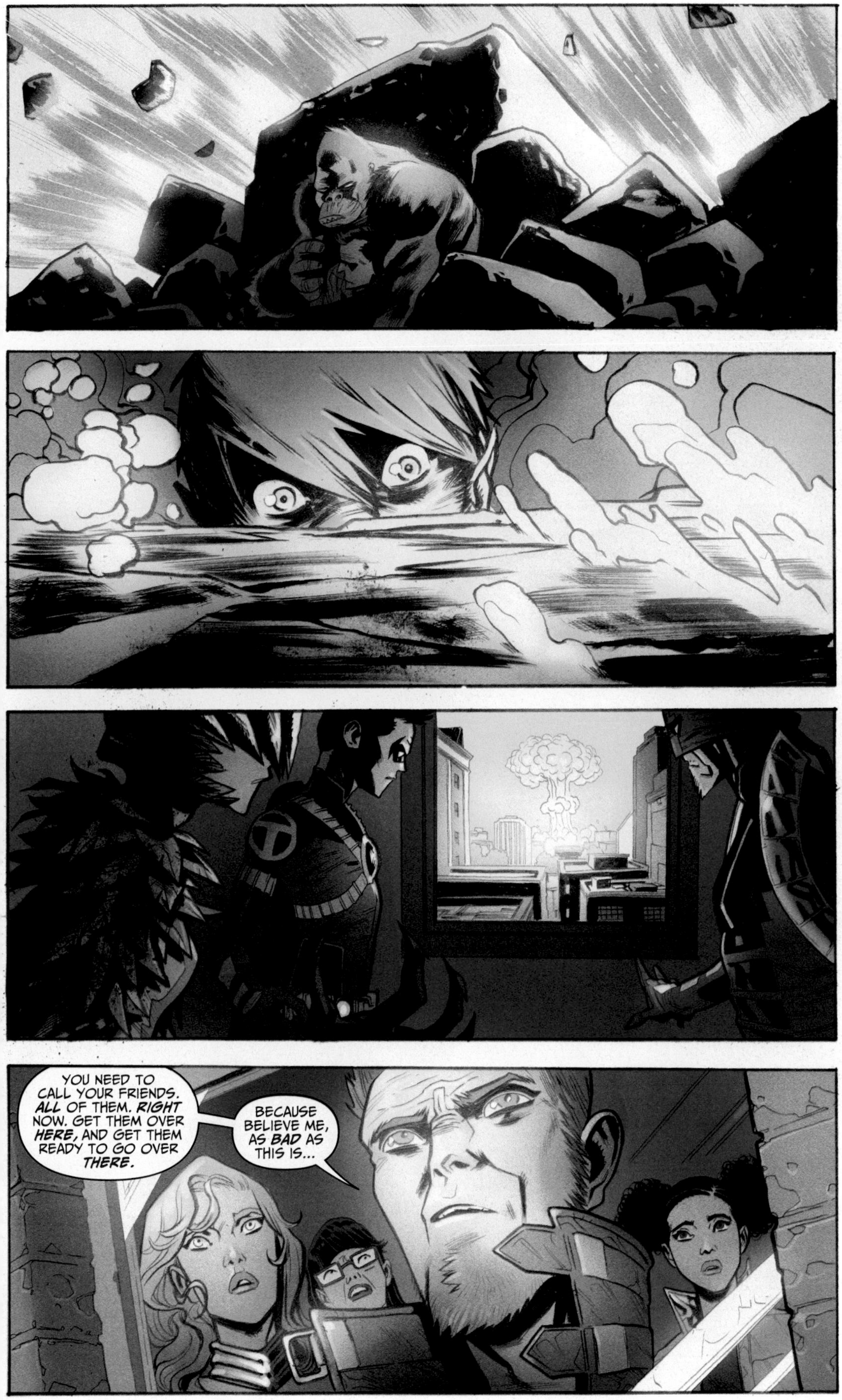
YOU NEED TO CALL YOUR FRIENDS. ALL OF THEM. RIGHT NOW. GET THEM OVER HERE, AND GET THEM READY TO GO OVER THERE.
BECAUSE BELIEVE ME, AS BAD AS THIS IS...

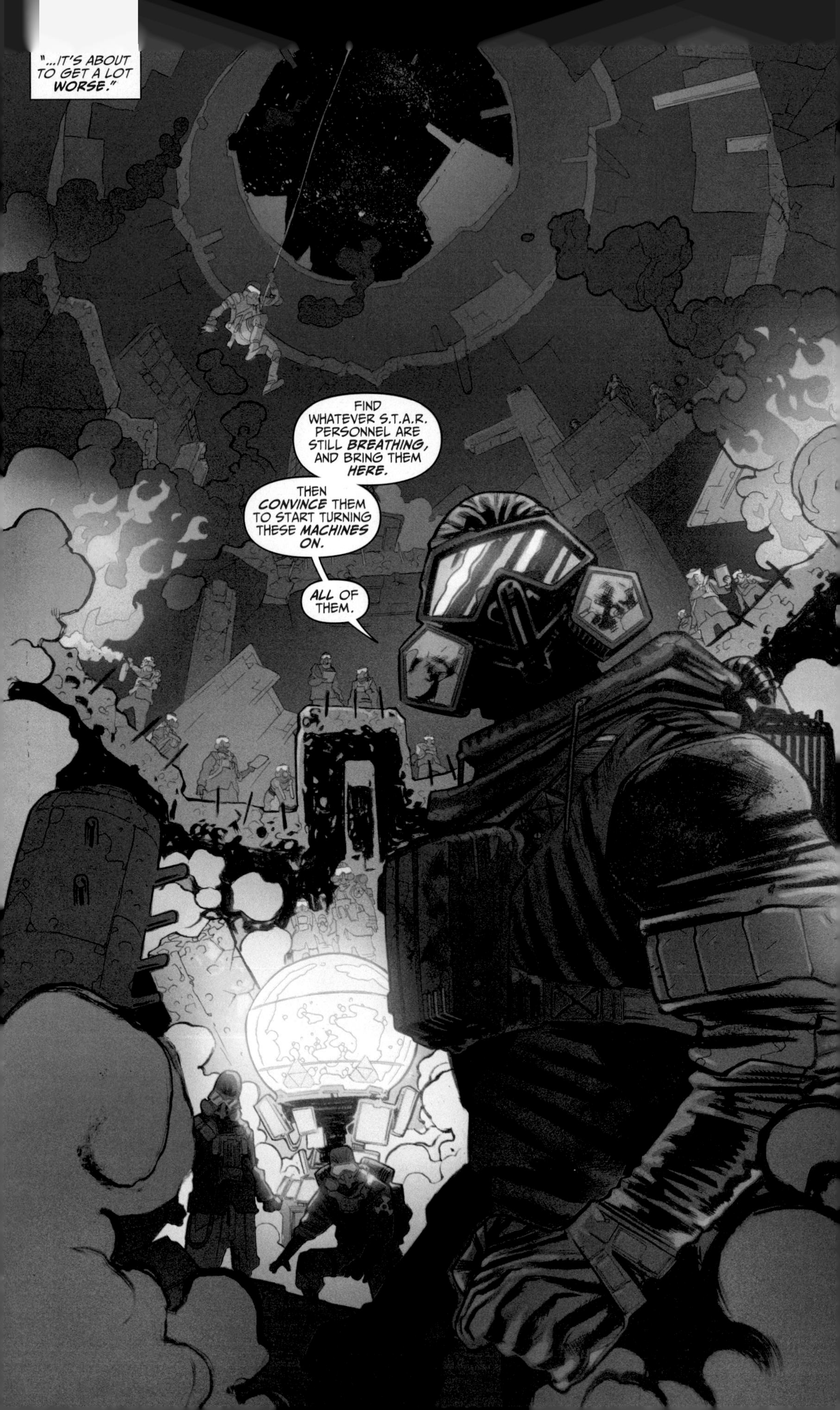

"...IT'S ABOUT TO GET A LOT WORSE."
FIND WHATEVER S.T.A.R. PERSONNEL ARE STILL BREATHING, AND BRING THEM HERE.
THEN CONVINCE THEM TO START TURNING THESE MACHINES ON.
ALL OF THEM.

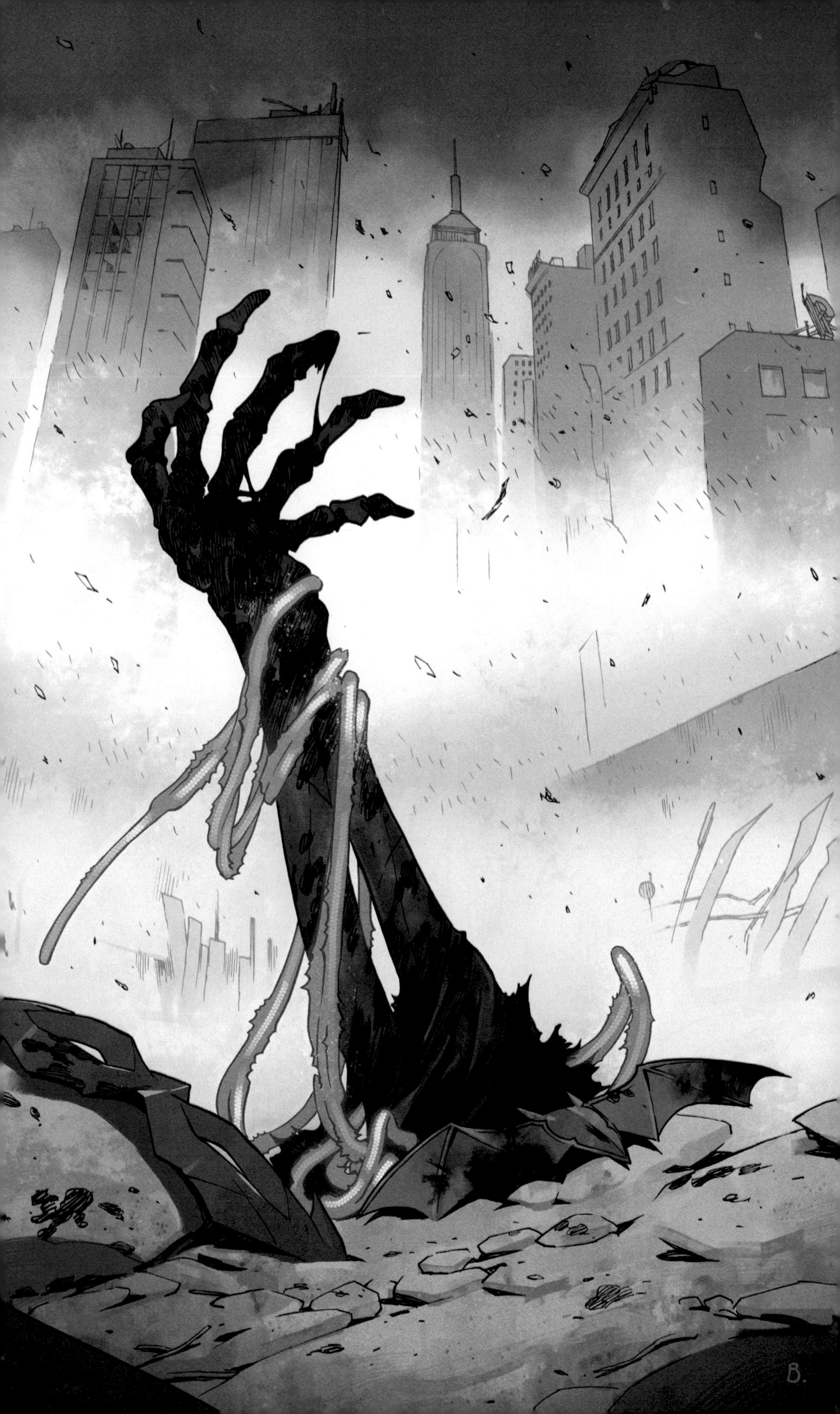

ONE BRIEF, SHINING MOMENT: PART 1

WILL PFEIFER writer KENNETH ROCAFORT artist DAN BROWN colorist JOHN J. HILL letterer cover art by BENGAL

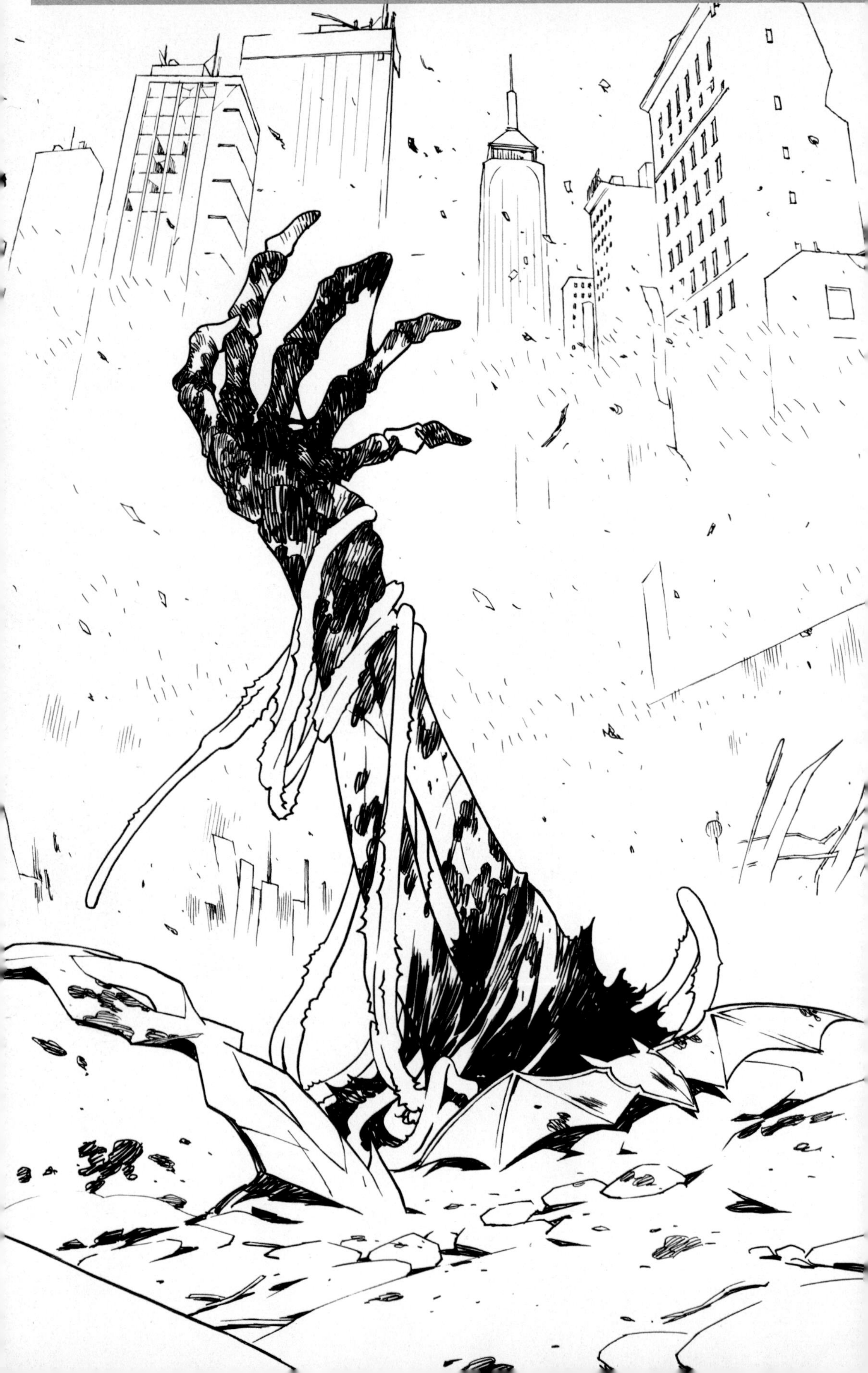

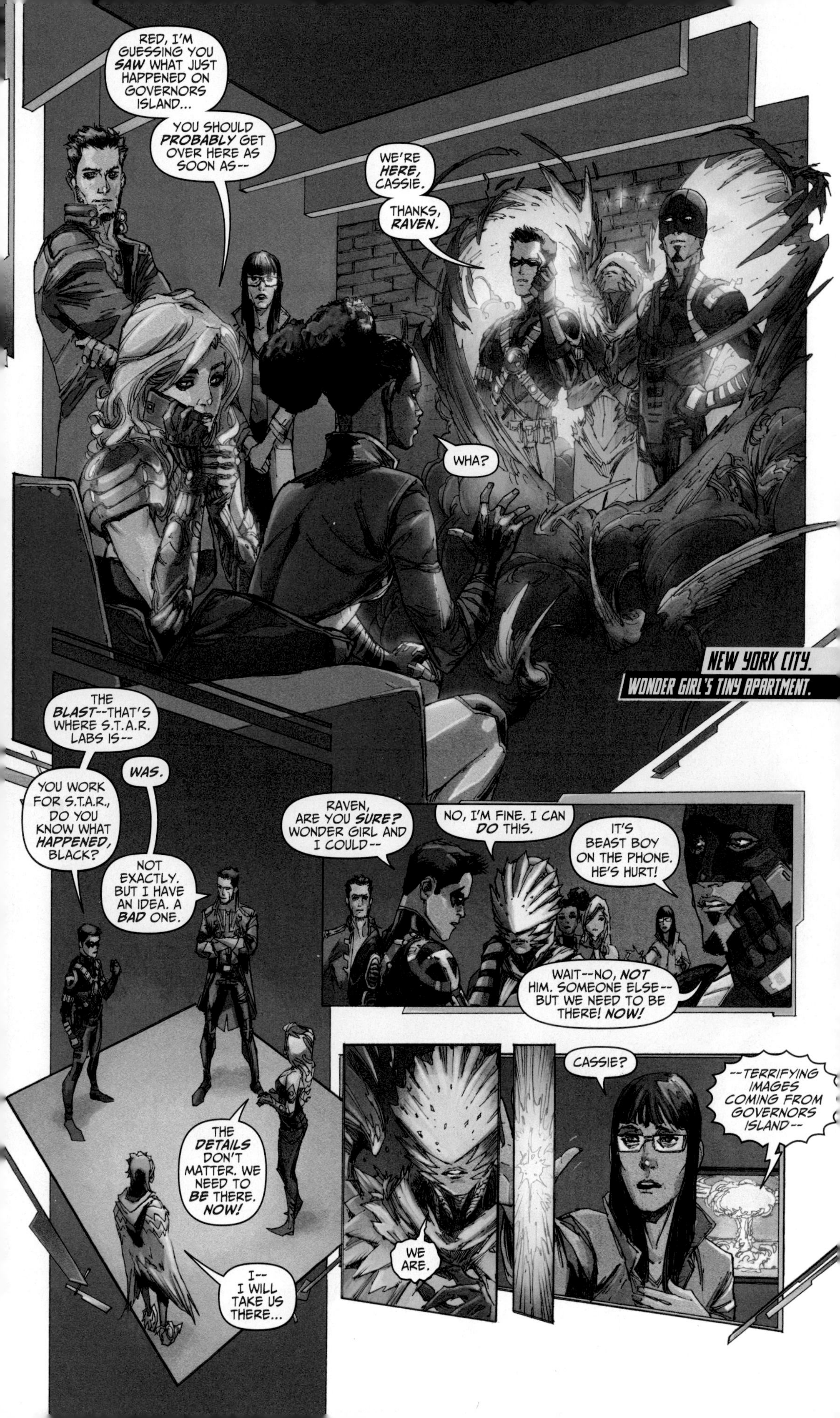
RED, I'M GUESSING YOU SAW WHAT JUST HAPPENED ON GOVERNORS ISLAND...
YOU SHOULD PROBABLY GET OVER HERE AS SOON AS--
WE'RE HERE, CASSIE.
THANKS, RAVEN.
WHA?
NEW YORK CITY.
WONDER GIRL'S TINY APARTMENT.
THE BLAST--THAT'S WHERE S.T.A.R. LABS IS--
WAS.
YOU WORK FOR S.T.A.R., DO YOU KNOW WHAT HAPPENED, BLACK?
NOT EXACTLY. BUT I HAVE AN IDEA. A BAD ONE.
THE DETAILS DON'T MATTER. WE NEED TO BE THERE. NOW!
I-- I WILL TAKE US THERE...
RAVEN, ARE YOU SURE? WONDER GIRL AND I COULD--
NO, I'M FINE. I CAN DO THIS.
IT'S BEAST BOY ON THE PHONE. HE'S HURT!
WAIT--NO, NOT HIM. SOMEONE ELSE-- BUT WE NEED TO BE THERE! NOW!
WE ARE.
CASSIE?
--TERRIFYING IMAGES COMING FROM GOVERNORS ISLAND--

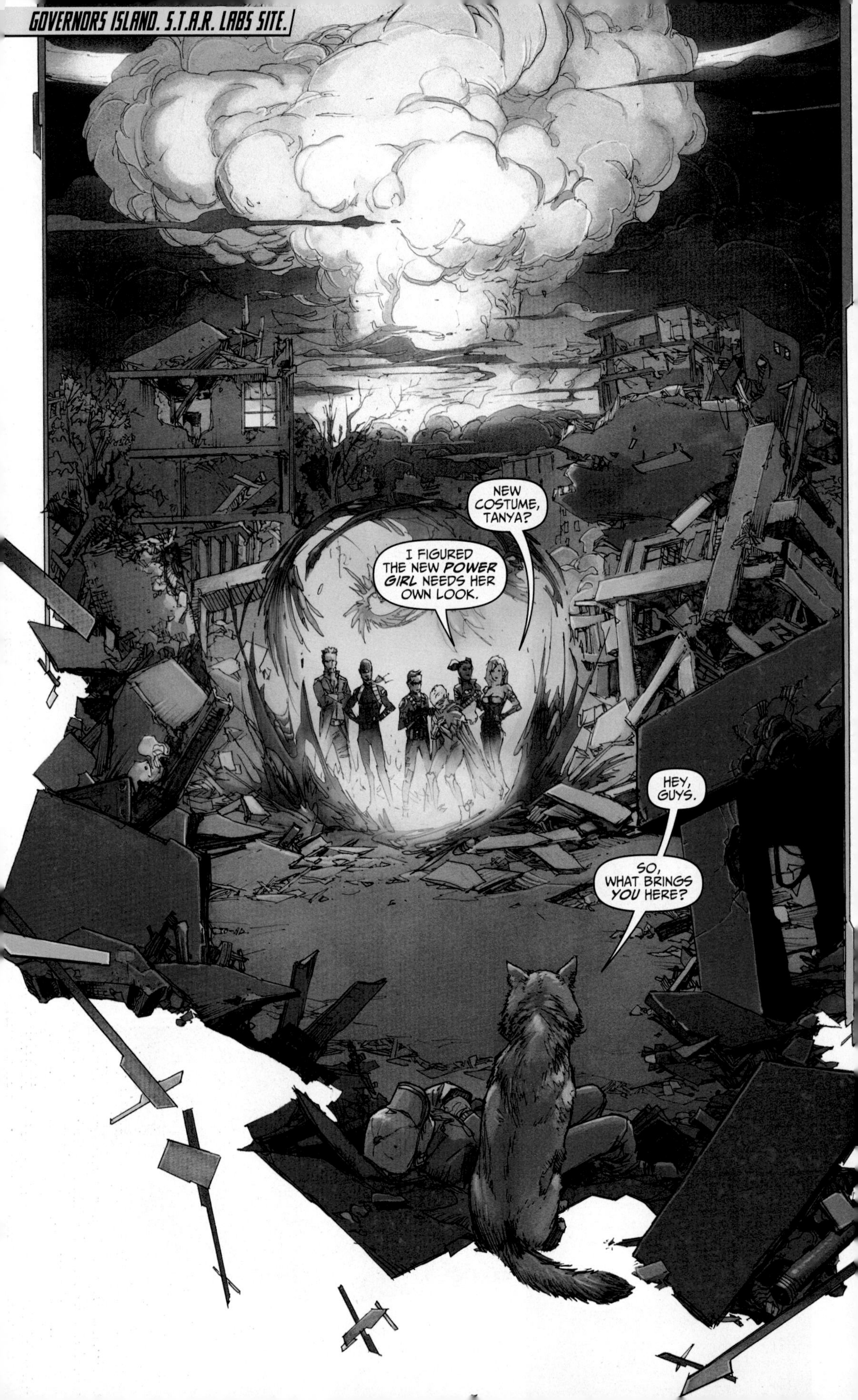
GOVERNORS ISLAND. S.T.A.R. LABS SITE.
NEW COSTUME, TANYA?
I FIGURED THE NEW POWER GIRL NEEDS HER OWN LOOK.
HEY, GUYS.
SO, WHAT BRINGS YOU HERE?

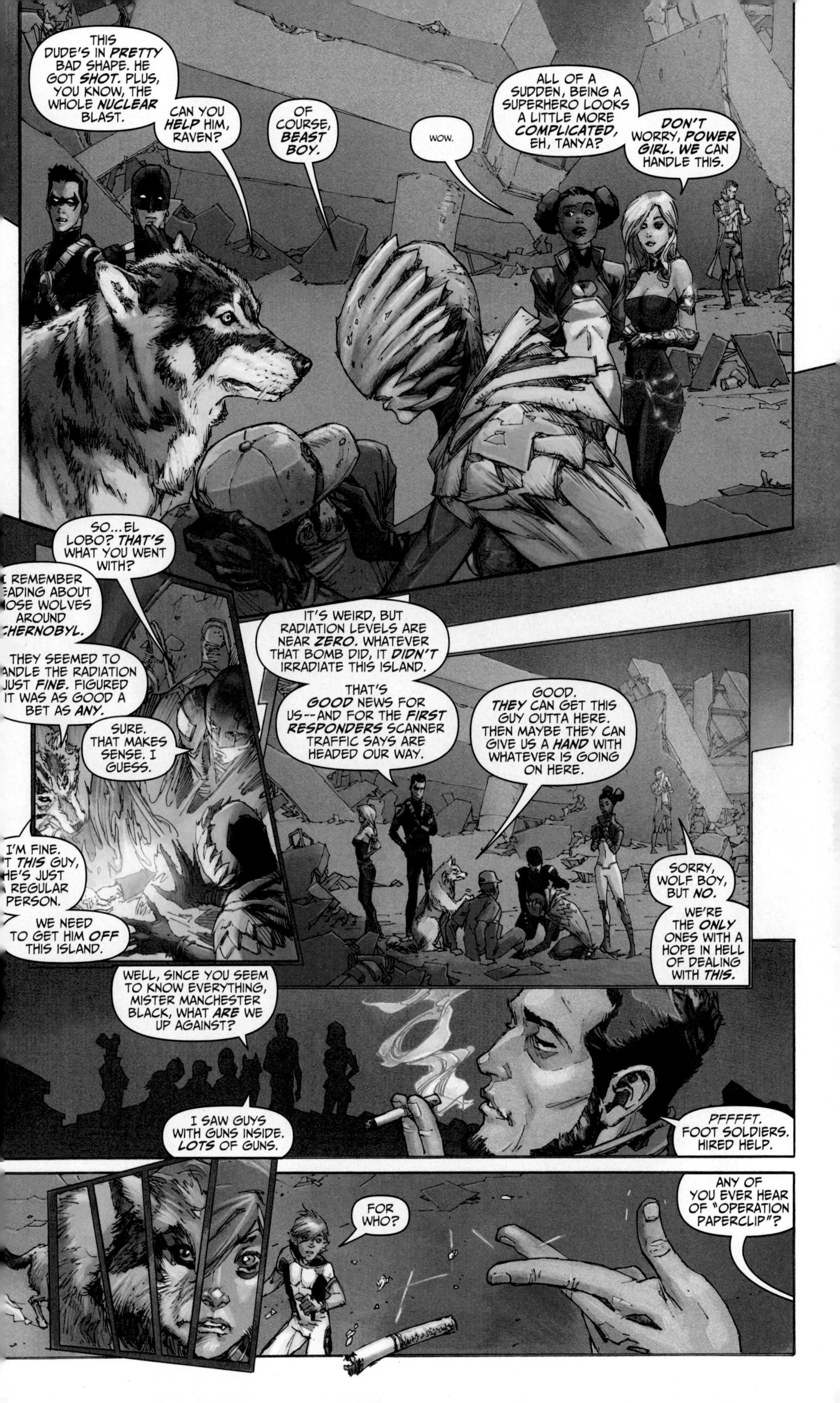

THIS DUDE'S IN PRETTY BAD SHAPE. HE GOT SHOT. PLUS, YOU KNOW, THE WHOLE NUCLEAR BLAST.
CAN YOU HELP HIM, RAVEN?
OF COURSE, BEAST BOY.
WOW.
ALL OF A SUDDEN, BEING A SUPERHERO LOOKS A LITTLE MORE COMPLICATED, EH, TANYA?
DON'T WORRY, POWER GIRL. WE CAN HANDLE THIS.
SO...EL LOBO? THAT'S WHAT YOU WENT WITH?
I REMEMBER READING ABOUT THOSE WOLVES AROUND CHERNOBYL.
THEY SEEMED TO HANDLE THE RADIATION JUST FINE. FIGURED IT WAS AS GOOD A BET AS ANY.
SURE. THAT MAKES SENSE. I GUESS.
I'M FINE. BUT THIS GUY, HE'S JUST A REGULAR PERSON.
WE NEED TO GET HIM OFF THIS ISLAND.
IT'S WEIRD, BUT RADIATION LEVELS ARE NEAR ZERO. WHATEVER THAT BOMB DID, IT DIDN'T IRRADIATE THIS ISLAND.
THAT'S GOOD NEWS FOR US--AND FOR THE FIRST RESPONDERS SCANNER TRAFFIC SAYS ARE HEADED OUR WAY.
GOOD. THEY CAN GET THIS GUY OUTTA HERE. THEN MAYBE THEY CAN GIVE US A HAND WITH WHATEVER IS GOING ON HERE.
SORRY, WOLF BOY, BUT NO.
WE'RE THE ONLY ONES WITH A HOPE IN HELL OF DEALING WITH THIS.
WELL, SINCE YOU SEEM TO KNOW EVERYTHING, MISTER MANCHESTER BLACK, WHAT ARE WE UP AGAINST?
I SAW GUYS WITH GUNS INSIDE. LOTS OF GUNS.
PFFFFT. FOOT SOLDIERS. HIRED HELP.
FOR WHO?
ANY OF YOU EVER HEAR OF "OPERATION PAPERCLIP"?

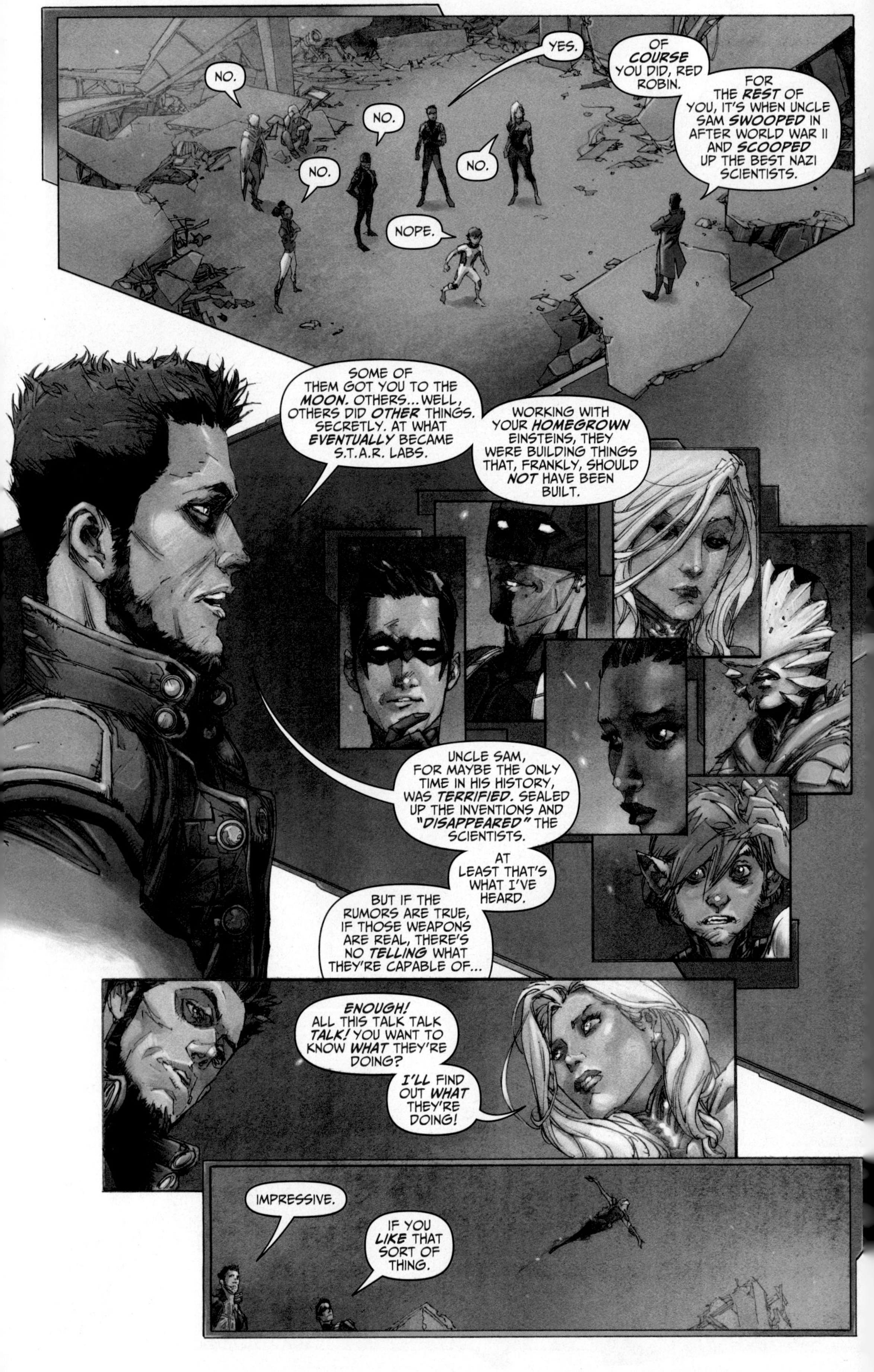
NO.
NO.
NO.
YES.
NO.
NOPE.
OF COURSE YOU DID, RED ROBIN.
FOR THE REST OF YOU, IT'S WHEN UNCLE SAM SWOOPED IN AFTER WORLD WAR II AND SCOOPED UP THE BEST NAZI SCIENTISTS.
SOME OF THEM GOT YOU TO THE MOON. OTHERS... WELL, OTHERS DID OTHER THINGS. SECRETLY. AT WHAT EVENTUALLY BECAME S.T.A.R. LABS.
WORKING WITH YOUR HOMEGROWN EINSTEINS, THEY WERE BUILDING THINGS THAT, FRANKLY, SHOULD NOT HAVE BEEN BUILT.
UNCLE SAM, FOR MAYBE THE ONLY TIME IN HIS HISTORY, WAS TERRIFIED. SEALED UP THE INVENTIONS AND "DISAPPEARED" THE SCIENTISTS.
AT LEAST THAT'S WHAT I'VE HEARD.
BUT IF THE RUMORS ARE TRUE, IF THOSE WEAPONS ARE REAL, THERE'S NO TELLING WHAT THEY'RE CAPABLE OF...
ENOUGH! ALL THIS TALK TALK TALK! YOU WANT TO KNOW WHAT THEY'RE DOING?
I'LL FIND OUT WHAT THEY'RE DOING!
IMPRESSIVE.
IF YOU LIKE THAT SORT OF THING.

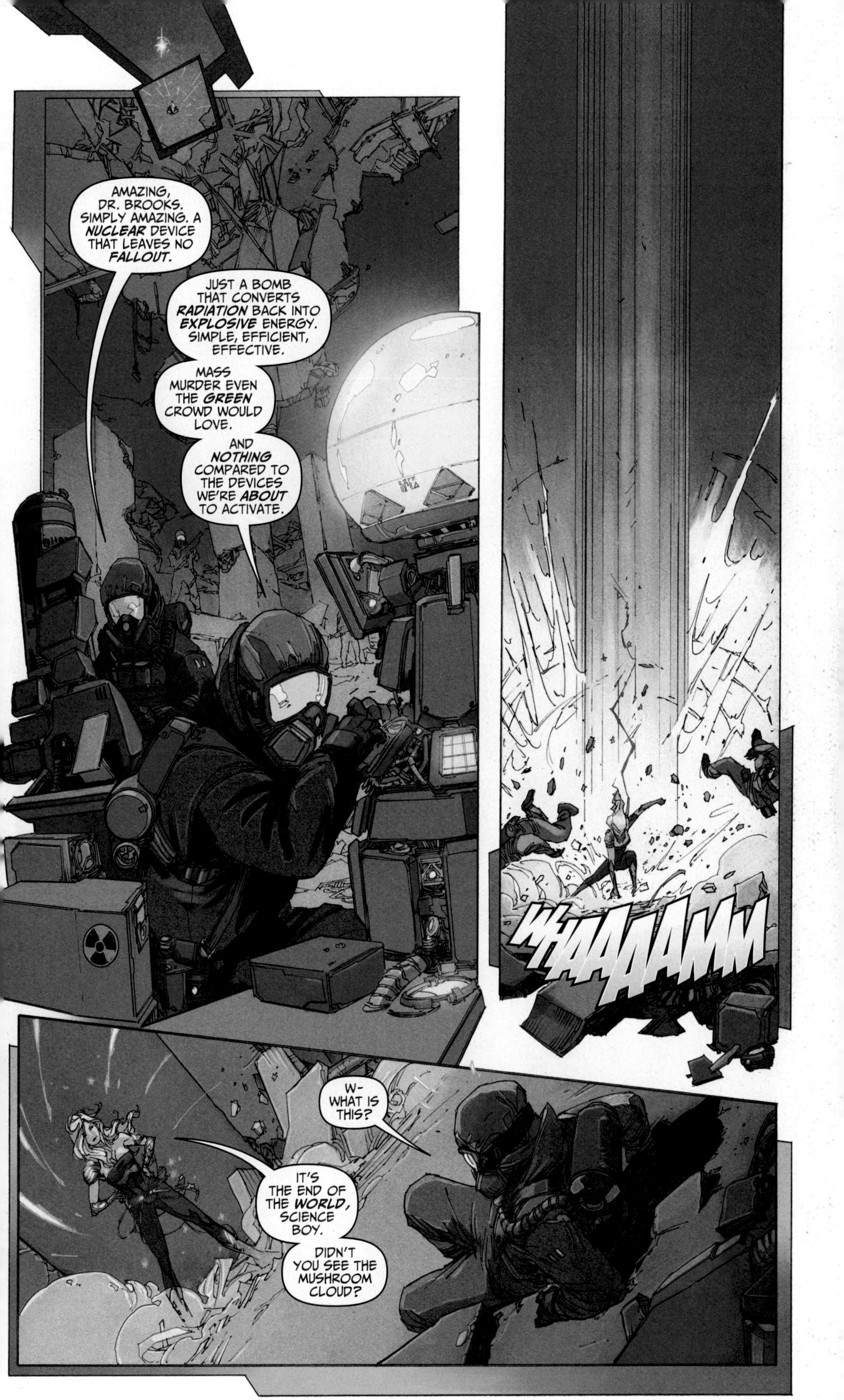
AMAZING, DR. BROOKS. SIMPLY AMAZING. A NUCLEAR DEVICE THAT LEAVES NO FALLOUT.
JUST A BOMB THAT CONVERTS RADIATION BACK INTO EXPLOSIVE ENERGY. SIMPLE, EFFICIENT, EFFECTIVE.
MASS MURDER EVEN THE GREEN CROWD WOULD LOVE.
AND NOTHING COMPARED TO THE DEVICES WE'RE ABOUT TO ACTIVATE.
WHAAAAMM
W- WHAT IS THIS?
IT'S THE END OF THE WORLD, SCIENCE BOY.
DIDN'T YOU SEE THE MUSHROOM CLOUD?

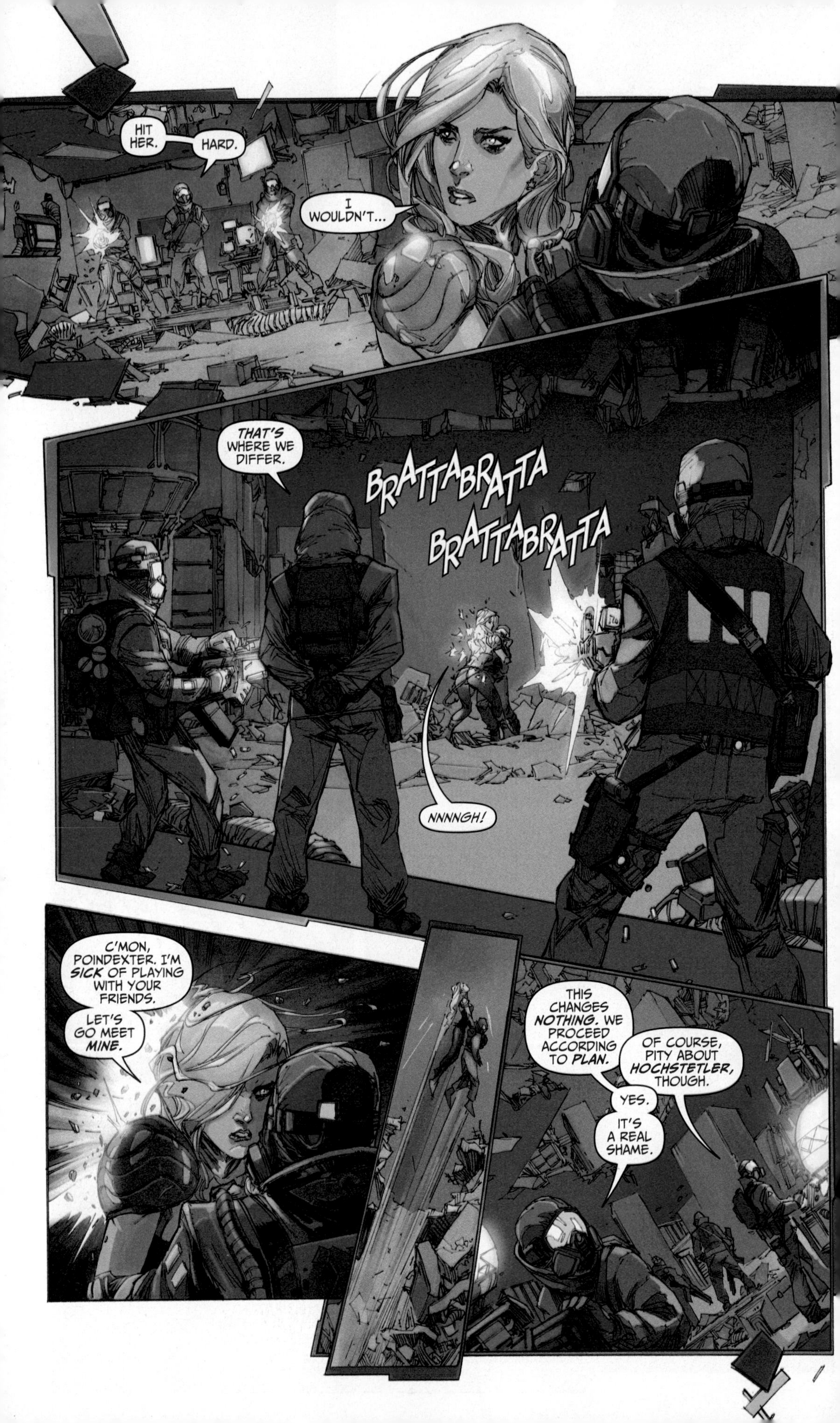
HIT HER.
HARD.
I WOULDN'T...
THAT'S WHERE WE DIFFER.
BRATTABRATTA BRATTABRATTA
NNNNGH!
C'MON, POINDEXTER. I'M SICK OF PLAYING WITH YOUR FRIENDS.
LET'S GO MEET MINE.
THIS CHANGES NOTHING. WE PROCEED ACCORDING TO PLAN.
OF COURSE, PITY ABOUT HOCHSTETLER, THOUGH.
YES.
IT'S A REAL SHAME.

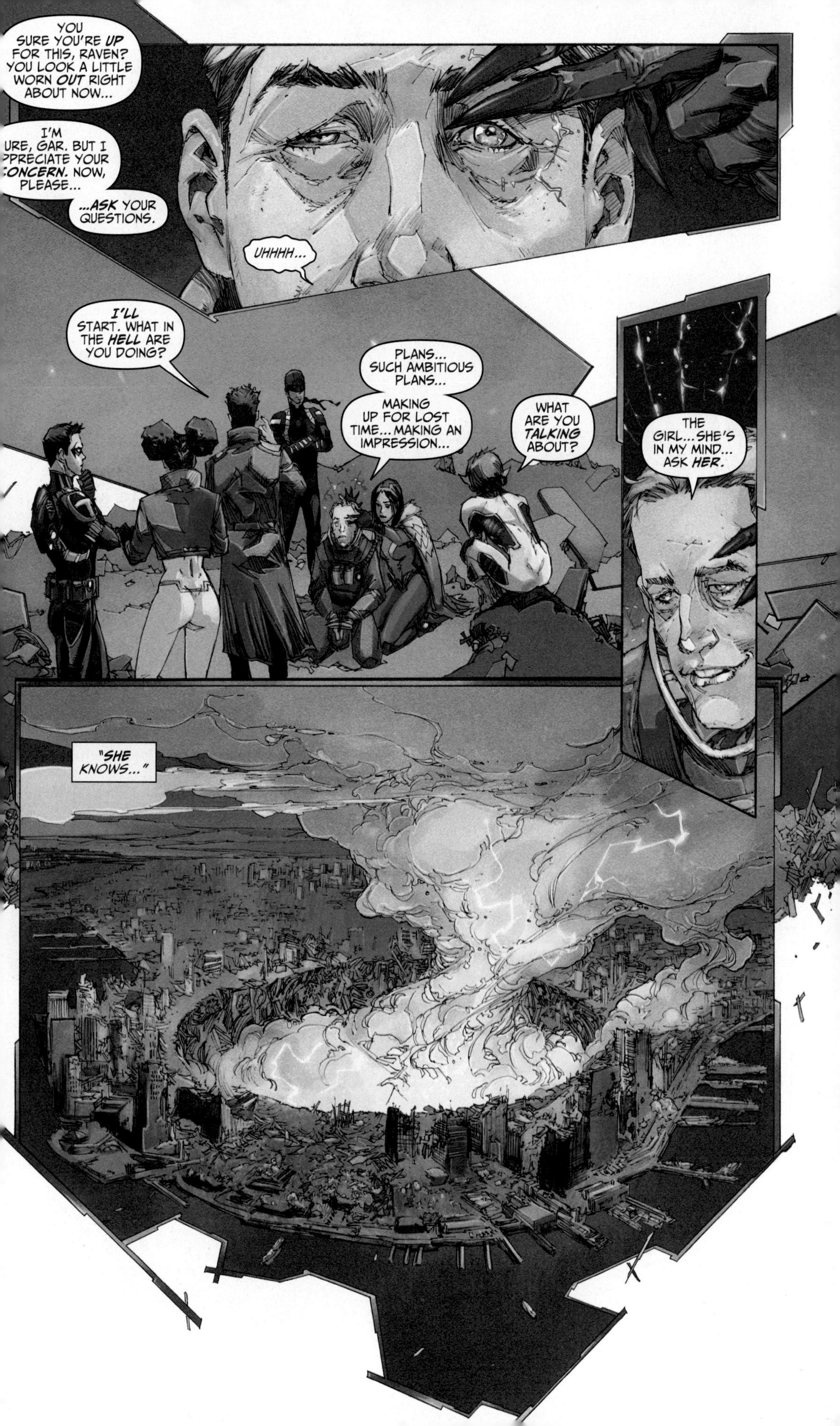

YOU SURE YOU'RE UP FOR THIS, RAVEN? YOU LOOK A LITTLE WORN OUT RIGHT ABOUT NOW...
I'M URE, GAR. BUT I PPRECIATE YOUR CONCERN. NOW, PLEASE...
...ASK YOUR QUESTIONS.
UHHHH...
I'LL START. WHAT IN THE HELL ARE YOU DOING?
PLANS... SUCH AMBITIOUS PLANS...
MAKING UP FOR LOST TIME... MAKING AN IMPRESSION...
WHAT ARE YOU TALKING ABOUT?
THE GIRL... SHE'S IN MY MIND... ASK HER.
"SHE KNOWS..."

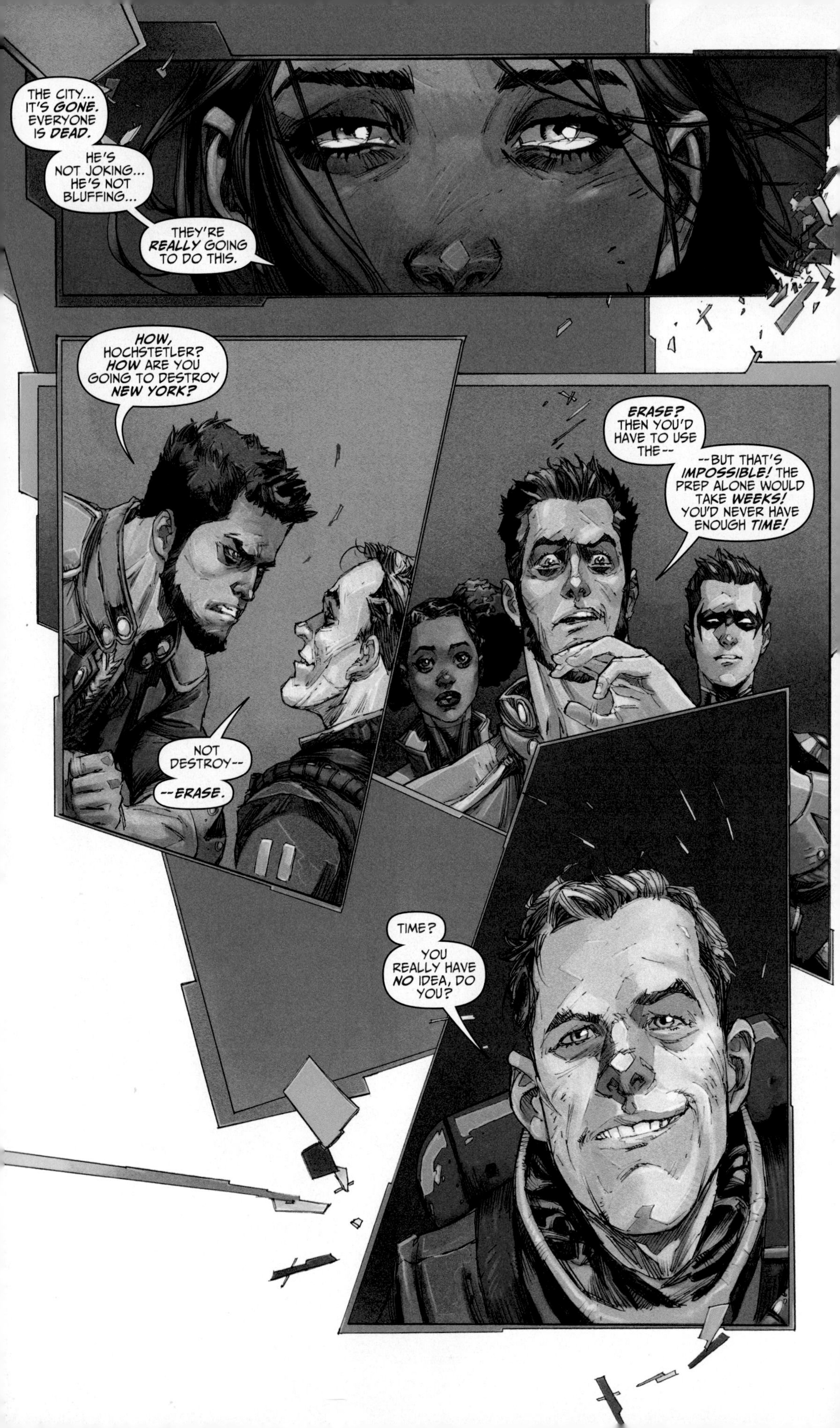
THE CITY... IT'S GONE. EVERYONE IS DEAD.
HE'S NOT JOKING... HE'S NOT BLUFFING...
THEY'RE REALLY GOING TO DO THIS.
HOW, HOCHSTETLER? HOW ARE YOU GOING TO DESTROY NEW YORK?
NOT DESTROY--
--ERASE.
ERASE? THEN YOU'D HAVE TO USE THE--
--BUT THAT'S IMPOSSIBLE! THE PREP ALONE WOULD TAKE WEEKS! YOU'D NEVER HAVE ENOUGH TIME!
TIME?
YOU REALLY HAVE NO IDEA, DO YOU?

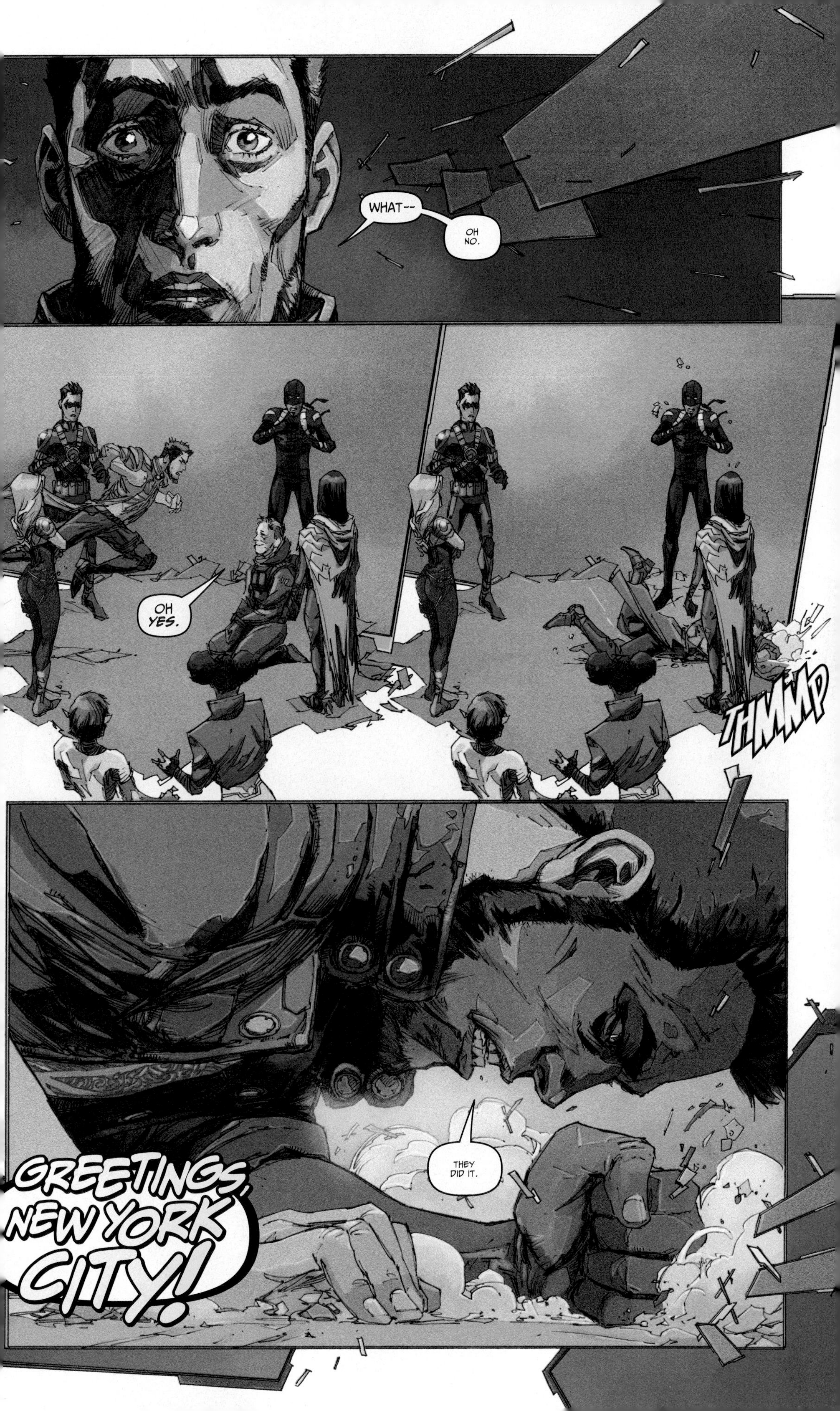
WHAT--
OH NO.
OH YES.
THMMP
THEY DID IT.
GREETINGS, NEW YORK CITY!

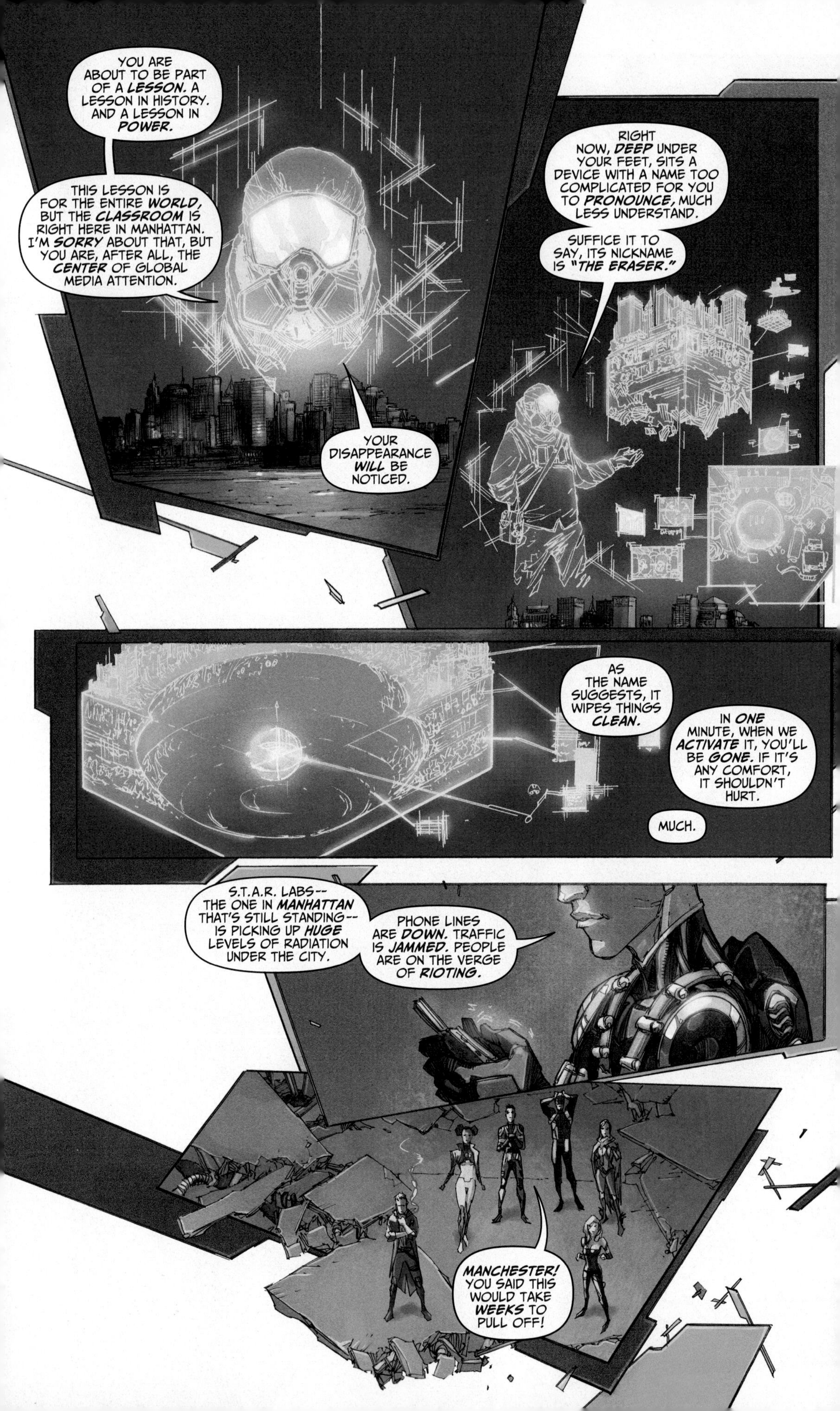
YOU ARE ABOUT TO BE PART OF A LESSON. A LESSON IN HISTORY. AND A LESSON IN POWER.
THIS LESSON IS FOR THE ENTIRE WORLD, BUT THE CLASSROOM IS RIGHT HERE IN MANHATTAN. I'M SORRY ABOUT THAT, BUT YOU ARE, AFTER ALL, THE CENTER OF GLOBAL MEDIA ATTENTION.
YOUR DISAPPEARANCE WILL BE NOTICED.
RIGHT NOW, DEEP UNDER YOUR FEET, SITS A DEVICE WITH A NAME TOO COMPLICATED FOR YOU TO PRONOUNCE, MUCH LESS UNDERSTAND.
SUFFICE IT TO SAY, ITS NICKNAME IS "THE ERASER."
AS THE NAME SUGGESTS, IT WIPES THINGS CLEAN.
IN ONE MINUTE, WHEN WE ACTIVATE IT, YOU'LL BE GONE. IF IT'S ANY COMFORT, IT SHOULDN'T HURT.
MUCH.
S.T.A.R. LABS-- THE ONE IN MANHATTAN THAT'S STILL STANDING-- IS PICKING UP HUGE LEVELS OF RADIATION UNDER THE CITY.
PHONE LINES ARE DOWN. TRAFFIC IS JAMMED. PEOPLE ARE ON THE VERGE OF RIOTING.
MANCHESTER! YOU SAID THIS WOULD TAKE WEEKS TO PULL OFF!

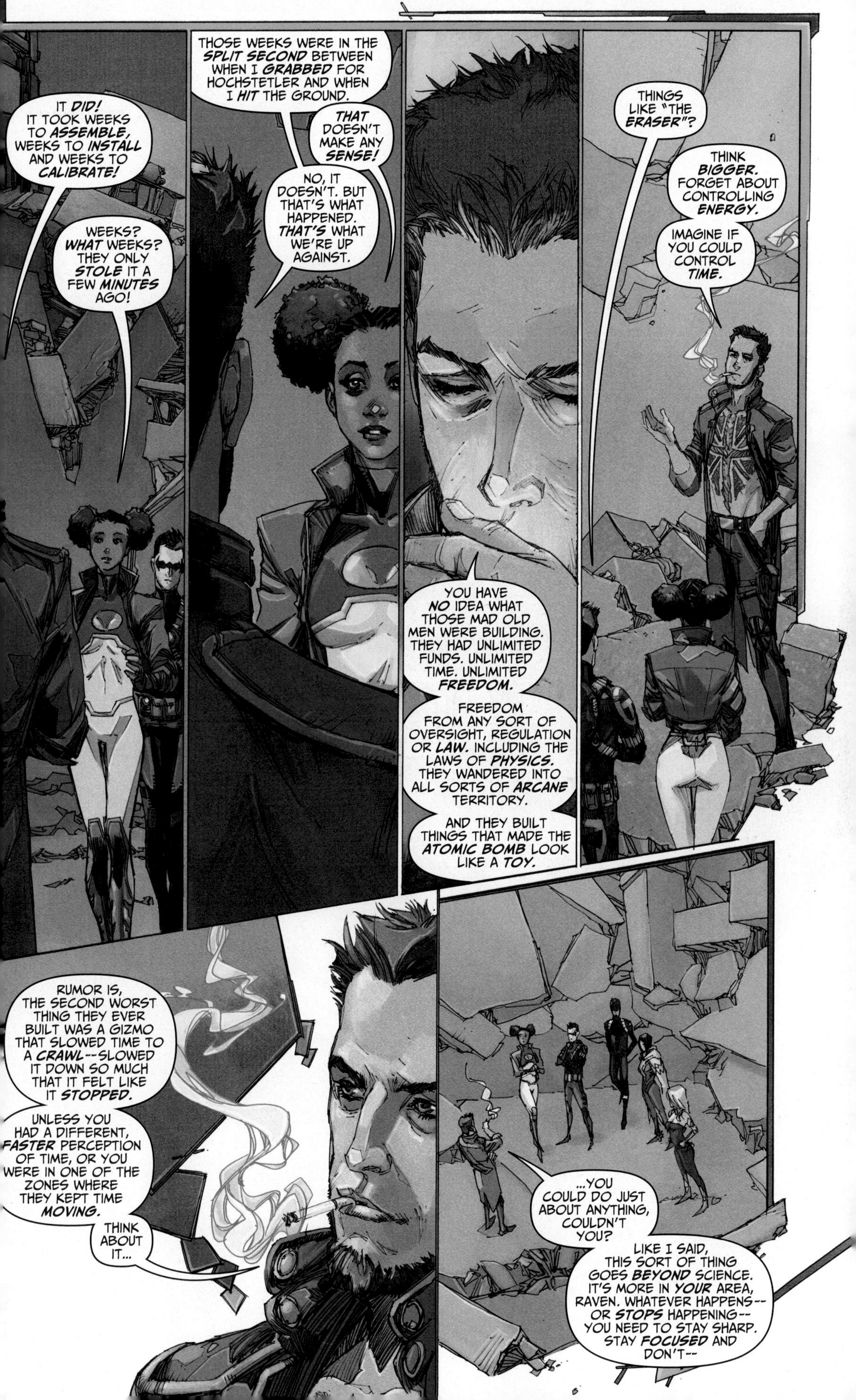

IT DID! IT TOOK WEEKS TO ASSEMBLE, WEEKS TO INSTALL AND WEEKS TO CALIBRATE!
WEEKS? WHAT WEEKS? THEY ONLY STOLE IT A FEW MINUTES AGO!
THOSE WEEKS WERE IN THE SPLIT SECOND BETWEEN WHEN I GRABBED FOR HOCHSTETLER AND WHEN I HIT THE GROUND.
THAT DOESN'T MAKE ANY SENSE!
NO, IT DOESN'T. BUT THAT'S WHAT HAPPENED. THAT'S WHAT WE'RE UP AGAINST.
YOU HAVE NO IDEA WHAT THOSE MAD OLD MEN WERE BUILDING. THEY HAD UNLIMITED FUNDS. UNLIMITED TIME. UNLIMITED FREEDOM.
FREEDOM FROM ANY SORT OF OVERSIGHT, REGULATION OR LAW. INCLUDING THE LAWS OF PHYSICS. THEY WANDERED INTO ALL SORTS OF ARCANE TERRITORY.
AND THEY BUILT THINGS THAT MADE THE ATOMIC BOMB LOOK LIKE A TOY.
THINGS LIKE "THE ERASER"?
THINK BIGGER. FORGET ABOUT CONTROLLING ENERGY.
IMAGINE IF YOU COULD CONTROL TIME.
RUMOR IS, THE SECOND WORST THING THEY EVER BUILT WAS A GIZMO THAT SLOWED TIME TO A CRAWL--SLOWED IT DOWN SO MUCH THAT IT FELT LIKE IT STOPPED.
UNLESS YOU HAD A DIFFERENT, FASTER PERCEPTION OF TIME, OR YOU WERE IN ONE OF THE ZONES WHERE THEY KEPT TIME MOVING.
THINK ABOUT IT...
...YOU COULD DO JUST ABOUT ANYTHING, COULDN'T YOU?
LIKE I SAID, THIS SORT OF THING GOES BEYOND SCIENCE. IT'S MORE IN YOUR AREA, RAVEN. WHATEVER HAPPENS-- OR STOPS HAPPENING-- YOU NEED TO STAY SHARP. STAY FOCUSED AND DON'T--

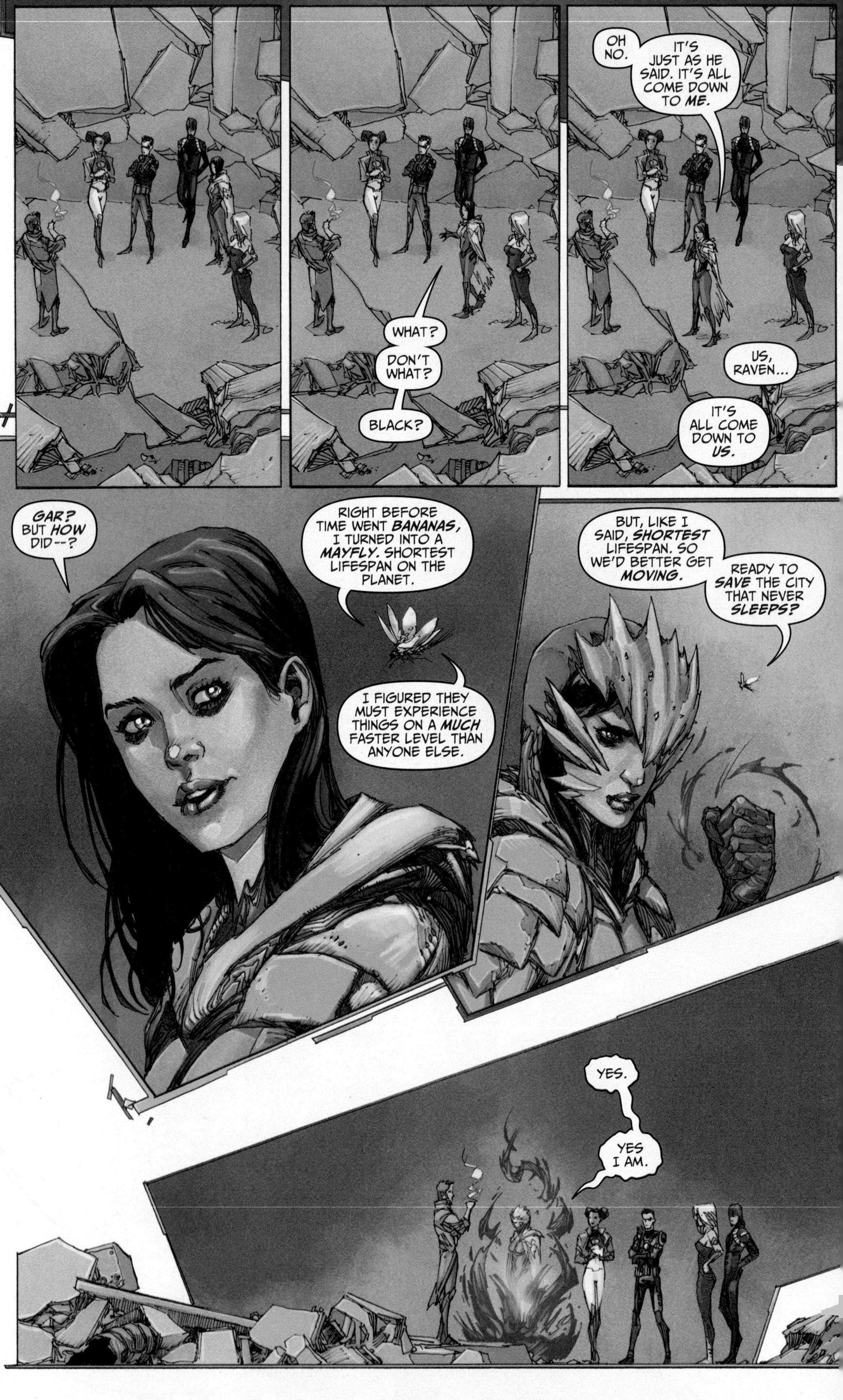

WHAT?
DON'T WHAT?
BLACK?
OH NO.
IT'S JUST AS HE SAID. IT'S ALL COME DOWN TO *ME.*
US, RAVEN...
IT'S ALL COME DOWN TO *US.*
GAR? BUT *HOW* DID--?
RIGHT BEFORE TIME WENT *BANANAS,* I TURNED INTO A *MAYFLY.* SHORTEST LIFESPAN ON THE PLANET.
I FIGURED THEY MUST EXPERIENCE THINGS ON A *MUCH* FASTER LEVEL THAN ANYONE ELSE.
BUT, LIKE I SAID, *SHORTEST* LIFESPAN. SO WE'D BETTER GET *MOVING.*
READY TO *SAVE* THE CITY THAT NEVER *SLEEPS?*
YES.
YES I AM.

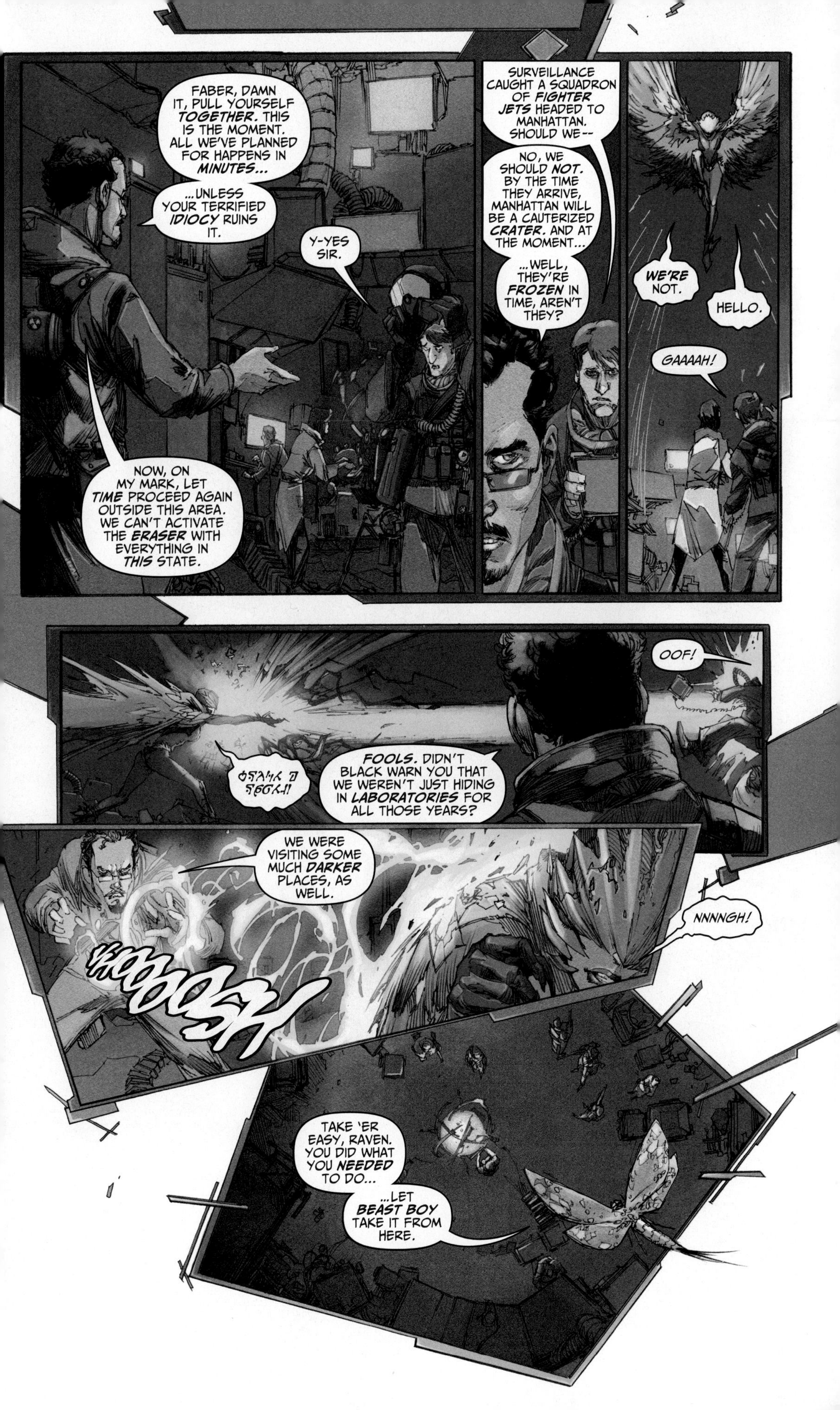
FABER, DAMN IT, PULL YOURSELF TOGETHER. THIS IS THE MOMENT. ALL WE'VE PLANNED FOR HAPPENS IN MINUTES...
...UNLESS YOUR TERRIFIED IDIOCY RUINS IT.
Y-YES SIR.
NOW, ON MY MARK, LET TIME PROCEED AGAIN OUTSIDE THIS AREA. WE CAN'T ACTIVATE THE ERASER WITH EVERYTHING IN THIS STATE.
SURVEILLANCE CAUGHT A SQUADRON OF FIGHTER JETS HEADED TO MANHATTAN. SHOULD WE--
NO, WE SHOULD NOT. BY THE TIME THEY ARRIVE, MANHATTAN WILL BE A CAUTERIZED CRATER. AND AT THE MOMENT...
...WELL, THEY'RE FROZEN IN TIME, AREN'T THEY?
WE'RE NOT.
HELLO.
GAAAAH!
OOF!
FOOLS. DIDN'T BLACK WARN YOU THAT WE WEREN'T JUST HIDING IN LABORATORIES FOR ALL THOSE YEARS?
WE WERE VISITING SOME MUCH DARKER PLACES, AS WELL.
NNNNGH!
KROOOSH
TAKE 'ER EASY, RAVEN. YOU DID WHAT YOU NEEDED TO DO...
...LET BEAST BOY TAKE IT FROM HERE.

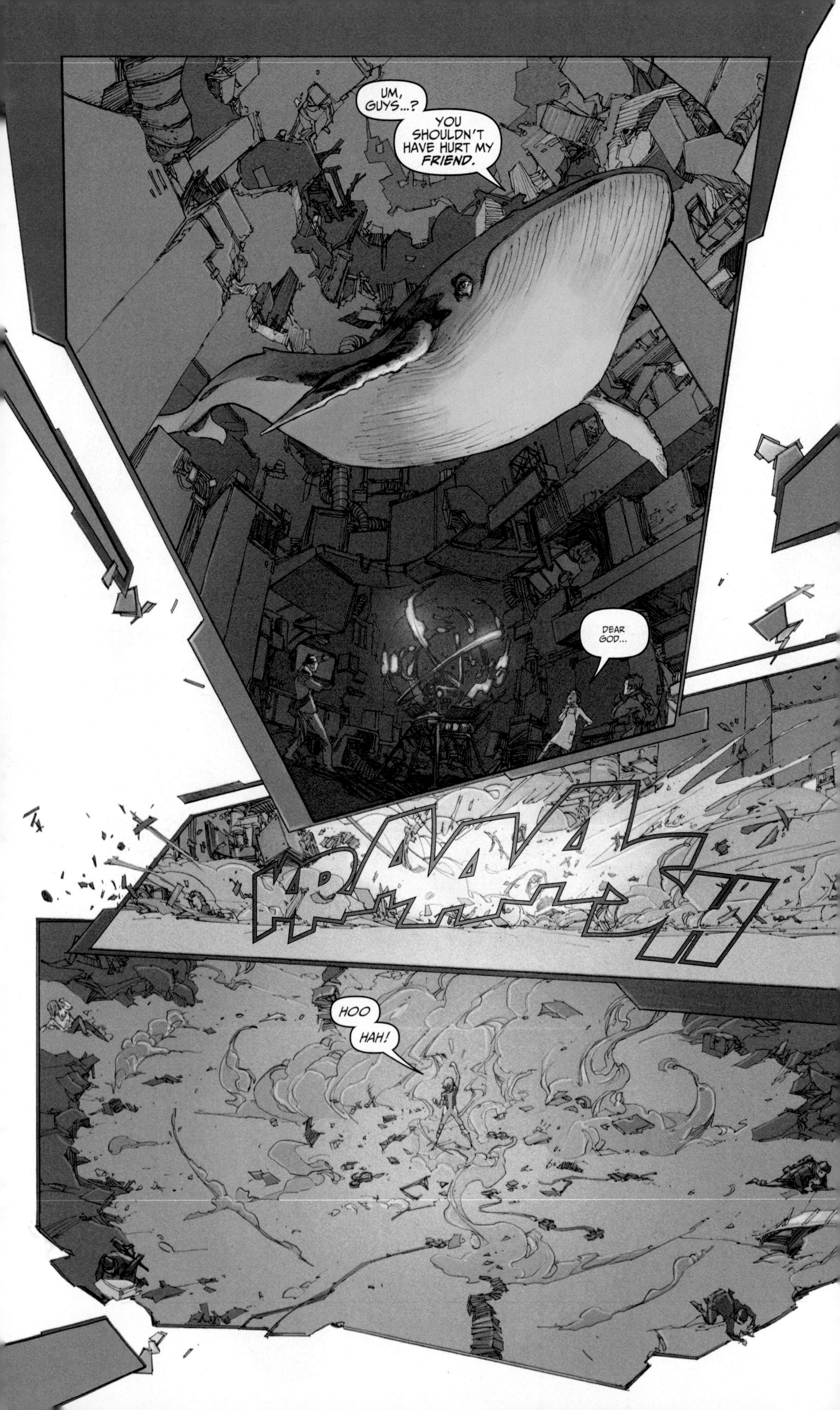
UM, GUYS...?
YOU SHOULDN'T HAVE HURT MY FRIEND.
DEAR GOD...
HOO
HAH!

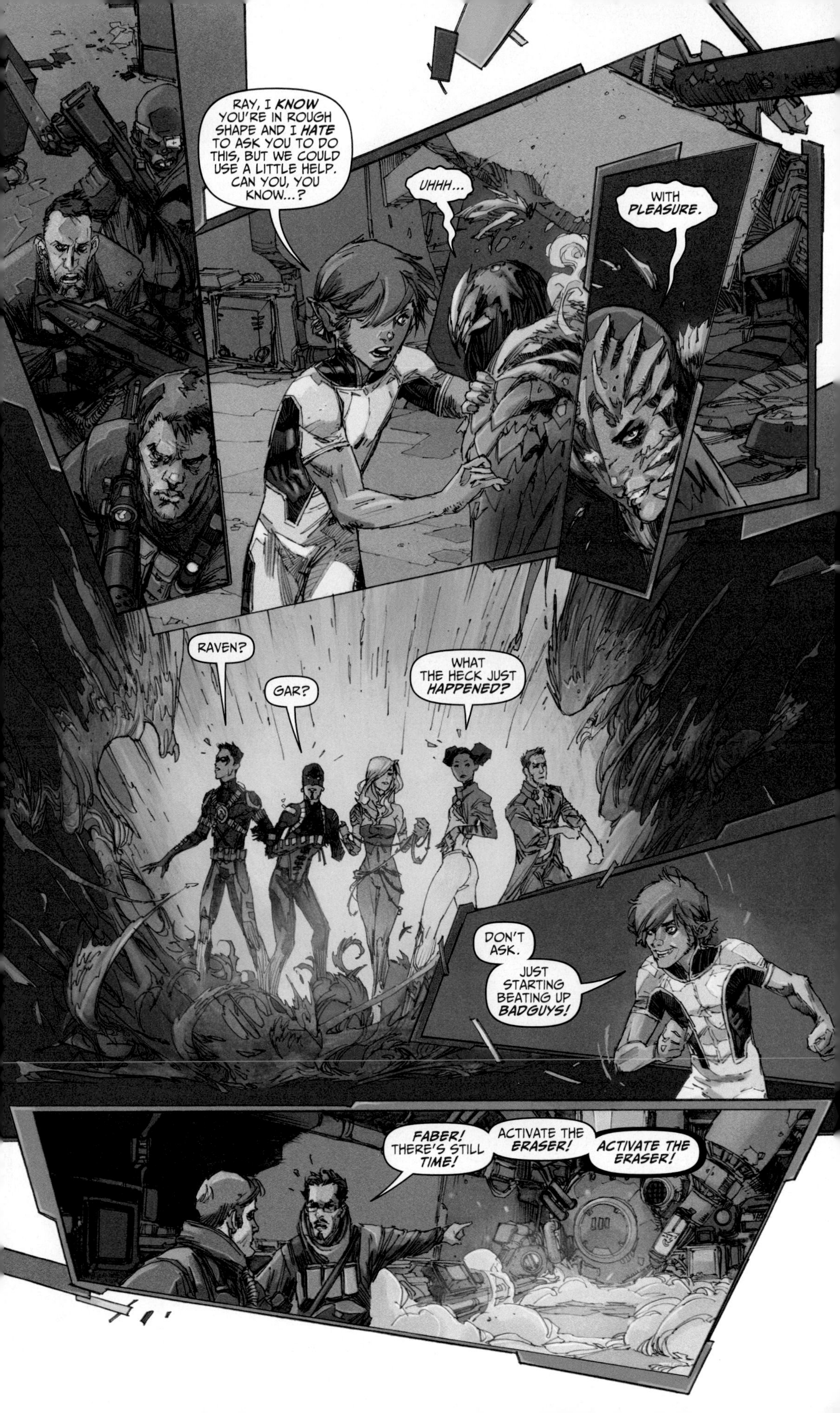
RAY, I KNOW YOU'RE IN ROUGH SHAPE AND I HATE TO ASK YOU TO DO THIS, BUT WE COULD USE A LITTLE HELP. CAN YOU, YOU KNOW...?
UHHH...
WITH PLEASURE.
RAVEN?
GAR?
WHAT THE HECK JUST HAPPENED?
DON'T ASK.
JUST STARTING BEATING UP BADGUYS!
FABER! THERE'S STILL TIME!
ACTIVATE THE ERASER!
ACTIVATE THE ERASER!

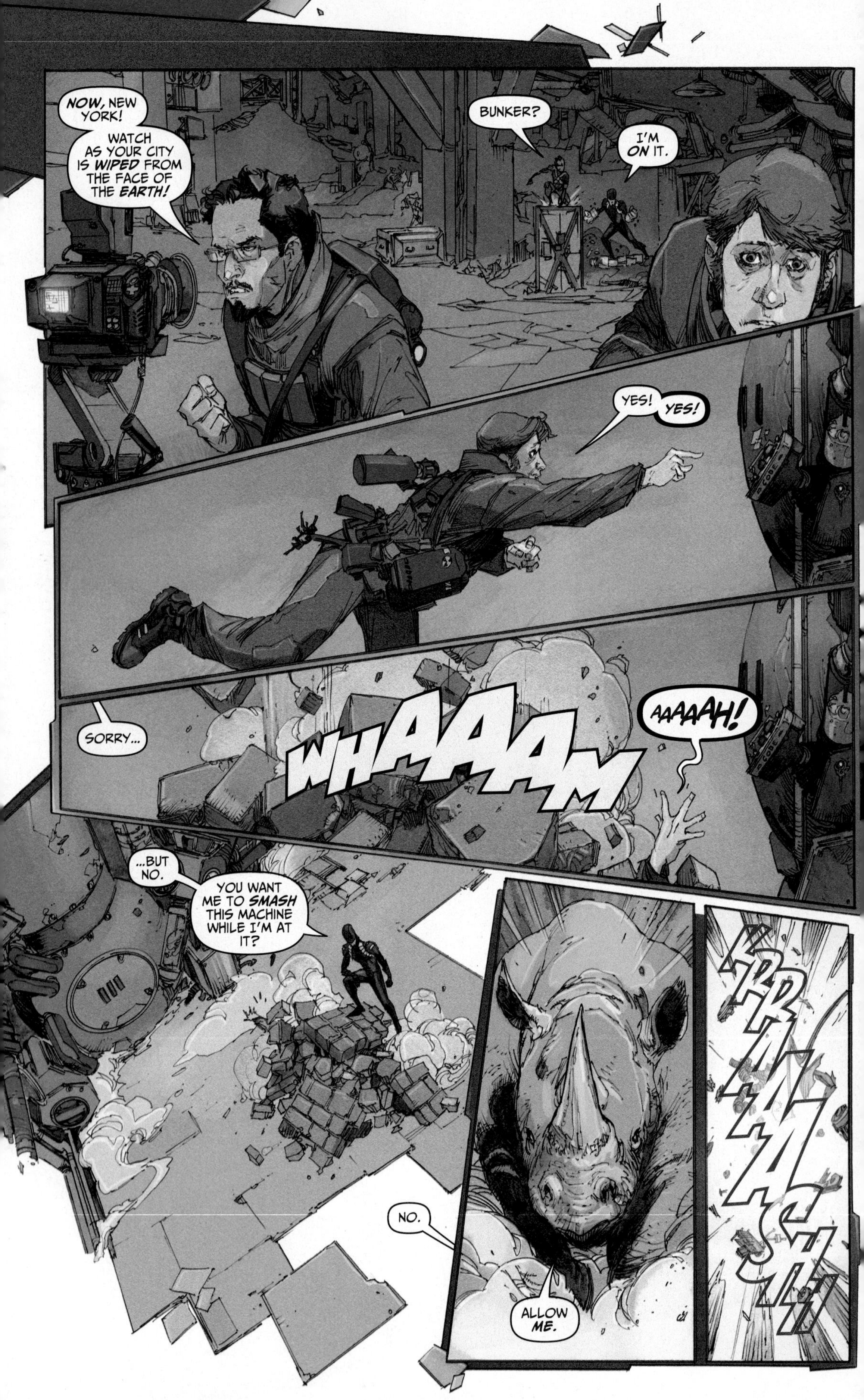

NOW, NEW YORK!
WATCH AS YOUR CITY IS WIPED FROM THE FACE OF THE EARTH!
BUNKER?
I'M ON IT.
YES! YES!
SORRY...
WHAAAAM
AAAAAH!
...BUT NO.
YOU WANT ME TO SMASH THIS MACHINE WHILE I'M AT IT?
NO.
ALLOW ME.

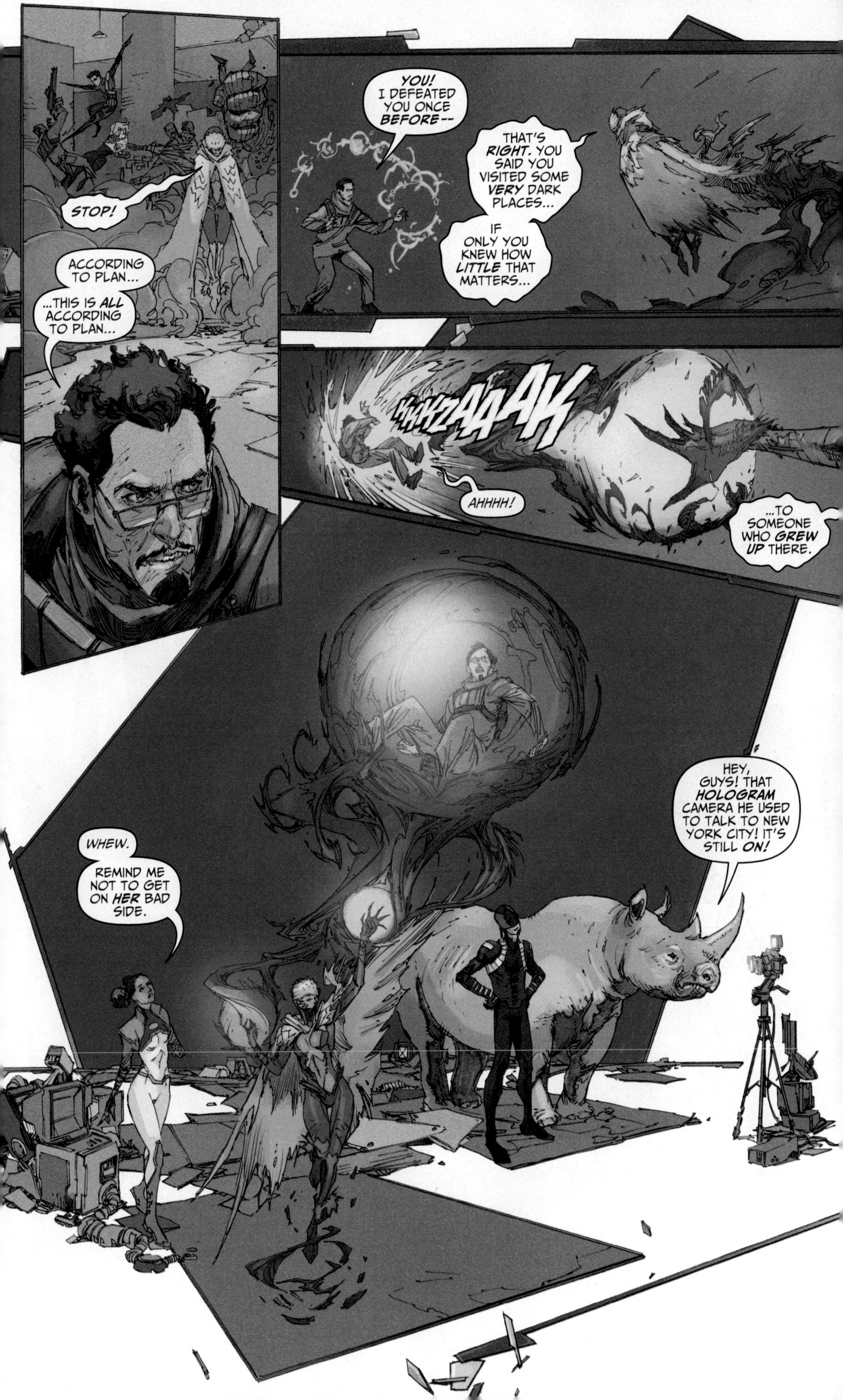
STOP!
ACCORDING TO PLAN...
...THIS IS ALL ACCORDING TO PLAN...
YOU! I DEFEATED YOU ONCE BEFORE--
THAT'S RIGHT. YOU SAID YOU VISITED SOME VERY DARK PLACES...
IF ONLY YOU KNEW HOW LITTLE THAT MATTERS...
HHKZAAAAK
AHHHH!
...TO SOMEONE WHO GREW UP THERE.
WHEW.
REMIND ME NOT TO GET ON HER BAD SIDE.
HEY, GUYS! THAT HOLOGRAM CAMERA HE USED TO TALK TO NEW YORK CITY! IT'S STILL ON!

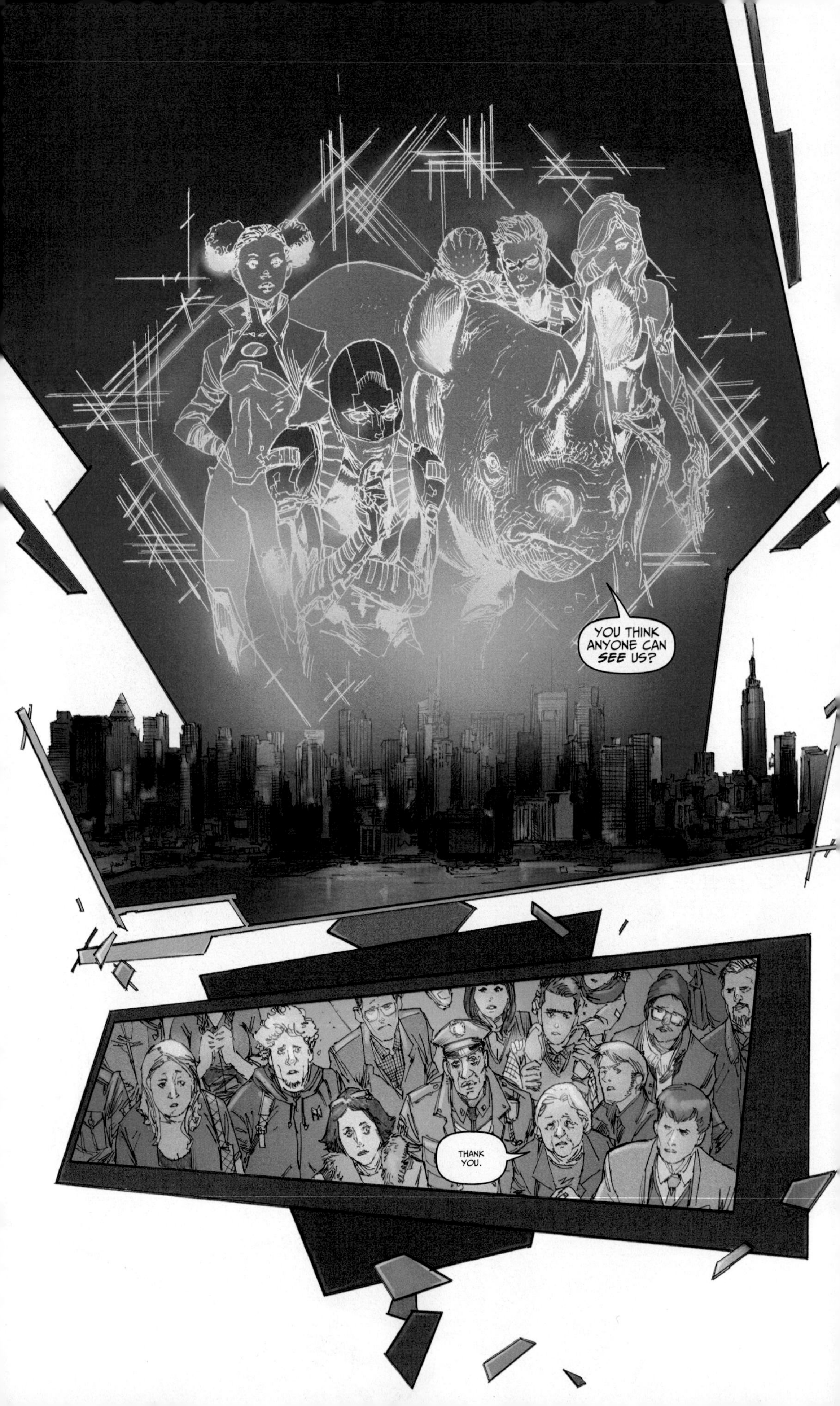
YOU THINK ANYONE CAN SEE US?
THANK YOU.

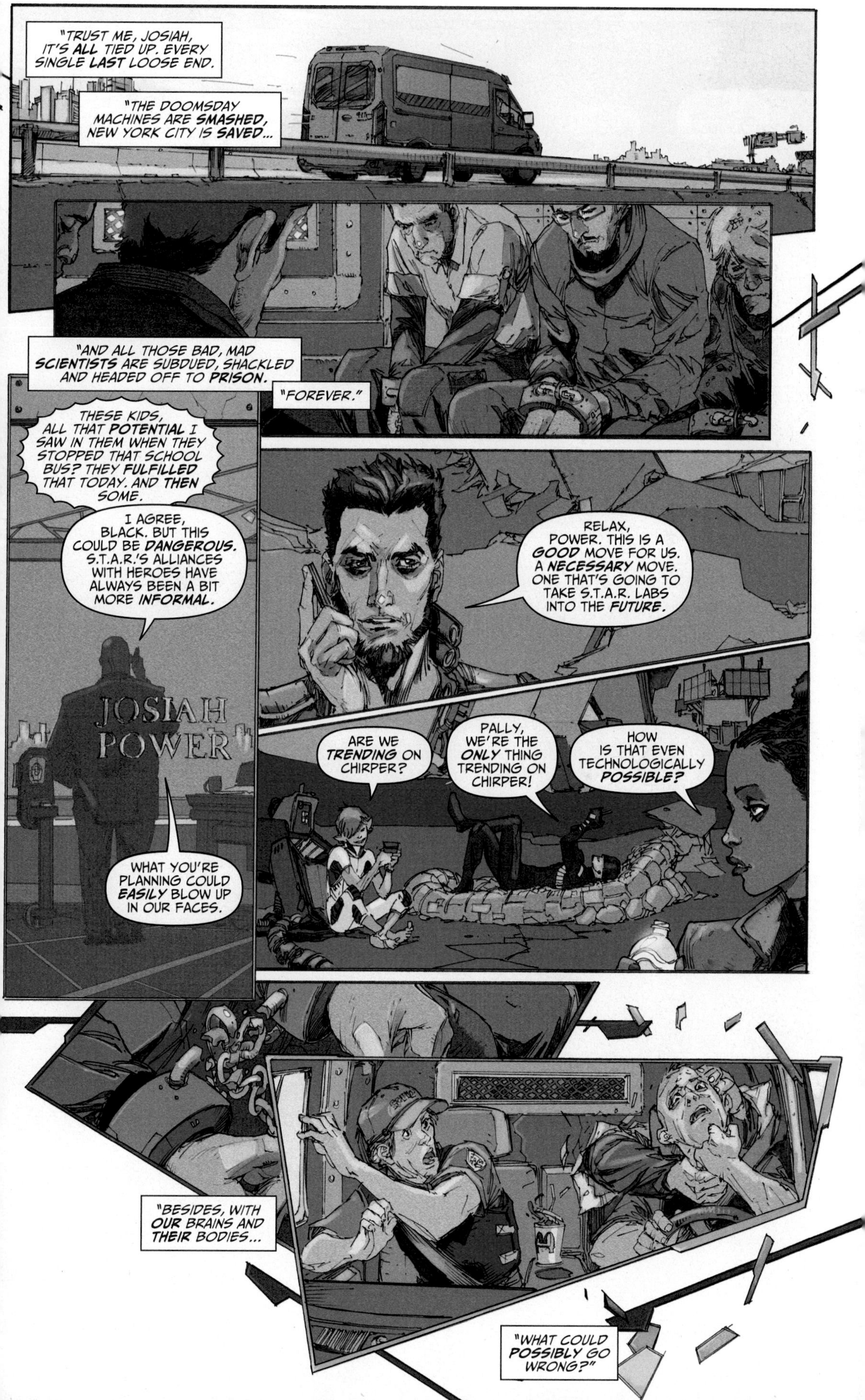
"TRUST ME, JOSIAH, IT'S ALL TIED UP. EVERY SINGLE LAST LOOSE END.
"THE DOOMSDAY MACHINES ARE SMASHED, NEW YORK CITY IS SAVED...
"AND ALL THOSE BAD, MAD SCIENTISTS ARE SUBDUED, SHACKLED AND HEADED OFF TO PRISON.
"FOREVER."
THESE KIDS, ALL THAT POTENTIAL I SAW IN THEM WHEN THEY STOPPED THAT SCHOOL BUS? THEY FULFILLED THAT TODAY. AND THEN SOME.
I AGREE, BLACK. BUT THIS COULD BE DANGEROUS. S.T.A.R.'S ALLIANCES WITH HEROES HAVE ALWAYS BEEN A BIT MORE INFORMAL.
JOSIAH POWER
RELAX, POWER. THIS IS A GOOD MOVE FOR US. A NECESSARY MOVE. ONE THAT'S GOING TO TAKE S.T.A.R. LABS INTO THE FUTURE.
WHAT YOU'RE PLANNING COULD EASILY BLOW UP IN OUR FACES.
ARE WE TRENDING ON CHIRPER?
PALLY, WE'RE THE ONLY THING TRENDING ON CHIRPER!
HOW IS THAT EVEN TECHNOLOGICALLY POSSIBLE?
"BESIDES, WITH OUR BRAINS AND THEIR BODIES...
"WHAT COULD POSSIBLY GO WRONG?"

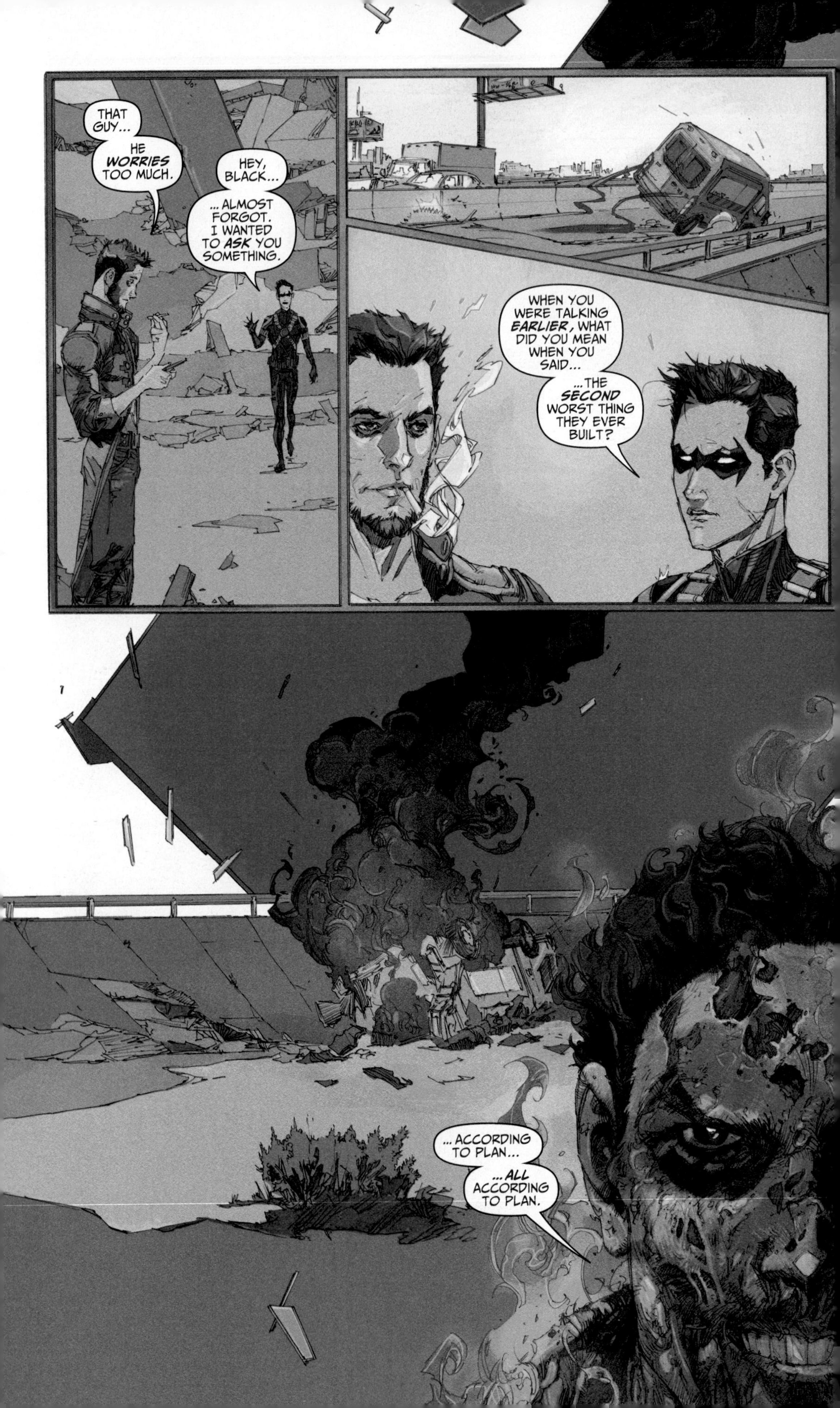

THAT GUY...
HE WORRIES TOO MUCH.
HEY, BLACK...
...ALMOST FORGOT. I WANTED TO ASK YOU SOMETHING.
WHEN YOU WERE TALKING EARLIER, WHAT DID YOU MEAN WHEN YOU SAID...
...THE SECOND WORST THING THEY EVER BUILT?
...ACCORDING TO PLAN...
...ALL ACCORDING TO PLAN.

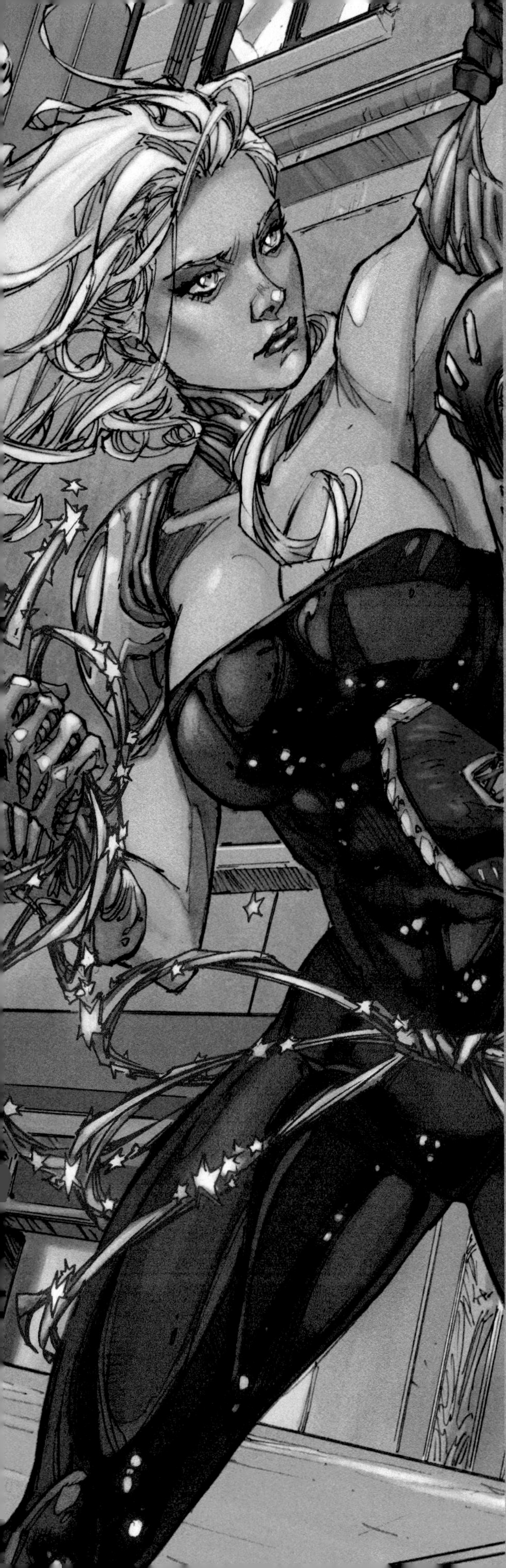

VARIANT COVER GALLERY

TEEN TITANS #1
VARIANT COVER BY
CLIFF CHIANG

TEEN TITANS #1
BATMAN 75TH ANNIVERSARY
COVER BY JOE QUINONES

TEEN TITANS #2
VARIANT COVER BY
CAMERON STEWART
WITH NATHAN FAIRBAIRN

TEEN TITANS #2
SELFIE COVER BY BEN CALDWELL

TEEN TITANS #3
VARIANT COVER BY KEVIN WADA

TEEN TITANS #3
VARIANT COVER BY GENE HA

TEEN TITANS #4
LEGO VARIANT COVER

TEEN TITANS #5
VARIANT COVER BY
DARWYN COOKE

TEEN TITANS #6
FLASH 75TH ANNIVERSARY
COVER BY MICHAEL ALLRED AND
LAURA ALLRED AFTER NICK CARDY

TEEN TITANS #7
VARIANT COVER BY
SEAN GALLOWAY

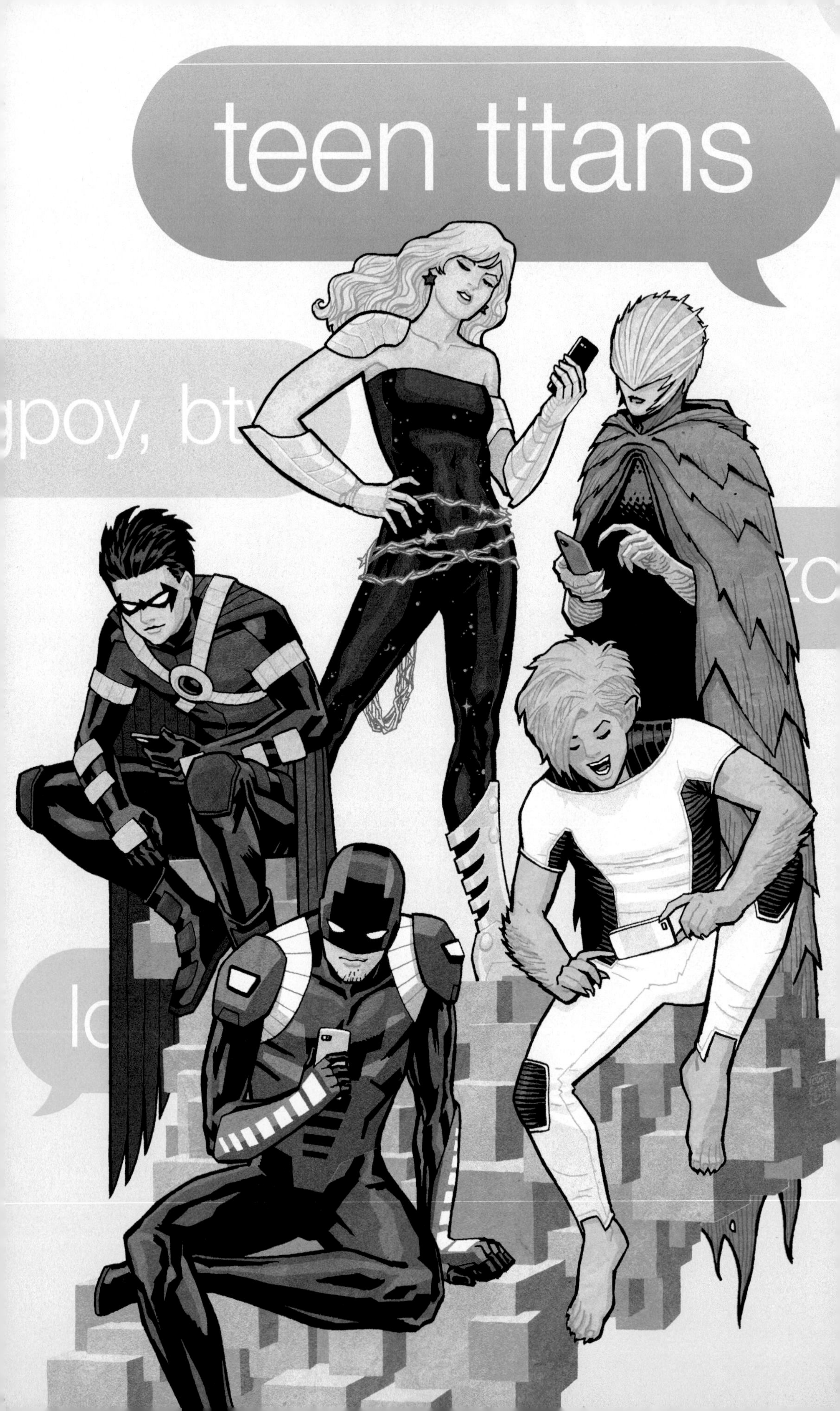
teen titans
gpoy, bt
zc
lo

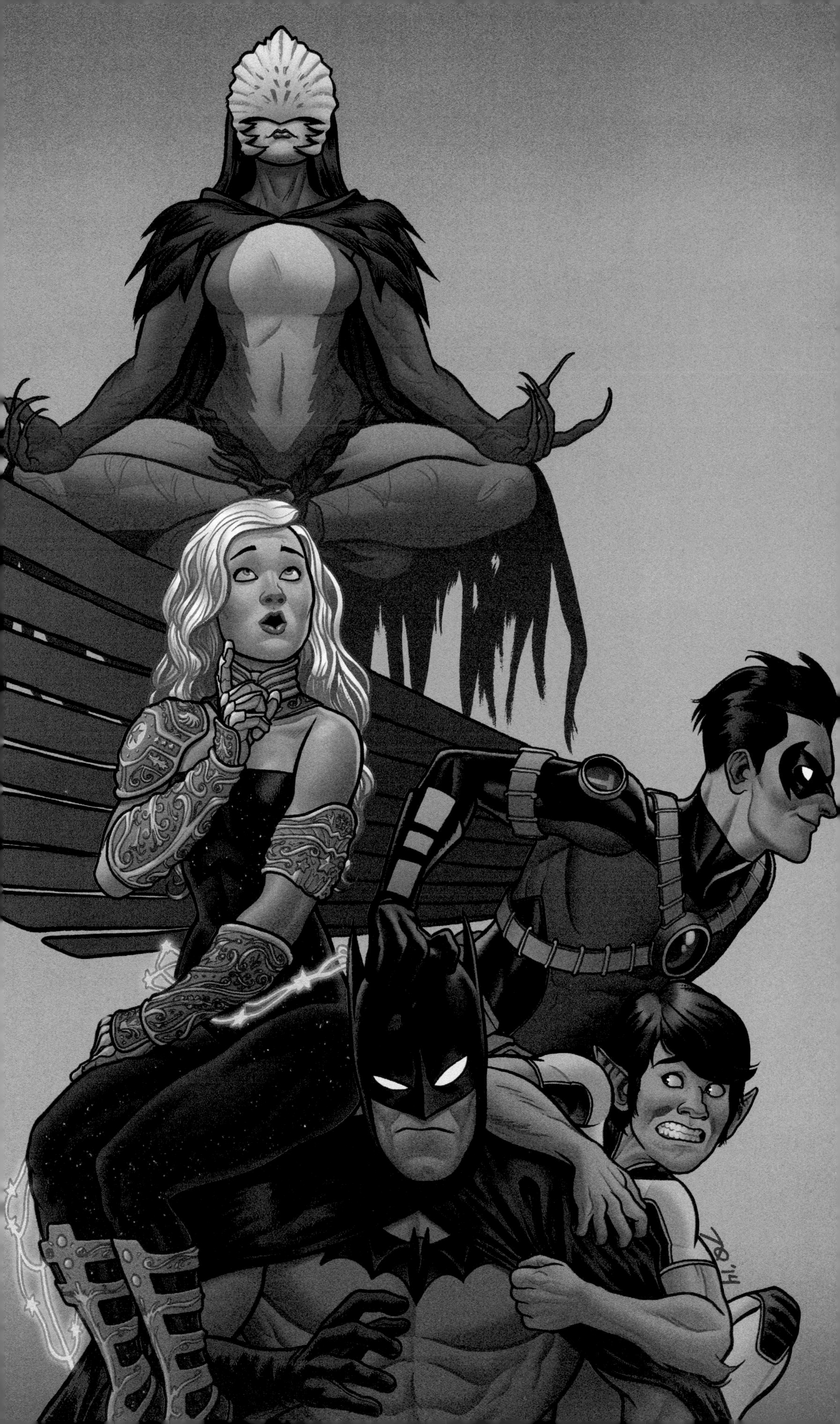

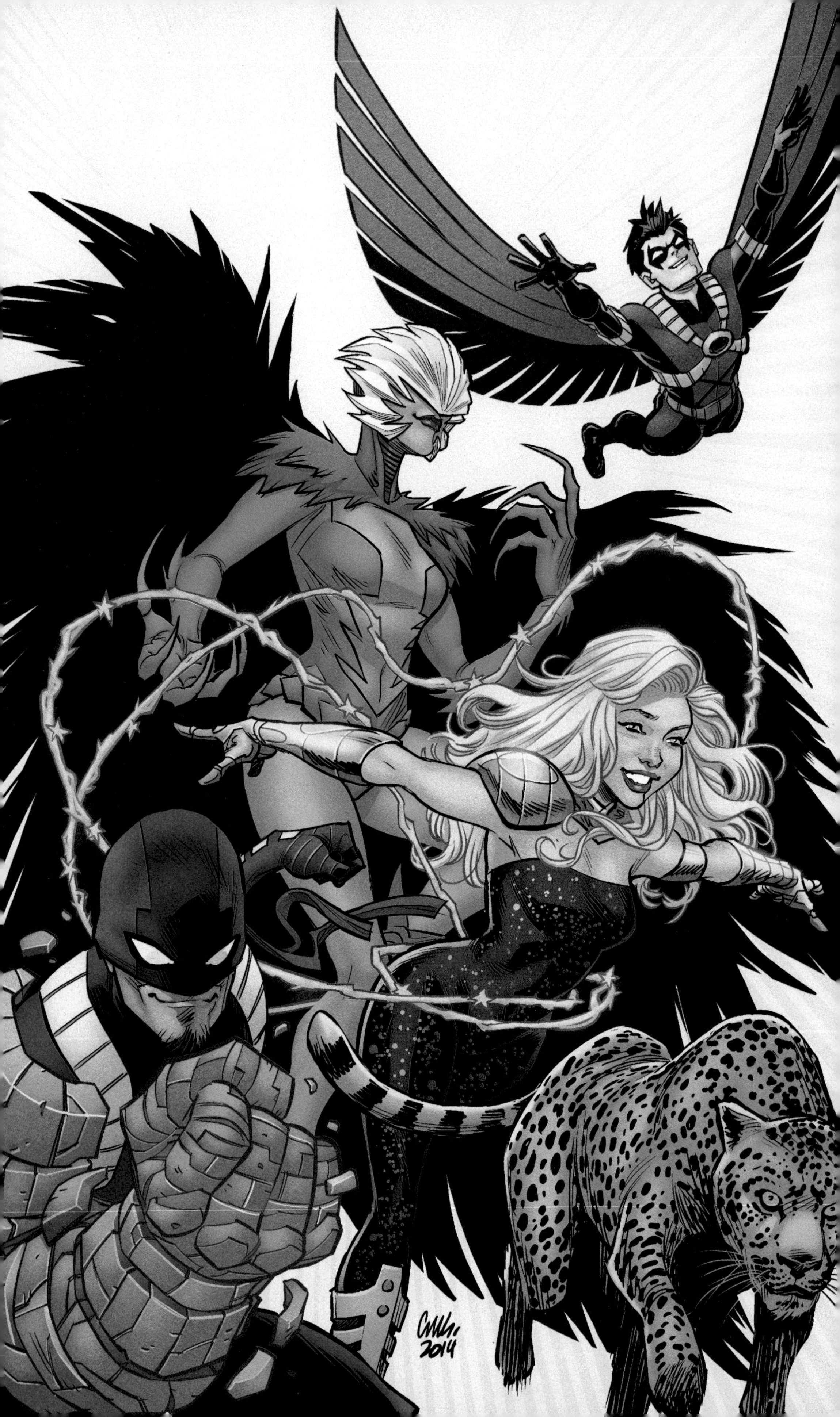

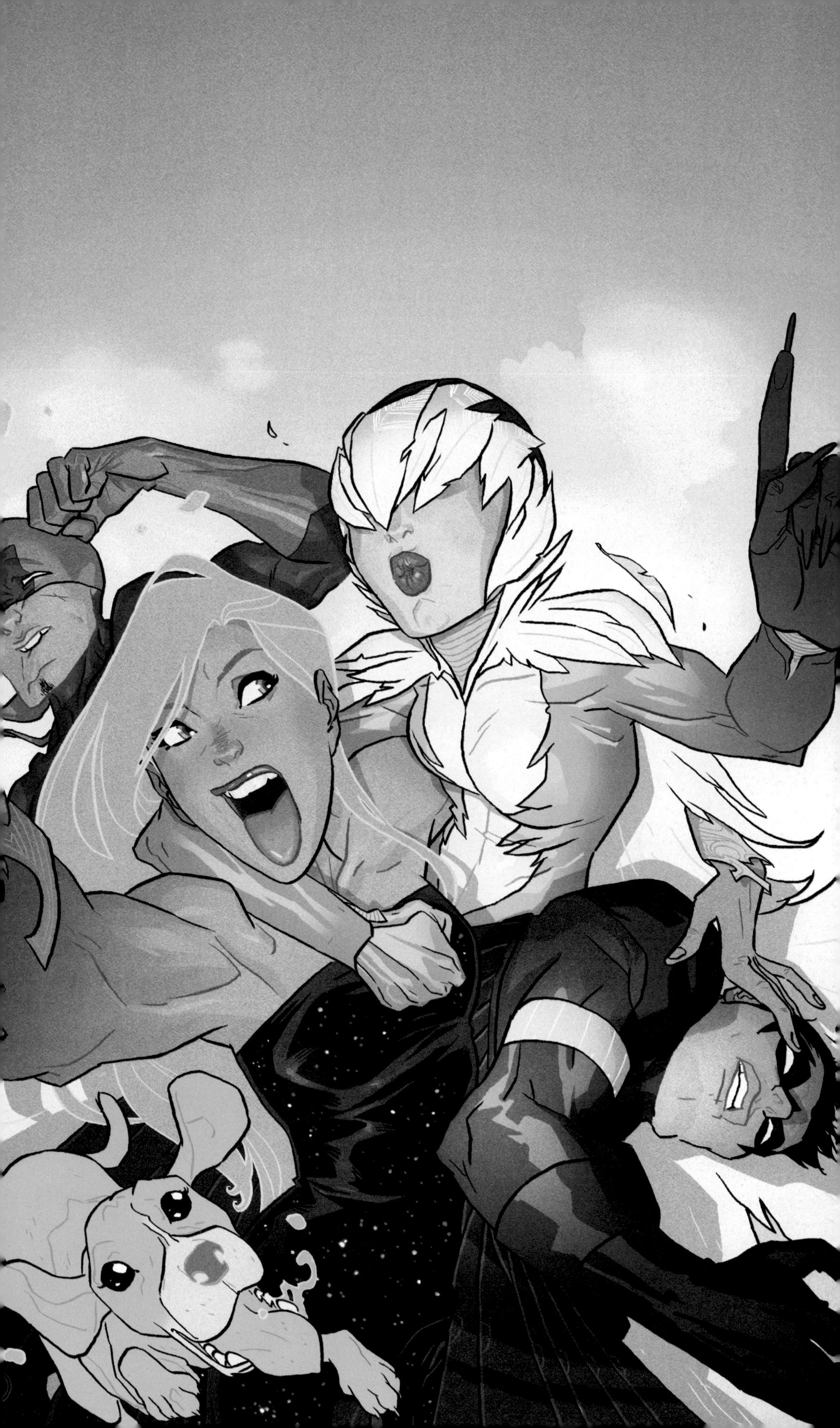

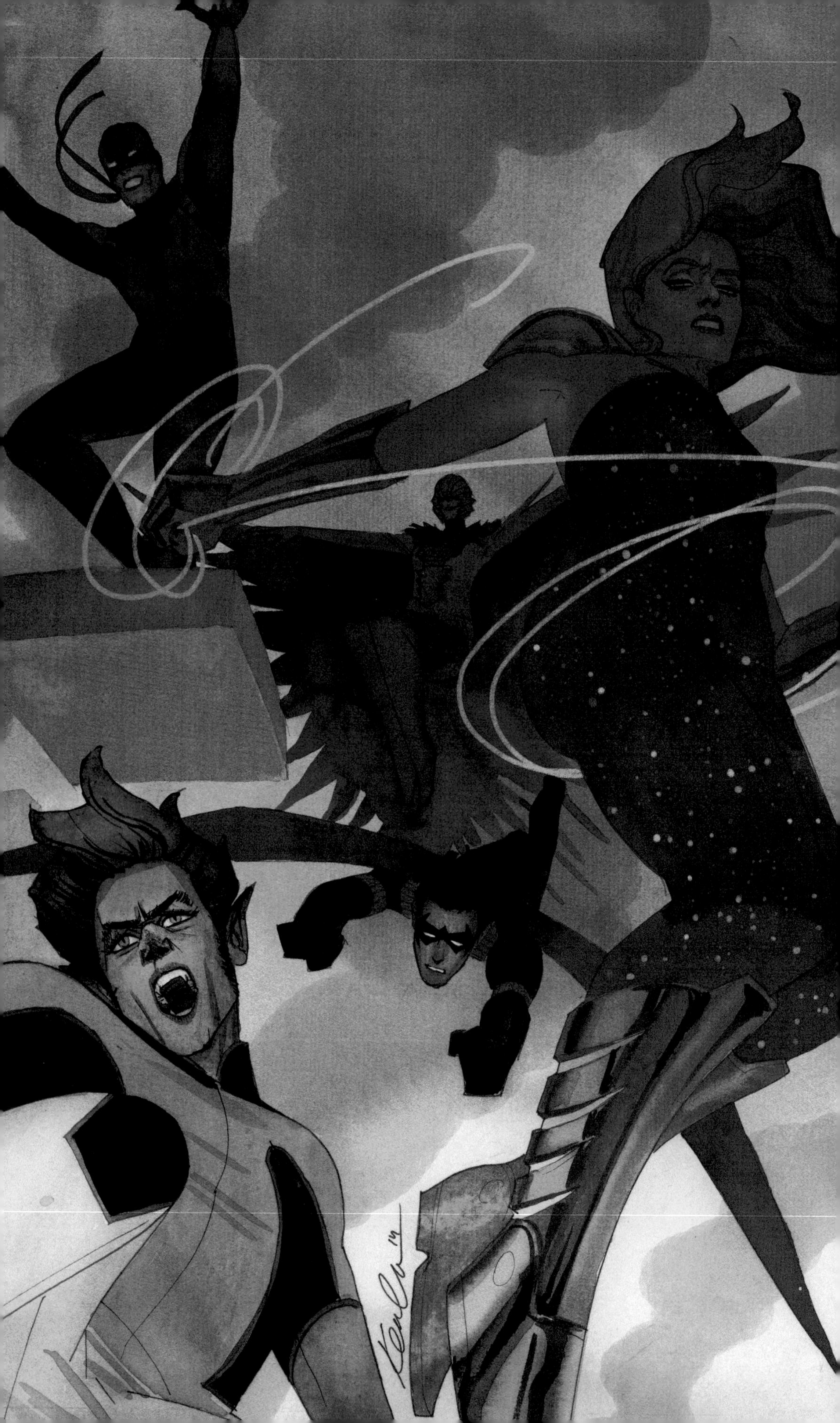

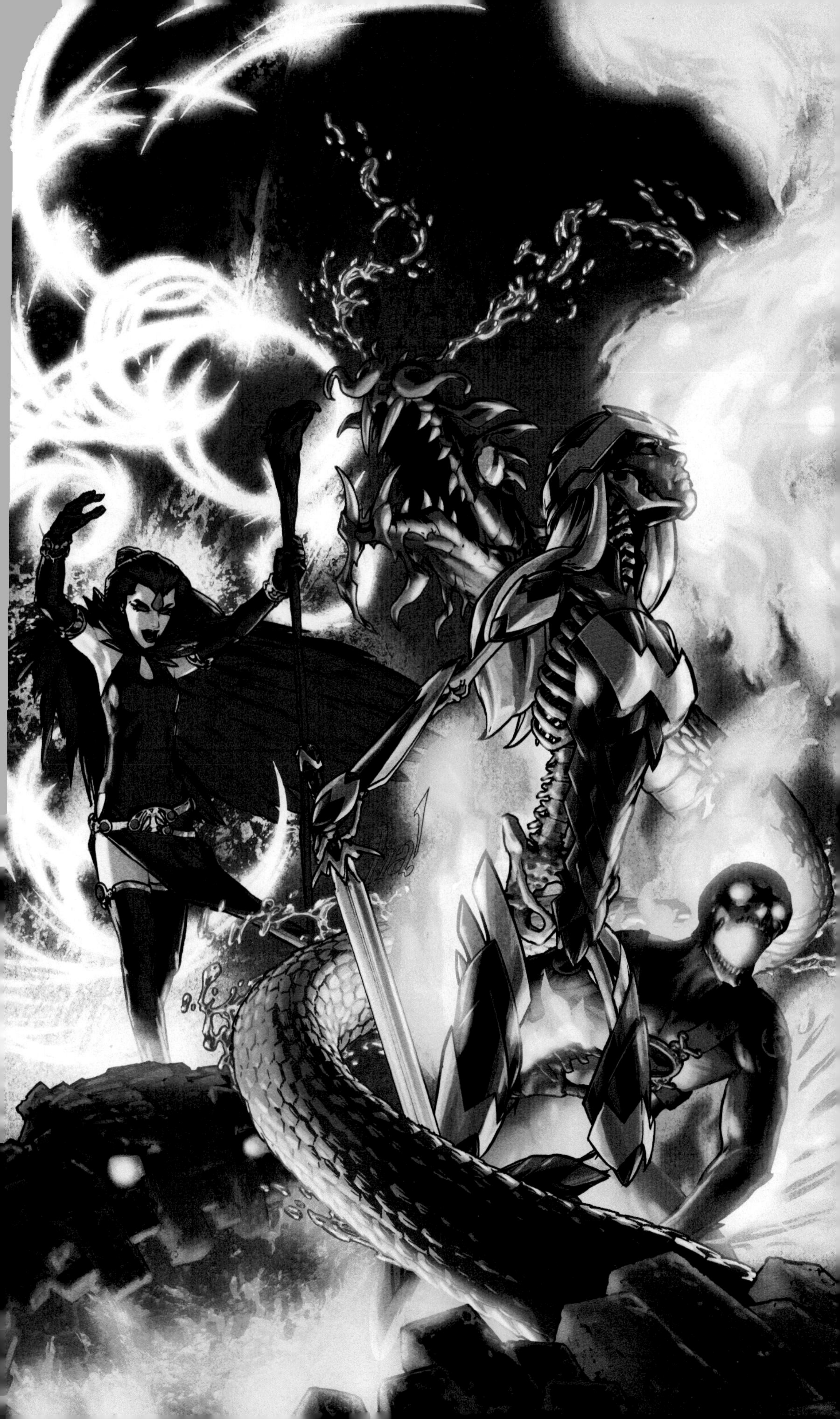

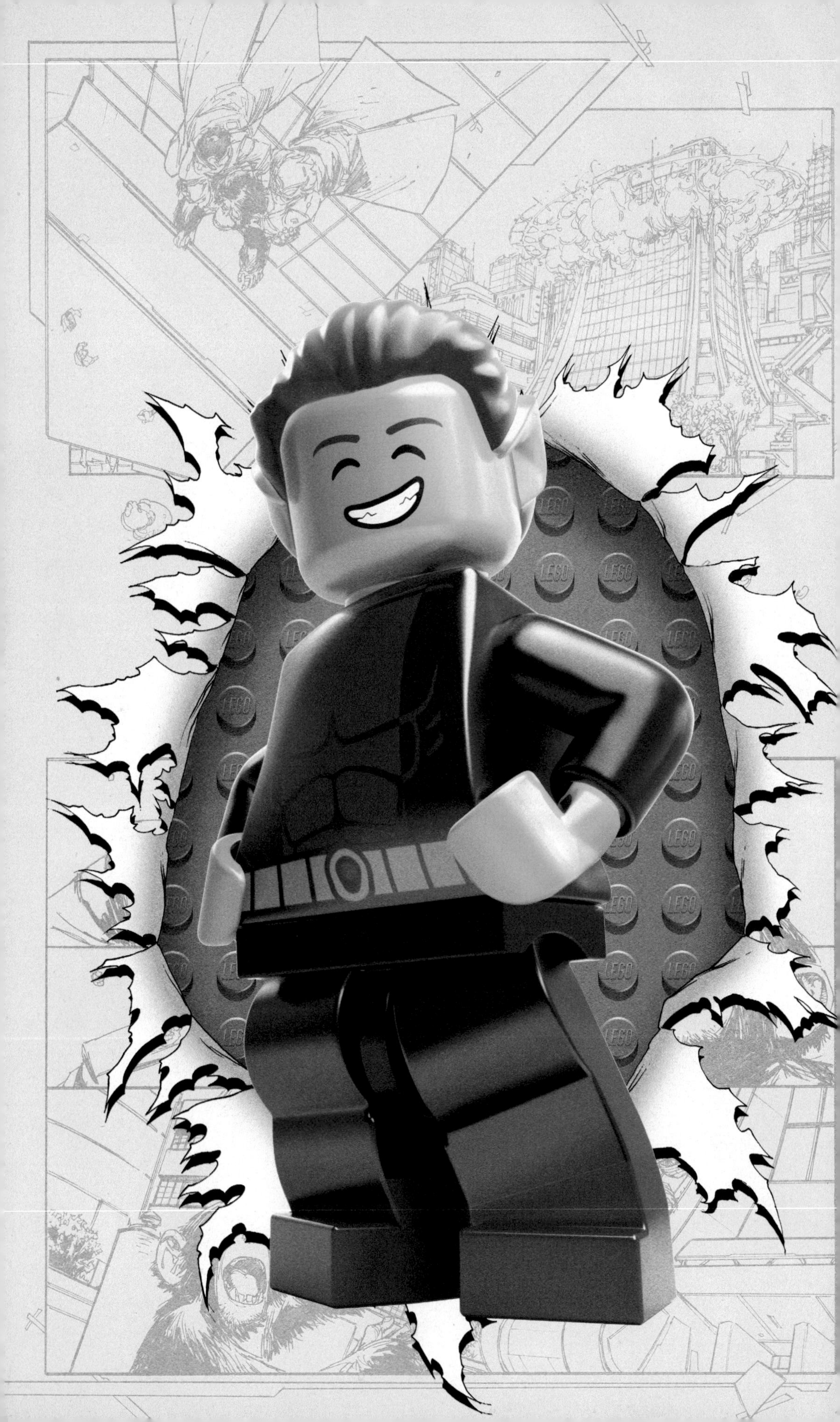

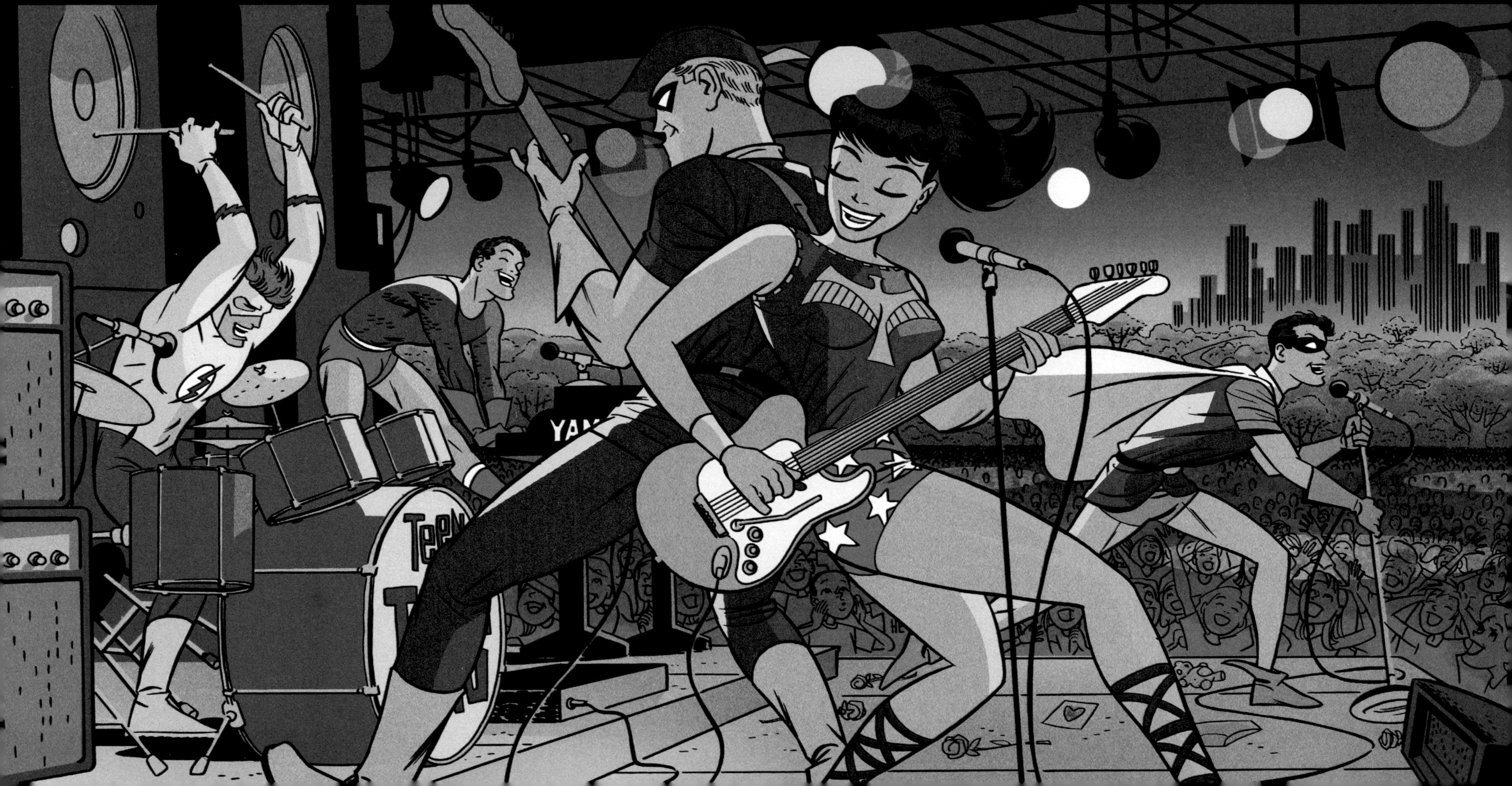

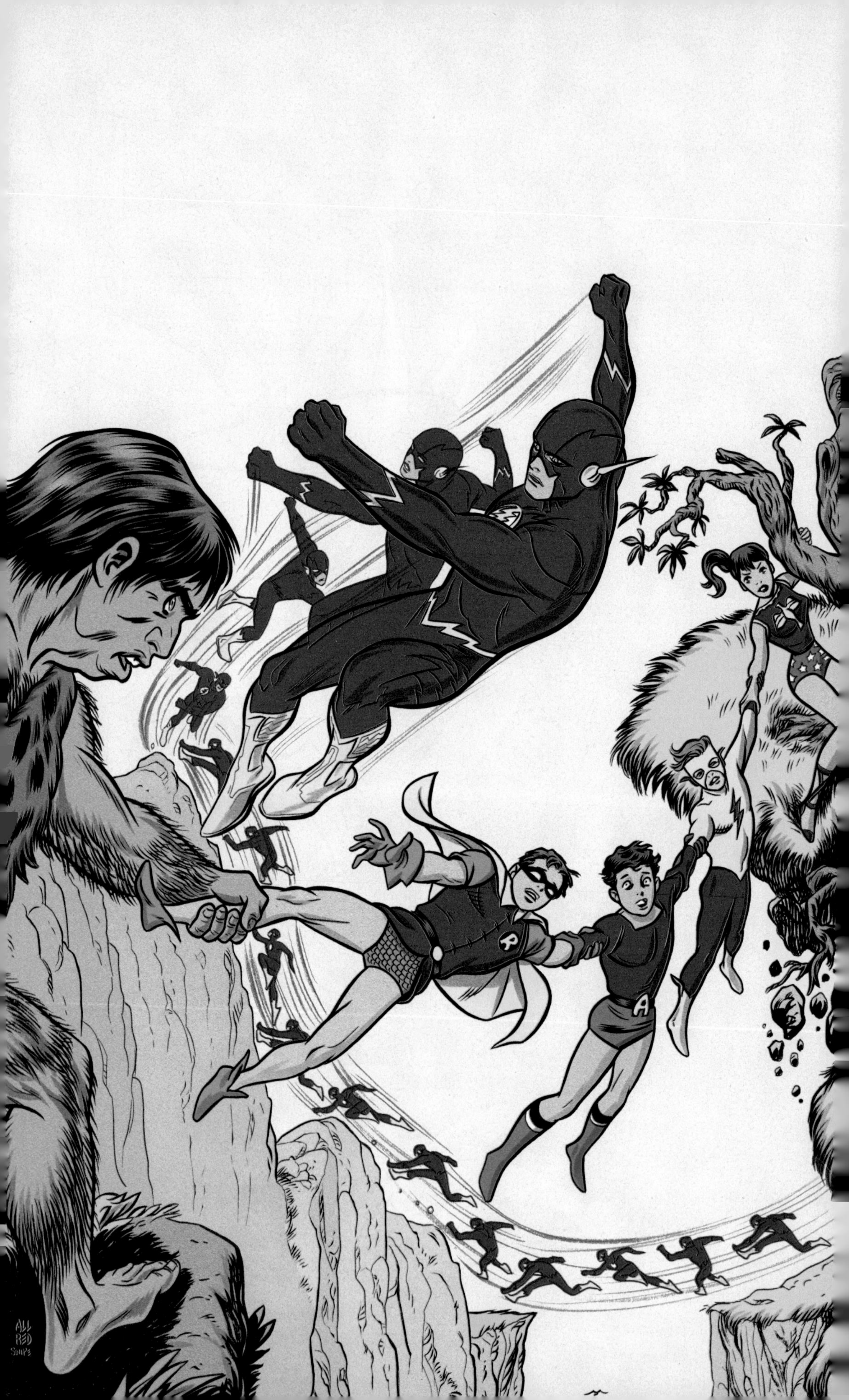
ALL RED

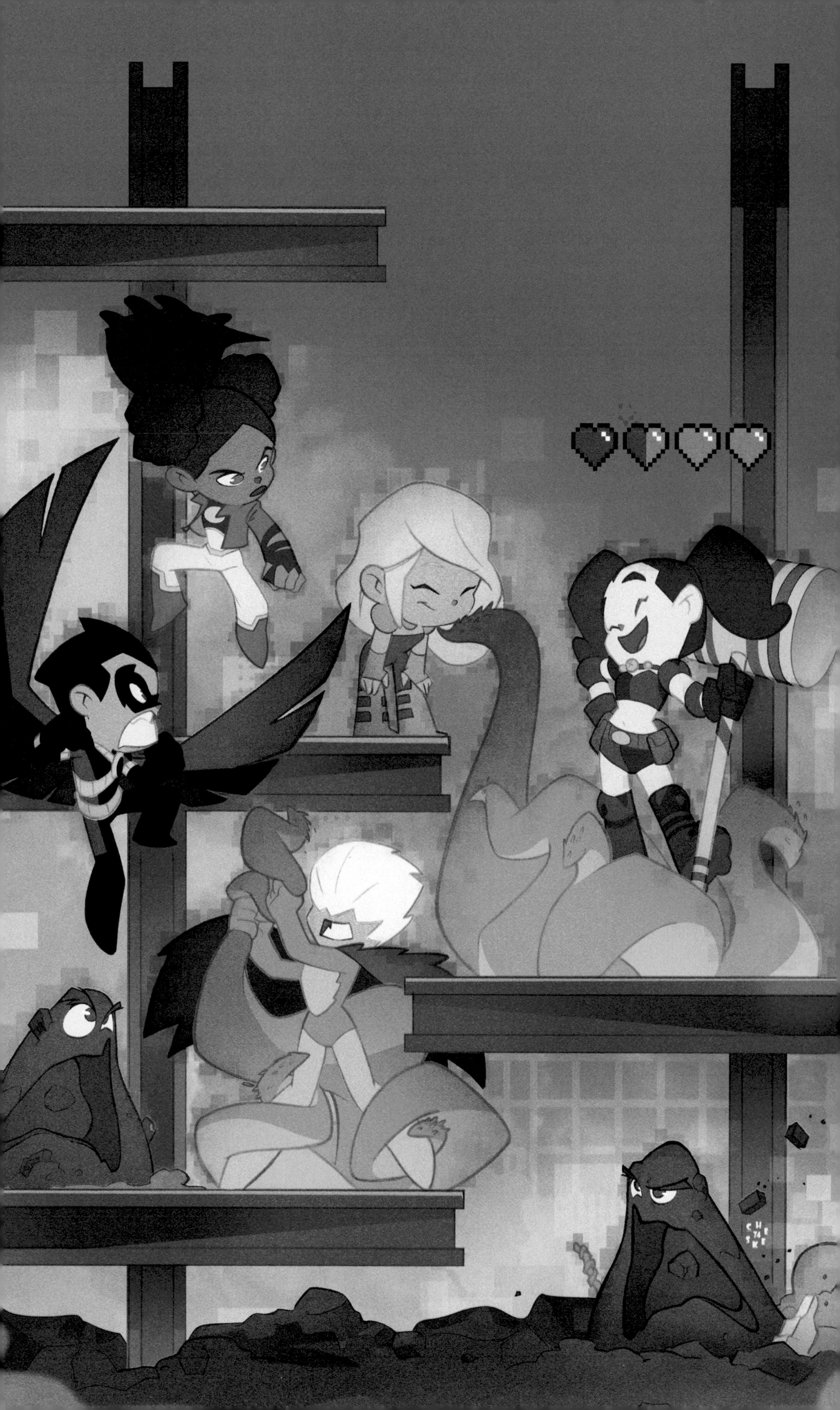

KENNETH ROCAFORT'S NEW AND TWEAKED DESIGNS FOR THE TEEN TITANS

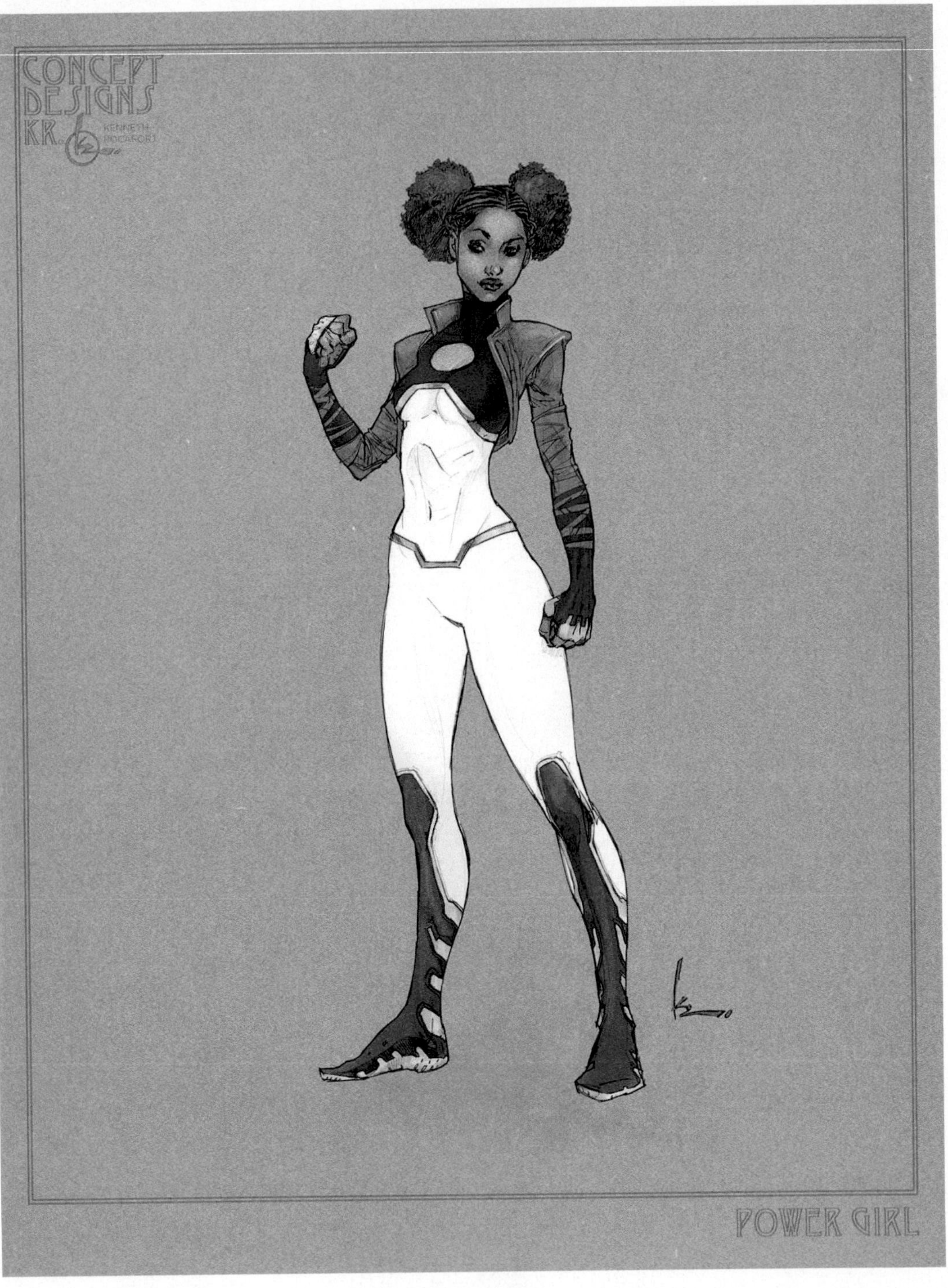
CONCEPT DESIGNS
KR.
KENNETH ROCAFORT
POWER GIRL

Originally introduced in WORLDS' FINEST, Power Girl was one of Rocafort's first designs for the new series.

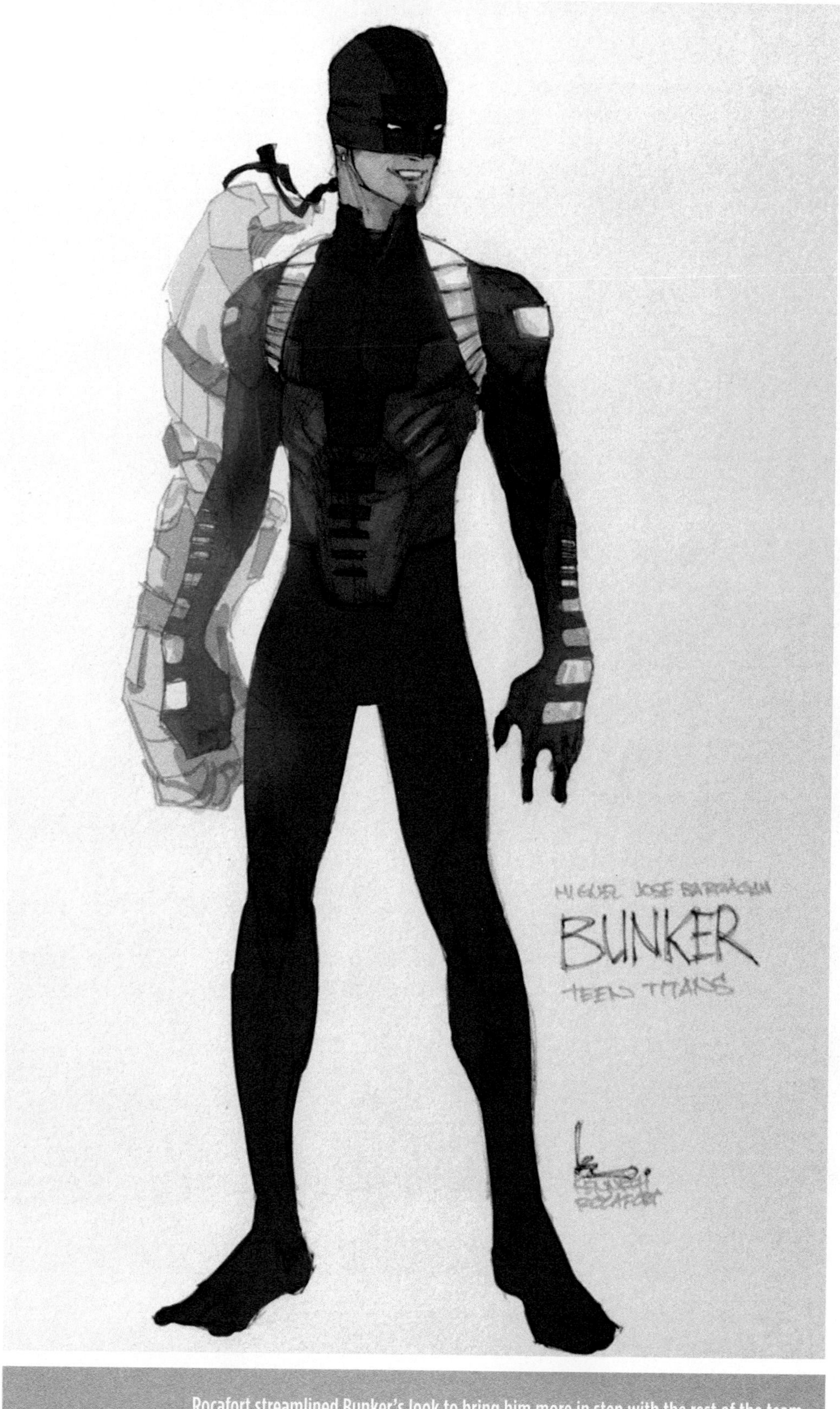
BUNKER
TEEN TITANS

Rocafort streamlined Bunker's look to bring him more in step with the rest of the team.

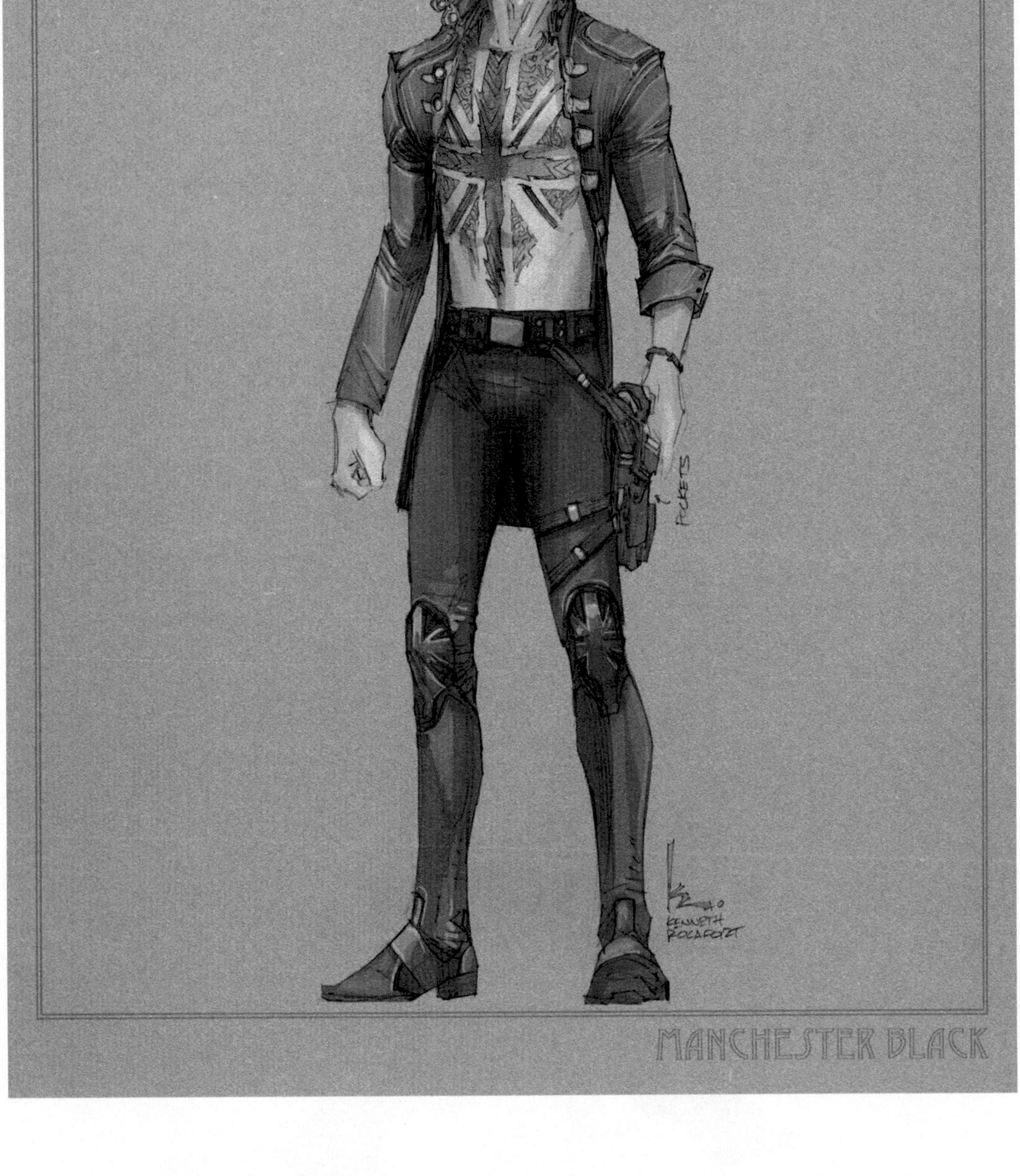
CONCEPT
DESIGNS
KR.
MANCHESTER
BLACK
POCKETS
KENNETH
ROCAFORT
MANCHESTER BLACK

Rocafort also reimagined Manchester Black for the Titans, with the character playing both hero and villain to the team.

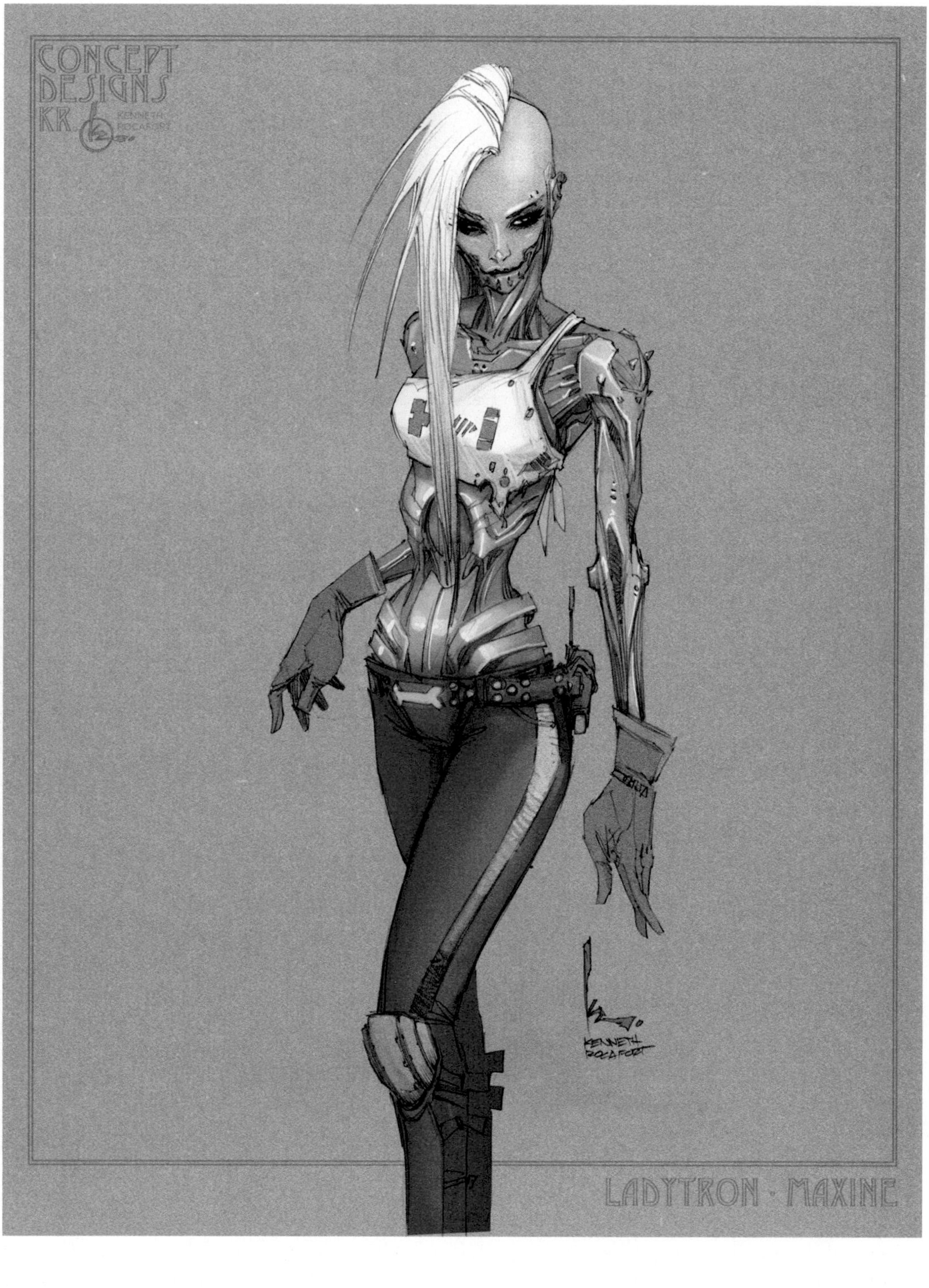
CONCEPT DESIGNS KR.
KENNETH ROCAFORT
LADYTRON - MAXINE

Although she eventually took on a different name and persona, Rocafort originally envisioned the villain of the first issue as an updated version of Ladytron.

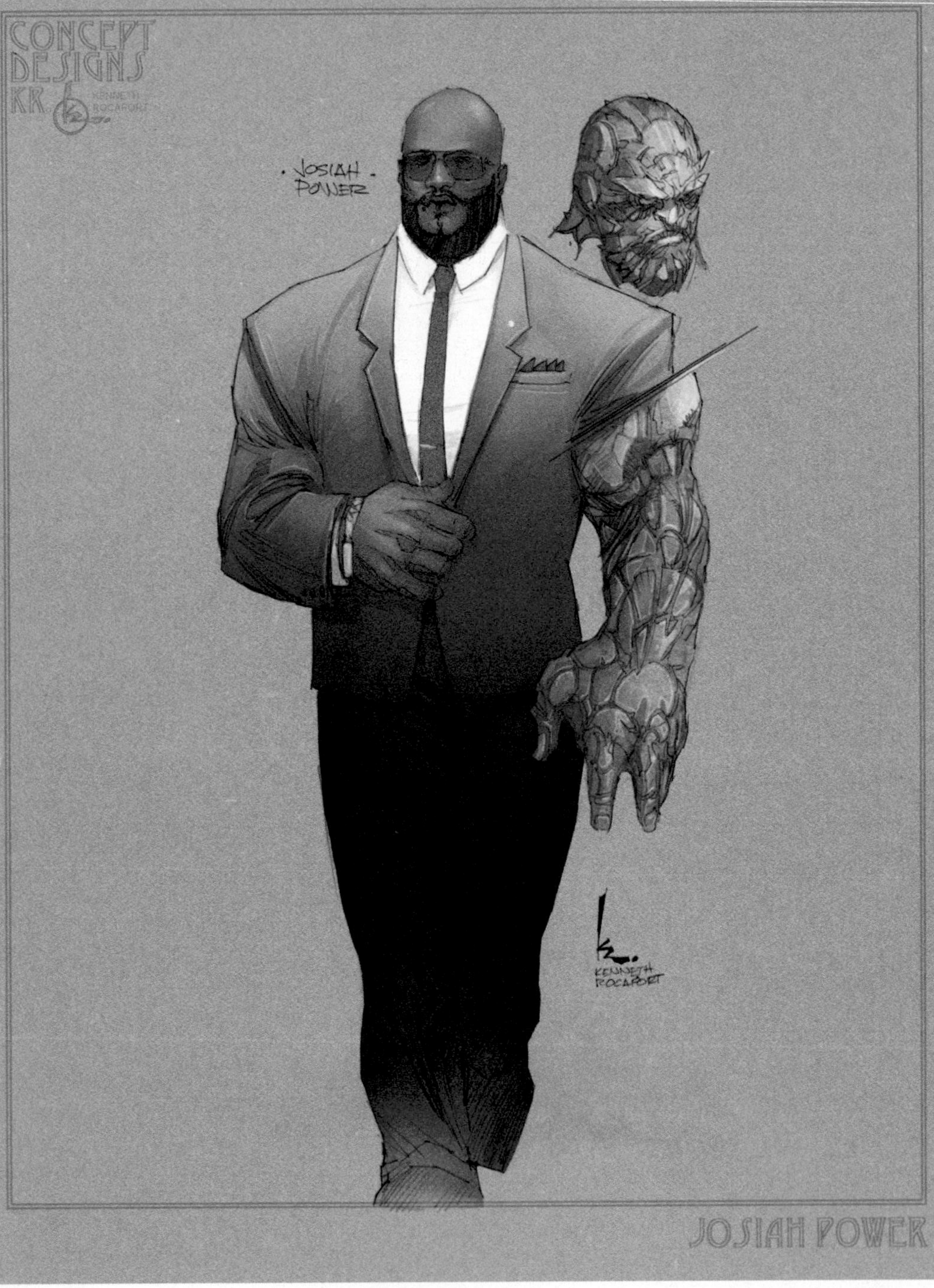
CONCEPT DESIGNS KR
KENNETH ROCAFORT
JOSIAH POWER
KENNETH ROCAFORT
JOSIAH POWER

Although we haven't seen it yet in the comic, Rocafort also did a pass at Josiah Power's superhuman alter ego.

START AT THE BEGINNING!

TEEN TITANS
VOLUME 1: IT'S OUR RIGHT TO FIGHT

**TEEN TITANS
VOL. 2: THE CULLING**

**TEEN TITANS VOL. 3:
DEATH OF THE FAMILY**

**THE CULLING: RISE OF
THE RAVAGERS**

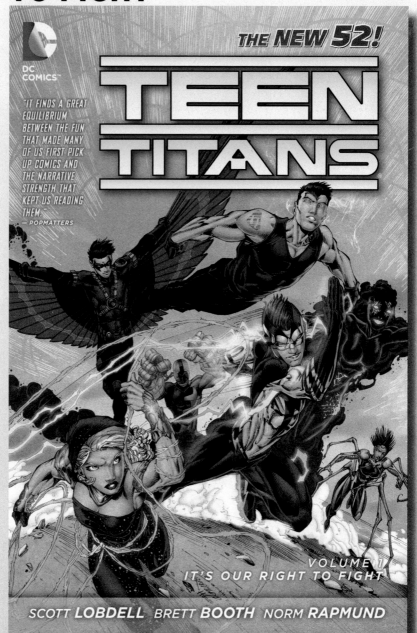

THE NEW 52!

DC COMICS™

TEEN TITANS

"IT FINDS A GREAT EQUILIBRIUM BETWEEN THE FUN THAT MADE MANY OF US FIRST PICK UP COMICS AND THE NARRATIVE STRENGTH THAT KEPT US READING THEM."
— POPMATTERS

VOLUME 1
IT'S OUR RIGHT TO FIGHT

SCOTT **LOBDELL** BRETT **BOOTH** NORM **RAPMUND**

DC COMICS™

"Brilliantly executed."
—IGN

"Morrison and Quitely have the magic touch that makes any book they collaborate on stand out from the rest." —MTV's Splash Page

"Thrilling and invigorating....Gotham City that has never looked this good, felt this strange, or been this deadly." —COMIC BOOK RESOURCES

GRANT MORRISON
with FRANK QUITELY & PHILIP TAN

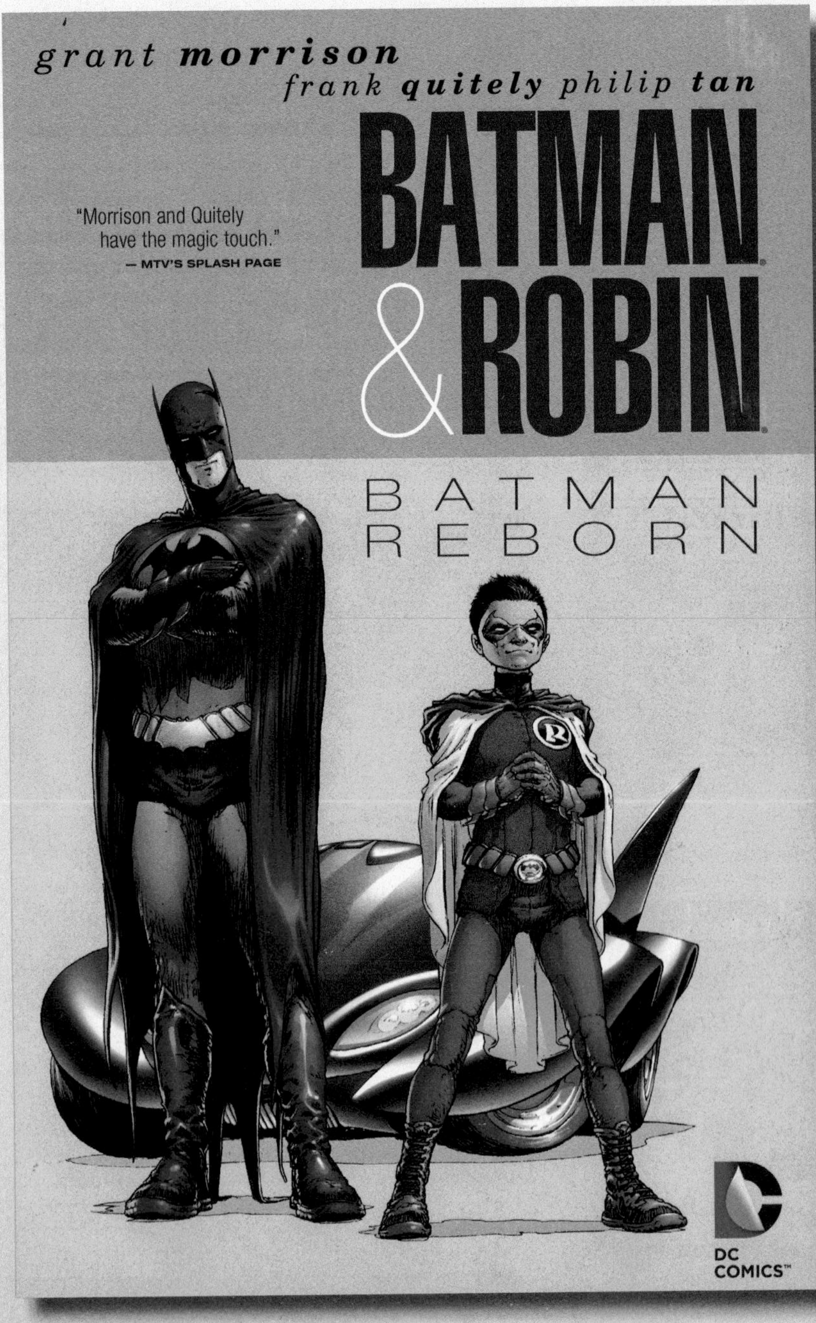
grant morrison
frank quitely philip tan
BATMAN & ROBIN
"Morrison and Quitely have the magic touch."
— MTV'S SPLASH PAGE
BATMAN REBORN
DC COMICS™

VOL. 2:
BATMAN VS. ROBIN

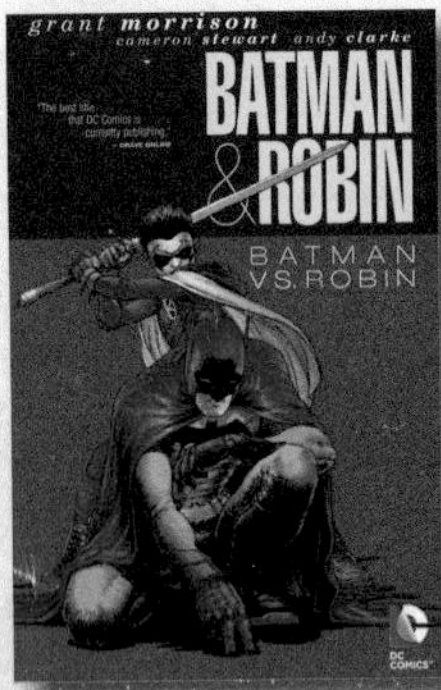
grant morrison
cameron stewart andy clarke
BATMAN & ROBIN
BATMAN VS. ROBIN

VOL. 3: BATMAN & ROBIN MUST DIE!

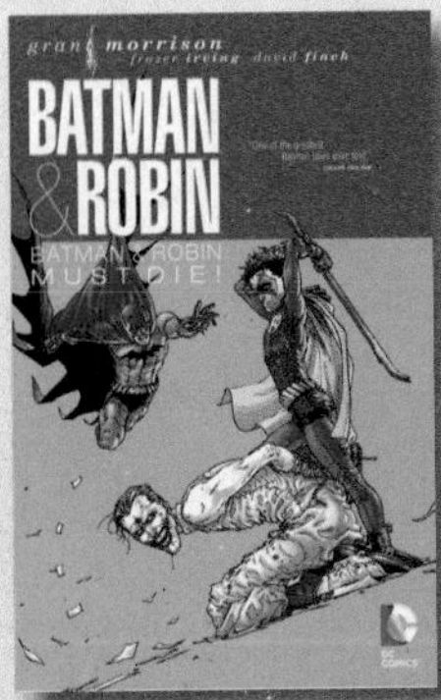
grant morrison
frazer irving david finch
BATMAN & ROBIN
BATMAN & ROBIN MUST DIE!

DARK KNIGHT VS. WHITE KNIGHT

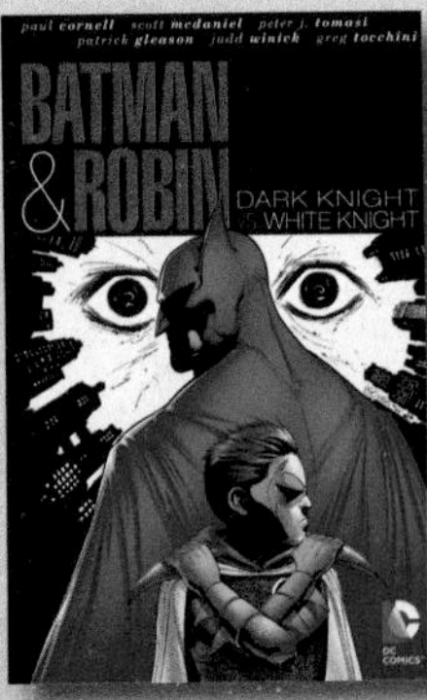
paul cornell scott mcdaniel peter j. tomasi
patrick gleason judd winick greg tocchini
BATMAN & ROBIN
DARK KNIGHT VS. WHITE KNIGHT